Contents at a Glance

iPod® + iTunes®
for Windows® and Mac®

Brian Tiemann

Sams Publishing, 800 East 96th Street, Indianapolis, Indiana 46240 USA

iPod® + iTunes® for Windows® and Mac® in a Snap

International Standard Book Number: 0-672-32811-9

Library of Congress Catalog Card Number: 2005902142

Printed in the United States of America

First Printing: July 2005

08 07 06 05 4 3 2 1

Trademarks

All terms mentioned in this book that are known to be trademarks or service marks have been appropriately capitalized. Sams Publishing cannot attest to the accuracy of this information. Use of a term in this book should not be regarded as affecting the validity of any trademark or service mark.

iPod, iTunes, Mac, FireWire, iPhoto, Apple, Mac OS, and Apple Store are either registered trademarks or trademarks of Apple. Windows is a registered trademark of Microsoft Corporation.

Warning and Disclaimer

Every effort has been made to make this book as complete and as accurate as possible, but no warranty or fitness is implied. The information provided is on an "as is" basis. The author and the publisher shall have neither liability nor responsibility to any person or entity with respect to any loss or damages arising from the information contained in this book.

Bulk Sales

Sams Publishing offers excellent discounts on this book when ordered in quantity for bulk purchases or special sales. For more information, please contact

U.S. Corporate and Government Sales

1-800-382-3419

corpsales@pearsontechgroup.com

For sales outside of the U.S., please contact

International Sales

international@pearsoned.com

Acquisitions Editor
Betsy Brown

Development Editor
Alice Martina Smith

Managing Editor
Charlotte Clapp

Project Editor
Dan Knott

Indexer
Erika Millen

Proofreader
Wendy Ostermeyer

Technical Editor
John Traekenschuh

Publishing Coordinator
Vanessa Evans

Designer
Gary Adair

About the Author

Brian Tiemann is a freelance technology columnist and software engineer who has written extensively in online magazines about the Macintosh, Apple software, and the philosophy of user-friendly design that has always been synonymous with them. A creative professional in the graphic arts and web design world as well as in networking and software quality, he enjoys software like iTunes and gadgets like the iPod not just as tools, but as prime expressions of the elusive art of the user experience.

A graduate of Caltech, author of *Mac OS X Tiger in a Snap*, and coauthor of *FreeBSD Unleashed* and *Sams Teach Yourself FreeBSD in 24 Hours*, Brian enjoys animation, motorcycles, photography, technological gadgets, the outdoors, and writing about them all. He lives in Silicon Valley with canines Capri and Banzai.

Dedication

To Mike and Julie, who said they could use a book like this.

Acknowledgments

I once thought three months was a short time to write a whole book; how about three *weeks*? This has got to be some kind of record. Naturally it couldn't have been done without the Sams editorial team working as tirelessly as they did pulling everything together: Alice Martina Smith for keeping me in good humor through the whole thing, and John Traekenschuh for keeping me encouraged (as well as for helping research the iPod photo); Tammy Graham and the folks in the art department for making the iPod screenshots work; and Betsy Brown for believing I could pull this thing off in the first place. I'd like to thank them and all the rest of the Sams team—and I'd also like to give special recognition to Ben, Tim, Albert, and Caley at the Oakridge Apple Store for being so helpful getting me the gadgets I needed for that in-store photo shoot.

I would also like to thank those who have continued to support and inspire me: James Lileks for bolstering my ego with his very presence; Steven Den Beste for toughening me up; Mike Hendrix for keeping that torch lit and that flag flying; and Paul, Mike, Damien, Kevin, Aziz, and J for always keeping me on my toes. Lance, Kris, Chris, David, John, Van, Trent, Marcus, Paul, and all the rest: Thanks again for being patient as I dropped off the face of the Earth yet again, and for remembering who I was when I emerged.

We Want to Hear from You!

As the reader of this book, *you* are our most important critic and commentator. We value your opinion and want to know what we're doing right, what we could do better, what areas you'd like to see us publish in, and any other words of wisdom you're willing to pass our way.

You can email or write me directly to let me know what you did or didn't like about this book—as well as what we can do to make our books stronger.

Please note that I cannot help you with technical problems related to the topic of this book, and that due to the high volume of mail I receive, I might not be able to reply to every message.

When you write, please be sure to include this book's title and author as well as your name and phone or email address. I will carefully review your comments and share them with the author and editors who worked on the book.

Email: consumer@samspublishing.com

Mail: Mark Taber
Associate Publisher
Sams Publishing
800 East 96th Street
Indianapolis, IN 46240 USA

Reader Services

For more information about this book or another Sams Publishing title, visit our website at www.samspublishing.com. Type the ISBN (excluding hyphens) or the title of a book in the Search field to find the page you're looking for.

1

✔ Start Here

For the first time in many years, Apple Computer Inc. finds itself in an enviable position in the technology industry: It's in nearly uncontested command of a product segment that's hip, extremely popular, and growing by leaps and bounds. This product is *digital music*, a field that blends the most cutting-edge aspects of personal computing, portable handheld devices, and the entertainment industry. With two key products—the music organizing "jukebox" software iTunes and the ubiquitous iPod portable music player—Apple has a commanding lead in this lucrative industry and shows no signs of slowing down.

Whether you're a long-time Mac user, a newcomer to the Apple fold, or a Windows user who might never have dreamed of using a product from Apple, the iTunes and iPod combination of products provides a complete solution for your music collecting and listening needs. iTunes runs as seamlessly on Windows PCs as it does on Macintosh computers, and the iPod—you must make sure to buy the right model for your kind of computer—is just as capable on one platform as it is on the other. The process of getting music on the iPod is even completely legal, thanks to the industry-leading iTunes **Music Store**.

iTunes and the iPod are designed with the utmost ease of use and convenience in mind. However, no matter what your computing background, the world of digital music can be a confusing place, full of esoteric acronyms and convoluted technical tasks. Even for a seasoned computer user, the little details necessary for making the fullest use of your digital music collection can be elusive.

▶ **NOTE**

Throughout this book, screenshots from both the Windows and Mac versions of iTunes will be used interchangeably. Because iTunes works almost identically on both platforms, a figure or procedure showing one version of iTunes applies the same way to the other version.

That's what this book is for. It's no lie on Apple's part that iTunes and the iPod are essentially pretty easy to figure out; but it's the little tricks, the side tasks, the streamlining procedures that really make the system sing that aren't immediately obvious. This book describes those tasks in a fully illustrated, step-by-step manner so that you can be as familiar with your iPod's esoteric functions as you are with its ubiquitous, white-and-stainless-steel case and the white earbuds you see dangling from so many pairs of ears on the street today.

What Is iTunes?

First introduced in January 2001, iTunes—Apple's "jukebox" or digital music organizer application—was the first in a long series of software applications developed by Apple after many long years of publishing almost nothing but the Mac Operating System (Mac OS) for the company's Macintosh computers. Indeed, iTunes in its original form was compatible only with Macintoshes running Mac OS 9 or the then-new Mac OS X. Many of Apple's applications developed since that time—iPhoto, iDVD, and many of the built-in applications and utilities found in recent versions of Mac OS X (10.3 "Panther" or 10.4 "Tiger")—share a common look and feel with iTunes, including its "brushed metal" skin, the list of data sources down the left side, and so on. Third-party application developers for Windows as well as the Mac platform have also jumped onto the bandwagon, using the iTunes style of interface for attractive, innovative software that's as pleasant to look at as it is easy to use. Many have argued, though, that few if any applications truly match iTunes' revolutionary unified design or accomplish their desired aims quite so well.

As discussed in "About Digital Music Technology," later in this chapter, the idea behind digital music is that instead of listening to songs from your favorite artists by putting a tape or CD into a standalone deck or player and playing it from beginning to end, the music that's on a CD can be copied—or *ripped*—into compressed data files on your computer. These data files don't just have the benefit of being freed from the bulky physical medium of the tape or CD, they also can contain all kinds of useful information built right into their structure, such as the name of each track, the name of the artist and album, the year it was released, the musical genre, even image data such as album art and user-defined information such as a "star" rating indicating how much you like a given song. These data files—usually stored in MPEG-1 layer 3 (or *MP3*) format—can be collected on your computer's hard drive, rearranged, selected individually, grouped by arbitrary criteria, and played back with very good clarity and audio quality. Doing this, however, requires software capable of making all this simple and intuitive.

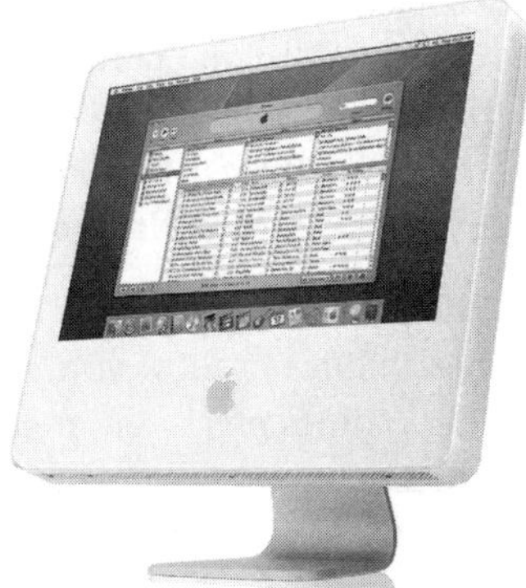

iTunes runs equally well on a Windows PC or a Macintosh.

Before the release of iTunes, digital music technology was the realm of technically astute music enthusiasts who did not mind wrestling with austere, difficult-to-master software. Digital music files were exchanged primarily through illegal, underground file-sharing channels, and it was all but unthinkable that digital music could become a mainstream medium to rival compact discs.

Ripping, Mixing, and Burning

After iTunes was released, however, under Apple's slogan "Rip. Mix. Burn," the first step toward legitimization of this new medium had been taken. Apple was actively encouraging computer users to extract the music from their compact discs (***rip***), rearrange it to their liking (***mix***), and create (***burn***) new CDs full of their own custom mixes. With iTunes, users finally had a tool that made these tasks easy. iTunes is built around these three fundamental functions—adding new music to your library, organizing it to your taste, and converting it to useful forms you can take with you. Changes to iTunes over the years since its release have only strengthened and expanded on these core functions, which are iTunes' essential reasons for being.

▶ KEY TERMS

Rip—To copy or import audio data from a CD.

Burn—To create a music CD using a writable disc (CD-R, CD-RW, or writable DVD).

Today, collecting music in iTunes has become a thoroughly mainstream and entirely legal affair, thanks to the iTunes **Music Store**, an Internet-based record store whose interface is built right into iTunes. Now there's no need to buy a physical CD of your favorite artist's latest album at all—you just click a button, and legitimately purchased music is downloaded directly into your iTunes **Library** for you to play with a click of the mouse. iTunes can also import music from your favorite CDs, and can play back individual digital music files that come from just about any source. You can even use iTunes to listen to "Internet Radio," a network of streams of audio data to which you can listen at any time by simply specifying the Web address of a desired channel.

The "mixing" aspect of iTunes is more robust than ever, giving you all kinds of possibilities for how you might choose to organize your music. In its basic interface, iTunes gives you great control over your music by letting you navigate quickly to a desired genre, artist, or album using the **Browse** lists; you can also go directly to a specific song by simply typing part of its title into the **Search** bar. This is only the beginning of your organizational options, though. Not only can you create a ***playlist*** of favorite songs by simply clicking and dragging them into order in the list, but with ***Smart Playlists***, you can tell iTunes to automatically filter through all your music according to criteria you specify—such as "released in the 1980s" or "played more than 10 times" or "in the Rock genre"—and produce a playlist that shows you all your music that matches these criteria in whatever order you choose.

Finally, sharing music—with other people, or just by giving you the option to take your music with you wherever you go—is what gives the iTunes digital music system the expandability and flexibility you crave as a music enthusiast. As it could since its initial release, iTunes can burn a playlist of music onto a writable optical disc such as a CD-R—if your computer has a drive that supports burning (most modern ones do). You can then play this burned CD in any standard CD player. You can also burn data discs full of compressed digital music files, which can then be played in any CD player capable of playing MP3 CDs (this way you can fit as much as 12 times as many songs on a single CD). iTunes even prints jewel-case inserts using album art so that you can keep your burned CDs organized attractively. Additionally, iTunes is a network-aware application, and multiple copies of iTunes running on the same home or corporate network can connect to each other and share music with each other. With AirPort Express, Apple's audio-capable wireless networking base station, iTunes can broadcast music to a speaker system of your choice, including the big stereo system hooked up to the A/V rig in your den.

None of these sharing options, however, holds a candle to the portability and seamlessness of the iPod, Apple's portable digital music player. The iPod was specifically designed to give you all the flexibility and ease of use you find in iTunes, in a compact device that fits right into your pocket.

What Is the iPod?

The iPod was released to much surprise and skepticism in November 2001. Revolutionary at the time, the iPod bucked the trends established by most existing digital music players (interchangeably called "MP3 players") in that instead of a small and clumsy LCD screen, it had a large and detailed one navigated by an innovative rotary thumb-wheel. And instead of a low-capacity Flash memory system that could hold only a few dozen MP3 files at a time, or a large and heavy full-size hard drive, it was built around a physically tiny hard drive that nonetheless packed a huge 5 gigabytes of storage. This was enough, as Apple's marketing noted with much fanfare, to fit a thousand songs onto a device the size of a deck of cards, and thus into your pocket—a benefit that handily offset the iPod's high retail price. A fast FireWire connection meant you could copy the entire contents of your iTunes' **Library** to the iPod in just a few minutes. With a straightforward navigation system that reflected the organizational structure of iTunes itself, the iPod quickly banished all naysayers and claimed the mantle of "iTunes to Go."

In the years since its release, the iPod has undergone many changes, the most obvious of which has been the gradual increase in capacity of its internal hard drive (although the device's physical dimensions, except for its thickness, have not varied): 10GB, then 20GB, and most recently 40GB and even 60GB models have appeared. iTunes' libraries comprising 5,000, 10,000, and even 15,000 songs can now fit easily on that same deck-of-cards-sized device. As Apple has refined the navigation system, recent iPods have sported subtly different interfaces, including versions with a touch-sensitive trackpad instead of a physically moving wheel, round buttons above the wheel instead of surrounding it, and (most recently) an integrated "click wheel" that incorporates all the iPod's controls into a single round rocking button. But the basics of the iPod's function have barely changed: You use your thumb to roll the selector up and down the menu on the screen, press the central button to select an option and move to the next screen, and navigate in that way until you find the music you want to listen to. Selecting that music starts it playing.

Other iPod models have joined the lineup as well. The iPod mini, available in a variety of metallic colors, uses an even smaller hard drive than the regular iPod's, giving it a capacity of 4GB or 6GB and a smaller and lighter body that can be strapped to your arm as you go jogging. The top-of-the-line iPod, the iPod photo, features a color screen that can display photographs as well as album art from your iTunes **Library**. The newest and smallest member of the iPod family, the Flash-based iPod shuffle, has no screen—instead, its 512MB or 1GB of storage can be "autofilled" by iTunes with a playlist of your choosing, with its contents optionally "shuffled" so that you're never sure what music might come up next.

▶ NOTE

In October 2004, Apple released a "U2 Special Edition" iPod with a black body and red click wheel, signed on the back by the members of the band U2. Aside from its flashy appearance, the special edition is functionally identical to a standard 20GB fourth-generation (4G) iPod.

In this book, the methods used to synchronize your iPod and navigate its contents are described in a way that's applicable to most if not all iPod models. On occasions where the methods described apply only to specific models, the following naming scheme is used:

- **1G**—First-generation iPod. FireWire port on the top. Freely rotating mechanical navigation wheel with control buttons surrounding it. Sharp front edge. 5GB or 10GB capacity.
- **2G**—Second-generation iPod. FireWire port on the top. Touch-sensitive navigation wheel with control buttons surrounding it. 10GB or 20GB capacity. Visually and functionally the same as the 1G iPod.
- **3G**—Third-generation iPod. Dock connector (combination FireWire/USB2) on the bottom, compatible with the separately available iPod Dock. Four small round control buttons above the touch-sensitive navigation wheel. Rounded front edge. Capacities ranging from 15GB to 40GB.
- **4G**—Fourth-generation iPod. Dock connector on the bottom. Integrated "click wheel" interface with the four control buttons embedded under the directional points of the touch-sensitive navigation wheel. 20GB or 40GB capacity.
- **iPod photo**—Similar in appearance and function to the 4G iPod, except for a full-color screen and a software interface capable of storing and displaying photographs downloaded to the iPod. 30GB, 40GB, or 60GB capacity.
- **iPod mini**—Smaller, rounded design; body in one of several metallic colors. Integrated "click wheel" interface similar to the 4G iPod. Dock connector on the bottom. 4GB or 6GB capacity.
- **iPod shuffle**—No display; small white body the approximate size and weight of a pack of gum. USB connector under a removable cap. Controls limited to Play/Pause, Back/Forward, Volume up/down, and a special "shuffle" switch. 512MB or 1GB capacity (using Flash memory).

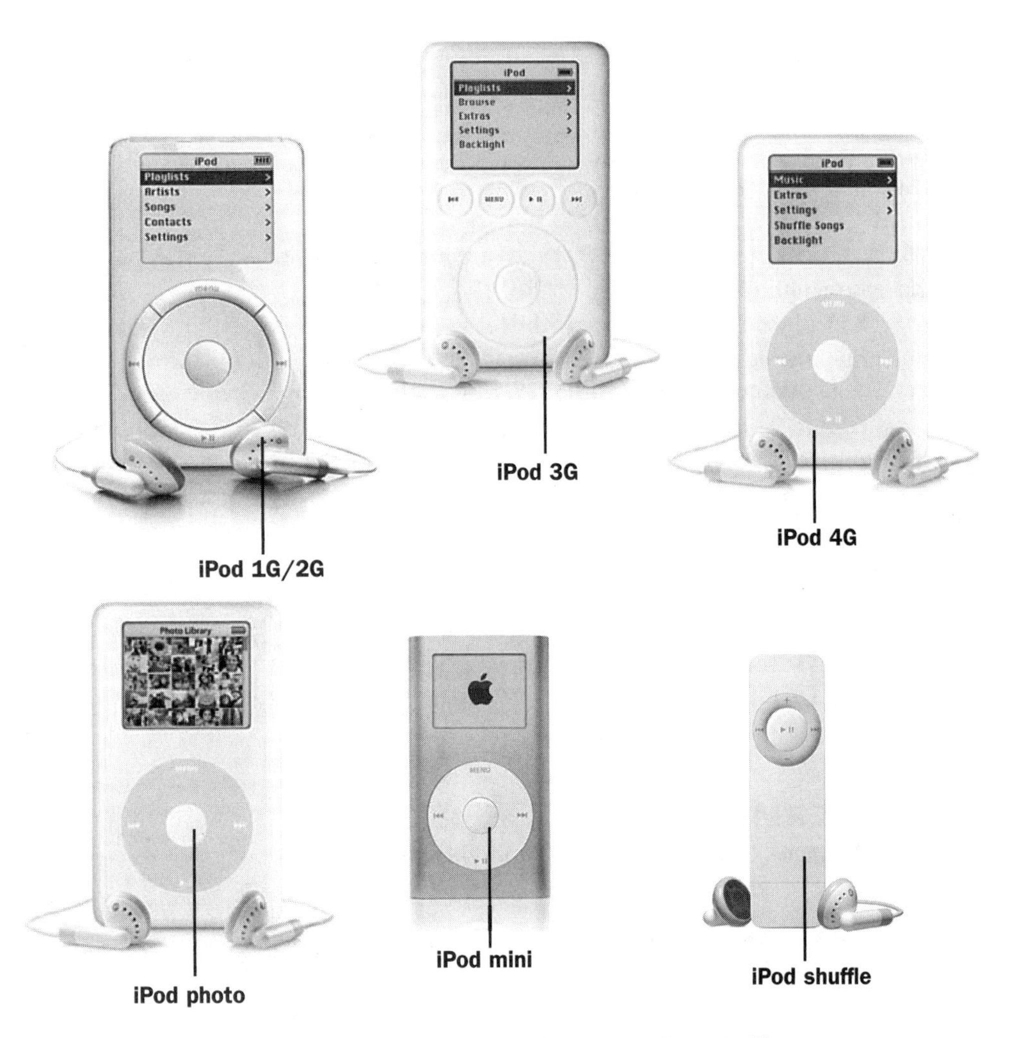

The iPod family: 1G/2G, 3G, 4G, iPod photo, iPod mini, and iPod shuffle.

Some features described in this book are not available on older iPod models. Additionally, screenshots used in this book to demonstrate iPod functions will generally use a non-color iPod screen. The color LCD screen found on the iPod photo is sharper and shows more shades than the monochrome screen on earlier iPod models; this allows it to show more and prettier details while you're navigating its interface, such as colorful icons, more engaging games, and additional playback features such as the display of album art. Except where necessary to demonstrate specific iPod photo features, the figures in this book reflect what you'd see on a standard monochrome 3G or 4G iPod.

▶ NOTE

Because the iPod photo's screen comprises more advanced color LCD technology, and the unit includes a composite A/V port for output instead of the usual headphone jack, a standard monochrome iPod cannot be upgraded through any software update to use the iPod photo's functions.

The iPod can carry music in either the standard MP3 format or Apple's proprietary, copyright-protected ***AAC format***. The iPod's use of AAC format means that it's specifically designed to work with iTunes and its system of obtaining legally purchased music from the iTunes Music Store. The iPod will not play music in Microsoft's ***Windows Media Audio (WMA)*** format (as found on any of the competing online digital music stores). Because the iPod controls the vast majority of the market for digital music players, and the iTunes **Music Store** leads all its competitors by a wide margin, this fundamental incompatibility is unlikely to cause you problems—unless you already own a lot of purchased music in WMA format. In that circumstance, you might have to use a technically advanced procedure similar to the one described in **56 Create an MP3 CD from Purchased AAC Music** to import this music into iTunes in MP3 or AAC format so that you can play it on your iPod. (In such a procedure, you'll have to burn audio CDs from your WMA files using Windows Media Player or a similar application because iTunes also won't play your purchased WMA music.)

▶ KEY TERMS

Windows Media Audio (WMA)—**Microsoft's competitor format to AAC, WMA files are similarly higher quality than MP3s, but their *DRM* is more restrictive.**

Advanced Audio Coding (AAC)—**A new digital audio format co-developed by Apple as part of the MPEG-4 definition; AAC has better quality than MP3, as well as optional built-in DRM.**

Regardless of the specific model, each iPod has the same basic mission at heart: To synchronize seamlessly with your iTunes **Library**, copy your music to its internal storage medium, and let you take your music collection wherever you go with the same ease of navigation and playback you enjoy in iTunes itself. The iPod is as much a part of the iTunes' experience as the iTunes **Music Store** is; without an iPod, you're only getting half the benefit of your digital music collection. Besides, without those telltale white earbud cords trailing into your clothes, how else will you show off to everyone on the street that you're on the cutting edge of the digital music revolution?

iPod Standard | **iPod photo**

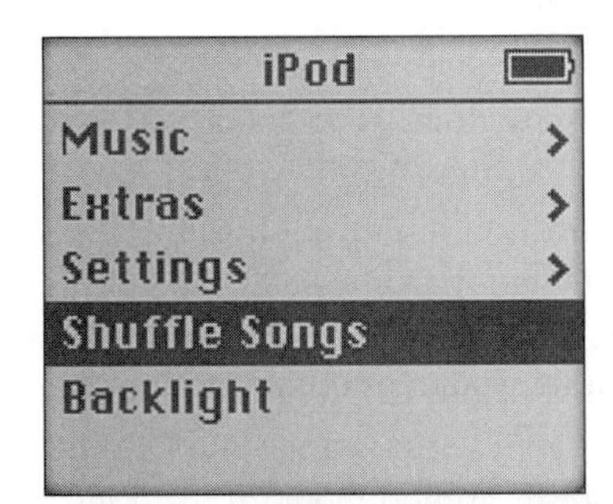

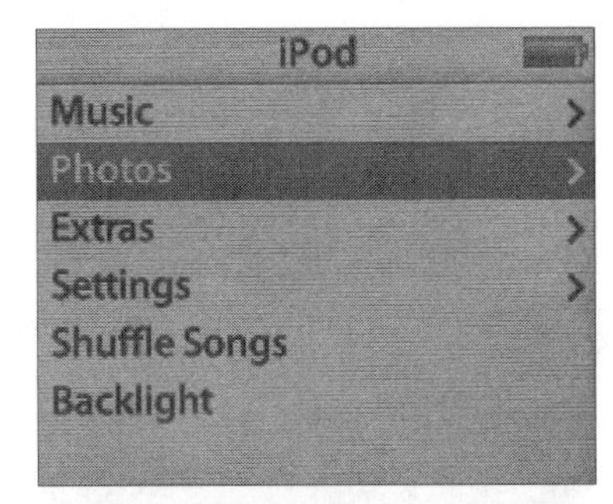

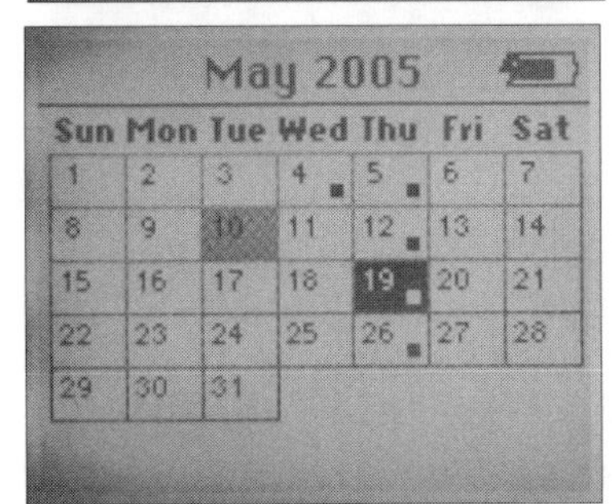

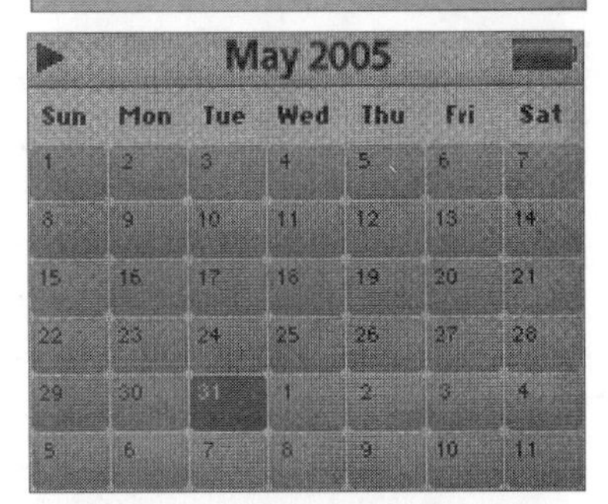

Comparison of analogous screens of the standard iPod and the iPod photo.

About Digital Music Technology

"But wait," you might be saying. "I thought compact discs were all about digital audio, which is what made them better than cassette tapes 20 years ago. How is that different from what is considered *digital music* in the iTunes' world?" And that's a fair question. In fact, it's got a good illustration built right into it. Think of digital music in the iTunes' age as being to CDs what CDs were to tapes. CDs are a digital medium, which means that the player can access any given song on the disc on command; with a CD, you can do such things as program the tracks to play in a certain order, randomly select songs from various discs in a changer, and so on. These features just weren't possible on an analog medium like the cassette tape, where the audio content consists of nothing more than a long, unbroken stream of magnetic material that is interpreted during playback as louder or softer sounds. The same huge leap in flexibility that we enjoyed in moving from tapes or vinyl records to CDs is now present as we move from CDs to pure digital music on our computers: Instead of the music data being stored on a physical disc that has to be moved around and manually loaded into a player, it's stored in the form of easily portable data files that can be played back in any order, modified, or copied from device to device by simply giving a command in software.

To accomplish this quantum leap in portability and control, a certain breakthrough or two was necessary. In the mid-1990s, these breakthroughs occurred. First, a compression algorithm was developed that shrunk the digital audio data from the uncompressed format in which it's stored on CDs (about 10MB per minute, far too large to be practical) to one in which large music collections could be conveniently stored on typical computer hard drives or transferred easily over the Internet. Additionally, processor speeds rose to the point where desktop computers could quickly and easily convert CD music data to the compressed format.

The MP3 Revolution

Developed in the early 1990s, ***MPEG-1 level 3 (MP3)*** became the first widely accepted encoding format that enabled the meteoric rise of digital music, even though it was underground and largely illicit at first. College students and young computer geeks with fast Internet connections used free or inexpensive encoding software (licensed from bodies such as the Fraunhofer Institute that holds the rights to the MP3 encoding algorithm) to convert its purchased CDs into MP3 format. After they were converted to the compressed digital form, these files immediately took on a life of their own, taking advantage of the files' relatively small size (usually 3 to 5 megabytes per song) and the explosive growth of the Internet to leap from computer to computer by way of the new breed of "peer-to-peer" software (such as Napster) that allowed MP3 collectors to seek out music on others' computers and quickly download it. Artists and record labels initially dismissed the threat that MP3 file sharing presented to their business model. However, soon it became apparent that the problem was not going to go away on its own—CD sales were slipping noticeably, and it would only get worse with time. A few high-profile lawsuits against MP3 collectors and broadcasters, and the legal shutdown of the Napster service, officially placed free music file sharing into the public eye—to some, an honorable form of rebellion against corporate tyranny; to others, the very act of killing the goose that lays the golden eggs.

▶ KEY TERM

MPEG-1 level 3 (MP3)—**The most widely used format for digital music, MP3 files sound pretty good but have no copy protection built in.**

There was no denying the benefit of digital music, after all. It's always been perfectly legal to copy a CD to MP3 format for your own use; it's just the unrestricted transmission of these unprotected music files to other, unrelated computer users that's illegal and a violation of copyright law. As long as you're using MP3s responsibly, if you've used them once, it's hard to go back. The convenience of playing a favorite song with a simple double-click—instead of digging out a CD and skipping to the appropriate numbered track as directed by the liner notes—is a difference of night and day. Similarly, CDs simply cannot compare to the organizational benefits of setting the ***info tags*** (or *ID3 tags*) on files so that you can immediately navigate to them by publication year, genre, track number, beats per minute, or even embedded album art images. Creating a mix CD from MP3 files is a giant leap above manually dubbing songs to a mix cassette tape as in the old days—then a laborious, hours-long process. Today, it involves little more than arranging the appropriate files in the right order, inserting a writable CD, and clicking a "burn" button.

▶ KEY TERM

Info tags—**Data fields built into a digital audio file that contain the song's title, artist, album, track number, album art, and other information. Often called *ID3 tags* in MP3 files; also referred to generically as *metadata*.**

The small size and platform-independence of MP3 files led to the inevitable creation of portable music players such as the iPod. Because MP3 files didn't actually take up any physical space to speak of (unlike music on CDs), the only limitation on how small a portable device could be made was in how large the screen and controls had to be to allow for easy navigation of your music. As an illustration, the iPod can't be made much smaller than the iPod mini variety—even if hard drive technology allowed the same storage capacity in a smaller package—because the user still has to work the wheel and buttons with her thumb, and the screen must be large enough to be readable while still retaining the six or seven lines of textual information that make the iPod's scrolling navigation so usable. These limitations are a far cry from the ones that dictate the shape of a portable CD player: no matter how small the technology of such a device gets, the overall unit can never get smaller than the five-inch bulk of a CD. (Also the user has to hold it horizontally and keep it from being jolted, which is all but an irrelevancy to digital music players—especially solid-state ones like the iPod shuffle.)

Going Legit

MP3 had its day in the sun, symbolizing the freedom of digital music as well as the irresponsibility that inevitably comes with such freedom. However, it was not to last. If digital music were to become a mainstream medium to rival or even replace CDs, it could not be on the MP3 format—because as soon as a record label sold an MP3, the purchaser could immediately turn around and broadcast it onto the peer-to-peer file-sharing networks (which have never gone away—rather, they've merely become more and more sneaky and undetectable by the authorities). Some online digital music stores, such as MP3.com and eMusic.com, have attempted to make a business case on selling MP3s created by artists who don't care about piracy and are only interested in exposure to their fans—but those artists are relatively few and don't include any of the big-name stars whose music most listeners want to buy.

The answer finally came when Apple introduced ***Advanced Audio Coding (AAC)***, a digital music format similar to MP3 but protected with digital signatures that ensure that only a limited number of "authorized" computers can open or play a given file. This format was introduced at the same time as the iTunes Music Store, which opened the doors of legal music downloads for both Mac and Windows users. AAC files' ***Digital Rights Management (DRM)*** technology gave the record industry the assurance it needed that the products it sold would not be devalued through immediate and uncontrollable duplication.

▶ KEY TERM

Digital Rights Management (DRM)—Software algorithms that provide "copy protection" for digital music, usually enforced with digital "keys."

Because of the DRM-protected flavor of the AAC format, record labels at last gave the nod to Apple, and it's because of the selection of popular music made available by that deal that the iTunes **Music Store** has become so popular where other similar ventures without industry-placating safeguards have failed. Built directly into iTunes, the Music Store is an online library of over a million downloadable tracks in thousands of albums by the most popular commercial artists and obscure cult idols alike. Leading the market by a wide margin, the iTunes

Music Store lets you buy music through an online account and download it directly into your iTunes **Music Library**. A single customer's purchased music, in AAC format, can be copied and played back on as many as five different computers, whether Windows PCs or Macs. This requires an Internet-based authorization process for each computer, however, and without that authorization the files cannot be opened. To read more about the details of the DRM technology used in iTunes and the AAC format, turn to 17 **About Digital Rights Management Technology**.

Fortunately, AAC files bring more to the table than just DRM restrictions; they also boast better audio quality and compression efficiency than MP3 files, making them smaller and clearer than MP3 files under most circumstances, with true separate stereo tracks and a more efficient codec (encoding and decoding) algorithm. This gives users their own good reasons to opt for AAC (which can be optionally encoded without any DRM restrictions, for example if you're importing your own CDs) instead of MP3.

▶ NOTE

Windows Media Audio (WMA) **provides similar features and benefits over MP3, although the DRM infrastructure used in WMA files (depending on the specific implementation used by a retailer) can be more restrictive than what is found in AAC.**

The downside of AAC files is that they're not as widely used as MP3 or even WMA files. Nearly all digital audio players can play MP3 files, and many can now handle WMA files as well. However, only the iPod can play AAC files. Considering that the iPod is the world's most popular portable digital music player by a huge margin, though, perhaps that is no drawback.

▶ NOTE

iTunes supports several digital music formats other than MP3 and AAC, as described in fuller detail in 8 **About Music Formats. AIFF** and **WAV**, both uncompressed formats, preserve flawless CD-quality audio at the expense of disk space. **Apple Lossless** is a format that halves the size of uncompressed CD audio with no loss of quality. iTunes for Windows can even import unprotected WMA files by converting them to AAC format; see 2 **Run iTunes for the First Time** and 11 **Add a Music File to Your iTunes Library** for more information.

With today's computer-component technology, a desktop PC or Mac can encode a full-length CD to MP3 or AAC format in as little as 1/20th the time it takes to play it all the way through at normal speed. The resulting files usually take up between 30 and 70 megabytes of space on your disk; this means that on a 120GB hard disk (a typical mid-range size for a desktop computer in 2005), you can potentially store about 2,500 CDs' worth of music, or 30,000 individual songs.

Besides which, with iTunes and the iPod, you can immediately dial up exactly the song, artist, or album you want to hear, without having to get up from your seat. That's a lot better than keeping your music discs in a disorganized, overflowing rack against your wall, isn't it?

iTunes and iPod on the Mac and Windows

Many Mac users—and Windows users, too—were stunned when in April 2003, along with opening the iTunes **Music Store**, Apple released a version of iTunes for Windows. Perhaps it was an inevitability. Before that release, Apple had sold iPods that were labeled for use with Windows; they were formatted to use Windows FAT32 file system format rather than the HFS+ file system on the Mac. Without a Windows version of iTunes to use in synchronizing them, however, these Windows iPods were only half a product. Apple had endorsed the MusicMatch Jukebox software for use with its Windows iPods. This solution was adequate, but hardly ideal. Thus, when Apple's iTunes **Music Store** finally debuted, bringing with it the first feasible system for legitimate and legal music downloads backed by the major record labels, it stood to reason that Apple would have to support it on the Windows side as well.

This move has paid off well. Most agree that iTunes' success on the Windows platform is what has really driven Apple's rise to popularity in the digital music industry; after all, even the most generous estimates place the market share of Macintosh users at about 5% of the computer industry, far too small to make any real impact on its own. Thus, when Apple released the Windows version of iTunes, its goal was to tap the hugely dominant Windows market as well as the already saturated Mac market, and to solidify its own AAC music file format as a Windows standard as well as a Mac one. Even though Apple is the only company to use AAC, and iTunes and the iPod are the only products to support it, their ubiquity across both platforms suggests that the gamble has worked.

▶ NOTE

A dirty little secret of the iTunes Music Store is that the store itself makes very little profit for Apple; each individual song's sale price almost completely goes to cover licensing fees, network storage and delivery costs, and Apple's own operating expenses. Apple makes its money from the music store by selling iPods, a revenue source its competitors can't claim.

Part of the success of iTunes on Windows is owed to customers' overall pleasant surprise at discovering that it is not merely a "port" of the Mac version; it's a stable, well-designed, well-integrated Windows application that's compatible with almost all popular CD drives (as is necessary for burning discs) and completely equal in all features with the Mac version of iTunes. Even such obscure features as third-party visualizers work on the Windows version. Part of this success is based on Apple's software design philosophy, which dictates that a piece of software should behave according to your expectations of it; so if a person is used to the Mac version of iTunes, he should be able to use the Windows version in the same way (and vice versa). The upshot is that Windows users believe that Apple is fully committed to making the Windows iTunes' experience every bit as good as the Mac iTunes' experience, and not merely treating the Windows world as an afterthought or its users as second-class citizens.

With all that background in mind, this book presents screenshots from both the Windows and Mac versions of iTunes when demonstrating techniques and features. Because iTunes works almost identically on both platforms, a figure or procedure showing one version of iTunes applies the same way to the other version. That said, however, there are a few minor caveats to keep in mind regarding iTunes' compatibility across platforms.

In Mac OS X, each application has its own Application menu (labeled with the application's own name) in the menu bar at the top of the screen. This convention is not present in Windows applications. Because iTunes was developed primarily with Mac OS X in mind, several options found in the Mac **iTunes** menu are instead found in other menus in the Windows version, primarily the **File** and **Help** menus (for example, **File, Exit** is the Windows equivalent of the Mac's **iTunes, Quit iTunes**). Also, the **Preferences** menu option, which appears in the **iTunes** menu on the Mac, is instead found in the **Edit** menu in the Windows version.

Another convention of the Mac operating system that can be confusing to newcomers to the Mac platform is its *modal* applications, meaning that the active application takes over the entire screen context, with its own menus appearing in the menu bar at the top. In contrast, Windows applications are all self-contained, each within its own window, with its menus shown under the window's title bar. iTunes on Windows has menus in this customary location. On the Mac, however, the menus don't appear in the iTunes' window itself—they're in the menu bar lining the top of the screen. iTunes must be the active application, in the foreground, for its menus to be accessible (however, iTunes' audio controls can be directly clicked and manipulated even if the application is not in the foreground).

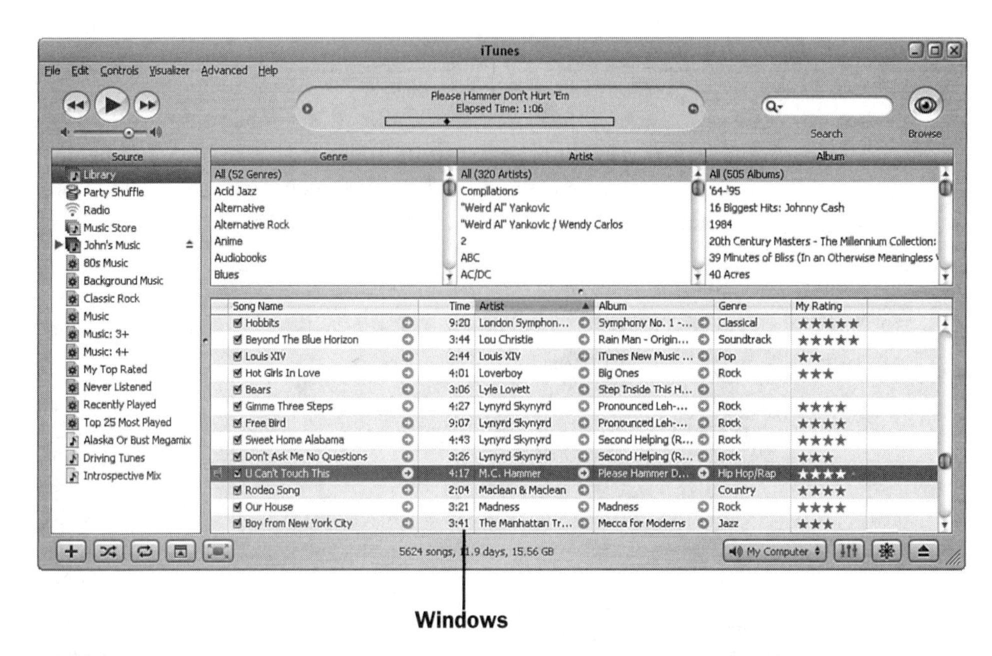

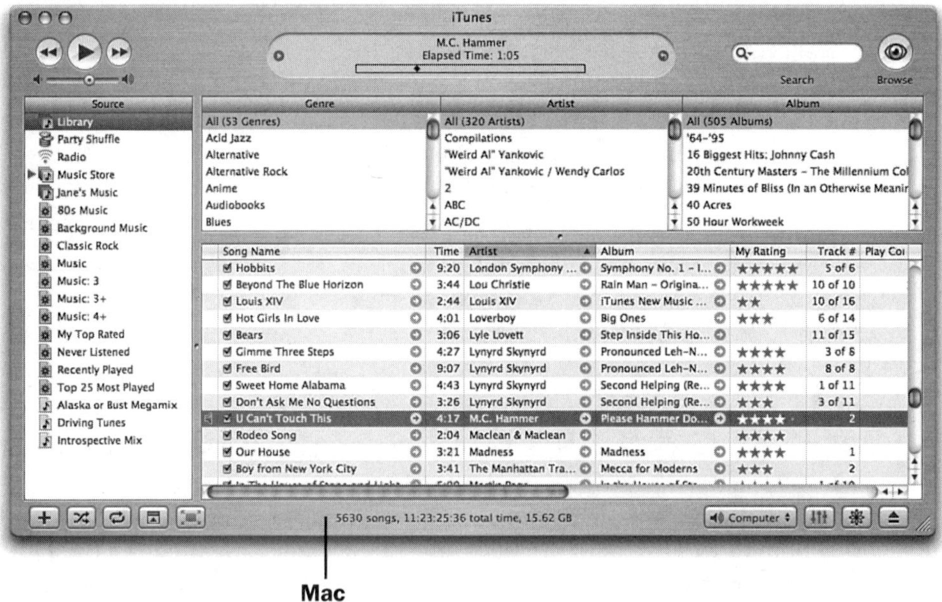

The Windows and Mac versions of iTunes compared.

One final esoteric feature of iTunes that differs across platforms is its handling of file paths. On the Mac, the HFS+ file system allows the operating system and applications (such as iTunes) to address each file by a unique ID number, not just by its path through the folders on the disk; thus iTunes can find a music file even if you move it to a completely different part of the disk. Windows, however, cannot track files this way; it can only use a file's path through the folders to locate the file. This means that if you move a file that's in the iTunes **Library** from one folder to another in Windows, iTunes will no longer be able to find that file if you try to play it. You'll have to reattach the link in the database using the method described in 62 **Repair a Missing Song Entry**.

The iPod theoretically works the same whether it's connected to a Windows PC or a Mac. However, you must be sure to buy the correct kind of iPod for your platform; a Windows iPod is formatted for the FAT32 file system, and a Mac iPod is formatted for HFS+ file system. Additionally, if you have an older iPod (1G or 2G), be aware that only FireWire connections are supported; you'll need to make sure that your PC has a FireWire card installed before you can connect your iPod. The same caution applies if your PC only supports USB 1.1 ("USB Full-speed") and not USB 2.0 ("USB High-speed"); all modern iPods except the iPod shuffle require either FireWire or USB 2.0. Add-on FireWire or USB 2.0 cards can be purchased for as little as $20 at computer or electronics stores.

▶ TIP

It's possible to convert a Mac iPod to a Windows iPod, or vice versa. First attach the iPod as a normal drive and format it for the target platform's native file system. Then restore the iPod's firmware and hard drive contents as described in 100 Restore Your iPod to Factory Settings. On older iPod models, be aware that this procedure is not supported by Apple and might void your warranty.

Get to Know the iTunes' Interface

If you are at all familiar with computer usage in general, interacting with your music in iTunes is generally a straightforward and intuitive affair. The sources of your music are listed in the **Source** pane on the left side of the window, including CDs, playlists, attached iPods, and any shared music libraries present on the network. The listings of songs—and the means for navigating them—are in the main body of the application window. This layout should not be too surprising, and you should be able to pick up iTunes' basic operation quickly. However, a few things about iTunes' more subtle behaviors might seem peculiar at first, and a good understanding of iTunes' structure and design intent are important in seeing why it does what it does.

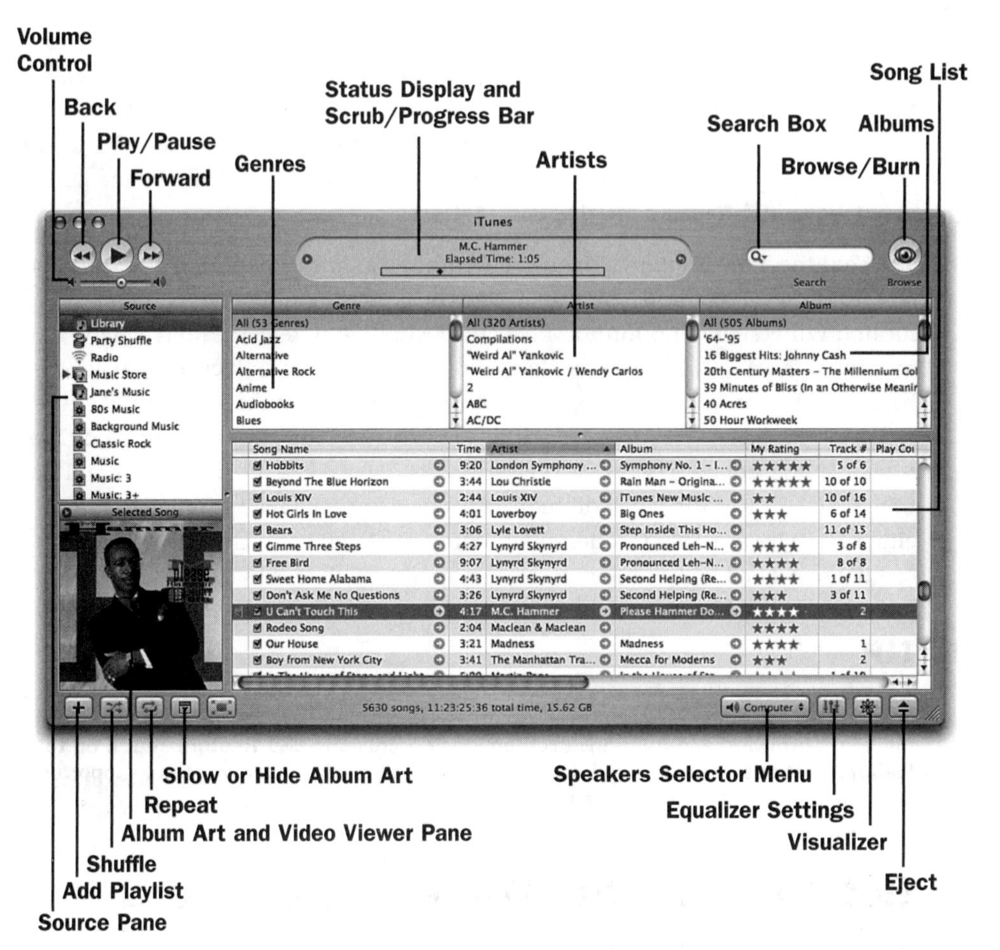

The main iTunes' window provides many features associated with recording and playing back audio files.

First of all, do not think of iTunes as merely a "player" for audio files you keep organized on your computer's hard disk. Rather, it is a separate, specialized interface for the *music* you own. It's a database, with references pointing to the music files on your hard disk and presenting them as usefully as possible. You manipulate these references in the database rather than representations of the files themselves. iTunes doesn't use the traditional "documents and folders" computing metaphor for organizing music; instead, it treats each individual audio file as a *song*, and organizes songs on the basis of their *artists*, *albums*, and *genres*, as well as in the custom *playlists* you can define. You don't "open an MP3 file" in iTunes as you would in a simple front-end program such as WinAmp. Rather, you select a song from iTunes' internal library and play it. The song you select corresponds to an MP3 or AAC file in a folder on your disk, and the folder it resides in is organized according to the artist and album—but you ideally never have to deal with the files themselves in the Finder or Windows Explorer in the course of your daily musical enjoyment. iTunes itself keeps track of all that for you.

Playing and controlling music in iTunes is analogous to the controls of most physical music players: The **Play/Pause** button starts and stops the music, the ***scrub bar*** lets you skip immediately to a specific place in a song by dragging the playhead, and the **Back** and **Forward** buttons skip from song to song in the current listing. Play a song by double-clicking it in the song list or by selecting it and clicking **Play**. There's nothing revolutionary about that. Where iTunes shines is in how it organizes your massive music collection and gets you to exactly the music you want.

KEY TERM

***Scrub bar*—A long, horizontal control with a sliding knob that allows you to skip directly to specific point in the timeline of a music or video file, as well as showing you your current position in the timeline.**

TIPS

If you click and hold the Back or Forward button, it will "rewind" or "fast-forward" the song in the same way most personal music players do.

Click the song information above the scrub bar to rotate between the song name, artist, and album, or to choose among Elapsed Time, Remaining Time, and Total Time readouts.

With **Library** selected in the **Source** pane, you can browse immediately to an artist (to see all the songs in that artist's albums) or to a particular album by using the **Browse** view (click the **Browse** button to reveal the navigation lists). The **Genre**, **Artist**, and **Album** lists operate in a manner similar to the Column view of the Mac OS X Finder: Selecting one or more items in one list narrows down the items shown in the columns to the right (so that if you select **Rock** from the **Genre** list, only Rock artists and albums are listed in the other two columns). You can also zoom straight to a song by typing part of its title into the **Search** box. By sorting the song list by its visible columns of data, you can put all your music in exactly the order you want to play it.

Songs in iTunes **Library** all have numerous pieces of data associated with them: Aside from the artist and album and genre, each song (potentially) has a track number, a "star" rating you can assign, a date when it was last played, and many other such fields—all specified in the ***info tags*** (or *ID3 tags*, for MP3 files) embedded within the file itself. iTunes' database structure works by managing songs by their info tags, which you can use to sort your songs into automatic ("Smart") playlists, filter them to your preference, and track how often you play them. By using this information, iTunes gradually molds itself to your listening style and preferences.

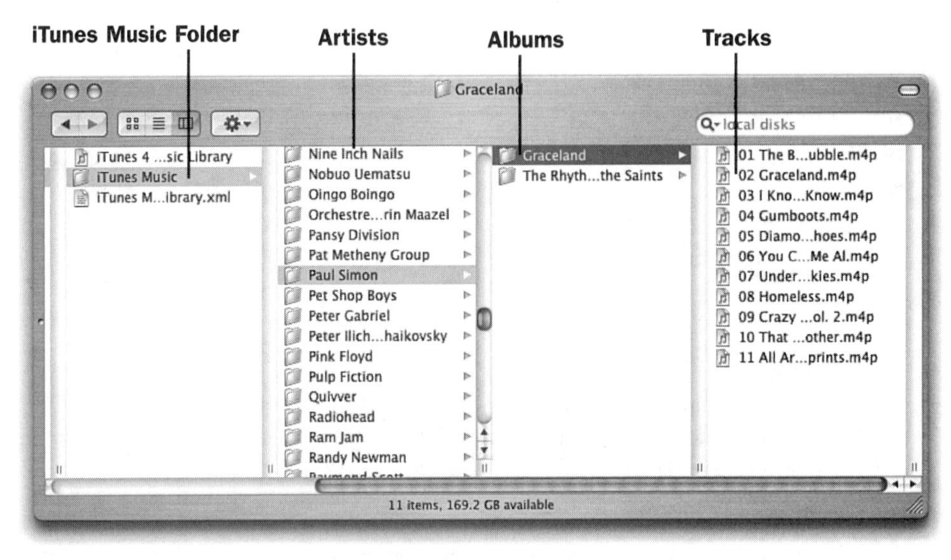

*The hierarchical structure of the **iTunes Music** folder, shown here in Mac OS X.*

Behind the scenes, iTunes keeps all its music files—MP3, AAC, and other formats it understands—in a special **iTunes Music** folder inside a folder called **iTunes** that also contains the main database file that iTunes reads and maintains. On the Mac, this folder resides inside the **Music** folder in your **Home** folder; on Windows, it's inside your **My Music** folder. Inside the **iTunes Music** folder are folders for every artist in the **Library**, and inside those folders are folders for each album by each artist. MP3 and AAC music files are sorted into those folders, with filenames kept in sync with the info tags you specify for the song name, track number, artist, and album. This way, you can always find your music files quickly using the Finder or Windows Explorer if you have to. iTunes can also keep track of music files that aren't in its **iTunes Music** folder, but those files won't be automatically organized if you change their info tags. See **12 Import Your Existing Music Collection into iTunes** if you're a seasoned MP3 collector and want to know more about what iTunes plans to do with your files.

For everyday musical enjoyment, you don't need to know much more than to choose the music source you want from the **Source** pane, then navigate to the music you want using the browser columns or by sorting on a column in the song listing. For example, find recently added music by clicking the header of the **Date Added** column; click the header again to reverse the direction in which the list is sorted. Find uncompressed AIFF files by sorting on the **Kind** column. Find all songs with "Night" in their song titles by typing **Night** into the **Search** box; sort the results by clicking one of the column headers. These controls and more are covered in greater detail in 33 **Find and Play Music.**

Selecting different music sources or methods of viewing your music puts iTunes into any of several "views" that are referred to from time to time in this book. Here are some of the most important views:

- **Library view.** With **Library** selected in the **Source** pane, you can view all your music in a single long list, sorted by the selected column.
- **Browse view.** Click the **Browse** button to see the **Genre**, **Artist**, and **Album** lists, which allow you to zero in on exactly the music you want. The **Browse** button is not always available (for example, in **Playlist** view, where there's a **Burn Disc** button instead), but you can always activate **Browse** view by selecting **Show Browser** from the **Edit** menu.
- **Playlist view.** Choose a playlist from the **Source** pane to see the songs in the list, which are only references to the songs in the **Library**. See 34 **Create a Playlist** and 35 **Create a Smart Playlist.**
- **Music Store view.** Select **Music Store** from the **Source** pane to browse and buy new music; see 19 **Browse the Music Store** for more information.
- **Shared Music view.** Choose any shared music library or playlist from the **Source** pane to browse and play music stored on someone else's computer. See 58 **Share Your Music over the Local Network.**

Get to Know the iPod Interface

In a world where clumsy, difficult-to-navigate MP3 players have been commonplace, the iPod—when it was released—was a much-needed breath of fresh air. Billed since the beginning as "iTunes to Go," the iPod presented a synthesis of iTunes' sensible organizational structure and a navigation system that worked *with* a human being's hand rather than rebelling against it. The revolutionary navigation wheel is several controls in one: someone who has never seen an iPod before might wonder where all the directional buttons and volume controls are; they're all incorporated into the wheel. While you're navigating the menus, the wheel moves the selection bar up and down, and the **Select** button chooses an option. When a song is playing, the wheel adjusts the volume. Additional wheel functions, such as seeking to a point within a song, are accessed by pressing the **Select** button one or more times to change the mode and then turning the wheel.

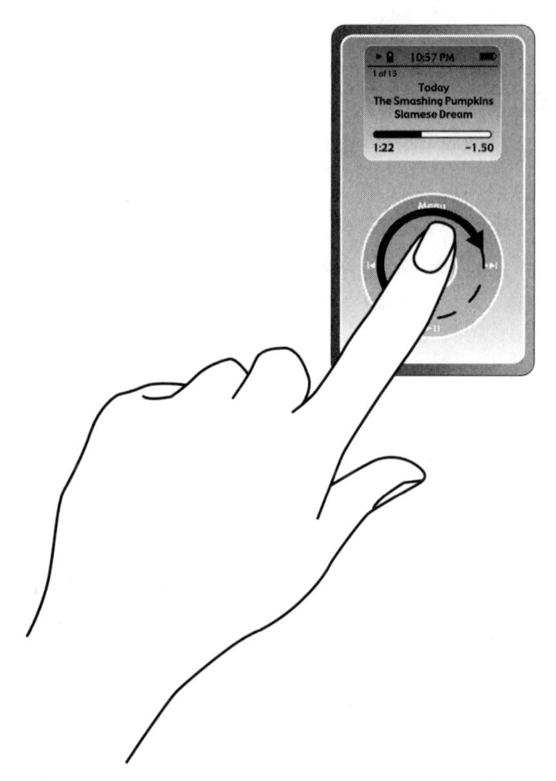

*Slide your finger or thumb in a circle on the wheel surface to navigate through the menu systems and control the volume. Press the **Select** button in the center to make a selection.*

The four remaining buttons are the minimum necessary for complete control of the device. Whether the buttons are arranged in a ring surrounding the wheel (as in the 1G and 2G iPods), in a row above the wheel (as in the 3G iPod), or incorporated into the wheel itself (as in the 4G iPod, iPod photo, and iPod mini), they cover the same functions: moving back and forward one track at a time (or, if you hold them down, fast-seeking backward and forward within the song), pausing and resuming the music, and moving up to the previous menu level.

▶ NOTE

The iPod shuffle, lacking both a screen and a navigation wheel, has separate volume control buttons in addition to Back, Forward, and Play/Pause buttons. The iPod remote has the same selection of controls that the iPod shuffle does.

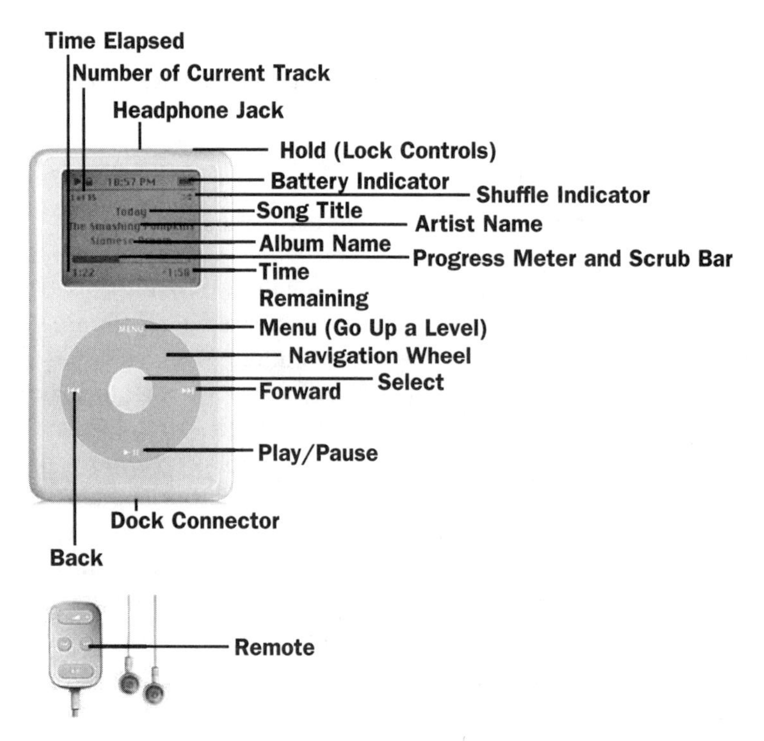

The iPod's controls allow you to delve into your music collection and zero in on the music you want with a spin of the dial.

The iPod remote, an accessory that comes standard with some iPod models and is also available separately, is designed to give you most of the control you need while listening to your music, without having to pull your iPod out of your pocket or its belt clip. The remote plugs directly into the top of the iPod, and your headphones or earbuds plug into the other side of the remote. You can then clip the remote to your lapel or the seam of your pants. The controls on the remote cover the necessary functionality of the iPod aside from direct navigation and manipulation of the source of music currently being played.

On both the iPod remote and the iPod itself, there's a **Hold** switch that disables all the iPod's controls when engaged, ensuring that your iPod can't be inadvertently jostled into switching music tracks or cranking up the volume to maximum while you're jogging or reaching for your loose change. The switch is deliberately hard to move so that you can't accidentally flip it on or off. When it's engaged, a "lock" icon appears on the iPod's screen, so check for this icon if your iPod's controls don't seem to be working.

▶ NOTE

The Hold switch on the iPod affects only the iPod's built-in controls; the Hold switch on the remote affects only the remote's controls.

▶ TIP

Holding down the **Menu** button for several seconds turns the backlight on or off.

If you leave the iPod undisturbed without playing music for two minutes, its screen shuts itself off automatically and the iPod enters its sleep mode (from which it can be awakened at the touch of any control button). If you're impatient, you can put the iPod to sleep immediately by holding down the **Play/Pause** button. When the iPod is asleep, it does not lose its place in the menus or in a song you're playing; when you wake it back up, it'll resume playing almost instantly, right where you left off. Even in sleep mode, however, the iPod uses a small amount of battery power; after two days of sitting unused, the iPod shuts down entirely. Pressing a button on a powered-down iPod causes it to go through its full boot procedure, which takes 10 to 15 seconds, and can be identified by the Apple logo that appears on the screen before the menus become visible.

On rare occasions, the iPod might become unresponsive and require you to reset it (which is equivalent to rebooting the system software). First toggle the **Hold** switch to its engaged position, and then back again to unlock it. For 3G and earlier iPods, hold down the **Menu** and **Play/Pause** buttons simultaneously for several seconds until the Apple logo appears on the screen. For the 4G iPod and iPod mini, because those two buttons are opposite each other on the click wheel and can't be pressed simultaneously, instead hold down the **Select** and **Menu** buttons to reset the unit.

To play music, use the navigation wheel to scroll through the Main Menu options to highlight **Playlists** (to access your playlists) or **Browse** (to select music by artist, album, or song name). Press the **Select** button to move to the next screen. Continue navigating in this way until you see the music you want to hear; press **Select** to begin playing it. Alternatively, select the name of any playlist, artist, or album and press **Play/Pause** to begin playing all the music categorized in that selection. These techniques and more are covered in greater detail in **46 Find and Play Music on the iPod**.

2

Setting Up iTunes and iPod

IN THIS CHAPTER:

1. Download and Install iTunes
2. Run iTunes for the First Time
3. Select Your iPod's Language
4. Connect Your iPod for the First Time
5. Set the iPod's Date and Time
6. Configure Your iPod for Your Headphones or Speakers
7. Configure the iPod's Backlight

Perhaps you've just bought a new iPod and are itching to get down to using it. Perhaps you've had an iPod and iTunes for a while now and are just now opening this book to see what tips and tricks you're missing. Either way, it's a good idea for you to use the tasks in this chapter to ensure that your copy of iTunes is installed and configured properly and that your iPod is set up according to your needs.

Whether you're using a Mac or a Windows PC, setting up iTunes is a pretty straightforward process—it's also a familiar procedure if you've ever installed software before. Nonetheless, the process involves some subtleties that might not be apparent to you at first. The same goes for the iPod, which has many hidden features and settings that it's important to set right away for optimal success in enjoying your music.

1 Download and Install iTunes

✔ BEFORE YOU BEGIN	→ SEE ALSO
Just jump right in!	2 Run iTunes for the First Time

If you're using a Mac, chances are you already have iTunes installed—it's bundled as part of the standard software loadout of every brand-new Mac. If you're using Windows, however (unless you're the owner of one of the few PC manufacturers that bundle iTunes with their new computers), you must download iTunes and install it on your system before you can use it.

Even Mac users should check periodically to make sure they have the newest version of iTunes with all the latest and greatest features. It's delivered by the standard Software Update mechanism in Mac OS X, or can be downloaded and installed manually using the procedure described in this task.

▶ NOTE

iTunes ships with every new iPod. If you just bought an iPod, install iTunes directly from the included software disc, according to the instructions packaged with the iPod, rather than following this procedure.

Before beginning this task, ensure that you are able to connect to the Internet properly. You must be able to reach Apple's website (**www.apple.com**) with your web browser to download iTunes, which is free of charge.

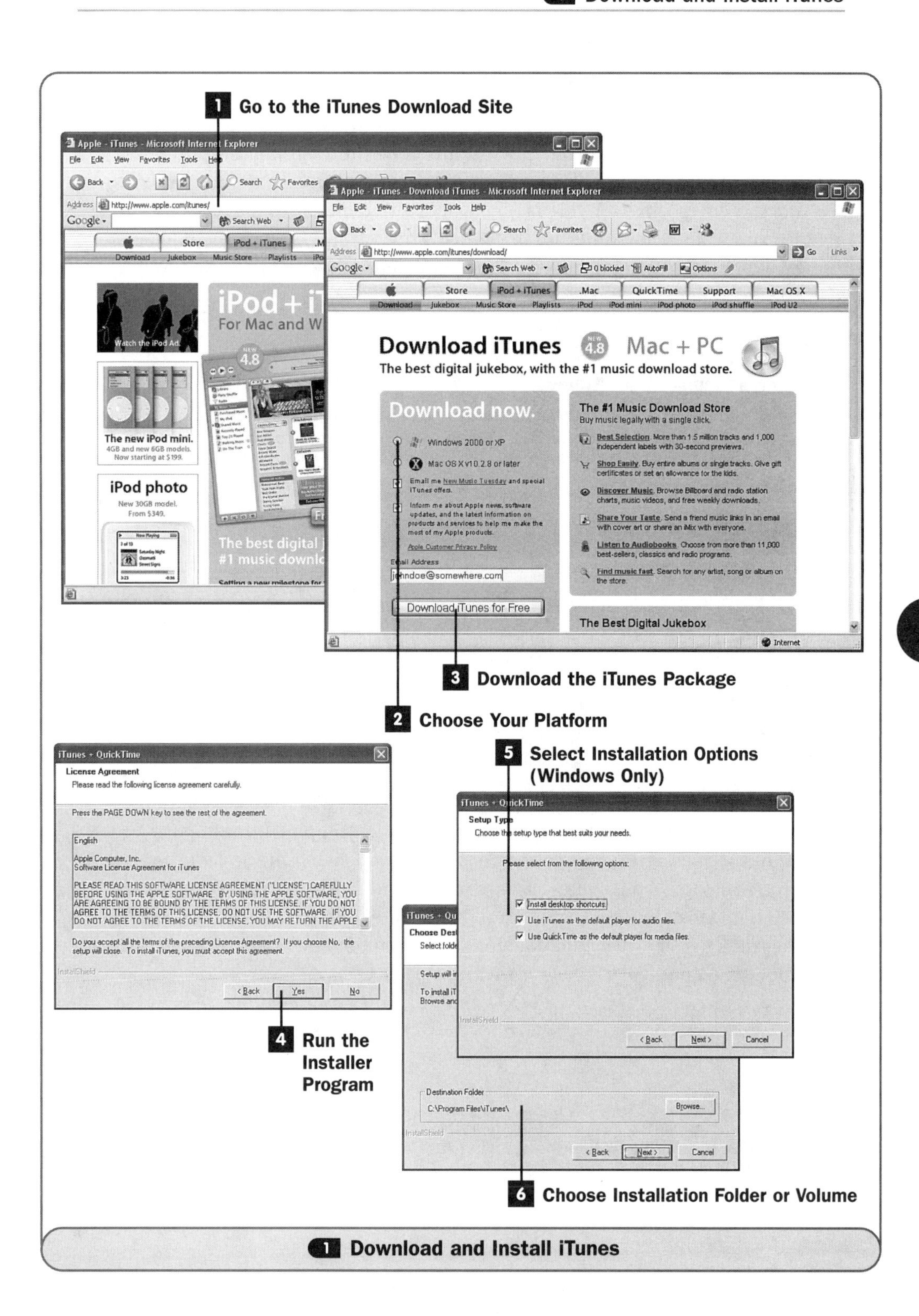

1 Download and Install iTunes

1 Go to the iTunes' Download Site

Open your web browser (Internet Explorer on Windows, or Safari on the Mac), type the address **http://www.apple.com/itunes**, and press **Enter**. If your computer is configured properly to access the Internet, the iTunes' website should appear, with its customary marketing materials that attempt to sell you iPods and songs from the iTunes **Music Store**. Right in the middle of the screen is a large link labeled **Free Download**; click this link to go to the download page.

▶ WEB RESOURCE

http://www.apple.com/itunes

Even after you install iTunes, the iTunes' website can be a useful place for you to start using some of its features; the site has links to pages where you can buy gift certificates, set up allowances, or get iTunes' technical support, among other functions.

2 Choose Your Platform

The download page first prompts you to select your platform. The radio button matching the operating system you're using should be selected automatically; if it isn't, choose **Mac OS X v10.2.8 or later** or **Windows 2000 or XP** accordingly.

1

3 Download the iTunes Package

First enable or disable the check boxes specifying whether you want Apple to send you promotional email messages and the weekly New Music Tuesdays notification. If you're concerned about privacy and don't like getting marketing email, disable these check boxes. However, if you plan on using the iTunes **Music Store**, you might want to consider leaving the box for the New Music Tuesdays notification checked. The iTunes **Music Store** is constantly being updated; hundreds of albums (from today and yesteryear) are added to the catalog every week, and the notification sent out every Tuesday lets you know when particularly noteworthy music has been made available. If you leave either of the two check boxes enabled, enter your email address in the text box provided, so that you can receive the messages.

▶ TIP

You can see a complete listing of all the new music added to the iTunes **Music Store** every week by clicking **See All** in the scrolling **Just Added** box on the iTunes **Music Store**'s main page.

When you're ready to begin downloading, click the **Download iTunes for Free** button. Your browser begins downloading the iTunes' installer package, and the main browser window changes to show a brief introduction to installing and using iTunes.

If you're using Internet Explorer on Windows, you might be prompted for several ways to handle the downloaded file. Click **Save** to save the installer package to your Desktop or click **Run** to run the installer from within the browser. Either option should suit your needs of installing the software, but choose **Save** if you want to keep the installer file around for future use.

4 Run the Installer Program

The installer package for Windows is about 20 megabytes in size, which should take about an hour to download on a 56K modem connection—less time on a broadband link such as DSL or cable. The package for Mac OS X is about half the size and takes about half the time to download.

After the package has finished downloading, unpack it if necessary. Mac OS X should unpack the file automatically into a mounted **iTunes 4.8.0** disk image—if it doesn't, double-click the downloaded **iTunes4.8.dmg** file that appears on the Desktop; Windows automatically saves the **iTunesSetup.exe** file to your selected download location. Double-click the resulting installer program icon—**iTunes4.mpkg** on the Mac, **iTunesSetup.exe** on Windows—to launch the iTunes installer.

▶ NOTE

The iTunes' installation folder for Mac OS X includes a file labeled **Read Before You Install iTunes**; it's a good idea to open and read this document, which describes system requirements and information about the most recent version's changes. This same document is available in the Windows version as one of the screens in the installer, as well as after installation as the **About iTunes** file in the **iTunes** program group.

The installer does essentially the same things on both Windows and the Mac, although the details of which screens appear in what order varies. An important distinction is that on Windows, the installer also includes *QuickTime,* which is Apple's audio/video framework that underlies and supports iTunes. QuickTime is built into Mac OS X, so the iTunes' installer does not need to install QuickTime on the Mac.

▶ KEY TERM

***QuickTime*—Apple's multimedia technology, built into Mac OS X; it must be installed on Windows for iTunes to work.**

The first screen of the installer contains information on the particular version of iTunes that you are installing, including system requirements, installation instructions, and notes about copyright. The next screen shows you the Software License Agreement, which you must accept by clicking **Agree** or **Yes** when prompted.

5 Select Installation Options (Windows Only)

On Windows, you are given the opportunity to disable any of three check boxes that define whether the installer will add iTunes' shortcuts to your Desktop, as well as whether you want to use QuickTime and iTunes as the default players for common multimedia files (such as JPEG and GIF images, MPEG and AVI movies, and individual MP3 audio files) on your computer. If you're happy with how image and movie files open on your computer already, disable the second and third check boxes; otherwise, leave them checked to use QuickTime, its included PictureViewer application, and iTunes to open those files in the future.

6 Choose Installation Folder or Volume

Finally, choose where on the disk you want to install iTunes (the default given location is usually okay) and click **Next** to begin the process of installing iTunes onto your disk. On Mac OS X, you are prompted instead to choose a destination volume (disk); iTunes is installed into the **Applications** folder of the volume you select on the Mac. Pick your startup disk if you have a choice.

On Windows 2000, you might be prompted to restart your computer at the completion of the installation process because parts of the setup process can be completed only after a restart.

After completing the installation, you can delete the downloaded package files (**iTunes4.8.dmg** on the Mac, **iTunesSetup.exe** on Windows). You're now ready to run iTunes for the first time.

2 Run iTunes for the First Time

✔ BEFORE YOU BEGIN	→ SEE ALSO
1 Download and Install iTunes	4 Connect Your iPod for the First Time 12 Import Your Existing Digital Music Collection into iTunes

Running iTunes for the first time is a little more complicated than any subsequent time you use it. This one-time process sets up iTunes by asking you a few questions about how you want to use iTunes; the options you're given can have some subtle but surprising consequences, so it pays to know what you're clicking during this procedure.

▶ NOTE

The options for organizing your music discussed in this task can be controlled in the Advanced pane of the iTunes Preferences window, if at any time you change your mind about them.

Apple has designed iTunes to be a total music management system, controlling every mile of the music-enjoyment process, from the purchasing or importing of new songs to the sharing of songs with others or transferring it to other devices. The entire process is governed not by definitive filenames and folder names, but by the contents of the info tags on each song in the database. This comprehensive design can be at odds with the way you expect digital music software to behave. One specific example is iTunes' capability to organize the filenames of your music files for you. With this option enabled, every name change you make to the info tags on songs within iTunes is automatically reflected in the filenames on the corresponding digital music files, which iTunes changes to keep up with your commands.

If you have an existing collection of MP3 files, and you allow iTunes to import them all into its library during this setup process, you might be caught by surprise to find that all your music files have been duplicated, renamed, and automatically filed into folders corresponding to the artists and albums in your library. Many unsuspecting first-time iTunes' users have been taken aback by this behavior or have been infuriated to find that all their carefully named and organized files have been copied into new folders and renamed (even if the original files were untouched). Yet if you take the time beforehand to ensure that iTunes doesn't do this to you—or, even better, to understand the intent of iTunes' design so that its reorganizing efforts are more of a benefit than an affront—you'll be a lot happier in the long run. See 12 **Import Your Existing Digital Music Collection into iTunes** after following this procedure if you've already got a digital music collection.

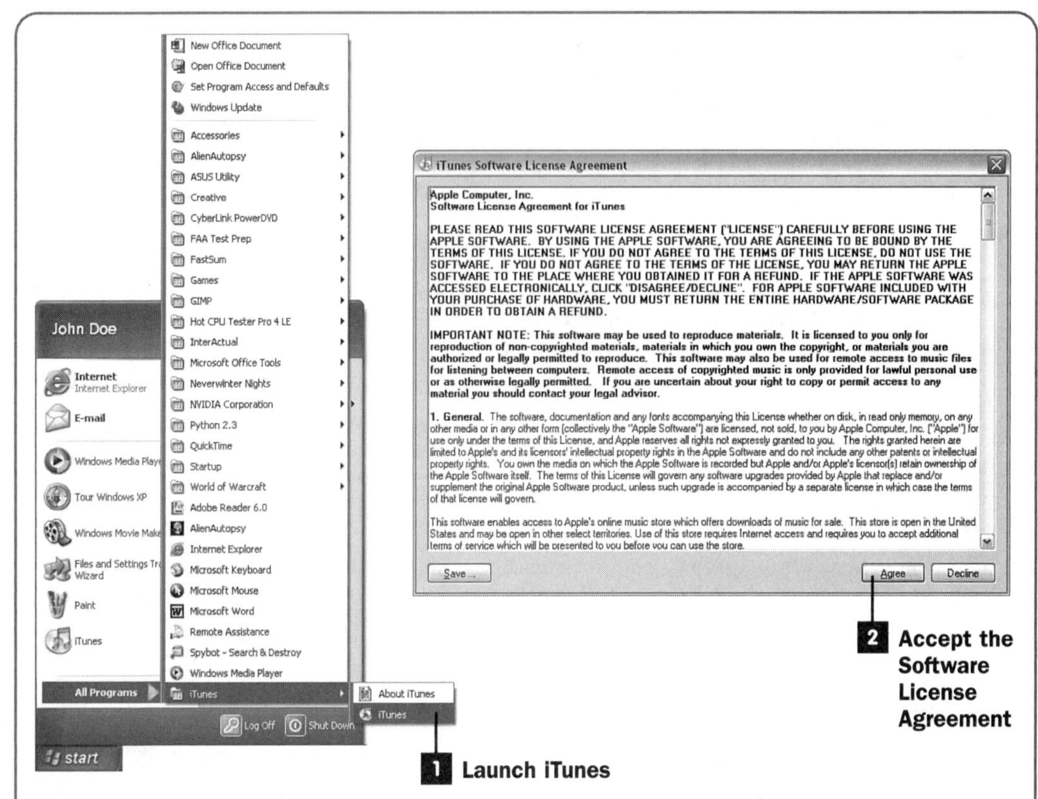

1 Launch iTunes

2 Accept the Software License Agreement

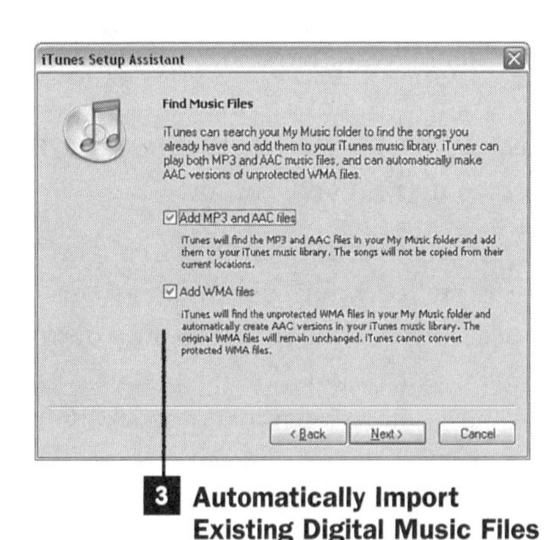

3 Automatically Import Existing Digital Music Files

4 Allow iTunes to Keep Your iTunes Music Folder Organized

5 Start with the iTunes Music Store

2 Run iTunes for the First Time

1 Launch iTunes

In Windows, navigate to **iTunes** in the **All Programs** submenu of the **Start** menu and select it to launch the application. In Mac OS X, click the **iTunes** icon in the Dock, or double-click the icon in the **Applications** folder.

2 Accept the Software License Agreement

Instead of the iTunes' window, which is what you'll see for every subsequent launch of the application, for this setup process you'll first see a window displaying the Software License Agreement. Read this document thoroughly if you want to be familiar with the rules of using iTunes; because it's a piece of software specifically designed to work with copyrighted materials that may or may not be used legally, it's a good idea to be familiar with what you're agreeing to. You have several options: **Save** lets you save the Agreement to a file for later perusal, **Print** (if available) sends the agreement straight to your printer, and **Decline** quits iTunes. Only if you click **Agree** will iTunes proceed with the setup screens.

From this point on, you can abort the initial setup process by clicking **Cancel**; if you do, iTunes will start normally. However, the next time you launch iTunes, you are prompted again to go through this setup process.

3 Automatically Import Existing Digital Music Files

iTunes can scour your hard drive looking for digital music files in MP3, AAC, or unprotected WMA format, and add them automatically to its library. If you've got an existing collection of music, you can leave the **Add MP3 and AAC Files** check box enabled and let iTunes import these files automatically. However, bear in mind that iTunes will find music files all throughout the system, not just where you like to keep your music; you might end up with the internal soundtracks from your video games imported into iTunes. If you disable this option, refer to 12 **Import Your Existing Digital Music Collection into iTunes** to bring your music into iTunes' **Library** in a more controlled manner.

You can change your mind about how your music is organized at a later time as well; see 67 **Consolidate Your Music Library** for more information.

▶ NOTE

If you leave the Add MP3 and AAC Files and Add WMA Files check boxes enabled, iTunes *copies* the music files to the iTunes, iTunes Music folder inside your Music or My Music folder—it doesn't *move* them. This approach ensures that your original music files remain untouched. However, it also means your disk space is suddenly taken up with *two copies* of every song you own. Be sure that you have plenty of disk space before proceeding; also, be sure to delete your unwanted original files when you're satisfied with the way iTunes has imported them!

The **Add WMA Files** option (which exists only on the Windows version, and is only available if you have Windows Media Player 9 Series or later installed—visit **http://www.windowsmedia.com** if you don't) works similarly to the **Add MP3 and AAC Files** option, except that when iTunes finds a WMA file, it converts it to AAC on-the-fly as it imports it, leaving the original WMA file untouched. iTunes cannot import *protected WMA files*, meaning purchased music files you might have obtained from a competing online digital music store. If you have a lot of these files, you might have to convert them to an unprotected format using a sneaky and painstaking method similar to the one described in 56 **Create an MP3 CD from Purchased AAC Music**.

When you've made your selection about the music files you want iTunes to automatically import, click **Next**.

4 Allow iTunes to Keep Your iTunes Music Folder Organized

The following setup screen gives you the option to allow iTunes to rename files and folders within the iTunes **Music** folder. This special folder is where iTunes keeps all the music it imports, as well as the songs it imported in the previous step (if you chose to let it do so). If you choose **No, I'll change the file and folder names myself** in this screen, changes you make to song titles, artist names, and album names within iTunes are not reflected in the file structure of the iTunes **Music** folder. However, if you choose **Yes, keep my iTunes Music folder organized,** every time you make such a change, iTunes automatically makes the same change in the names of the files in the iTunes **Music** folder. This means that if you ever have a need to navigate into that folder to pull out the bare music files—for example, to copy them to another system or send them through email—you can be sure that the files are named exactly the way you expect. Each file's name reflects the disc number (if that info tag is set), track number, and song title, and is organized into a folder for the album, within a folder for the artist. This behavior can be turned off later in the **Advanced** pane of the iTunes **Preferences** window (see 12 **Import Your Existing Digital Music Collection into iTunes**).

5 Start with the iTunes Music Store

The final choice you're given is whether to start iTunes this very first time by opening the iTunes **Music Store**, or by going straight to your music library. Choose the option that's best for you; this is most likely to be the second because you'll likely prefer to browse your music collection rather than jump straight into buying more music. It's the best way to get acquainted with iTunes, after all.

Click **Finish** to complete the setup process and arrive at the iTunes' window. If you chose to have iTunes search your hard disk for existing music files in Step 3, this search process takes place now; it may take a minute or two, so be patient while iTunes works. When the process is complete, all your existing music appears in iTunes' song listing pane.

3 Select Your iPod's Language

✔ BEFORE YOU BEGIN	→ SEE ALSO
Just jump right in!	4 Connect Your iPod for the First Time 5 Set the iPod's Date and Time 100 Restore Your iPod to Factory Settings

After you unwrap your new iPod, the first thing you have to do is pick a language. The iPod supports 14 languages in its interface, including Spanish, German, French, Swedish, Danish, Japanese, Korean, Simplified and Traditional Chinese, and others. The language you select when you first take the iPod out of its box defines the presentation of the entire iPod menu system.

1 Turn On the iPod

Make sure that the **Hold** button is not engaged. Press any button, such as the **Select** button, to wake up the iPod from sleep mode.

▶ NOTE

Most iPods have a partial battery charge when they're removed from their retail boxes. You should completely charge your iPod's battery as soon as you get it home from the store, but there is usually plenty of power to wake it from sleep and explore the menus after you set its language.

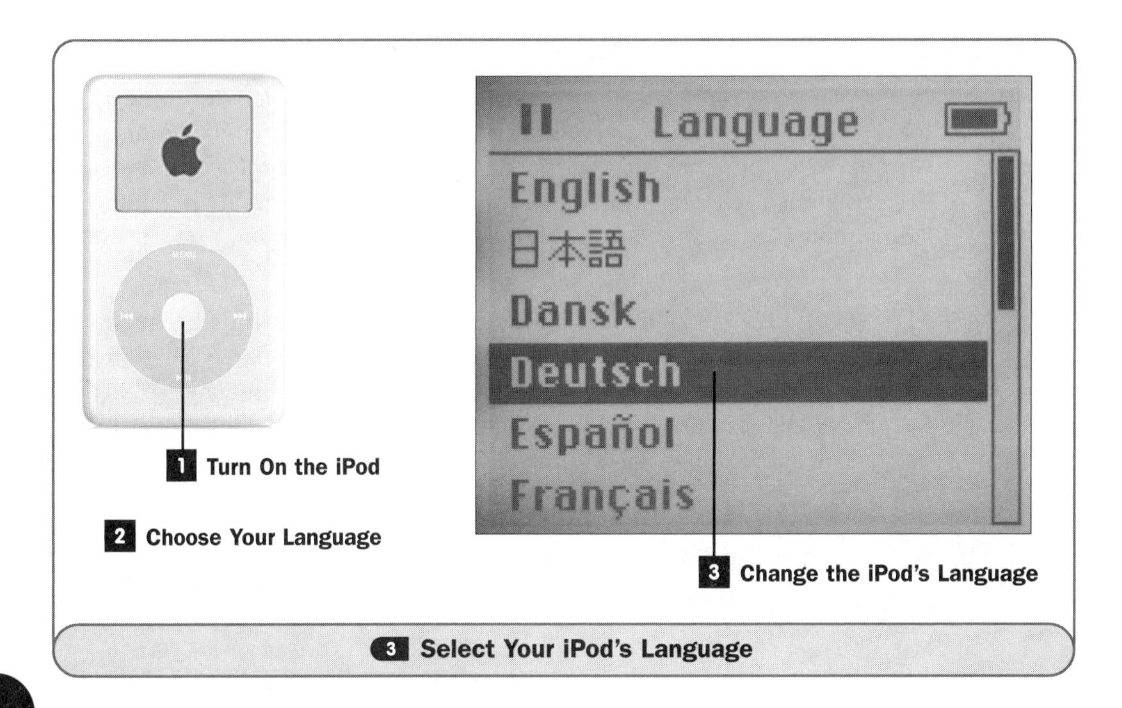

2 Choose Your Language

If the iPod's language has not yet been set (as is the case with brand-new units) the first screen you see is a list of languages. This will be your first opportunity to see how the navigation wheel works. Move your thumb in a circular path around the wheel to move the selection cursor up and down until your language of choice is highlighted. Press the **Select** button (in the center of the wheel) to choose this language and go to the iPod's Main Menu.

3 Change the iPod's Language

If you want to change the iPod's language, you can do so at any time by navigating into the **Settings** menu, then choosing the **Language** option.

▶ TIP

If you accidentally set the iPod to a language you can't read, you can get to the **Language** menu as follows: Press the **Menu** button a few times until you're at the Main Menu (the top of the screen reads **iPod**). Unless you have customized your Main Menu (see 82 **Customize the iPod's Main Menu**), the **Settings** menu—whatever it's called in the language you have selected—is the third option from the top. Select that option; in the next screen, **Language** is the third option from the bottom. Select that option and then choose your correct language from the screen that follows.

4 Connect Your iPod for the First Time

✔ BEFORE YOU BEGIN

2 Run iTunes for the First Time
3 Select Your iPod's Language

→ SEE ALSO

42 Transfer Your Music to Your iPod
100 Restore Your iPod to Factory Settings

The first time you plug in your iPod, you're led through a brief setup process that's necessary for the future usability of the iPod's synchronization features. iTunes launches whenever an iPod is plugged in; if iTunes detects that a new iPod has been connected that has not yet been set up, a series of dialog boxes prompts you for a name by which iTunes should address the iPod whenever you connect it in the future. You're also prompted to choose whether the iPod should be automatically synchronized with your iTunes **Library**, and you're given the chance to register your iPod with Apple for support benefits.

1 Connect Your iPod Using FireWire or USB2

Using the iPod Dock (if you have one), or a direct USB 2.0 or FireWire cable plugged in at one end to your computer, connect your new iPod at the Dock connector port, located on the bottom edge of the iPod. The iPod wakes from sleep, then immediately switches to the **Do Not Disconnect** icon, which indicates that it's being mounted as an external device by the computer. Do not disconnect your iPod while this icon is shown because you could damage the data on the iPod. (This doesn't matter with a new and empty iPod, but it's important to follow this rule at all times.)

iTunes launches automatically. When it detects your iPod connected to the computer, it presents a dialog box labeled **iPod Setup Assistant**. (See step 5 if your iPod is not automatically detected.)

4

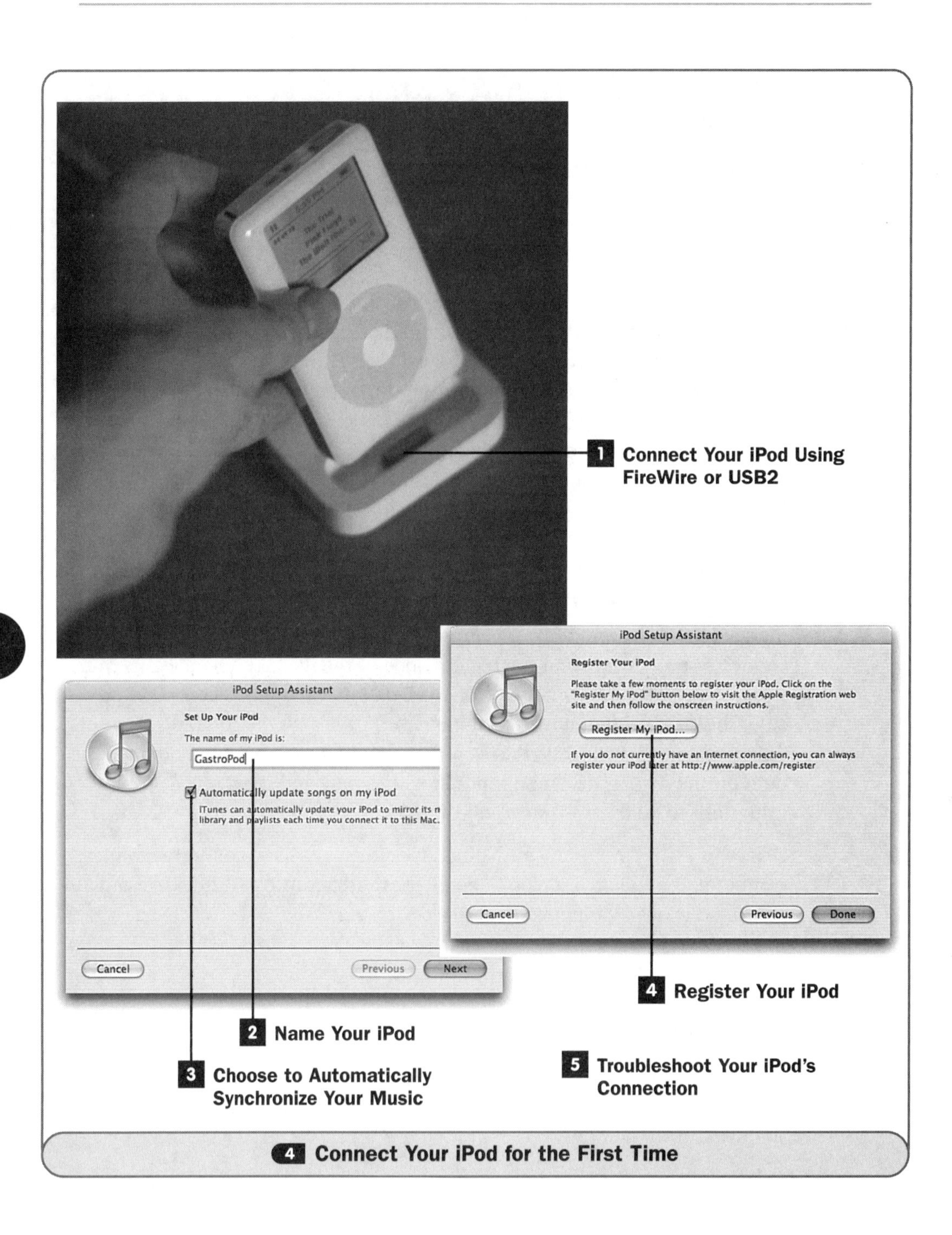

4 Connect Your iPod for the First Time

2 Name Your iPod

Choose a name for your iPod. For a Mac iPod, this name can be as long as you like (to a practical maximum of 68 characters) and should uniquely identify your iPod so that you can easily see when it's connected in iTunes. The name can contain any special characters except for the colon (:). However, if you have a Windows iPod or an iPod shuffle, because these units use a FAT32 file system instead of the Mac's native HFS+ file system, you must also avoid spaces and special characters such as . " / \ [ ] : ; | = , when you name your iPod.

▶ TIP

You can change your iPod's name at any time by renaming it in the **Source** pane in iTunes or by renaming the volume while it's mounted as an external disk.

3 Choose to Automatically Synchronize Your Music

The **Automatically update songs on my iPod** check box is automatically selected. If you leave it this way, all your songs, artists, albums, and playlists will be automatically copied to your iPod and updated each time you connect it so that the contents of your iPod are always in sync with what's in your iTunes **Library**. If your iPod's capacity is larger than your iTunes **Library**, it's best to leave this box selected. If your music collection is larger than your iPod, however, disable the check box and refer to 43 **Use a Large iTunes Library with a Small iPod** for more information on how to make the best use of your iPod.

4

▶ NOTE

If you have an iPod shuffle, the check box is labeled **Automatically choose songs for my iPod**. If you enable this check box, iTunes copies a random selection of songs to "autofill" the iPod shuffle. See 44 **Autofill Your iPod Shuffle** for details.

4 Register Your iPod

Click **Next** to apply your chosen name and configuration to the iPod. In the following screen, you can simply click **Done** to exit the assistant and return to using iTunes. However, before you do that, it's a good idea to click the **Register My iPod** button to visit the support website where you can provide your iPod's serial number and other information to Apple. Registering your iPod in this way ensures that, in the future, if you have a technical problem with your iPod, Apple's support technicians will be able to quickly find your product's information on file and save time in diagnosing and solving your problem.

When you click **Done**, iTunes begins synchronizing your iPod's contents and copying all the music in its library to the iPod's hard drive (if you chose to do so in Step 3). If you already have a lot of music in iTunes, this might take several minutes; don't disconnect the iPod until iTunes' display reads **iPod update is complete**, and the **Do not disconnect** icon on the iPod disappears and is replaced with the navigation menus. Skip to 42 **Transfer Your Music to Your iPod** for more information on synchronizing your iPod.

▶ TIP

After loading your iPod with music, let it remain connected to your computer until its battery is fully charged (three hours or so). It's a good idea to leave it in the charger as often as possible. See 51 About the Care and Feeding of Your iPod for more information about battery care.

5 Troubleshoot Your iPod's Connection

It's possible, for Windows users in particular, that your iPod might not immediately show up in iTunes—and might stubbornly refuse to appear no matter what you do or which port you plug it into. This can result from any of a myriad of different hardware issues, and a thorough discussion of all possible things that can go wrong is beyond the scope of this book. However, there are a few things you can try.

4

Perhaps the most common problem with iPod connectivity is a bad FireWire or USB 2.0 connection. This can be the result of a faulty connector or a bad hub that doesn't properly transfer the complete signal to your operating system. iPods sold for Windows computers are packaged with a USB 2.0 cable. The first thing to check is that your computer supports USB 2.0, because USB 1.1 is not supported except on the iPod shuffle (which is small enough to be filled in a reasonable time by the older and slower USB 1.1).

If your computer doesn't support USB 2.0, or if it does support it but it doesn't seem to be working (make sure that you try the USB cable in every USB port on your computer), try using FireWire instead. Most modern computers have at least one FireWire port, also known as IEEE 1394. Apple sells a separate FireWire cable for your iPod for $19.00. If you don't have any FireWire ports on your computer, you can get a card for your computer with USB 2.0 *and* FireWire ports for as little as $20 (although, naturally, more money gets you better quality).

If you're using the iPod Dock, try connecting the USB 2.0 or FireWire cable directly to the iPod's Dock connector instead. If this approach fixes the problem, you'll know that the Dock is the culprit and must be replaced.

If neither FireWire nor USB 2.0 work for you, it's possible that you need to update your installation of Windows. Run Windows Update to ensure that all drivers and libraries for FireWire and USB 2.0 are installed on your computer.

Finally, if all else fails, contact Apple Support; you get a year of free service with your new iPod, and Apple's on the hook to make sure that you can get it running properly. It could be that you have a faulty iPod. Perhaps your Dock or cable is bad. Whatever the cause, you've spent a lot of money on that shiny new iPod, and you have the right to Apple's help in getting it clicking away.

5 Set the iPod's Date and Time

✔ BEFORE YOU BEGIN	→ SEE ALSO
3 Select Your iPod's Language 4 Connect Your iPod for the First Time	89 Use Your iPod as an Alarm Clock

After you've named your iPod, the next step in getting your iPod ready for use is setting its internal clock. It's important that the iPod have an accurate internal time for a variety of reasons. The alarm clock functions and calendaring features, clearly, require the iPod's time to be correct in order to work (see 84 **Transfer and View iCal Calendar Items (Mac only)** and 89 **Use Your iPod as an Alarm Clock** for more information). Furthermore, during normal playback of your music, the iPod keeps track of which songs it plays and when; when you synchronize your iPod back to iTunes, the time when each song was last played is transferred into the iTunes' database so that your navigation within iTunes can take accurate advantage of which songs you've played most recently. For example, if you have a ***Smart Playlist*** that keeps track of the last 100 songs you've played in order (see 35 **Create a Smart Playlist** for more details), having the correct time set on your iPod as well as on your computer ensures that the songs are all shown in order.

▶ NOTE

Your iPod's date and time are set automatically each time you synchronize it with iTunes. However, you might have a need to set the time manually, for example if you don't have access to your computer for an extended period of time, or if you go on a trip across time zone lines.

1 Navigate to the Date & Time Settings

Navigate into the iPod's **Settings** menu. Highlight the **Date & Time** option and press the **Select** button.

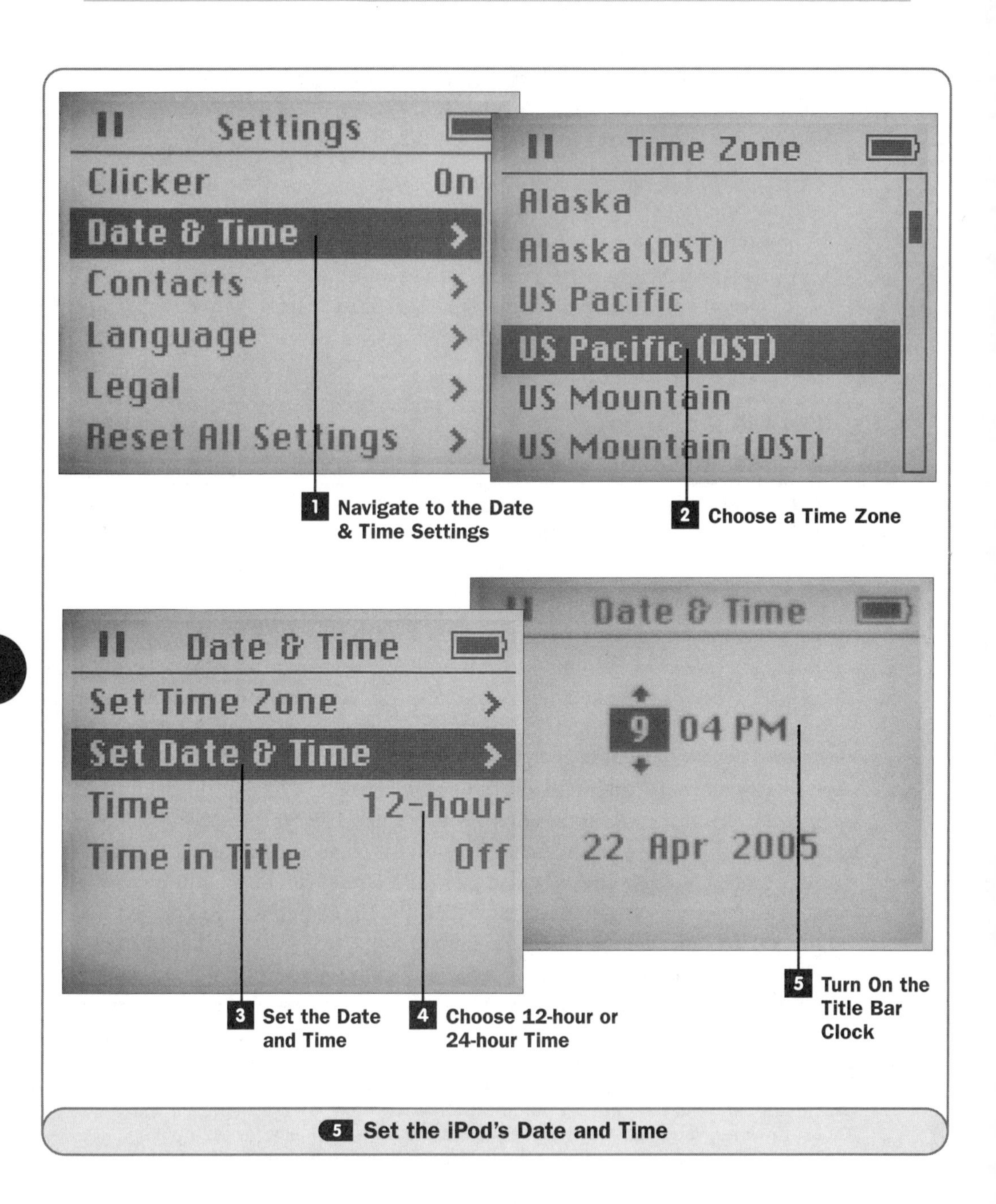

5 Set the iPod's Date and Time

2 Choose a Time Zone

In the **Date & Time Settings** menu, scroll to the **Set Time Zone** option and press the **Select** button. In the **Set Time Zone** submenu, scroll to the appropriate time zone setting for your location. Make sure that you select correctly whether Daylight Saving Time (labeled **DST**) is in effect at the current date. Time zones are identified by a region or a large city located in each zone. Press the **Select** button to choose a time zone and return to the **Date & Time Settings** menu.

3 Set the Date and Time

Choose the **Set Date & Time** option. In this screen, use the navigation wheel to raise or lower the value of each selected field (such as the hour, day or month, or year), and the **Select** button to accept each field's correct value and move to the next field. Be sure to set **AM** or **PM** correctly. After you press **Select** on the final field (the year), you returned to the **Date & Time Settings** menu.

4 Choose 12-hour or 24-hour Time

Select the **Time** option and use the **Select** button to toggle between 12-hour and 24-hour time formats. This setting is purely a matter of taste, and how you like to view the time—the option you select does not affect the iPod's internal timekeeping.

5 Turn On the Title Bar Clock

Select the **Time in Title** option and use the **Select** button to toggle the feature on and off. With this feature enabled, the title of each screen in the iPod's navigation system switches to display the current time a few seconds after you navigate to that screen.

Press the **Menu** button several times to back out of the **Settings** menu system when you're done.

6 Configure Your iPod for Your Headphones or Speakers

✔ BEFORE YOU BEGIN	→ SEE ALSO
4 Connect Your iPod for the First Time	40 Auto-Level Song Volumes 74 Adjust the Global Equalizer 75 Adjust Equalizer Settings for Individual Songs

The iPod comes with a wide selection of internal "graphic equalizer" presets—adjustment curves applied to the spectrum of audio output frequencies, amplifying some frequency ranges and quieting others—that you can select to compensate for the frequency range of your speakers or headphones. Because the iPod can be used with any of a nearly infinite range of sound output devices, from tiny in-ear headphones to large powered speakers, it's necessary to be able to choose an equalizer curve that matches the capabilities of the speakers you're using. For instance, earbuds with poor bass response might need to have the high frequencies dulled and the bass boosted; whereas large, deep stereo speakers might need to have the midranges and high frequencies boosted according to their own weak areas. Certain genres of music also have equalizer curves that enhance their typical range of frequencies, so you can set an appropriate equalizer preset if you're going to be listening to a certain style of music a lot (such as **Rock** or **Dance**). You'll want to experiment with various equalizer settings until you get sound response that you find satisfying.

▶ TIP

Return to this task after you've filled your iPod with music and spent some time listening to it; after you've become familiar with the iPod's operation, you can select an appropriate equalizer setting with more accuracy.

1 Navigate to the Equalizer Settings

Navigate into the iPod's **Settings** menu. Highlight the **EQ** (Equalizer) option and press the **Select** button.

2 Choose an Equalizer Preset

Use the navigation wheel to browse the list of equalizer presets. The presets are named in ways that should help you choose an appropriate one. If you listen primarily to Rock music, for example, the **Rock** preset might be for you; if you have a small pair of earbuds or a small set of external speakers, try the **Small Speakers** or **Treble Reducer** preset.

It can be helpful to use iTunes to examine each equalizer preset's profile visually. Click the **Equalizer Settings** button in the lower-right corner of the iTunes window. All the same presets are present in iTunes' **Equalizer** window as are available in the iPod; simply choose one from the drop-down menu to see the amplification curve described by the blue sliders.

The **Off** setting (at the top of the **EQ** menu) means that the iPod doesn't apply any special amplification curve to the music as it sends it out to the headphones or speakers.

▶ TIP

If you define custom equalizer presets in iTunes (see 74 Adjust the Global Equalizer), the iPod cannot synchronize those presets; the iPod's list of presets is fixed in its firmware and cannot expand to include any customized presets you have created.

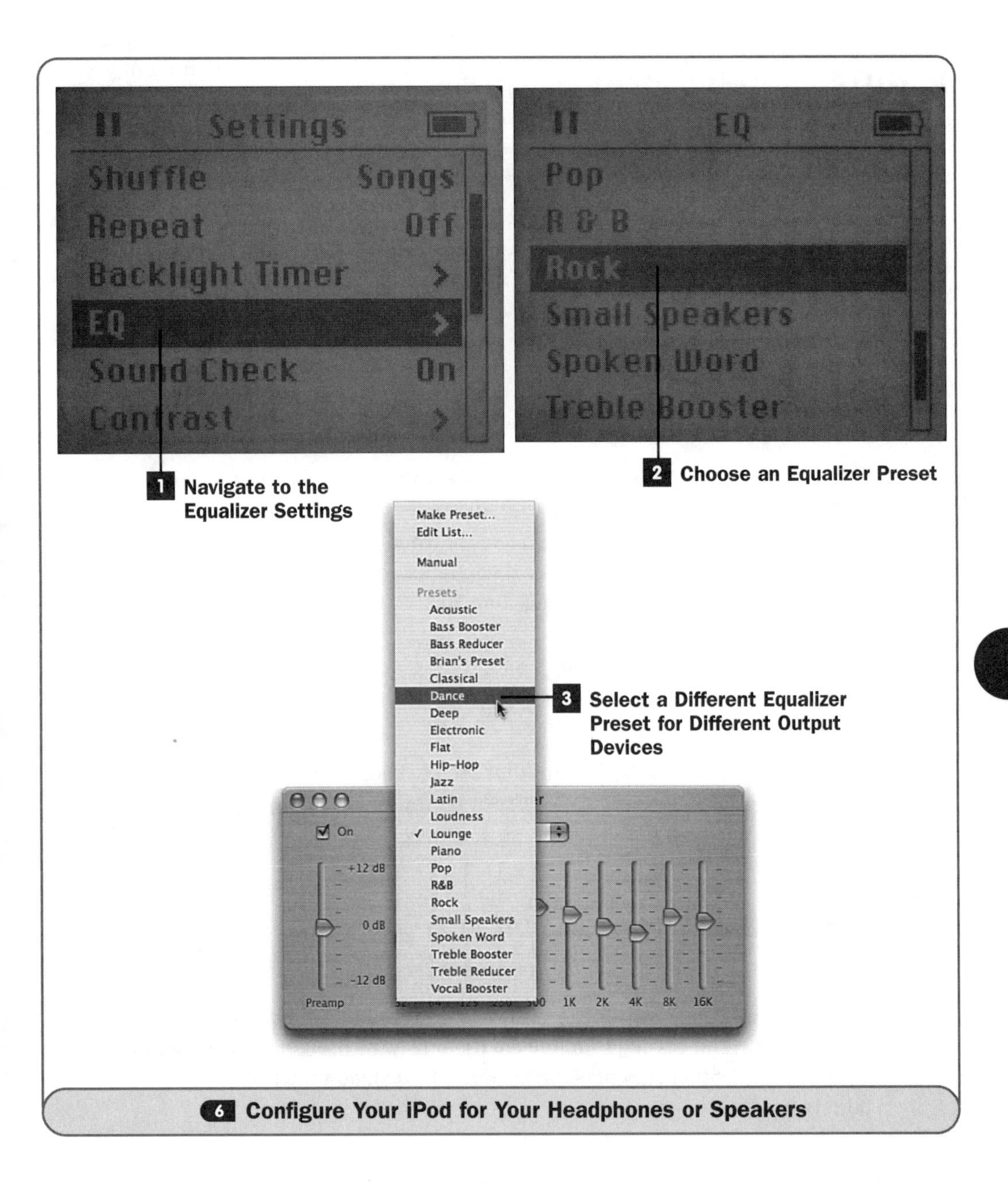

3 Select a Different Equalizer Preset for Different Output Devices

Repeat steps 1 and 2 anytime you connect a different set of speakers or headphones to your iPod.

▶ NOTE

If you have set equalizer presets for individual songs in iTunes (see 75 Adjust Equalizer Settings for Individual Songs), those presets do not affect how the songs are played in the iPod—the iPod uses only the equalizer preset you've selected manually.

7 Configure the iPod's Backlight

✔ BEFORE YOU BEGIN	→ SEE ALSO
4 Connect Your iPod for the First Time	90 Listen to Your iPod in the Car 91 Turn Your iPod into a Boom Box with Remote Control

The iPod's backlight and contrast settings allow you to view its screen even in insufficient light. This is clearly beneficial anytime you want to use your iPod at night; additional uses for the backlit screen are when your iPod is mounted in your car as a portable audio system, or if you're using it in conjunction with a set of docking speakers (as described in **91 Turn Your iPod into a Boom Box with Remote Control**), where you need to be able to read the screen in a dimly lit room. In these circumstances, it's especially useful to be able to configure the backlight to remain illuminated for a long time after it's been turned on, or even for it to stay on permanently until you turn it off yourself.

Beware of the additional battery drain that the backlight causes. If you set the backlight to remain on for long periods or at all times, be sure that your iPod is connected to an external power source, such as a car adapter—if you don't, expect reduced battery life.

1 Turn the Backlight On and Off

Hold down the **Menu** button for several seconds to turn on the backlight. Hold it down again for the same amount of time to turn the backlight off.

If you turn on the backlight and leave it on, it turns itself off automatically 20 seconds after you stop pressing buttons on the iPod's interface, thus saving battery power.

▶ TIP

You can enable a Main Menu option to turn the backlight on and off, if you prefer doing it that way instead of just pressing the **Menu** button. See **82 Customize the iPod's Main Menu** for more information.

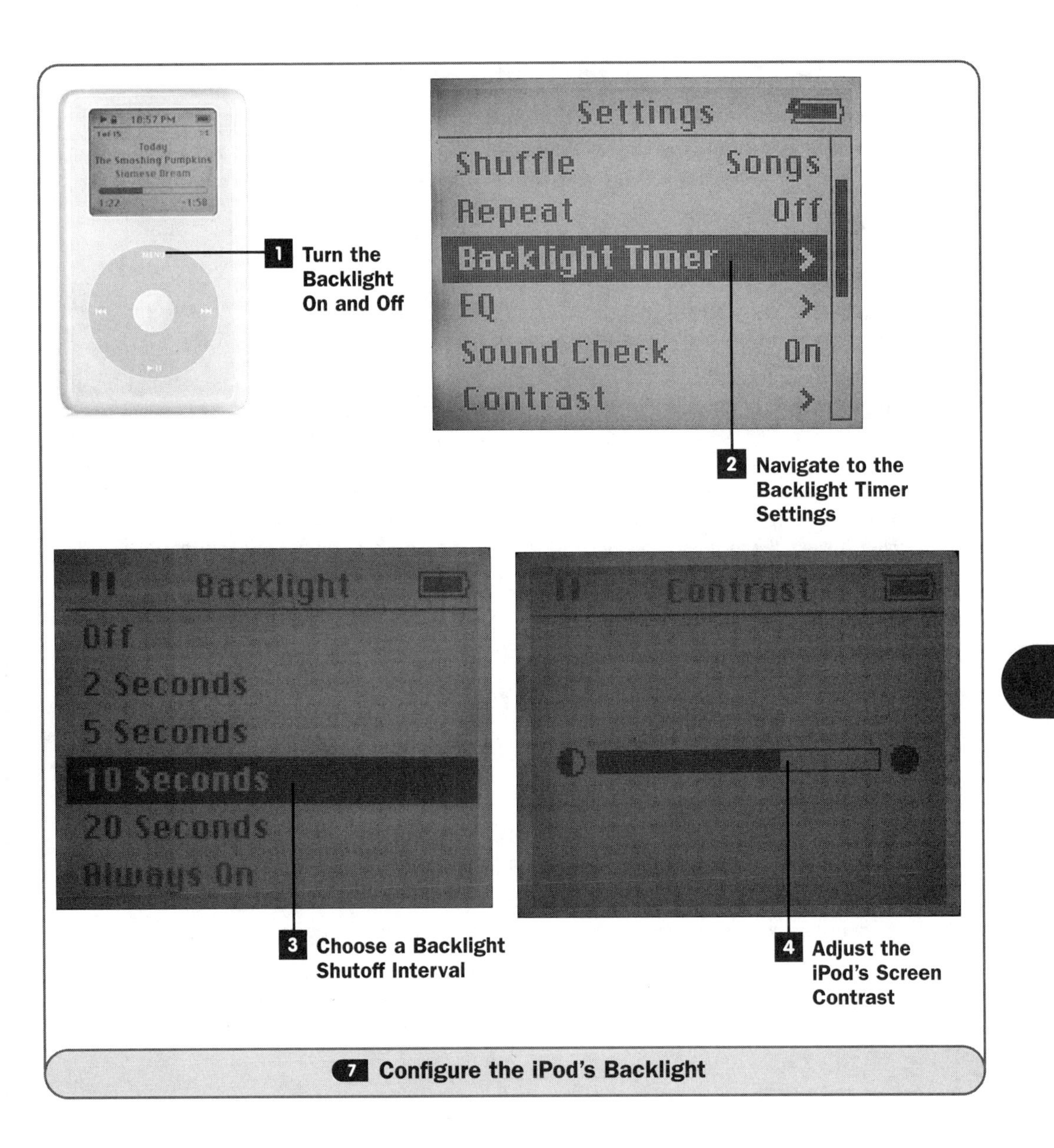

7 Configure the iPod's Backlight

2 Navigate to the Backlight Timer Settings

You can configure the amount of time the backlight stays on after being turned on. Navigate into the iPod's **Settings** menu. Highlight the **Backlight Timer** option and press the **Select** button.

3 Choose a Backlight Shutoff Interval

From the next screen, choose a time interval and press **Select**. The interval you select is the time between when you stop pressing buttons on the iPod and when the backlight automatically shuts off.

If you select the **Off** setting, the backlight is turned on manually by holding down the **Menu** button; it automatically shuts off after about 20 seconds.

If you choose any number of seconds, the backlight automatically turns on as soon as you touch any of the controls, and stays illuminated for the specified time after you stop touching buttons.

If you select **Always On**, the backlight remains on at all times.

▶ NOTE

If the **Hold** button is engaged, the backlight shuts off after two minutes, even if you selected **Always On** for the backlight timer. Make sure that you do not engage the **Hold** button if you want the backlight to stay on at all times. Remember, though, that the iPod goes into sleep mode (and the backlight shuts off) after two minutes of complete inactivity. Turn the iPod (and its backlight) back on by pressing any button.

7

4 Adjust the iPod's Screen Contrast

Choose **Contrast** from the **Settings** menu. The next screen allows you to adjust the screen's contrast using the trackwheel. At one extreme of the scale, a minimum of power is given to the screen, preventing the background from becoming dark enough to interfere with the text; at the other, the screen is given more power, so that the text is darker, but the background may darken, too. Adjust the slider until you can read the text at a comfortable level; be sure to check the contrast with the backlight turned on as well.

Press the **Select** button to set the contrast level; press the **Menu** button to return to the Main Menu screen. Your iPod is now ready to be filled with music and used on the go!

▶ NOTES

Your iPod's screen might become darker if it gets hot, for example if its hard disk is running continuously as you fill it with music. Don't adjust its contrast during this anomalous time—when it returns to normal operating temperature, the contrast you select might not be readable anymore. Wait until the screen cools before adjusting the contrast.

The **Contrast** setting is not available on the iPod photo because its color screen uses much more sophisticated electronics that ensure a readable display.

3

Building Your Digital Music Library

IN THIS CHAPTER:

iTunes' foremost function is as a digital music organizer, a way for you to replace your bulky CD collection with a flexible, programmable digital music library that all fits inside your computer. To accomplish this, naturally, you'll have to get your music into iTunes somehow.

Music you add to the iTunes **Library** comes from any of the following sources:

- Imported (***ripped***) from CDs that you already own
- Imported from your existing collection of MP3, AAC, or unprotected WMA files
- Imported as an individual music file you receive or create yourself, or convert from an analog format such as a tape or vinyl LP
- Copied in automatically by iTunes during installation (see **2 Run iTunes for the First Time**)
- Purchased from the iTunes **Music** Store

The iTunes **Music** Store, the method for acquiring new music that requires the least effort and the fewest middlemen, is covered in **18 Sign Up for the iTunes Music Store** and related tasks in Chapter 4, "Using the iTunes **Music Store**." The tasks in this chapter cover the remaining methods of importing music, particularly the one for which iTunes' interface was primarily designed: importing the music from your existing CD collection.

8

8 About Music Formats

✔ BEFORE YOU BEGIN	→ SEE ALSO
Just jump right in!	66 Convert Audio Files to Other Formats

No matter how easy to use a piece of software is, there are some trivialities of computer technology that just can't be escaped. One of these bits of esoterica is the plethora of digital music file formats you'll encounter while using iTunes. Ideally, and for the most common paths of use, file formats are little more than a curiosity you never have to deal with yourself; but the moment you try to do anything at all advanced with your music, you'll find yourself surrounded by what seems an alphabet soup of acronyms and labels, lurking malevolently just under iTunes' polished surface. It pays to know what each of these formats is all about and how to deal effectively with it.

The ***format*** of a digital music file refers to the specific structure of the data within it. All digital music files follow essentially the same idea: a series of numbers that describe the pitch and intensity of the sound waveform at each particular instant in the audio stream, all adding up to a familiar musical sound when it's interpreted by software such as iTunes at normal playback speed. Different kinds of files differ, though, in exactly what form those numbers take. Some music formats support ***compression*** (the ability to reduce the file size by discarding relatively unimportant sound information, or by indexing small repeated fragments of sound instead of encoding them all directly—as well as other, ingeniously mathematical methods). Some formats support ***Digital Rights Management (DRM)***, enforcing copy protection. Some forms of digital audio files encode stereo data differently from others, resulting in a somewhat different sound quality. These subtle but important differences are what make some formats more suitable for certain tasks than others, and explain why we have to deal with so many different file formats in the world of digital music.

KEY TERMS

Format—**The specific internal data structure of a digital music file.**

Compression—**Fitting more music into a fewer number of bytes by discarding unimportant musical data or indexing repeated patterns.**

The following audio file formats are either supported directly by iTunes or destined to be a part of your life as you work with iTunes. Except where noted, the customary filename extension—the three or four letters after the final period (.) in a file's name—is the same as the acronym of the format listed.

- **CDDA (Compact Disc Digital Audio)**—An uncompressed, true stereo digital audio stream made up of a simple series of audio samples. This is the standard format in which every commercial audio CD is encoded and the format in which iTunes burns audio CDs. The CDDA format is essentially interchangeable with AIFF and WAV formats, and is almost never used directly on computers.
- **AIFF (Audio Interchange File Format)**—An uncompressed audio stream format developed by Apple and popularized as the default sound format of the Macintosh platform. Still the preferred format for raw audio editing on the Mac. AIFF files can be converted without loss of quality to WAV format and back.
- **WAV (Windows WAVeform file)**—An uncompressed audio stream format developed by Microsoft and IBM; equivalent to AIFF in its supported features and file size, WAV is the default raw audio format for Windows. WAV files can be converted without loss of quality to AIFF format and back.

- **MP3 (MPEG-1 Audio Layer 3)**—Developed in the early 1990s as part of the MPEG video/audio compression specification, MP3 is the first audio format to have brought the file size of individual song tracks down to the point where they could be easily transferred across the Internet while still sounding nearly true to the original CD-quality sound from which they were derived. Encoding technology for MP3 files is subject to patents held by Thomson Consumer Electronics and the Fraunhofer Institute, who contributed to the format's original design. MP3 is a ***lossy*** compression format, meaning that any music converted to MP3 format cannot be flawlessly converted back to its original format; some music data is inevitably lost. The benefit is that an MP3 file usually achieves about a 12:1 compression ratio over the uncompressed source, depending on the ***bit rate*** selected during encoding.

KEY TERMS

Lossy—A compression or conversion process in which some sound information or resolution is irretrievably lost, as when encoding a CD to MP3 format. The converse is ***lossless*** compression, meaning a reversible process in which no information is lost.

Lossless—A compression or conversion process where perfect sound quality from the original source is preserved. Lossless compression doesn't achieve such small file sizes as ***lossy*** compression, but it's reversible.

Bit rate—The number of bits per second consumed by an audio stream; the bit rate can be constant or variable, and if constant can be used to calculate how much disk space a song file will take up.

MP3's compression is achieved through a number of techniques, including the discarding of superfluous (inaudible) audio data and the application of psychoacoustics. Stereo information is usually done in "joint stereo" mode, meaning that instead of two separate tracks for the left and right channels, most information is recorded as a "mono" track and a separate channel records the separation from left to right, which saves on file size. Also, Variable Bit Rate (VBR) encoding is frequently employed to encode lower-complexity sections of music at a lower bit rate, saving space without sacrificing audio quality.

MP3 files have no Digital Rights Management (DRM) technology built in, meaning that there is no way for a copyright holder to control or track the spread of an MP3 version of a song. MP3 files do, however, have ***info tags***—also known as ID3 tags—that allow the user to embed a wide variety of organizational information into the file's text headers. This information does not interfere with the audio stream at all, but gives software such as iTunes the ability to organize MP3 files with much better control and flexibility than with filenames alone.

- **AAC (Advanced Audio Coding)**—The official successor to MP3, AAC (another lossy compression format) is the latest iteration of the audio specification in the MPEG standard, part of the MPEG-4 framework that underlies modern versions of ***QuickTime***. Apple is currently the most visible company using AAC in its products, although it is far from being a "proprietary" format; the only thing proprietary about AAC as used in the iTunes **Music** Store is how the DRM scheme (known as FairPlay) is keyed to individual purchasers. Functionally, however, as far as any company that wants to interoperate with music purchased through iTunes, Apple's format is essentially closed.

AAC files incorporate many advances over the earlier MP3 format, including as many as 48 distinct audio channels, a more dynamic form of stereo encoding, and a notably smaller file size for files encoded with the same subjective sound quality. This means that if you encode your CD collection in AAC format instead of MP3, you can save about 25% of your disk space (which, remember, also applies to the space available on your iPod). AAC supports all the same info tags as MP3 does.

There are two flavors to AAC as used in iTunes: *protected* and *unprotected*. Protected AAC files are keyed to an individual purchaser's identity and cannot be opened on a given computer unless that computer has been authorized with the central iTunes' authorization servers; as many as five separate computers can be authorized at one time for a single purchaser account. (See 23 **Authorize a Computer to Play Purchased Music** for more information.) Unprotected AAC files are as freely portable and playable as MP3 files are; you can send an unprotected AAC file to anyone else with iTunes or any other software capable of reading AAC files, and the recipient can play it successfully. When you import music from your CD collection, iTunes creates the digital music files by default in unprotected AAC format.

AAC files are identified by either a **.m4a** (MPEG-4 Audio) or **.m4p** (MPEG-4 Protected) filename extension, depending on whether or not the files are protected with DRM.

- **WMA (Windows Media Audio)**—Microsoft's answer to MP3 (and later, to AAC as used in iTunes), WMA is a lossy compression format that is entirely proprietary and owned by Microsoft. Its capabilities are comparable to those of AAC—the audio quality for a given file size is considerably better than with MP3, and thus for the same audio quality you get significant file size savings. WMA also comes in both protected and unprotected flavors. iTunes for Windows can import unprotected WMA files by converting them to AAC on-the-fly.

The DRM scheme in WMA files as sold through the online music stores that compete with the iTunes **Music Store** is very flexible and is implemented differently by various sellers. Some stores restrict copying and playback to a certain number of computers, like iTunes does. Others, like Napster's subscription service, enforce an expiration date beyond which a file cannot be opened; periodic authorization is required to extend the expiration date on these files. Still other services set a limit on the number of times a given song can be played before it becomes locked.

- **Apple Lossless**—A format developed by Apple and released with iTunes 4.5 in April 2004, with the intention of supporting high-quality audio storage for professional musicians and audiophiles without requiring the full amount of disk space required by uncompressed AIFF, WAV, or CDDA data. Apple Lossless achieves compression of about 2:1 over the uncompressed source data by using techniques similar to those found in GIF or ZIP files, both compression formats that must by their nature be totally lossless. If you encode your music using Apple Lossless, expect to consume about 5 megabytes of disk space for every minute of music; but this music will be at true CD quality without even the minimal degradation of quality found in MP3 or AAC formats. Apple Lossless files are encapsulated in MPEG-4 wrappers, and thus have a **.m4a** filename extension. These files are not, however, AAC files.
- **MIDI (Musical Instrument Digital Interface)**—Completely unlike all the preceding formats, MIDI is not a series of samples at all, but a synthesized music format. MIDI files are generally tiny compared to sampled music files such as AAC and MP3—only 20 to 50 kilobytes—because all they contain are lists of commands comparable to what you'd see on a piece of sheet music. MIDI files depend on a library of playback technology to interpret these commands, as an orchestra would read the sheet music in front of it; both Windows and Mac OS X can play MIDI files natively, but the playback quality of a MIDI file depends greatly on the quality of the synthesized instruments in the software you use. iTunes can add MIDI files to its library and play them using the QuickTime MIDI instruments, but these files cannot be transferred to the iPod. MIDI files generally have a **.mid** extension.
- **Internet Radio**—A "stream" of audio data (usually in MP3 format) coming from a source on the Internet, Internet Radio data cannot be saved directly

by iTunes, paused, rewound, or scanned using the scrub bar—it's a live stream to which you connect by specifying a web address to listen to. Favorite Internet Radio streams are added to your iTunes library as you listen to them so that you can return to them whenever you want, but (naturally) they cannot be transferred to your iPod. Internet Radio streams sometimes use downloaded "playlist" files to schedule the playback of tracks stored on the server. Refer to 37 **Listen to an Internet Radio Station** for more information.

iTunes gives you the ability to convert between most of these formats, if not bidirectionally, at least from each to a native format such as AAC or MP3. In the tasks in this chapter, you will see how to take advantage of the strengths of these different formats as you bring in your music from varying sources to consolidate it all into your digital iTunes **Library**.

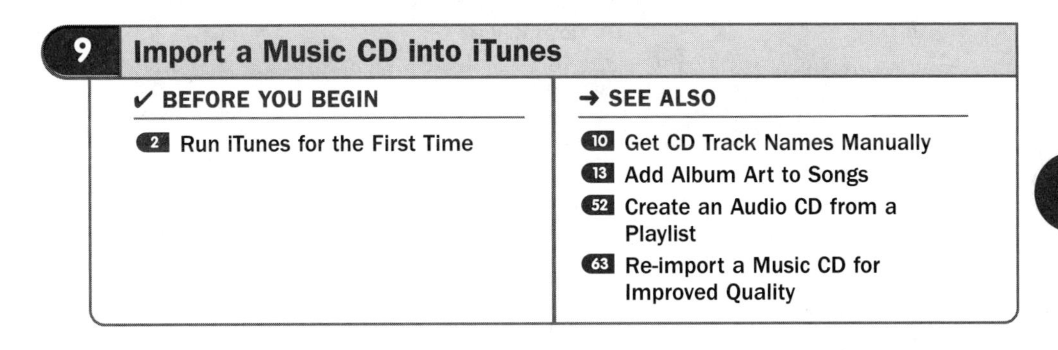

9 Import a Music CD into iTunes

✓ BEFORE YOU BEGIN

2 Run iTunes for the First Time

→ SEE ALSO

10 Get CD Track Names Manually
13 Add Album Art to Songs
52 Create an Audio CD from a Playlist
63 Re-import a Music CD for Improved Quality

Chances are that you've already got a collection of music on compact discs. In fact, you may have dozens of discs taking up room in organizers, spilling out onto shelves, getting their contents mixed up with their jewel cases, slowly driving you mad. Finding and playing music on your CDs, unless you're superhumanly organized, might be getting to be more of a hassle than it's worth.

Now that you have iTunes, it's time to put an end to all that. With a couple of clicks of the mouse, you can convert each of your commercial CDs into a catalog entry in the iTunes **Library**—ready for you to select and play at a moment's notice.

▶ TIP

iTunes also makes a dandy player for any of your CDs, even if you don't want to import its music into the iTunes **Library**. Just insert the disc as shown in this task, wait for the track names to be downloaded, and then play the tracks as described in 33 **Find and Play Music**. iTunes also keeps records of the downloaded track names and applies them to the files on the CD if you look at them in the Finder or Windows Explorer.

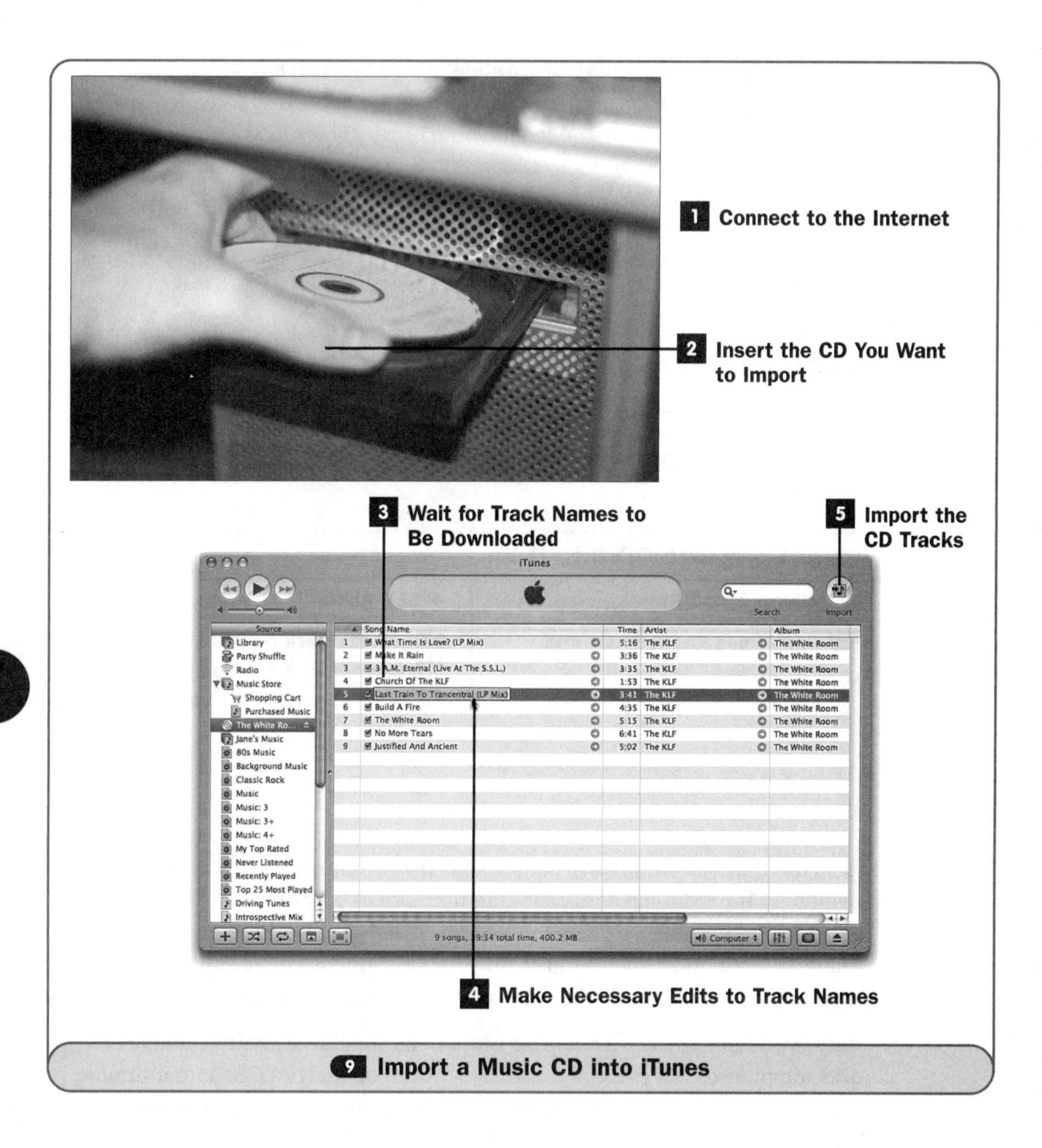

9 Import a Music CD into iTunes

1 Connect to the Internet

This step is optional, but highly recommended. iTunes has to be able to connect to the Internet to download the album name and the titles of the tracks included on each of your CDs. Standard music CDs don't have this track name information embedded into them—the information on the CD itself is just several tracks of raw CDDA audio data, and the only way the disc can address the data is by track numbers. The titles and album name are included only in the printed liner notes.

This is the reason for the existence of Gracenote (**http://www.gracenote.com**), also known as the CDDB, or CD Database. Gracenote is a publicly accessible database of CD names and track titles, defined using each CD's unique combination of track lengths. It's highly unlikely that any two different discs will have the exact same number of tracks, each with the same length. The unique arrangement of each disc's tracks and lengths enables iTunes to submit your CD's raw track information to Gracenote and immediately get back a response containing all the CD's track names, which are then applied to all the tracks on the CD in iTunes.

▶ **NOTE**

Gracenote's database is populated through the volunteer efforts of millions of ordinary computer users like yourself. Its information may thus be inaccurate or incomplete. If you find errors in the downloaded track names from Gracenote, make the changes necessary (as shown in Step 4) and submit them to Gracenote as described in 14 Submit CD Track Names to the Gracenote Database.

2 Insert the CD You Want to Import

First select an audio CD that you want to add to iTunes **Library**. Open your computer's CD drive and insert the disc. Close the drive door and wait for the disc to spin up.

▶ **TIP**

If you have a lot of music CDs to import, you can save time by setting up iTunes to automatically begin importing the music off every disc you insert. In the **General** tab of the iTunes **Preferences** window (choose **Edit, Preferences** in Windows or **iTunes, Preferences** on the Mac), choose the **Import Songs** or **Import Songs and Eject** option from the **On CD Insert** drop-down menu.

3 Wait for Track Names to Be Downloaded

If you're connected to the Internet, iTunes contacts the Gracenote database and submits your CD's track lengths; if Gracenote finds a match, it returns the name of the CD album and the titles of all the tracks. In iTunes' song listing, the track names are applied to the tracks, and the disc is labeled with its album name.

▶ **NOTE**

If you're on a dial-up modem connection, depending on your system configuration, iTunes may cause your modem to automatically connect to the Internet so that it can obtain the track names.

In the unlikely event that two or more disc entries in the Gracenote database have exactly the same sets of track lengths, you are prompted to select the appropriate one. If you can't tell which one is correct (for instance, if two different people submitted significantly different information for the same disc), choose one; if you don't like the results, query the Gracenote database again as explained in 10 **Get CD Track Names Manually**.

If you do not have an active Internet connection, iTunes lists the disc as **Untitled CD**, and shows the tracks with names such as **Track 01**, **Track 02**, and so on. See 10 **Get CD Track Names Manually** if you inserted the CD before you connected to the Internet.

4 Make Necessary Edits to Track Names

Gracenote's information might contain typos or outright errors—as a volunteer project dependent on user input, it's not perfect. You can correct these errors before importing the tracks. In fact, it's best to do it now instead of after importing so that if you insert the CD again in the future, iTunes remembers the corrected information and not the erroneous data from Gracenote.

Click once on any song shown in the song listing to select it; click again in any of the displayed fields, such as the **Song Name** field. The field turns into an editable text box showing the field's current contents. You can type a new name for any track, change the artist name, adjust the genre (the style of music), change the year when the album was released, or make other similar changes. Alter the disc's album name by clicking its text label in the **Source** pane. Press **Return** or **Enter** to accept the changes to the name.

An alternate way to make changes to track information—and a more complete one that gives you access to far more fields than just the ones visible in the listing—is to select a song and then choose **File**, **Get Info** (or right-click the song and choose **Get Info** from the context menu). In the dialog box that appears, make any changes you want to that track's information, then click **OK** to apply them.

Select multiple tracks (hold down **Space** as you click to select a range of songs, or hold down **Ctrl** or ⌘ to select individual non-contiguous tracks); then choose **Get Info** to edit certain fields of all the selected tracks at once. This is an excellent way to change (for example) the **Genre** field of all the tracks at once, if Gracenote supplied information claiming that the CD is a Rock album whereas you would classify it as Pop or Alternative.

▶ TIP

If you want to import only certain tracks and skip others, disable the small check box next to each track that you don't want to import.

5 Import the CD Tracks

When the track names are all adjusted to your liking, click the round **Import** button in the upper-right corner of the iTunes' window. The disc spins up and iTunes starts copying the music data onto your computer. Internally, iTunes is copying the raw CDDA music streams to memory, and then encoding them to AAC format, into which it copies all your edited track information as it saves each song file to the hard disk. The speed of this process depends greatly on the performance of your computer. A high-end Pentium IV or Power Mac G5 can import at 25x or higher (25 times the speed of raw playback), and is in fact limited more by the data transfer rate of the CD drive itself than of the speed of the CPU. Older computers can import only at slower speeds such as 10x or even as little as 5x.

▶ TIP

By default, your music is imported in unprotected AAC format, the most efficient and high-quality format iTunes supports. If you want to use a different format, such as MP3 or a *lossless* format such as AIFF or Apple Lossless, or if you want to adjust the bit rate or other options on the imported files, see **65 Import a CD in CD-Quality (Lossless) Format.**

By default, iTunes plays the songs on the CD as you import the tracks. You can turn off this behavior in the **Importing** section of the iTunes **Preferences** window.

▶ NOTE

Tracks toward the end of the disc import faster than the ones at the beginning because CD audio is encoded from the center of the disc outward, and the outside of the disc moves faster—moving more data linearly past the sensor per second—than the inside of the disc.

As iTunes completes importing each track, a green check mark appears next to that track in the song listing, and you can switch to the **Library** view to see the tracks in your library. (Incomplete tracks are shown in gray and cannot be played.) When all the tracks have finished importing and you hear the musical tone that signals the completion of the process, click the **Eject** icon next to the disc name in the **Source** pane, or simply eject the disc from your CD drive.

If your CD is damaged and iTunes has difficulty importing the tracks, refer to 63 **Re-import a Music CD for Improved Quality** for some techniques you can try.

For the finishing touch, see 13 **Add Album Art to Songs** to give your imported music the graphical content they need to really give you the full experience of your old physical CDs.

10 Get CD Track Names Manually

✔ BEFORE YOU BEGIN	➔ SEE ALSO
9 Import a Music CD into iTunes	14 Submit CD Track Names to the Gracenote Database 16 Extract a "Secret Track" into the iTunes Library

If you forgot to connect to the Internet before inserting an audio CD, don't panic—even though it looks like you're stuck with an **Untitled CD** with tracks unhelpfully labeled **Track 01**, **Track 02**, and so on, you're not out of options. A command in the iTunes **Advanced** menu lets you send a new query to the Gracenote database even after iTunes has given up trying to find the disc's correct track listing, and you don't have to painstakingly type in all the track information yourself.

▶ NOTE

If you already imported a CD with generic track names, you can type all the names in manually, or you can import the CD again (making sure that you connect to the Internet first). See 63 Re-import a Music CD for Improved Quality for the procedure.

1 Insert an Audio CD

Select an audio CD that you want to add to your iTunes **Library**. Insert it into the computer's CD drive and close the drive door. Wait for iTunes to populate the CD's track listing; if you don't have an Internet connection, the tracks are given generic names, such as **Track 01**, **Track 02**, and so on.

2 Connect to the Internet

You must have an active Internet connection at this point. Kick your teenager off the phone and dial up your modem; or connect your laptop to the local wireless network. Make sure that your connection is active by trying to connect with your browser to a website or two.

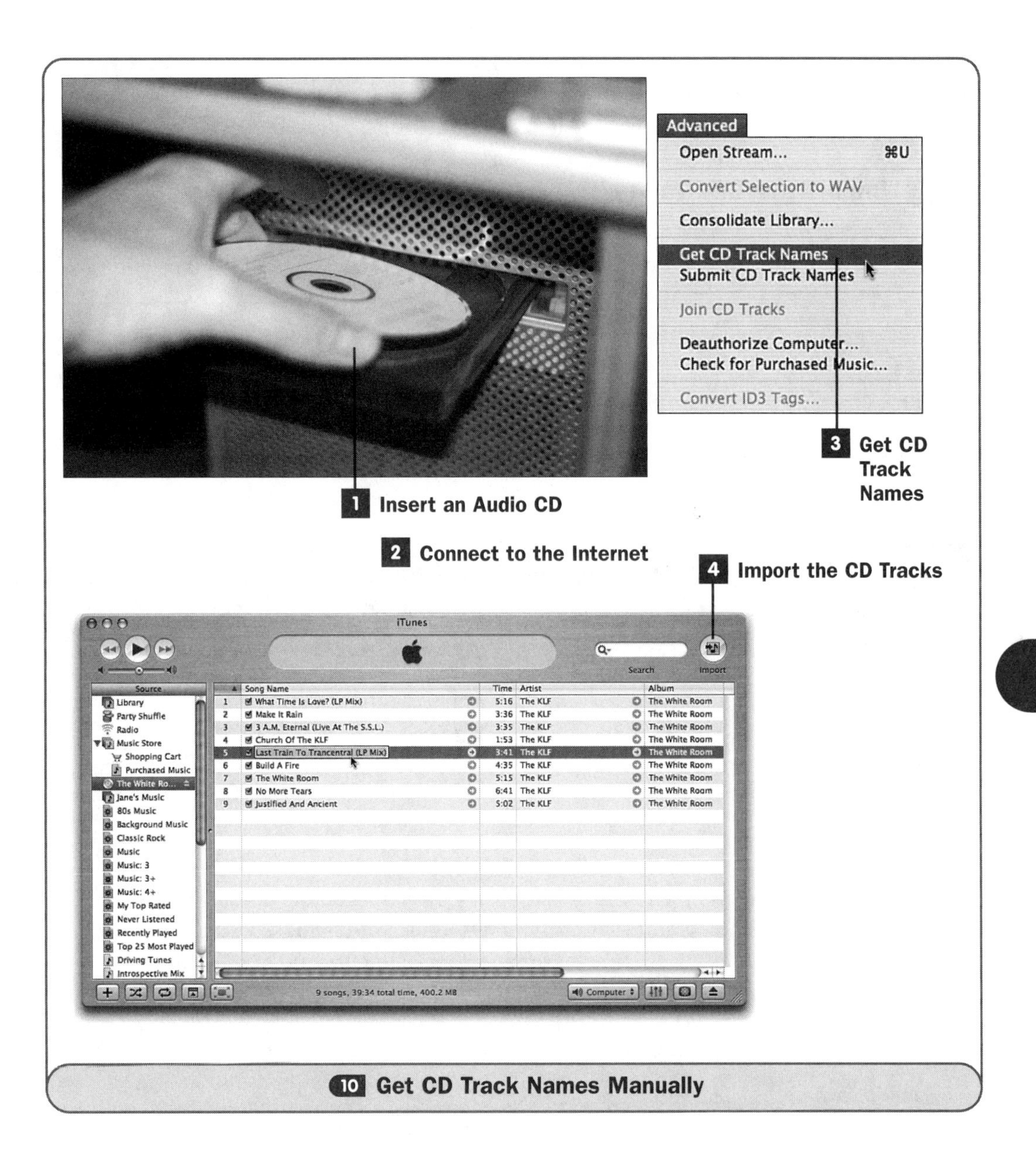

3 Get CD Track Names

Choose **Get CD Track Names** from the **Advanced** menu. iTunes makes a fresh attempt to contact the Gracenote database and replace its existing list of generic track names with the correct names from the database.

If you were presented earlier with multiple choices of disc entries, and you picked one whose contents turned out not to be correct, you should be given the same choices again; be sure to pick another disc entry this time around.

4 Import the CD Tracks

Click **Import** to copy the music from the CD into your iTunes **Library**. When you hear the musical tone, eject the CD and switch back to the **Library** view (click **Library** in the **Source** pane) to enjoy your imported music.

▶ TIP

Some CDs simply don't have entries in the Gracenote database. If you can't get track names for your CD no matter what you do, enter all the track names yourself and see 14 Submit CD Track Names to the Gracenote Database to do a good deed for your fellow fans.

11 Add a Music File to Your iTunes Library

✔ BEFORE YOU BEGIN

2 Run iTunes for the First Time

→ SEE ALSO

12 Import Your Existing Digital Music Collection into iTunes

64 Customize Importing Options

66 Convert Audio Files to Other Formats

69 Examine and Modify Song Information

Not all your music files are found on physical CDs. Chances are, if you've been on the Internet for any length of time, you've received or discovered music files (usually in MP3 format) from time to time—whether the files are of popular songs or of any other nature, such as comedy routines, political speeches, demo songs from a friend, or archived radio broadcasts. Perhaps you're an amateur or professional musician creating music using applications such as Ejay or GarageBand, and you want to add your productions to the iTunes **Library** so that you can enjoy them with the rest of your music and transfer them to your iPod to take with you. Or perhaps, you've just found a lot of music you like using file-sharing services. (But of course, you wouldn't do that.)

Fortunately, adding these files to iTunes is pretty easy, and you can do it one of two ways: by navigating to the file's location or by dragging and dropping. iTunes can import songs in MP3, AAC, AIFF, WAV, or MIDI format; on Windows, it can also import unprotected WMA files, which it automatically converts to AAC format during the import process.

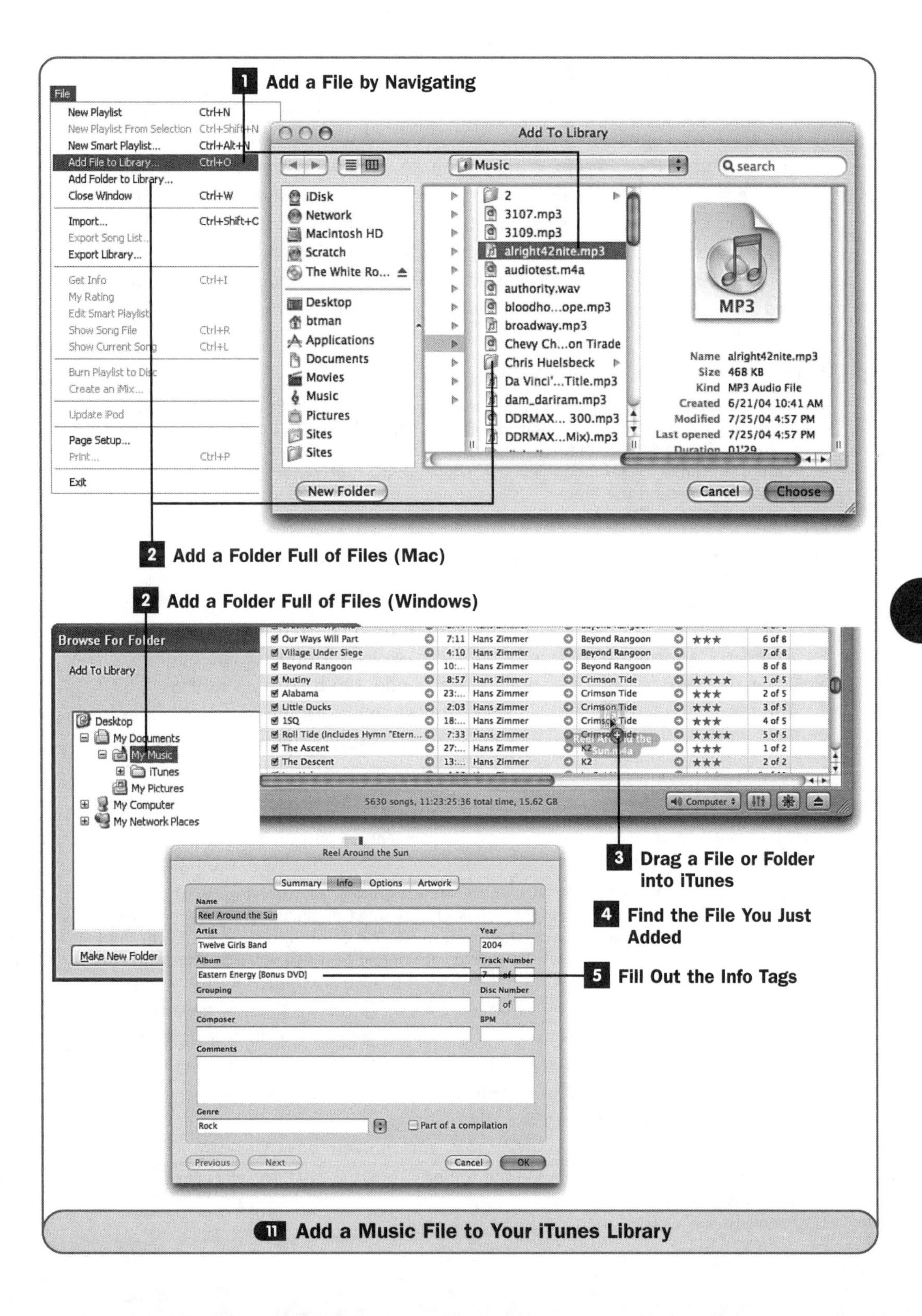

11 Add a Music File to Your iTunes Library

1 Add a File by Navigating

Choose **File, Add File to Library** (in Windows) or **File, Add to Library** (on the Mac). A file picker dialog box appears. Use this picker (which is in the standard form for your operating system) to navigate to the location on the hard disk of the music file you want to import. Select the file and click **Open** or **Choose**. (You can also select multiple files at once by holding down **Shift**, **Ctrl**, or ⌘ as you click.) iTunes copies the file into an appropriate place in your iTunes **Music** folder, filing it into folders named according to the embedded info tags (if present); the original file is left untouched on your hard disk.

TIP

If you prefer, you can have iTunes **Library** point directly to the file in the location where you added it, instead of copying it into the iTunes **Music** folder. To do this, turn off the **Copy files to iTunes Music folder when adding to library** check box in the **Advanced** section of the iTunes **Preferences** window (choose **Edit, Preferences** in Windows, or **iTunes, Preferences** on the Mac).

2 Add a Folder Full of Files

11

Suppose that you like to keep all your MP3 files in a certain folder on your disk; or suppose that you have a folder that resulted from unpacking a ZIP archive of a certain collection of MP3 files, such as a ripped CD album. Instead of picking each file individually to add it to the iTunes **Library**, you can instead choose the whole folder. iTunes imports all the importable files in that folder and ignores any non-music files; it even searches subfolders for files to import as well, making it a one-step process to add a whole folder-tree full of music files.

NOTE

Adding a large number of files at once to the iTunes **Library**, as when importing a whole folder tree, can be a time-consuming process. iTunes must duplicate every file and sort all the copies into the iTunes **Music** folder. You must also be sure to have sufficient hard disk space to hold all the copies of the music you import because you'll end up with *two* copies of everything.

On the Mac, the process for adding a folder is the same as in Step 1: In the file picker window, simply select the folder name (instead of selecting an individual file within the folder) and click **Choose**. On Windows, however, choose **Add Folder to Library** from the **File** menu; a separate kind of picker appears, showing you the folder tree structure beginning with your **Desktop**. Open folders in the tree until you see the folder you want; click to select it and then click **OK**.

▶ NOTE

iTunes does not create duplicate entries in its database for the same audio files. You can drag a file into iTunes as many times as you want, but it will not create an additional entry or lose track of the file. This means you can safely and cleanly add a whole folder full of MP3s, even if you've already added some of the individual MP3 files to the iTunes Library. The Date Added field for those files won't even be updated.

3 Drag a File or Folder into iTunes

An alternate, more direct way to add a file or folder to iTunes is to simply drag and drop it into iTunes. In the Finder or Windows Explorer, navigate to where the file or folder is that you want to import; with the iTunes' window open, click and drag the item into the song listing pane of iTunes (the main body of the window, below the **Browse** lists). The + icon on the mouse pointer indicates that the item will be added to iTunes when you release the mouse button. When the mouse is in the iTunes' window and the + icon is visible, drop the item into iTunes to add it to the library.

▶ TIP

You can also drag files or folders to the iTunes' icon in the Dock in Mac OS X to add them to the iTunes Library.

4 Find the File You Just Added

iTunes doesn't automatically scroll to show you the file you just added. If you want to find the file, the easiest way is to type its filename into the **Search** bar while the **Library** item is selected in the **Source** pane; as you type, the song listing narrows to show you only the matching songs in the library.

Another way to locate the newly added song is to scroll horizontally to the **Date Added** column in the song listing pane (see 71 **Customize Which Information Columns Are Displayed** if this column is not there) and then click the column heading twice to sort the songs on that column in descending order. The newly added song (or songs) should be at the top of the list.

5 Fill Out the Info Tags

If the song files you imported weren't created using iTunes or a similar program with access to the Gracenote database, chances are that the ***info tags*** aren't completely filled out. Without all the info tags properly set, you won't be able to navigate to the song using the **Artist** and **Album** lists, as you can with tracks you imported properly from CD. Select a song and click in various fields to make changes to its fields. Alternatively, select the song and choose **File**, **Get Info** (or right-click the song and choose **Get Info** from the context menu) and make the changes in the comprehensive info tag editor window.

12 Import Your Existing Digital Music Collection into iTunes

✓ BEFORE YOU BEGIN

2 Run iTunes for the First Time
11 Add a Music File to Your iTunes Library

→ SEE ALSO

13 Add Album Art to Songs
69 Examine and Modify Song Information
70 Eliminate Duplicate Tracks
97 Restore Your Music Library Database from a Backup Copy

Let's face it: You probably already have a number of MP3 files on your computer. If you've been using the Internet for a while, you might have hundreds or even thousands of MP3s, either imported from your CD collection using other software, or obtained from the Internet. iTunes makes no judgments about where your music comes from; it organizes it all equally, letting you transform your flat listing of music files in a folder somewhere on your computer into the multilevel database that makes iTunes' music navigation so easy.

This task lets you bring your collection of MP3 files—no matter how large—into iTunes with a full understanding of the consequences of the organizational options iTunes gives you. First you set iTunes to treat imported files the way you want it to; then you simply import your music collection—as lengthy a process as that might be—as described in 11 **Add a Music File to Your iTunes Library**.

1 Open the Preferences Window

Open the iTunes **Preferences** window (in Windows, choose **Edit**, **Preferences**; on the Mac, choose **iTunes**, **Preferences**). Click the **Advanced** tab.

2 Choose to Copy Music Files to the iTunes Music Folder

The **Copy files to iTunes Music folder when adding to library** check box determines exactly what happens when you import a new file or group of files into the iTunes' database. If the check box is enabled, iTunes makes a duplicate of each imported file and places it into an appropriate place in the iTunes **Music** folder, in folders based on the **Artist** and **Album** ***info tags***. If the check box is disabled, iTunes' database instead points to added music files wherever in the system they happen to be.

The default behavior is to allow iTunes to copy newly added files into its managed folder, which keeps all your music files neatly organized in a single location. You might want to turn this feature off if you like keeping certain "one-off" MP3 files in a certain folder outside your iTunes **Music** folder for quick access in the Finder or Windows Explorer or by other applications but also like to use iTunes to play those files.

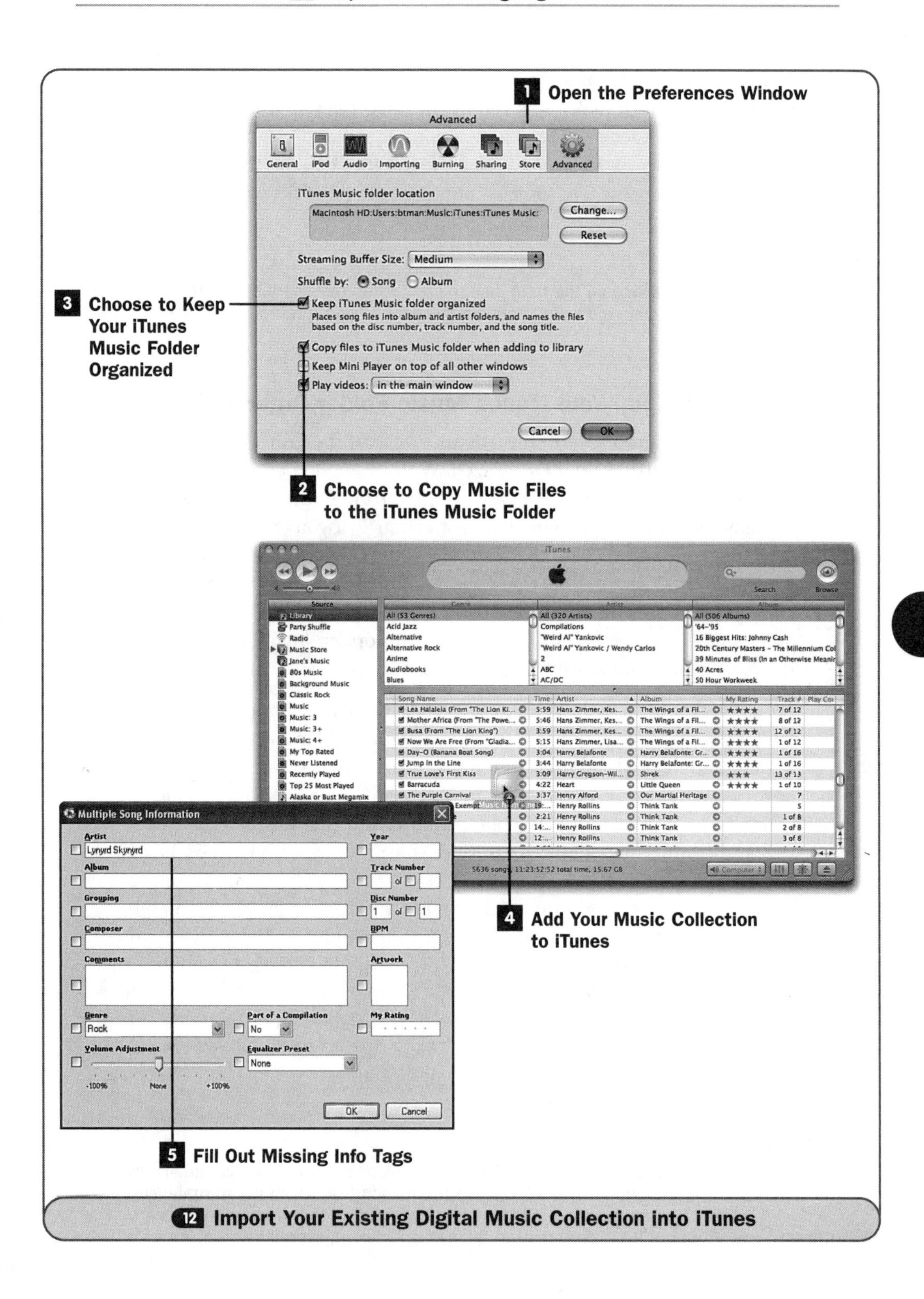

12 Import Your Existing Digital Music Collection into iTunes

Enable the option if you want iTunes to be able to keep its own copy of each music file in its own folder, to do with whatever it needs, while leaving your original copy untouched. Disable the option if you don't want iTunes making duplicates of all your imported files, a process that doubles the disk space needed by your music files (at least until you get rid of the originals).

NOTE

If there isn't enough space on the hard disk to create the necessary duplicates, iTunes stops copying and reports the error condition so that you can free up some space before trying again.

3 Choose to Keep Your iTunes Music Folder Organized

The other relevant option in the **Advanced** tab of the **Preferences** window is **Keep iTunes Music Folder Organized**. With this option enabled, every change you make to the info tags of a file in iTunes' interface is reflected immediately in the files themselves. For instance, if you change the title of a song, the file is renamed to match (with a prefix reflecting the disc number, if it's part of a CD set, and the track number). If you change the artist name or album name, the folders into which the file is organized are also renamed and the file is moved accordingly. Disable this option if you don't want iTunes messing around with your files' names.

For example, if you want to import all your music into iTunes while leaving the files in their original locations on your hard disk and with their original names, disable the **Copy files to iTunes Music folder when adding to library** option. If you want iTunes to copy your music files to the iTunes **Music** folder and add them to appropriate locations in the folder tree depending on the initial state of the **Artist** and **Album** info tags in each of the files, but *not* to update the folders or filenames after they've been imported, enable the **Copy files to iTunes Music folder when adding to library** option but disable the **Keep iTunes Music Folder Organized** option. If, however, you want to allow iTunes to perform all the organizational duties for which it was designed, taking full advantage of all the flexibility of music files with rich info tag data, leave both options enabled; this means you'll always be able to navigate to your appropriately named music files in the Finder or Windows Explorer, just as easily as you can in iTunes itself.

NOTE

If you re-enable the **Keep iTunes Music Folder Organized** option after you initially disabled it, iTunes must perform a check against all the songs in its library to make sure that all the filenames are accurate. This process can take a long time, and you can quit it by clicking **Stop**; but it's a good idea to let it finish making everything neat, so be patient.

4 Add Your Music Collection to iTunes

When the two important settings are configured to your liking, click **OK** to close the **Preferences** window. Now you're ready to bring all your music into iTunes.

If you have several music folders and a lot of time on your hands, you can import each folder individually into iTunes as described in 11 **Add a Music File to Your iTunes Library**. However, the most fun way—especially if you enabled both organizational options in Steps 2 and 3—is to throw all your files into iTunes at once, even if you have thousands of songs in your collection. To do this, first consolidate your music collection by placing all your folders of MP3s into a single parent folder. Then drag the parent folder into the song listing area of the iTunes' window and release the mouse button when you see the + icon on your mouse pointer.

Depending on the speed of your computer, the length of the ensuing process can be several minutes or more, even up to the better part of an hour. As iTunes copies and sorts your music files, you can watch them being filed away into the appropriate folders within your iTunes **Music** folder; iTunes itself will be unresponsive, but you can watch your music collection be organized for you while you wait.

▶ NOTE

If any unprotected WMA files are among your music collection, iTunes pops up a window that notifies you that it will be converting these files to AAC format as it imports them. The AAC files are organized into the appropriate folders, and the original WMA files are left untouched on your hard disk.

5 Fill Out Missing Info Tags

Now begins a task that will probably take you days, if not weeks or months, to finish to your satisfaction, depending on how obsessively neat you are: editing all the newly imported entries in the iTunes' database so that all their info tags are properly filled out. Whether you've chosen to let iTunes update the underlying filenames or not, keeping the info tags correctly updated is important to allowing you to navigate efficiently, set up ***Smart Playlists*** based on the info tags, and share the music over the local network or to your iPod in such a way that it can be navigated smoothly. See 69 **Examine and Modify Song Information** for more information on updating your songs' details, and 13 **Add Album Art to Songs** to enhance your songs with appropriate album art.

13 Add Album Art to Songs

✔ BEFORE YOU BEGIN	→ SEE ALSO
9 Import a Music CD into iTunes	77 Carry Your Photos on an iPod photo
11 Add a Music File to Your iTunes Library	

As convenient and versatile as digital music files are, there are some things about CDs that they can't replace. There's just something special about being able to pick up a CD case and identify it by the artwork on its cover; a listing of songs in bare text format just doesn't bring with it quite the same cachet, especially when the listing for a Mozart symphony looks just the same as the one for a ska band or stand-up comedian's routine. Furthermore, CD albums tend to come with booklets full of more artwork, including lyric sheets, interviews, cast and crew information, and more—some very extensive and thick. Where is the equivalent of these things in the digital music world?

iTunes can't quite provide the same experience as these features of CDs give you. However, you *can* add album art in the form of digital image data to the headers of your MP3 or AAC files. A scanned picture file, even a high-resolution one, is only a few hundred kilobytes at most, compared to the three or four megabytes of a complete digital audio file; thus, adding a piece of album art to a song, or even several pictures at once, doesn't materially increase the impact on your disk space. It can, however, greatly enhance your enjoyment of your music by showing you what the album looked like that the song to which you're listening came from.

▶ NOTE

Songs purchased from the iTunes Music Store come with their own high-resolution album art already built in; some, in fact, have additional files attached, such as printable PDFs and lyric sheets. You can also buy videos from the iTunes Music Store; these play in the same display pane used to show album art or in a separate window.

1 Obtain Album Art Images

The first step is to get one or more images of the album art for a given CD album. If you have a scanner, you might choose to scan the cover of your CD jewel case insert, as well as some of the pages from the interior of the insert booklet. Consult the documentation for your scanner if you choose to do it this way; save the final picture files with at least 500 pixels of resolution in both width and height, but don't make it much bigger than 1000 pixels square. Save the image file in JPEG format for the best compression/quality balance. Try to keep each picture under 200 kilobytes in size.

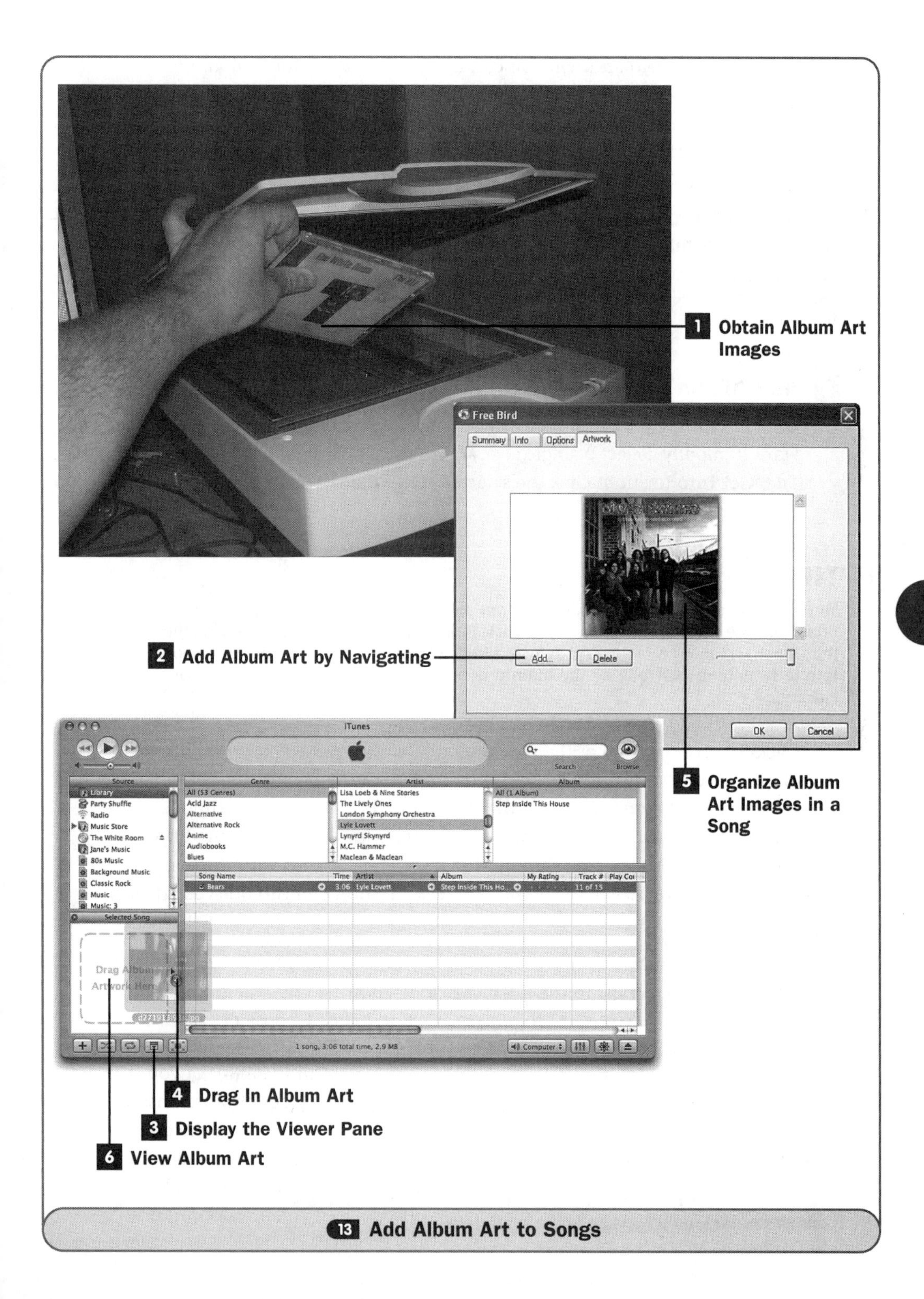

13 Add Album Art to Songs

If you don't have a scanner, you can usually find acceptable album art images on the Internet. AMG's Allmusic service (**http://www.allmusic.com**) has comprehensive discographies for almost all major bands, including album art that—while not very high-resolution—will do in a pinch.

▶ WEB RESOURCE

http://www.allmusic.com

The Allmusic site, run by the All Media Guide (AMG), contains comprehensive discography listings of most well-known bands, including album art you can use in your imported music files.

2 Add Album Art by Navigating

Use the **Library** view and the **Browse** columns to navigate to the music you want to modify. Select a single song, or a group of songs, and then choose **File, Get Info** (or right-click the selected song and choose **Get Info** from the context menu).

▶ TIP

You can select an entire album, or all of an artist's works, by choosing it from the appropriate Browse list. For instance, if you click **Phil Collins** in the **Artist** listing at the top of the iTunes window, and leave **All** selected in the **Album** listing, you can then choose **Get Info** to simultaneously edit all the information of all the Phil Collins songs in your Library.

Click the **Artwork** tab of the **Info** dialog box. This pane shows you all the album art currently embedded in the selected song or songs. Use the slider in the lower-right corner to adjust the size of the thumbnails of the images; you can view the thumbnails one at a time at maximum size (click the **Previous** and **Next** buttons to scroll through the images associated with the selected songs), or at any size down to 32 on-screen at once. You can add more than 32 images if you want.

Click the **Add** button to add another piece of art to the information for the selected song or songs. In the file picker that appears, navigate to the location of the picture you want to add; select it and click **Choose** or **Open**. The picture is added to the display pane. Repeat for all the pictures you want to add to this song or set of songs (you can't add more than one picture at a time). Click **OK** to dismiss the **Info** window.

▶ TIP

You can remove a piece of album art from a song or songs by selecting it in the display pane of the **Info** dialog box and clicking **Delete**.

3 Display the Viewer Pane

Click the **Show Album Art** button under the **Source** pane in the iTunes' window. A smaller pane, labeled **Selected Song**, opens above the button; this **Viewer** pane shows you any album art that already exists in a selected song, or a gray dashed box with a *Drag Album Artwork Here* message if there is no album art in the song.

▶ NOTE

Click the Selected Song heading to switch the Viewer pane to Now Playing if music is playing; this action toggles between viewing the album art for the selected song or for the currently playing track (if the track art is different from what's selected).

4 Drag in Album Art

A quicker way to add album art than the one described in Step 2 is to simply drag picture files from the Finder or Windows Explorer into the **Viewer** pane. You can add multiple pictures at once this way—just select multiple files and drag them all into the **Viewer** pane with one motion. You can even drag pictures directly from your web browser into the pane, without having to save them to your computer first.

5 Organize Album Art Images in a Song

When you have added multiple pictures to a song or group of songs, you will probably want to set the order in which that artwork appears; this way you can be sure that the album cover artwork appears first, and as you browse the pictures they appear in the correct sequence. Open the **Info** window again for a song or group of songs; click the **Artwork** tab. Adjust the slider until all the pictures are visible at once. Now click and drag the pictures into the order you want them to appear; the first one should go at the upper left, and so on in the normal order you'd expect in reading a page left to right.

6 View Album Art

In iTunes, click the small thumbnail image in the **Viewer** pane to display the full-resolution image in its own window. If there is more than one picture embedded in a song, use the **Left** and **Right** arrow buttons to page through the available pictures.

▶ TIP

Drag the vertical divider to widen or narrow the Source pane. As the Source pane grows wider, the Viewer pane gets larger accordingly, keeping a square shape.

If you have an iPod with a color screen (such as the iPod photo), the album art for the current song appears on the **Now Playing** screen; if you press the **Select** button several times to switch through the various control modes, you can view the artwork at the full size of the iPod's screen.

14 Submit CD Track Names to the Gracenote Database

✔ BEFORE YOU BEGIN	→ SEE ALSO
9 Import a Music CD into iTunes	69 Examine and Modify Song Information

The reason Apple uses the Gracenote database to provide track names for inserted CDs is that it's the largest public database of track names available. It's the largest because it gets information from the millions of people using software like iTunes every day. Apple could have chosen to provide its own internal music database, with professionally entered information—as Microsoft did in the past—but the inevitable result would be that its information would be much more limited. Apple chose to go with Gracenote's much greater coverage of all the thousands, if not millions, of CD albums available in the world, because the risk of occasional erroneous information was a small price to pay for the much vaster field of information that is available.

▶ NOTE

The same philosophy is present in Wikipedia (http://www.wikipedia.org), the online collaborative encyclopedia whose contents are edited daily by everyone who happens to want to add anything. The risk of abuse is more than mitigated by the wealth of accurate and useful information that users provide.

As an iTunes' user, you can do your part to make sure that the Gracenote database has the most accurate information possible. If you notice any errors in the track name data it provides, simply make the necessary corrections and submit the changes back to Gracenote.

To submit CD track information, you have to start with a complete commercial CD, not just a collection of tracks in your library.

1 Insert an Audio CD

Select an audio CD that you want to add to your iTunes **Library**. Insert it into the computer's CD drive and close the drive door. Wait for iTunes to populate the CD's track listing; if you don't have an Internet connection, the tracks are given generic names, such as **Track 01**, **Track 02**, and so on.

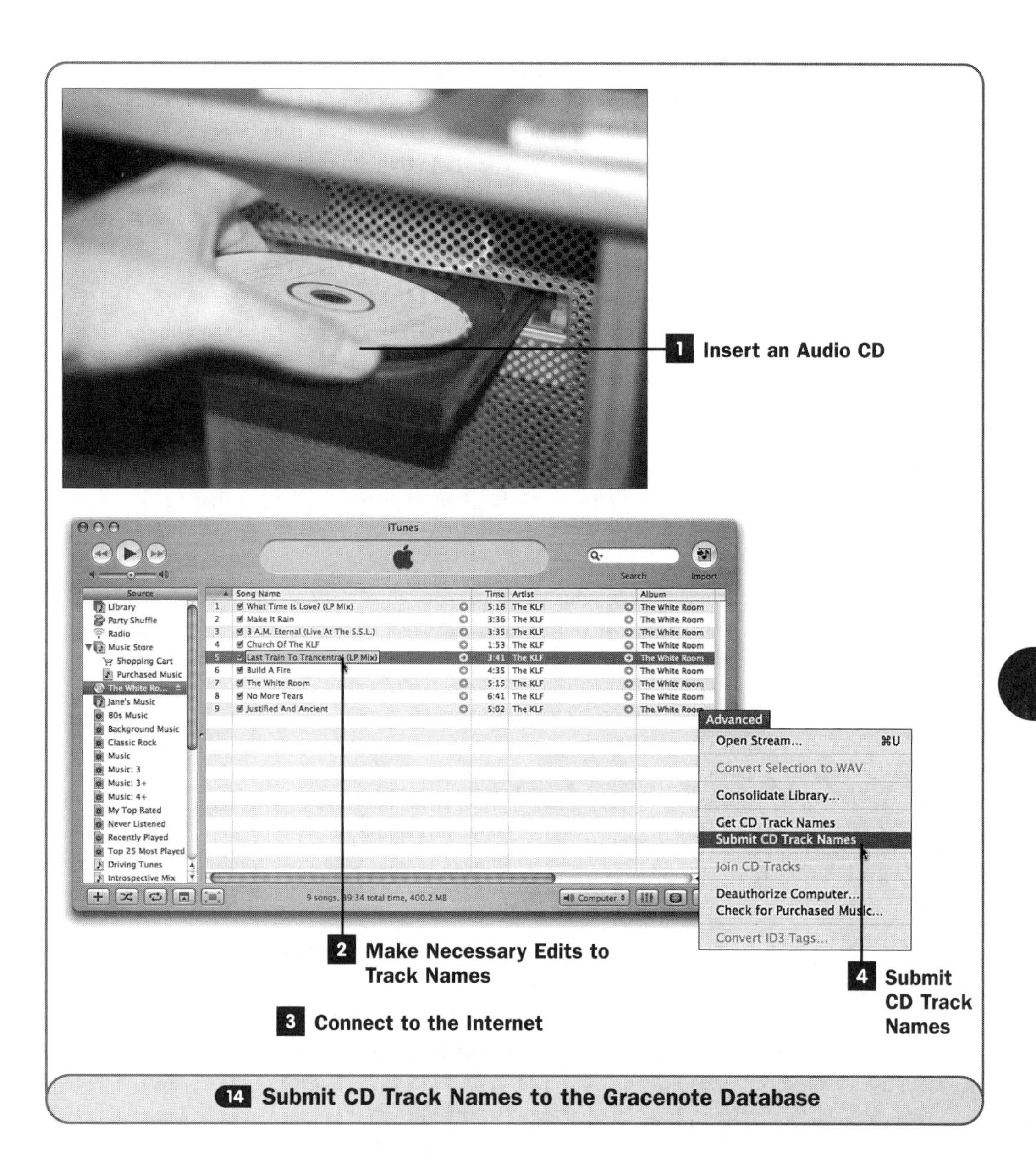

14 Submit CD Track Names to the Gracenote Database

2 Make Necessary Edits to Track Names

Using the **Info** window or the displayed fields in the song listing pane, enter the proper names for the tracks on the CD. The best approach is to select all the songs on the disc, choose **File, Get Info** or right-click the song and choose **Get Info** from the context menu, and make all the changes at once to as many fields as possible. Make sure that the CD's title is correct; if it's part of a multiple-disc set, fill in the **Disc Number** fields rather than putting an identifier such as [1/3] in the title. If you can, fill in the **Composer**, **Genre**, and **Year** fields as well (**Year** should reflect the original release date of the album so that the music on the disc can be accurately pegged to a certain era in musical history). Click **OK** when you're done; the fields are all updated to reflect your changes.

3 Connect to the Internet

If you're not connected to the Internet already, connect now. Dial up your modem or connect to the wireless or wired network, depending on your circumstances.

4 Submit CD Track Names

Choose **Advanced, Submit CD Track Names**. iTunes connects to the Gracenote site, checks the available categories, and submits your information. That's all there is to it. The Gracenote staff will check your submission for accuracy and add it to the database usually within a day or two. Don't expect any feedback from Gracenote or a thank-you—but from now on, anyone trying to import the same CD whose information you just submitted will get your more accurate information instead of what was available before.

15 Import a CD with Joined Tracks

✔ BEFORE YOU BEGIN	→ SEE ALSO
9 Import a Music CD into iTunes	64 Customize Importing Options

Most CDs are designed so that individual songs can be played out of order, selected at random, mixed in with tracks from other discs, and so on. However, that's not the case with all CDs. Some discs—for example CDs of live performances (in which audience applause carries over from one track to the next) or spoken-word renditions of popular books—don't sound very good when their tracks are shuffled around. Also, the technically inevitable "hiccup" that occurs between tracks (particularly on the iPod) can disrupt the flow of these unified streams of audio enjoyment.

iTunes provides a solution for this problem: You can import groups of CD tracks as *joined* tracks, meaning that several tracks are merged into a single unbroken digital audio file with no "hiccups" or internal breaks of any kind.

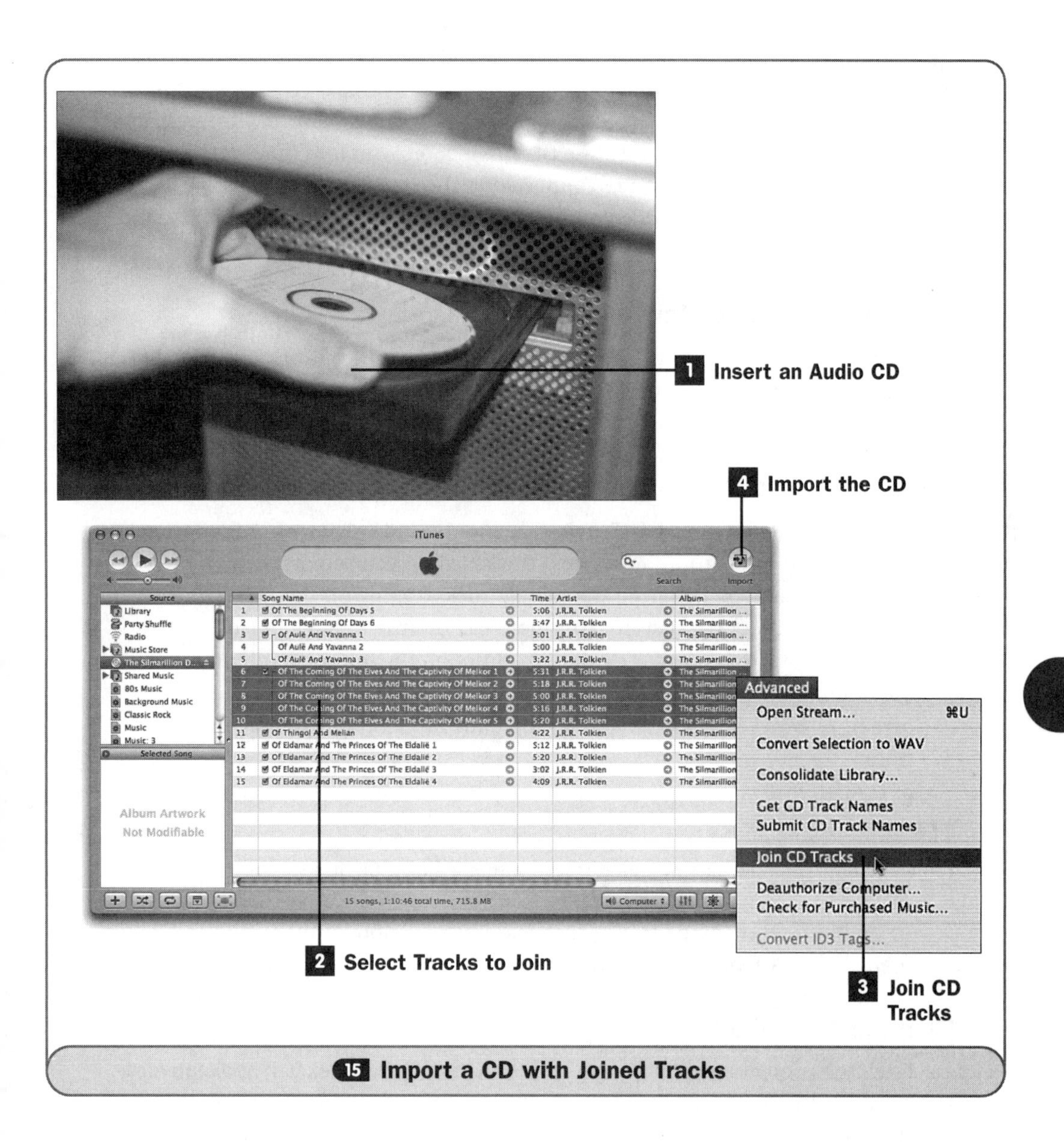

15 Import a CD with Joined Tracks

15

▶ NOTE

You can join tracks only when you are importing them from a CD. If you want to join tracks that are already in your iTunes **Library**, burn them to an audio CD, then join and import the tracks. See 52 **Create an Audio CD from a Playlist** for more information.

1 Insert an Audio CD

Select an audio CD that you want to add to your iTunes **Library**. Insert it into the computer's CD drive and close the drive door. Wait for iTunes to populate the CD's track listing; if you're connected to the Internet, the correct track names should be downloaded automatically from Gracenote and applied to the tracks.

2 Select Tracks to Join

In the iTunes' song listing, select two or more consecutive tracks on the CD (hold down **Shift** as you click). Note that the tracks must be listed according to the track numbers (the first column) for the purpose of this task.

3 Join CD Tracks

Choose **Advanced, Join CD Tracks**. This command creates what is effectively a single long track from the selected tracks; when you import the CD, only one audio file is created from the joined tracks, taking on the name and other track info of the first track in the selection (the individual track names and numbers are no longer available, although the imported album retains the original number of total tracks, and non-joined tracks are not renumbered). A "bracket" appears next to the joined tracks, indicating their joined status.

▶ TIP

You can create multiple sets of joined tracks within a single CD, if necessary.

To unjoin a set of joined tracks, first select one or more of the joined tracks, then choose **Advanced, Unjoin CD Tracks**.

4 Import the CD

Click the **Import** button to begin importing the CD into your iTunes **Library**. Examine the resulting songs in your library when the process is done; you should see only a single long track in place of the set of joined tracks you selected, and their flow will be uninterrupted when you play the track back.

16 Extract a "Secret Track" into the iTunes Library

✔ BEFORE YOU BEGIN

9 Import a Music CD into iTunes
11 Add a Music File to Your iTunes Library

➜ SEE ALSO

68 Find Music Files from iTunes Entries
70 Eliminate Duplicate Tracks

Sometimes the authors of CDs get sneaky on us. Sometimes they like to slip in a "secret" track, right at the end of the disc, after a long period of silence following the end of the final track. This practice is left over from the days of cassette tapes, when the tape might have several minutes of dead time left over at the end. An unsuspecting listener might hear silence after the end of the last track and, thinking that the tape was over, simply stop the player and rewind the tape. Only the true die-hard fans of the band would listen to the silence all the way to the physical end of the tape; these fans would be rewarded for their trouble by the occasional hidden, "secret" track stuck in right before the end of the tape.

In the age of CDs, this practice made less sense because any quick perusal of the track lengths would indicate that there was something fishy about a Track 12 that lasted for 14 minutes, especially if the song itself didn't run for more than the usual 3 or 4 minutes. However, some CD authors continued to do this, hiding "secret" tracks in plain sight.

But it's the iTunes' age now, and we've got control over our music that just wasn't possible in the earlier days. Now we can snip up that final 14-minute track, crop out the useless silence from the middle, and turn the "secret" track into a full-fledged track with its own rightful place in the song listing. We can listen to it without having to go through the preceding "real" track and the intervening silence first. After we've enjoyed the band's little joke, we can move on to organizing our music the "right" way.

1 Find the Song with the Secret Track

Navigate to the song in the library listing that has the hidden track buried inside it. Select this song by clicking it; then choose **File**, **Show Song File** (or right-click the song and choose **Show Song File** from the context menu). This command opens a Finder or Windows Explorer window showing the selected song file.

2 Create a Duplicate of the Song File

In Mac OS X, click the song file to select it, then choose **File**, **Duplicate** to create an identical copy. In Windows, right-click the file and choose **Copy**; then right-click in the same window and choose **Paste** to create a duplicate of the file.

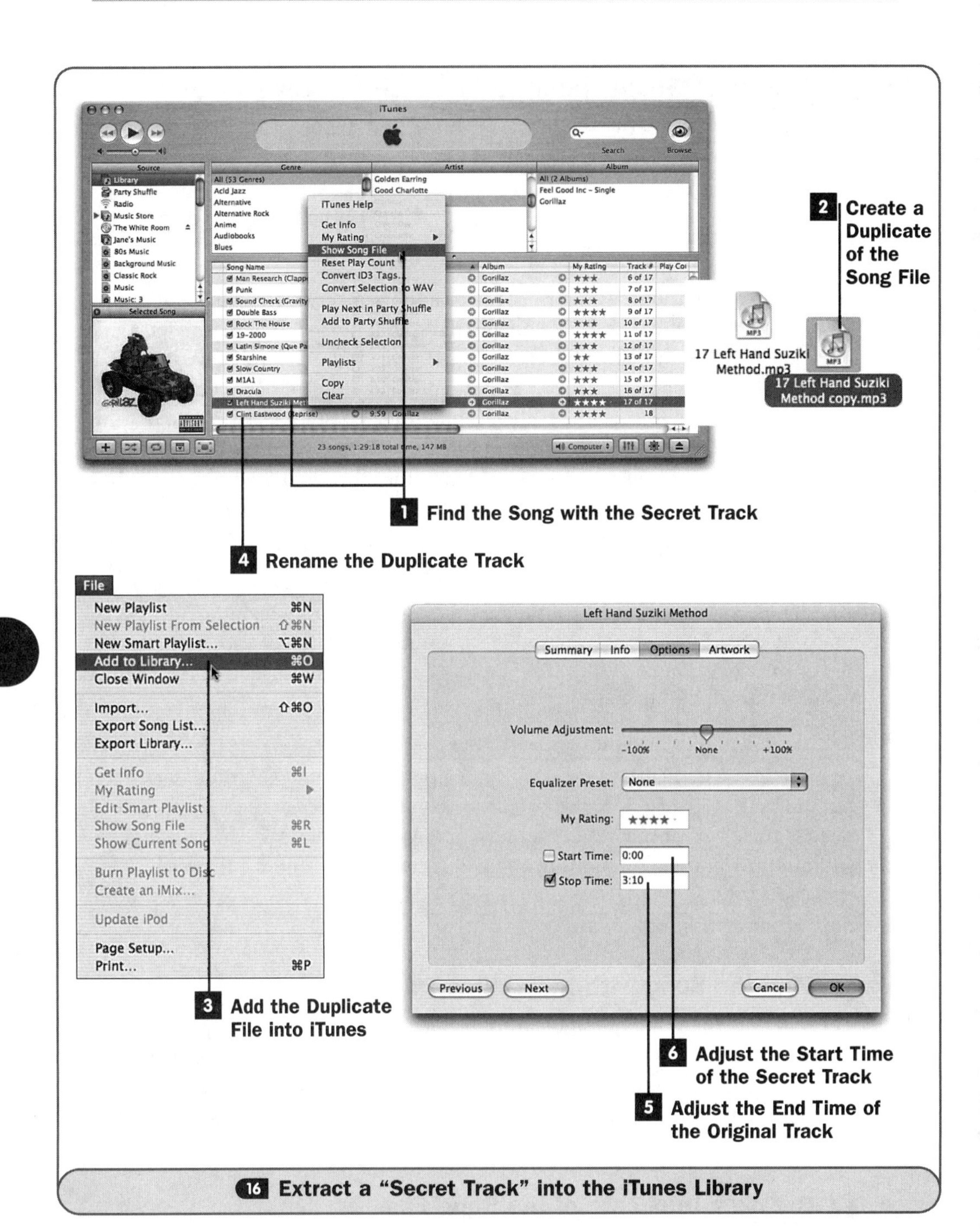

16 Extract a "Secret Track" into the iTunes Library

3 Add the Duplicate File into iTunes

Drag the newly created duplicate into iTunes to add it to the library as described in 11 **Add a Music File to Your iTunes Library**. There should now be two identical copies of the same song right next to each other in the library view.

4 Name the Duplicate Track

Now it's time to choose a song name for the newly unhidden not-so-secret track. By their nature, these songs aren't normally shown in CD track listings, so you'll have to choose an appropriate title yourself. Type the new song name using the editable fields in the song listing pane or the **Info** window.

It's also a good idea to choose an appropriate track number for this song. If there are 12 "official" tracks on the disc, and you enter **13** for the track number for the new song, the **12** in the "total" field (after the **of**) gets blanked out (because it's no longer valid). You might want to make a quick change to all the tracks in the album and update them all so that there are **13** total tracks. To do this, select all the tracks in the album (or select the album title in the **Album** list), choose **File**, **Get Info**, and update the "total" field (located after the **of** under in the **Track #** column).

5 Adjust the End Time of the Original Track

Select the original track, the one from which the secret track was extracted. Play the track and move the scrub bar to the end of the first segment of audio, the end of the "real" track. Click the second line of the display until it reads **Elapsed Time**; write down the time signature it reports one or two seconds after the real track ends.

Move the playhead to the point where the secret track begins. Write down the time signature when this occurs; make sure to pick a time about one second before the track starts so that you don't end up missing the first sounds of the secret track.

Choose **File**, **Get Info** to display the **Info** window; click the **Options** tab. In this tab, you can customize the effective starting and ending time for individual tracks; that's ideal for your needs here, because what you want to do is snip out the silence in the middle of both the original and new files—and get rid of the irrelevant track of music from each of them as well. For the original song, set the **Stop Time** field to the time signature you wrote down for the end of the original track.

6 Adjust the Start Time of the Secret Track

Click **Next** to select the duplicate track. (Make sure that you have the right file by switching to the **Info** tab temporarily.) Set the **Start Time** field to the time signature you wrote down for the beginning of the hidden track. Click **OK**.

Now you've got two separate tracks, for all intents and purposes the same as if they'd come off the CD that way. True, both tracks still have an erroneously long running time, but if you play either song—in iTunes or on the iPod—all that plays is the actual music, the part you care about.

4

Using the iTunes Music Store

IN THIS CHAPTER:

Now that we're all used to buying our books online from Amazon.com, participating in auctions online on eBay.com, and even getting all our news and entertainment online, it seems silly that in the age of digital music, when song files can be transmitted more easily from computer to computer than albums carried from the record store to our house, we should still be limited to buying physical CDs when we want to add to our record collections.

Well, with the iTunes **Music Store**, all that has changed. At the time of this writing, the iTunes **Music Store** has sold over 400 million songs to customers on both the Mac and Windows platforms, at a pace that continues to climb daily as more and more people discover iTunes and the selection of music that grows by hundreds of albums every week. Priced at a constant 99 cents per track, or $9.99 per album, and offering customers the ability to buy just their favorite tracks instead of whole albums full of filler, iTunes offers a value that's hard for competitors to undercut and easy for the big record labels to like. With the built-in ***Digital Rights Management*** technology in protected AAC files, customers get the flexibility they need and true ownership of the music they buy, and the labels get the assurance that they're not just giving out freely distributable digital songs at a dollar a pop. After all, the record companies also have to make a profit if digital music is to become a mainstream medium to supplant CDs.

The iTunes **Music Store** is designed to be as intuitive to use as iTunes itself is; but that doesn't mean it's completely without its quirks or hidden features. With the tasks in this chapter, you should become fully familiar with how the iTunes **Music Store** works, how to take advantage of its lesser-known features, and how to get the most bang for your buck as you build your iTunes Library through the fastest-growing legal means of music delivery on Earth.

17 About Digital Rights Management Technology

✔ **BEFORE YOU BEGIN**

8 About Music Formats

By 1997 or so, the world had accepted ***MPEG-1 level 3 (MP3)*** as the *de facto* standard format for digital audio; it was versatile, ubiquitous, and mostly free. MP3 files, which are as little as 1/12 the size of their CD audio counterparts with almost no noticeable degradation in quality, can be played just about anywhere and by anything, from PDAs to cell phones to car stereos. Best of all, they have no ***Digital Rights Management (DRM)*** technology. Or, perhaps (depending on who you ask), that's the *worst* aspect of MP3 files. MP3s have been the scourge of the commercial music industry in recent years, enabling music enthusiasts to trade songs freely and amass huge collections of commercial music without paying for it. The large record labels demanded a form of MP3-like digital audio that gave users the flexibility they craved, and yet allowed copyright holders to protect their property by only allowing users to make a limited number of copies of the files; they got it in ***Advanced Audio Coding (AAC).*** AAC is a component of the MPEG-4 standard brought to life in part by Apple and has been incorporated into iTunes since version 4.

In the iTunes **Music Store**, the restrictions placed on the purchaser by the protected AAC files it sells are as follows: You can play purchased songs on as many as five different computers, following an Internet-based authorization process that unlocks your digital ID for those five computers. You can burn purchased AAC files to regular audio CDs by first putting them in a playlist, then burning a disc from that playlist as described in 52 **Create an Audio CD from a Playlist**; however, you can burn only seven copies of the same unaltered playlist before iTunes makes you stop. Individual songs can be burned to CD an unlimited number of times, however. iTunes' users on the same network can connect to each other to listen to shared music libraries, but they must be authorized on their own computers to listen to shared protected music, and only five different listeners can connect to a single copy of iTunes in a given day.

The proposition of Apple's AAC copy-protection is an acknowledgment that *some* piracy, or willful breaking of the DRM, is inevitable. No copy-protection scheme is totally effective because any music that can be played through speakers can be re-recorded into an unprotected format (such as MP3) using a simple audio loop-back cable and recording software. However, because each song must be purchased before it can be downloaded, the would-be pirate must spend the money to buy each song and then painstakingly re-record each song to the new unprotected format, a process that takes as long as it does every track to play at normal speed. This means that the risk of piracy is a *linear* one, requiring a commensurate amount of effort and payment by the would-be pirate for each stolen track—and the gamble is that pirates won't consider it worthwhile. Furthermore, people who are otherwise willing to search for free music on file-sharing services (which might be of poor quality) are likely to think $1 per track is a fair price for peace of mind and an assurance of quality. The same philosophy underlies the iTunes **Music Store**'s restriction on being able to burn a single playlist of purchased songs to a CD seven times. Sure, a pirate can then simply re-create the playlist and continue burning bootlegged audio CDs of purchased music. But he can't do it in an automated fashion, without hands-on supervision, altering the playlist every seven copies. This is a small speed-bump standing in the way of pirates, but it is a speed-bump nonetheless—and it's doing the job, to judge by the fact that in two years, iTunes' reputation as a trustworthy provider of well-protected music has grown, and industry participation has grown with it.

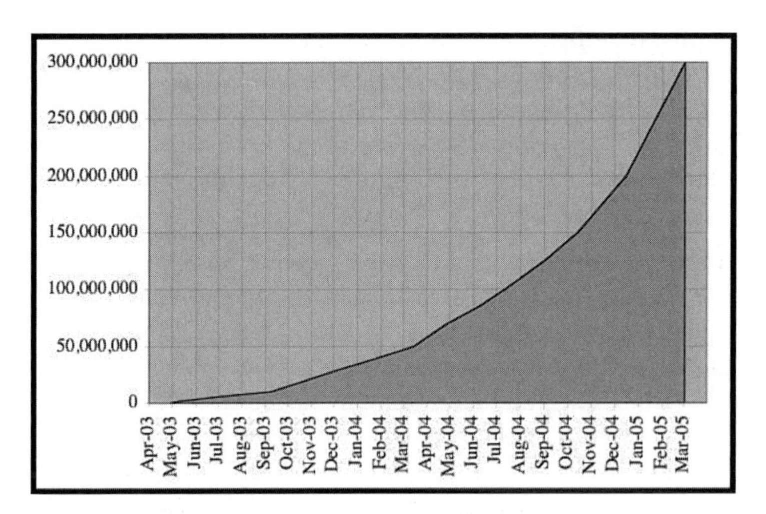

*Sales through the iTunes **Music Store** have skyrocketed since it was first opened.*

In contrast to the way some competing DRM systems (such as the one used by Napster's subscription service) work, in iTunes' AAC system you pay individually for each song at the time you download it, but the song files are yours to keep once you've bought them. Each file is keyed with your ID in the iTunes **Music Store**; this means that once a computer you use has been unlocked with your ID, all the music files on that computer that were purchased using that ID can be freely played. If you should ever need to unlock your files in the future, all you have to do is authorize your computer using your ID with a simple communication over the network to the iTunes' servers. There is no time limit to your ownership of the files or to your ability to authorize.

17

▶ NOTE

You can authorize up to five computers to play music you bought, and you can deauthorize any authorized computer later at your discretion. See 23 Authorize a Computer to Play Purchased Music for more information.

In contrast, competing subscription services such as Napster allow you to freely download as many songs as you want, as long as your subscription is kept current. Each month you must re-authorize your computer through a transaction with the central server to retain access to your files. If your subscription lapses, your files become useless. For some users who prefer to browse with unlimited freedom and who don't mind paying a subscription fee forever, this kind of system might be acceptable. But Apple's bet is that most people prefer to own their music, not rent it.

Authorizing your computer in iTunes to gain access to downloaded AAC files.

The relationship between Apple and the labels, and between both of them and the customers, is a fluid one that continues to change. Apple periodically renegotiates the terms of the deal it has with the labels, sometimes because it wants to adjust the user experience to be more useful to the customer, sometimes because the labels want to bump up the restrictions. For example, in mid-2004, Apple raised the limit on the number of authorized computers a customer could have from 3 to 5; at the same time, it reduced the number of playlists you could burn to a CD from 10 to 7. This was part of a negotiation with the labels in which Apple gained more usability for its customers, while giving the labels more assurance against piracy. (Who really needs more than 7 copies of the same CD, anyway?)

DRM restrictions will always rankle some people, and with good reason: Copyright in the digital age is far from an established science. But in the meantime, you'd be hard put to find a fairer or more generous purveyor of DRM-protected digital music than Apple and the iTunes **Music Store**.

18 Sign Up for the iTunes Music Store

✔ BEFORE YOU BEGIN	→ SEE ALSO
2 Run iTunes for the First Time	20 Purchase Audio from the iTunes Music Store
17 About Digital Rights Management Technology	21 Purchase Music Using a Shopping Cart

As with nearly all online purchasing systems these days, the iTunes **Music Store** requires a credit card for instant verification of purchases. Furthermore, because the ideal way for the store to work is that you can select a song or album on an impulse and buy it with a single click, your credit card information must be saved in an account so that it can be accessed automatically whenever you make a purchase.

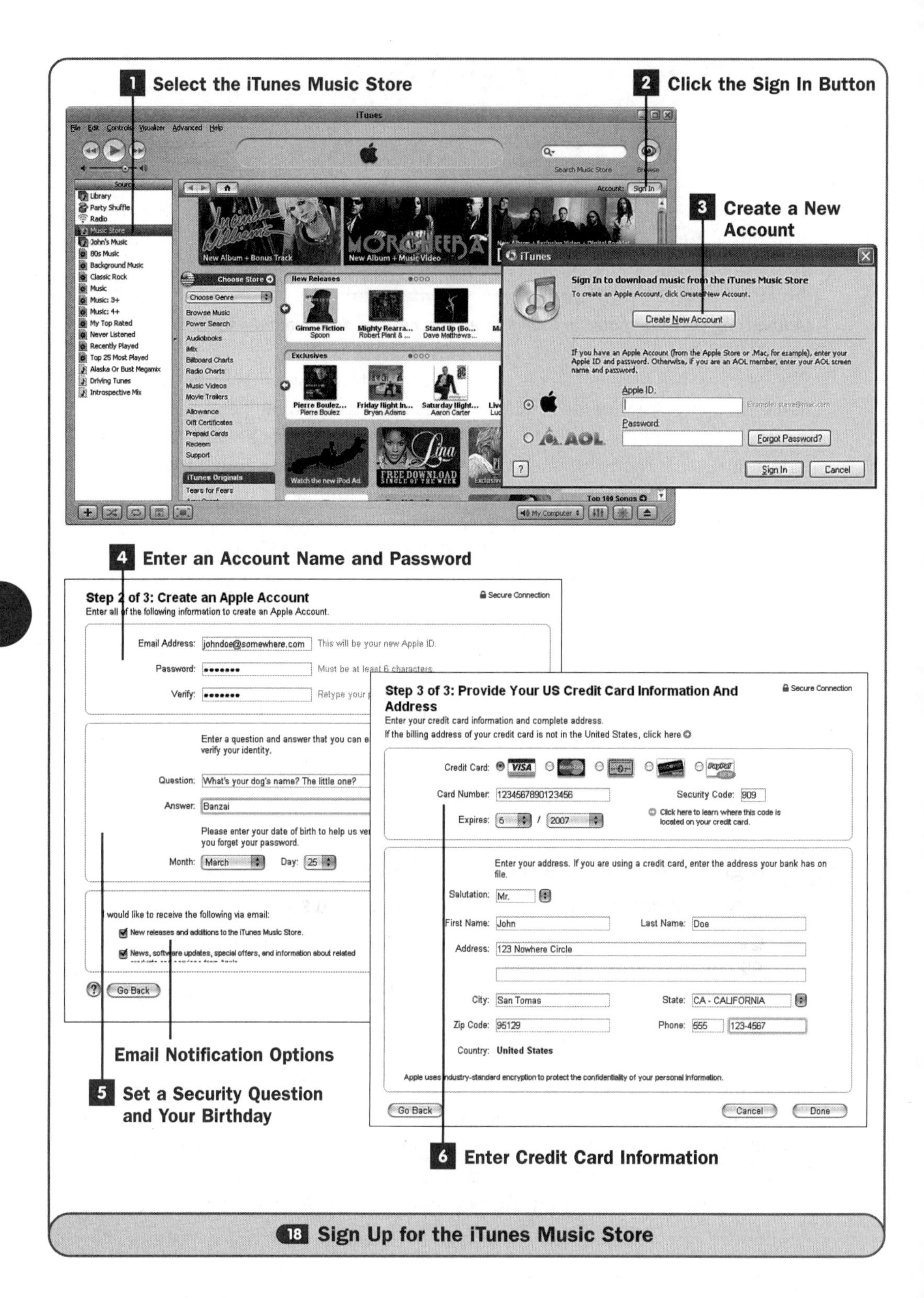

18 Sign Up for the iTunes Music Store

If you're security-conscious, this probably sounds risky—and it is, somewhat. With companies that are less than reputable, you would never want to store your complete credit card information invisibly on a central server where it can be accessed without your knowledge. However, the inherent risk in such a configuration is diminished when you're dealing with a large company whose reputation is on the line with every customer interaction it makes. If Apple were to be the target of accusations that it was ripping off its customers or giving out their credit card information, that would be the end—not only of the iTunes **Music Store**, but probably of Apple altogether. Apple can't afford to breach customers' trust by treating their sensitive information with anything less than the utmost care. Besides, Apple's method for storing credit cards centrally is no different from the "1-Click" settings you might have used at Amazon.com, a company that has as much to lose as Apple does from any credit-card-related scandal.

The bottom line is that you don't have to worry about something unsavory happening with your credit card as you use the iTunes **Music Store**. Millions of users have found that the benefits of using the store far outweigh any risks, and you likely will, too.

1 Select the iTunes Music Store

Make sure that you have a valid Internet connection. As with all tasks related to the iTunes **Music Store**, you can't connect to the store unless you're able to access the Internet.

Click the **Music Store** option in the iTunes **Source** pane. iTunes connects to the music store, an online service similar to a web page but contained entirely within the iTunes' window. You should see the iTunes **Music Store**'s main page, which includes many sections for navigating to music for purchase as well as banner advertisements and special offers. In the upper-right corner of the iTunes' window is an **Account** box that currently reads **Sign In**.

2 Click the Sign In Button

You can't buy any music without signing in, and you can't sign in until you have an account. Click **Sign In** to begin the account-creation process.

3 Create a New Account

In the dialog box that appears, you can either enter an Apple ID (a .Mac email address, such as **johndoe@mac.com**, is a valid Apple ID if you have one) or an AOL screen name to sign in. If you don't have either a .Mac email address or an AOL screen name, or if you want to create a new iTunes **Music Store** account for any other reason, click the **Create New Account** button.

4 Enter an Account Name and Password

When you click the **Create New Account** button, iTunes begins a three-step process to set up your Apple ID and user account. First read the **Terms of Service** agreement and click **Agree** to proceed.

In the next screen, you set up your Apple ID—which should be equal to your existing email address—and set a password by entering it twice (in the **Password** and **Verify** fields). Be sure to choose a good password—use a mixture of capital and lowercase letters, numbers, and special symbols, and don't use a word that can be found in the dictionary or any other sequence of characters that is easy to guess (especially for a computer).

▶ NOTE

Apple's convention for creating new user IDs (used for the online Apple Store and .Mac as well as the iTunes Music Store) is to use your existing valid email address, provided by your ISP, as your Apple ID name. If you have a choice of working email addresses, you might want to use as short an address as possible when signing up to avoid excessive typing when you log in.

5 Set a Security Question and Your Birthday

Provide a security question—a question that the iTunes' servers can ask you if you forget your password—that only you can answer. The security question is a way to identify yourself to the server. For example, a good question would be "What is your favorite food?" or "What is your city of birth?" Type a simple answer that you can provide exactly as you type it here if Apple ever has to ask you the question to verify your identity.

Also specify your birth date, an additional security precaution. Finally, use the check boxes to determine whether you want to receive regular notification emails from Apple regarding newly added music or special offers. Click **Continue** to move to the final screen.

6 Enter Credit Card Information

Choose the credit card type you want to use to pay for your music purchases and enter the card number and expiration date. You can also opt to use a ***PayPal*** account; if you select the **PayPal** option, a web link appears instead of the credit card number verification that you can use to validate your PayPal account and link it to your iTunes' purchases. Click this link and go through the approval process to authenticate your PayPal details.

▶ KEY TERM

PayPal—An online financial broker that makes it easy for money to be exchanged between any two parties, found at **http://www.paypal.com**.

Next, enter your credit card billing details as they are registered with your credit card company. Click **Done** to save the information and create your Apple ID.

You should be automatically logged in at the end of the process; your Apple ID appears in the **Account** box in the upper-right corner of the iTunes' window. If not, click the **Sign In** button and provide your Apple ID where prompted to sign in.

19 Browse the iTunes Music Store

✔ BEFORE YOU BEGIN	→ SEE ALSO
18 Sign Up for the iTunes Music Store	20 Purchase Audio from the iTunes Music Store 21 Purchase Music Using a Shopping Cart

With or without an iTunes' account, you can browse through the more than one and a half million songs in the iTunes **Music Store** and see what it's got to offer. However, if you want to purchase any music, you'll have to sign in with a valid Apple ID.

There are a number of ways to search for music in the store: You can go to a favorite genre and see top-selling artists, you can use the featured sections of newly added or popular albums on the main page, or you can go straight to a piece of music you know you want by searching directly for it by name. You can even browse all the categories of music in a columnar text browser similar to the navigation lists in iTunes itself.

1 Sign In to the iTunes Music Store

In the iTunes' window, choose **Music Store** from the **Source** pane and connect to the store. If you are not already signed in, click the **Sign In** button in the upper-right corner of the screen and provide your Apple ID (or AOL screen name) and password to sign yourself in.

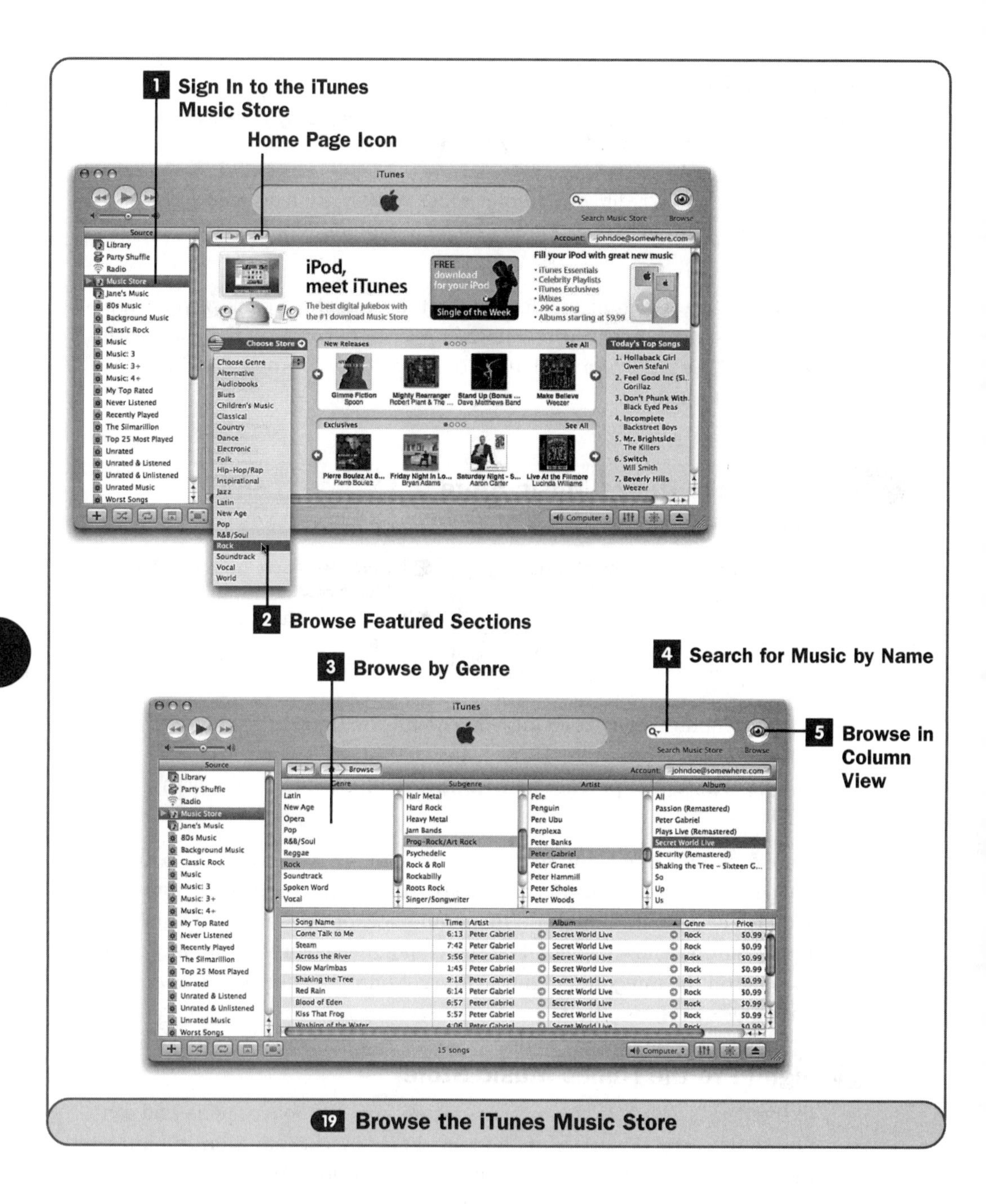

19 Browse the iTunes Music Store

2 Browse Featured Sections

In the middle of the music store's Home page, stacked vertically and scrolling horizontally, are several sections showing newly available music in various categories: **New Releases**, **Exclusives**, **Pre-Releases**, **Just Added**, and **Staff**

Favorites. Four albums are shown in each display; the little bubbles in the top center of each display area indicate how many pages of music there are for each category (usually 4, for a total of 16 albums per section). Use the left and right arrows to scroll from page to page (the colored bubble moves to show which page you're currently viewing), and click any displayed album to go to that album's download page.

▶ TIP

No matter how far you navigate into the music store, you can see the path from the Home page (indicated by a house icon) down to your current location in the bar above the Music Store display pane. Click any of the links in this path to return to that level; click the house icon to go back to the music store Home page. Use the left and right arrows to the left of the house icon to move back and forth through the history of your navigation throughout the store—no matter where a link takes you, you can always return to the previous page with the **Back** (left arrow) button.

3 Browse by Genre

Return to the Home page of the music store by clicking the house icon in the navigation path. Use the drop-down list on the left side of the page to select a genre to browse. Each genre page has the same layout as the Home page, with scrollable sections arranged horizontally so that you can discover featured albums.

▶ TIP

From any of the major genre pages), you can click the names of the featured tracks in sections such as **Today's Top Songs** or **Today's Top Albums**; these links take you to the download pages of the songs or albums in question.

4 Search for Music by Name

If you know the name of the music you want, type it into the **Search Music Store** bar in the upper-right corner of the iTunes' window and press **Return** or **Enter**. The results that match your search terms are listed in the page that appears; you can go to the album or artist page for any of the matching songs by clicking the right-arrow icon next to any of the fields on the listed songs.

To narrow your search to a specific scope (for example, if you want to see results only when the album name matches your search term, not the artist or song name), click the magnifying glass icon to select the scope you want to use.

▶ TIP

The **Power Search** option (also available from the Home page by clicking the magnifying glass icon in the **Search Music Store** bar and choosing **Power Search** from the menu that drops down) lets you search for specific combinations of music, such as for tracks with a certain name on a specific album, or within a certain genre.

5 Browse in Column View

One final way to browse the music store is to use the columnar **Browse** view, in which music is organized similarly to how you navigate iTunes itself in the **Library** view. Click the **Browse** button in the upper-right corner of the iTunes' window. The screen changes to a much more austere view, lacking any ads or unnecessarily attractive presentations, with nothing standing between you and the artist and albums you want.

First choose a **Genre** from the top-left list, then a **Subgenre** if available; then select an **Artist** from the next list (which is filtered by the selection you made in the first list or lists). You can double-click an artist name to go to that artist's discography, or instead select a single album from the **Album** list in the top-right list to see that album's available tracks. Double-click an album name to go to that album's download page.

20 Purchase Audio from the iTunes Music Store

✓ BEFORE YOU BEGIN	→ SEE ALSO
18 Sign Up for the iTunes Music Store	21 Purchase Music Using a Shopping Cart
19 Browse the iTunes Music Store	22 Check for Purchased Music

After you've signed in to the music store using your Apple ID or AOL screen name, buying music or ***audiobooks*** from the iTunes **Music Store** is no more complicated than finding the music you want and clicking the appropriate **Buy Song** or **Buy Album** button. Purchased music goes straight into your iTunes **Library** and the special **Purchased Music** playlist, where you can play each track as soon as it's finished downloading.

▶ KEY TERM

Audiobook—The digital equivalent of the spoken-word tape. It's a special kind of digital audio file that plays for a long time as its content (the text of a book or speech) is read. The file includes additional technology such that, if you pause listening to the audio stream, iTunes remembers where you left off and picks up again at that point when you resume listening. This technology even works if you move from iTunes to iPod as you listen to the audiobook.

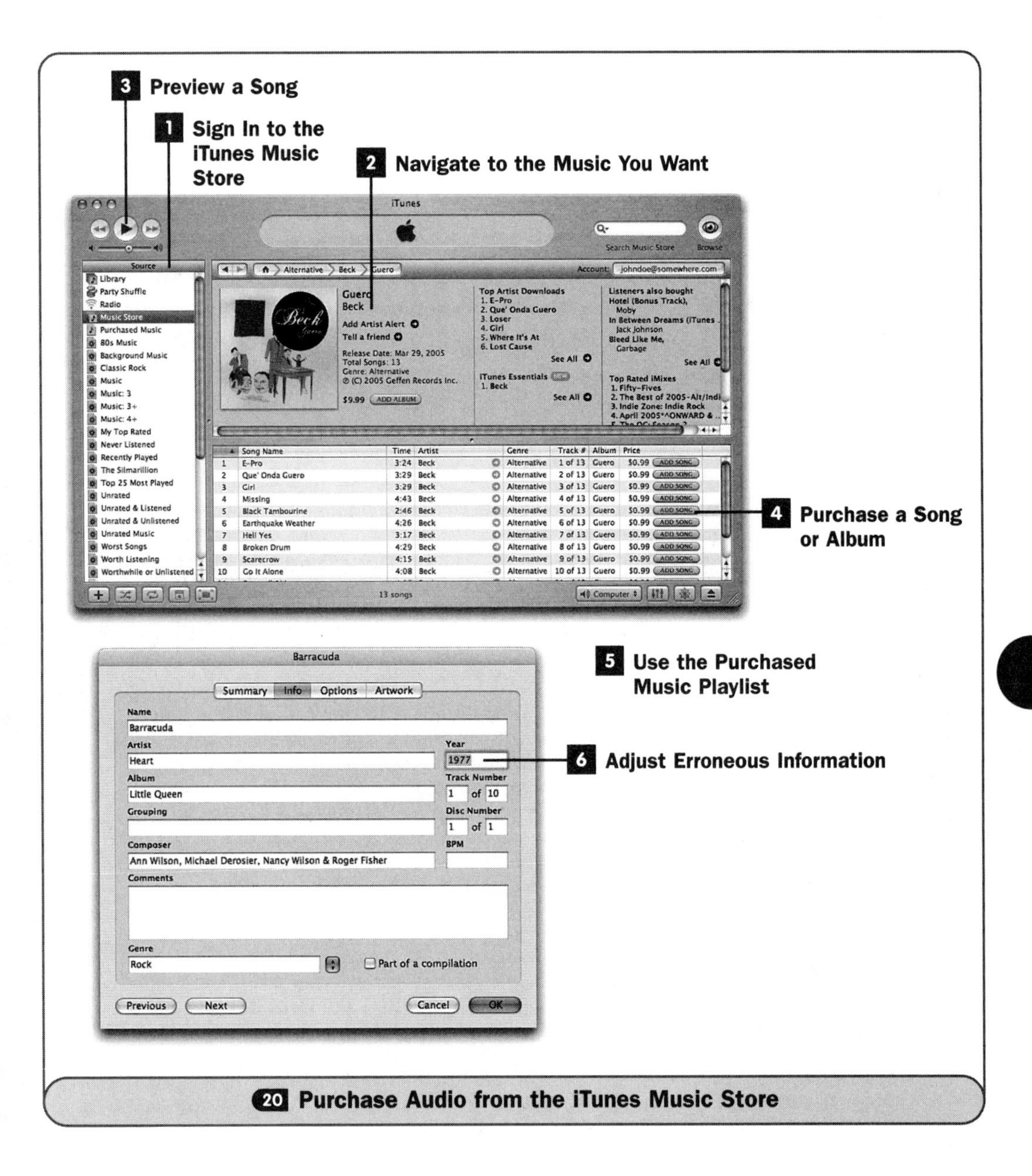

1 Sign In to the iTunes Music Store

Choose **Music Store** from the **Source** pane and connect to the store. If you are not already signed in, click the **Sign In** button in the upper-right corner of the window and provide your Apple ID (or AOL screen name) and password to sign yourself in.

2 Navigate to the Music You Want

As described in 19 **Browse the iTunes Music Store**, navigate the iTunes **Music Store** to find music you're interested in buying.

3 Preview a Song

Every album has its own download page, which is divided into two sections with the album information (including cover art) and links to related tracks on the top, and the list of the album's tracks on the bottom. Double-click any track name to hear a 30-second clip of the song, chosen from the middle of the track so that you get as good an idea as possible of the texture of the song (including its chorus). Previewing tracks is free of charge.

▶ TIP

If you have a slow network connection, the preview clips might not play very well—they might stutter a lot and stall for rebuffering. To minimize this problem, choose **Edit, Preferences** (Windows) or **iTunes, Preferences** (Mac) to display the iTunes **Preferences** window, click the **Store** tab, and enable the **Load complete preview before playing** check box.

▶ NOTE

Some tracks in an album may have a note saying **Album Only** instead of a **Buy Song** button; this means the track is available only if you buy the entire album. This condition might be the result of a licensing agreement in which the label allowed a particularly popular track to be purchased only if the customer bought the entire album it's on; these cases are relatively rare. So are cases where an album is listed as a **Partial Album**, or if it has a **By Track Only** note. These conditions can come about if tracks are particularly short or long and don't fit the 99-cent/track or $9.99/album price structure well, or if a licensing deal failed to get the rights to certain songs on an album.

4 Purchase a Song or Album

When you decide you want to buy a song, click the **Buy Song** button at the right end of the song's information row at the bottom of the window. A dialog box confirms that you really want to buy the song; you can suppress this confirmation box for future purchases by enabling the **Don't warn me about buying Songs again** check box. Similarly, buy an entire album by clicking the **Buy Album** button in the top of the window and confirming the purchase in the dialog box that appears.

▶ TIP

If you chose to suppress confirmation messages and you want to re-enable them, first click your Apple ID in the **Account** box, enter your Apple ID and password, and click the **View Account** button. In the screen that appears, click the **Reset Warnings** button to reset your account to show you all the routine confirmation messages when you buy music.

5 Use the Purchased Music Playlist

The selected song, or the songs in the selected album, begin downloading into your iTunes **Library**. Click **Purchased Music** in the **Source** pane; this is a special playlist associated with the music store that shows you all the songs you've bought. It's a great way to get immediate access to the music you buy, as well as to keep an eye on just how much money you've spent on the iTunes **Music Store** (look at the **Date Added** column to see when you purchased each track). Tracks that are not completely downloaded yet appear in gray type; as each track finishes downloading, the type turns black, and you can double-click it to listen to the track.

▶ TIPS

If for some reason your download of purchased music is interrupted (your Internet connection goes down, for example, or your computer crashes), you haven't lost your money or your music; see 22 **Check for Purchased Music** for how to recover in this situation.

Another way to review your purchases is to view your account information (click your **Apple ID** in the **Account** box, enter your ID and password, and click **View Account**) and then click the **Purchase History** button.

6 Adjust Erroneous Information

Many of the albums in the iTunes **Music Store** have an incorrect date of release set in their ***info tags***; this usually results from the album being encoded from a re-released version—you will seldom see a classic Elvis Presley or Eagles album listed with the correct year. Having the correct year set for all your music is especially important when you create ***Smart Playlists*** based on musical era, as you will see in 35 **Create a Smart Playlist**.

Fortunately, incorrect info tags are easy enough to correct. Navigate to the purchased tracks or album in the **Library** view; select them all and choose **File, Get Info**. Enter the correct release year in the **Year** field and click **OK**.

▶ WEB RESOURCE

http://www.allmusic.com

Refer to the All Music Guide for accurate album release information.

▶ TIP

Sometimes, unfortunately, the only way to buy a certain track in the music store is on a "Greatest Hits" album. You might be a musical stickler who likes to have all tracks marked according to their original albums. You can set the info tags to reflect the track's original album name, release year, and track number, as reported by the All Music Guide; you can even add new album art to make it look as if the track came from the original album. See 13 **Add Album Art to Songs** for more about adding album art and arranging it in the proper order.

21 Purchase Music Using a Shopping Cart

✔ BEFORE YOU BEGIN

18 Sign Up for the iTunes Music Store

20 Purchase Audio from the iTunes Music Store

➜ SEE ALSO

22 Check for Purchased Music

Normally, the iTunes **Music Store** is set up so that a single click of a **Buy Song** or **Buy Album** button charges your credit card and immediately downloads your selected music. However, this might not be the best solution for you; if you have a slow dial-up connection, or if you prefer to keep your purchases in a holding area while you decide how and when to purchase them (for example, if you want to keep yourself on a budget but want to keep track of the music you want to get someday), a "shopping cart" might be just the thing you need.

When you use a shopping cart, instead of **Buy Song** and **Buy Album** buttons, you'll see **Add Song** and **Add Album** buttons; clicking these buttons adds the music to your shopping cart rather than downloading it immediately. You aren't charged for any music in your shopping cart until you decide to download it. You can remove items from the cart or buy individual songs or albums from the cart without paying for everything at once.

▶ TIP

A shopping cart gives you versatility you wouldn't otherwise have, especially if you use iTunes on more than one computer. As an example, you can browse the music store and add music to the shopping cart while you're at work (while you're on break, of course), and then open up the shopping cart from your home computer and purchase its contents. Your Apple ID and password keep your shopping cart safe and secure.

1 Sign In to the iTunes Music Store

Choose **Music Store** from the **Source** pane in the iTunes' window and connect to the store. If you are not already signed in, click the **Sign In** button in the upper-right corner and provide your Apple ID (or AOL screen name) and password to sign yourself in.

2 Set iTunes to Purchase Using a Shopping Cart

Choose **Edit**, **Preferences** (Windows) or **iTunes**, **Preferences** (Mac) to display the **Preferences** window. Click the **Store** tab.

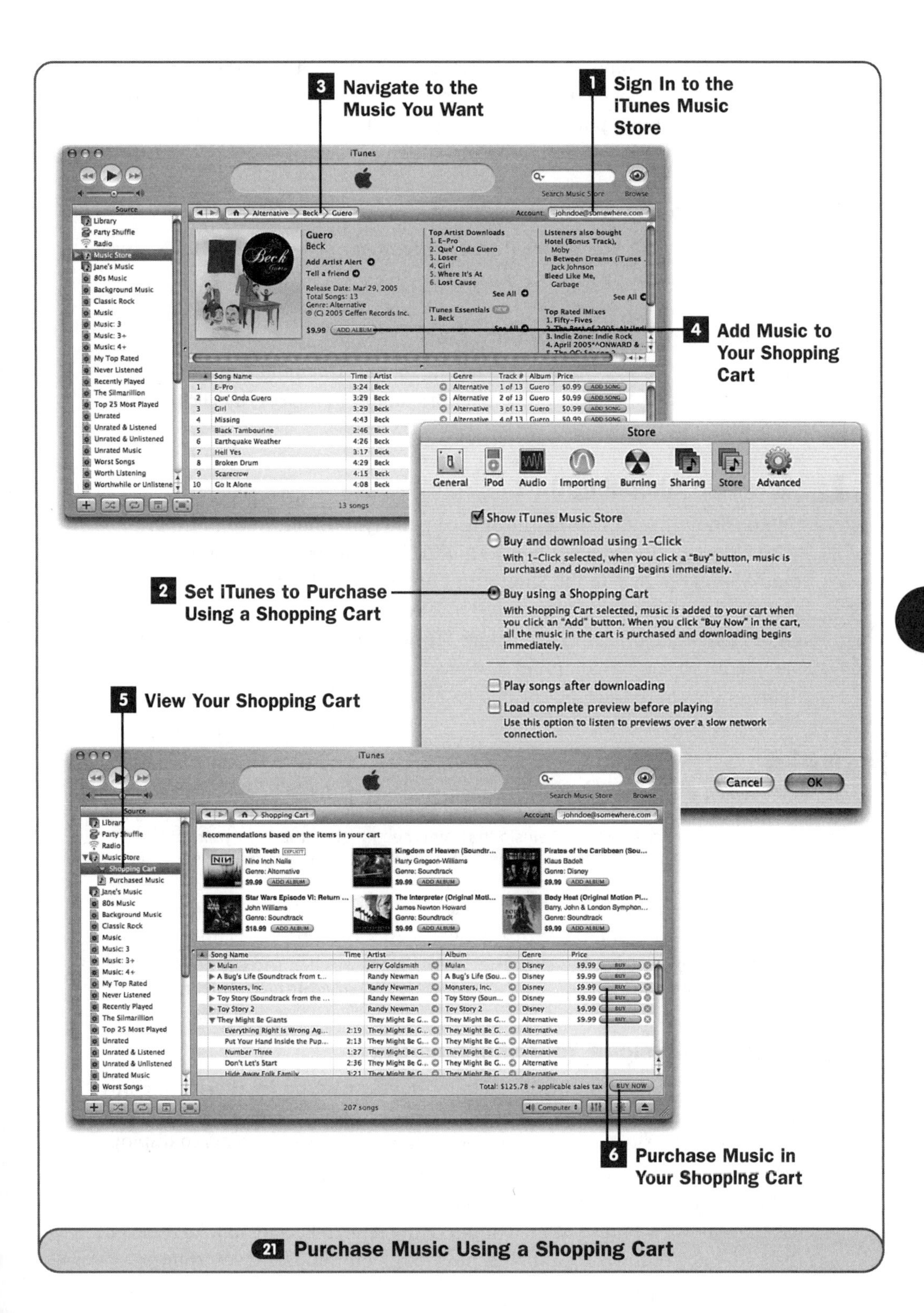

3 Navigate to the Music You Want
1 Sign In to the iTunes Music Store
4 Add Music to Your Shopping Cart
2 Set iTunes to Purchase Using a Shopping Cart
5 View Your Shopping Cart
6 Purchase Music in Your Shopping Cart
Store
General
iPod
Audio
Importing
Burning
Sharing
Store
Advanced
Show iTunes Music Store
Buy and download using 1-Click
With 1-Click selected, when you click a "Buy" button, music is purchased and downloading begins immediately.
Buy using a Shopping Cart
With Shopping Cart selected, music is added to your cart when you click an "Add" button. When you click "Buy Now" in the cart, all the music in the cart is purchased and downloading begins immediately.
Play songs after downloading
Load complete preview before playing
Use this option to listen to previews over a slow network connection.
Cancel
OK
21
21 Purchase Music Using a Shopping Cart

Change your shopping mode by selecting the **Buy Using a Shopping Cart** radio button and click **OK**. When you change this setting, the **Music Store** option in the **Source** pane becomes a first-tier item with both the **Purchased Music** playlist and the **Shopping Cart** option beneath it.

3 Navigate to the Music You Want

As described in 19 **Browse the iTunes Music Store**, navigate the iTunes **Music Store** to find music you're interested in buying.

4 Add Music to Your Shopping Cart

When you decide you want to add a song to your shopping cart, click the **Add Song** button. Similarly, add an entire album to the cart by clicking the **Add Album** button.

5 View Your Shopping Cart

Choose **Shopping Cart** from the **Source** pane (you might have to expand the **Music Store** option to see it by clicking the triangle icon to the left of the **Music Store** option). In the **Shopping Cart** screen, all the tracks and albums you placed in the cart are listed at the bottom; the top of the screen shows a set of albums suggested by the iTunes **Music Store** database as being of possible interest to you based on the contents of your cart. You can add any of these albums to the cart by clicking its **Add Album** button.

▶ NOTE

If you try adding a song or album that's already in the cart, iTunes gives you an error message explaining that you can't add the same music twice. If you're not using a shopping cart and you try to download music that matches music already in your library, iTunes gives you a warning asking whether you really want to download the same song again.

Double-click any song in the cart to hear a 30-second preview clip. For albums in the cart, double-click the album entry or click the triangle icon next to the album's name to see all the tracks in the album.

6 Purchase Music in Your Shopping Cart

You can purchase any individual album that's in the cart by clicking the **Buy** button; this process is the same as if you weren't using a shopping cart and clicked the **Buy Album** button on the album's download page. Similarly, click **Buy Song** to purchase any individual song in your shopping cart. If you're feeling wealthy and want to buy everything in your shopping cart at once, use the **Buy Now** button at the bottom of the screen. Be sure to take a look at the total price of the cart's contents next to the button before you splurge!

Click the round **X** icon to the right of the **Buy** or **Buy Song** button to remove any item (album or song) from your shopping cart.

22 Check for Purchased Music

✔ BEFORE YOU BEGIN	➜ SEE ALSO
18 Sign Up for the iTunes Music Store	94 Back Up Your Music to CD or DVD
20 Purchase Audio from the iTunes Music Store	

The iTunes **Music Store** keeps track of the status of your downloads and makes sure that you get every byte of each song you purchase. If a download is interrupted, the store keeps a note of that fact and makes sure that you have the opportunity to download all the tracks to which you're entitled.

1 Sign In to the iTunes Music Store

Choose **Music Store** from the **Source** pane in the iTunes' window and connect to the store. If you are not already signed in, click the **Sign In** button in the upper-right corner and provide your Apple ID (or AOL screen name) and password to sign yourself in.

2 Check for Purchased Music

Choose **Advanced, Check for Purchased Music**. iTunes connects to the music store and checks the download queue for your account for any incomplete tracks.

▶ NOTE

iTunes periodically (about once a week) checks for purchased music automatically when you launch it.

3 Download Interrupted Tracks

If iTunes finds any tracks in the download queue still waiting to be retrieved, it begins to download them again automatically. Use the **Purchased Music** playlist to see which tracks are in the queue and are now being downloaded (they're the ones shown in gray type).

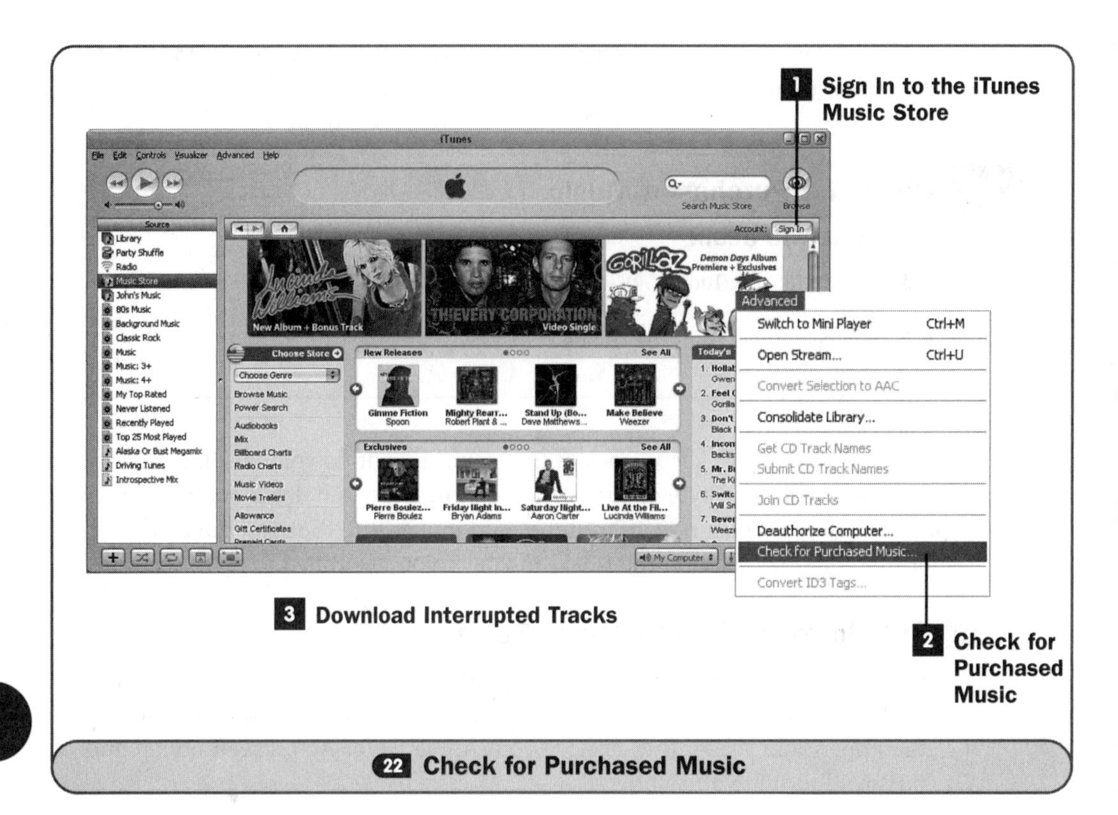

22 Check for Purchased Music

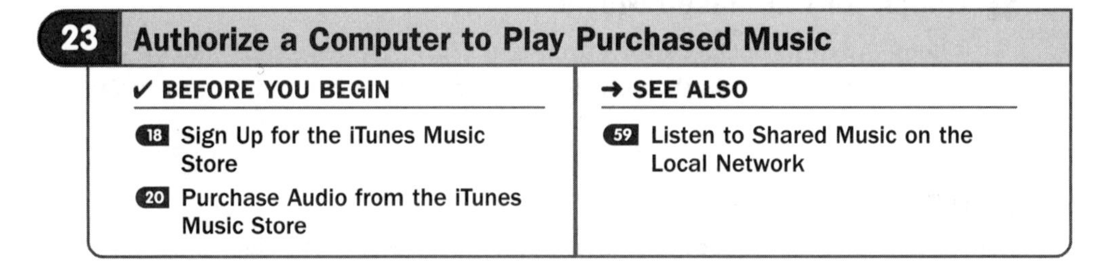

23 Authorize a Computer to Play Purchased Music

✔ BEFORE YOU BEGIN

18 Sign Up for the iTunes Music Store

20 Purchase Audio from the iTunes Music Store

➜ SEE ALSO

59 Listen to Shared Music on the Local Network

When you set up an iTunes **Music Store** account, the computer you used to set it up automatically becomes ***authorized*** to play protected AAC music files that you purchase from the store. You're entitled to authorize up to five total computers (Macs or Windows PCs) that can play back any protected songs purchased using your account. Authorizing a computer for a given account is a process that involves entering your iTunes **Music Store** account ID and password when prompted after you attempt to play a protected music file. The software you use to play the file (iTunes—or, on the Mac, QuickTime using the Finder) connects to the central iTunes' authorization servers and assigns one of the five authorizations to the computer you're currently using; subsequently, any protected files purchased with that ID can be played on that computer without any further interference from the ***DRM***.

▶ KEY TERMS

Authorize—**Register a computer over the network to be able to play protected AAC files purchased using a particular iTunes Music Store account.**

Deauthorize—**Revoke the ability for a computer to play protected AAC files purchased using a particular iTunes Music Store account, freeing up one of the available authorizations.**

The limit of five authorizations per account is intended to reflect the basic needs of a household, analogous to the everyday usefulness of a physical CD. Imagine a customer who wants to play his purchased music on his primary computer, his laptop, and his computer at work; furthermore, he wants another computer or two in his home to be able to connect to his copy of iTunes over the network and play the music he purchased. That's five total places where one person's purchased music can be played. If the music-permission scheme allowed much more than that, one would wonder whether it's fair to the music publishers for a single purchased copy of the music to be enjoyed by that many people. Hence the limit of five authorizations.

You can revoke the authorization of a certain computer in a process known as ***deauthorization***, as you will see in this task, and reassign that authorization to another computer as necessary.

To authorize a computer to use your purchased music, you must have an active Internet connection. If you're not connected to the Internet and your computer has not been authorized to open a protected AAC file, you won't be able to authorize your computer to play the file.

1 Add a Protected AAC File to iTunes

On a computer other than the one where a protected AAC file was purchased and downloaded, add a copy of a protected AAC file to your iTunes **Library** as described in 11 **Add a Music File to Your iTunes Library**. This file might be copied to your computer over the network or sent as an email attachment, or it might be a song in a shared iTunes **Library** to which you connect as described in 59 **Listen to Shared Music on the Local Network**. Regardless of how you got access to the file, the ***DRM*** restrictions on it ensure that you cannot open the file without proper authorization.

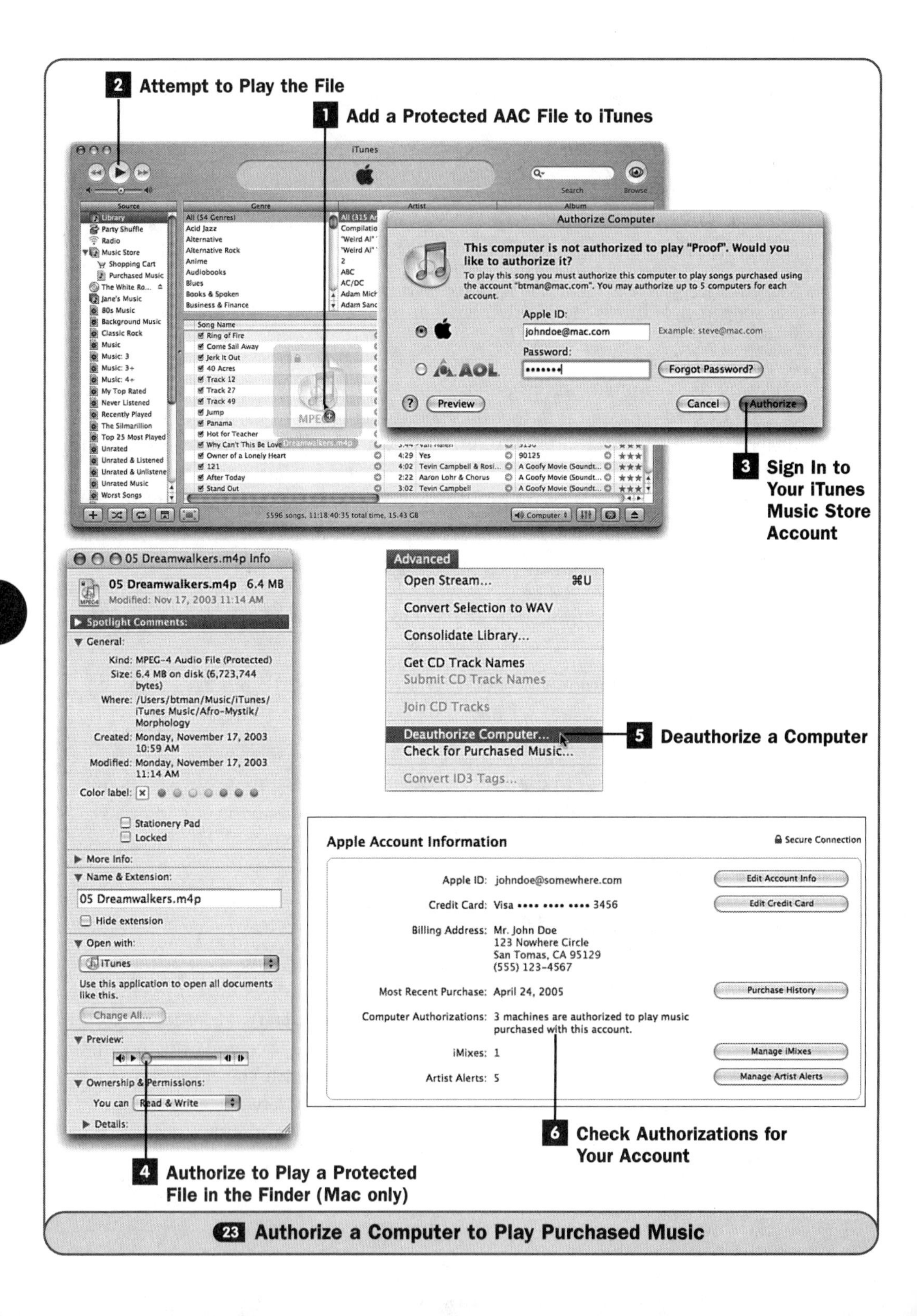

23 Authorize a Computer to Play Purchased Music

2 Attempt to Play the File

Select the protected AAC song and click the **Play** button. The song doesn't begin playing; instead, a dialog box similar to the **Sign In** window in the iTunes **Music Store** appears. The Apple ID for the account used to download the track is already filled in, and you must enter the password for the account, proving that you're the person who purchased the music (or someone to whom the purchaser has given access privileges), to proceed.

3 Sign In to Your iTunes Music Store Account

When you enter your password and click **Authorize**, iTunes connects to the central authorization server and checks your credentials. It also makes sure that one of the five authorization slots for your account is available; if so, you get a message saying that the current computer has been successfully authorized, and the song begins to play.

From this point forward, you won't need to authorize to play any other protected AAC files on that same computer, provided those files were all purchased with the same account. iTunes keeps track of whether it has been authorized for a certain Apple ID; if you have a catastrophic failure such that you need to reinstall your operating system or rebuild your computer from scratch, you have only to perform the steps in this task again to reestablish the authorization for your computer (it doesn't use up another authorization slot to re-authorize a computer that the iTunes' servers already know about). However, you should deauthorize your computer before you sell it, or if you need to send it in for service; deauthorizing prevents potential situations in which a single computer might be assigned multiple, redundant authorizations.

▶ NOTE

You can have more than one Apple ID authorized on a single computer—for example, if two people share a computer but use separate music-buying accounts. Even having two authorization slots mistakenly used by a computer is not in itself a problem—it just means that one of your five authorization slots is being wasted. Deauthorizing a computer multiple times until it's no longer possible to do so is one way to clear up this problem.

4 Authorize to Play a Protected File in the Finder (Mac only)

In Mac OS X, you can play protected AAC files in the Finder, by previewing them in Column view or by using the **Preview** pane in the **Info** window (available by selecting the file and choosing **File, Get Info**). Because the authorization process is handled ultimately by QuickTime, which is built into the Finder, attempting to play a protected AAC file in the Finder on a computer that isn't authorized results in the same dialog box appearing as in Step 2. Enter your password for the Apple ID and click **Authorize** to play the AAC file and any others purchased with the same account.

5 Deauthorize a Computer

If you want to revoke the authorization for a computer to play your purchased music—for example, if you want to authorize an additional computer to play your music, and your five authorization slots are all used up—you can do so. Choose **Advanced, Deauthorize Computer** from the menu bar in iTunes. You are prompted to enter your account password; type it in and click **Deauthorize**. iTunes makes the necessary transaction with the Apple servers, and a message tells you that the computer has been successfully deauthorized.

It's a very good idea to deauthorize your computer before you sell it or send it in for service to avoid confusing the server into assigning more than one authorization to your computer. If you suspect that this has happened, view the related documents at the **iTunes and Music Store Service and Support** (Mac) or **Music Store Customer Service** (Windows) web links available under the **Help** menu in the iTunes menu bar.

▶ NOTE

Deauthorization requires your password as a security measure. You wouldn't want just anybody to be able to come along and revoke your computer's ability to play your own files, would you?

6 Check Authorizations for Your Account

If you're not sure how many authorizations your account is using, you can check this information using the account information page in the iTunes **Music Store**. Click your Apple ID in the **Account** box, enter your Apple ID and password in the dialog box that appears, and click the **View Account** button. The screen that appears shows you how many computers are authorized to play music for your account. Compare this number against the number of computers you know to be authorized for your music. If there's a discrepancy, contact the iTunes **Music Store** support staff—choose **iTunes Music Store Service and Support** (Mac) or **Music Store Customer Service** (Windows) web links available under the **Help** menu—to have the support staff revoke incorrect authorizations and free up those slots.

24 Find More Music by Artists in Your Library

✔ BEFORE YOU BEGIN

9 Import a Music CD into iTunes
20 Purchase Audio from the iTunes Music Store

➔ SEE ALSO

29 Request Music from the Music Store
30 Watch for Newly Added Music Using an RSS Feed

As you browse your music in the iTunes **Library**, you'll see little gray right-arrow icons next to song names, artists, and albums in the song listing. These arrows are links—known as *QuickLinks*—that take you to matching pages in the iTunes **Music Store**, allowing you to quickly find more music by any artist in your library. You can disable these links if you find they clutter up your music-browsing experience.

▶ KEY TERM

QuickLinks—Gray "arrow" icons in song info fields in iTunes that lead to similar music in the iTunes **Music Store**.

24

1 Add Music to Your iTunes Library

First build your iTunes **Library** by adding CDs to it (9 **Import a Music CD into iTunes**) or purchasing music from the music store. Every distinct artist name is listed in the **Artist** list at the top of the iTunes' window in **Library** view; likewise, every distinct **Album** name is shown in its own list.

2 Show Links to Music Store

Open the iTunes **Preferences** window—choose **Edit, Preferences** (Windows) or **iTunes, Preferences** (Mac). Click to the **General** tab. Find the check box labeled **Show links to Music Store**. Make sure that this check box is enabled if you want to show the little gray QuickLinks in the iTunes' window; click **OK**.

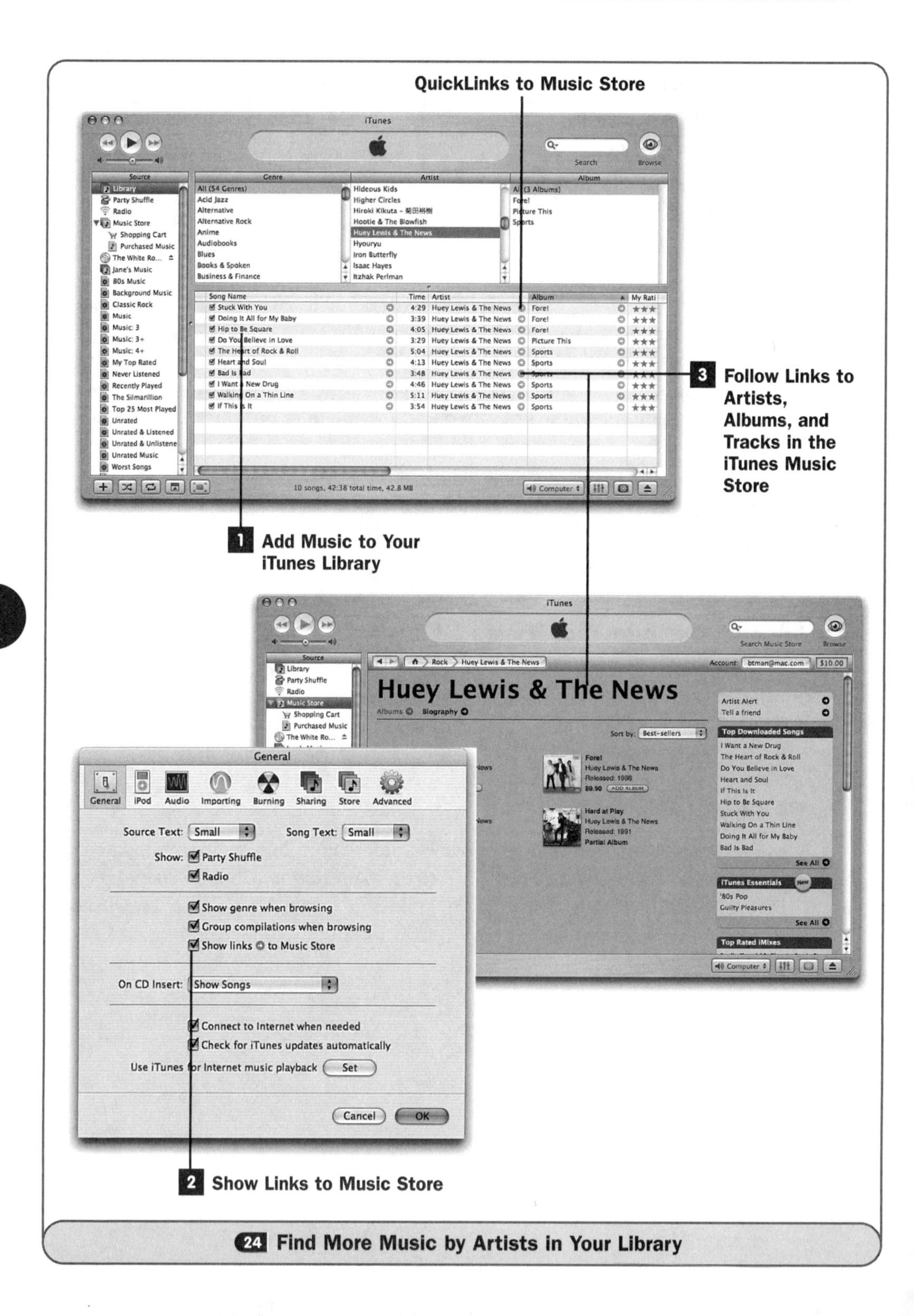

24 Find More Music by Artists in Your Library

3 Follow Links to Artists, Albums, and Tracks in the iTunes Music Store

As you browse your music in iTunes, notice the gray arrow icons next to every song name, artist, or genre. If you have an active Internet connection, click any of these QuickLink icons to take you to a corresponding page in the iTunes **Music Store**. Each link is aware of the context formed by the other ***info tags*** on the song whose links you follow. For example, clicking the arrow icon on a song name tries to find a song not just with the same name in the music store, but also with the same artist and album names; this way you're sure to reach the download page for the album containing the same track whose icon you clicked in case you want to download more tracks from that same album. Clicking the arrow icon on an artist takes you to that artist's discography page.

If the artist or album name you click isn't found in the music store database, you're instead shown a list of the closest matches. Notice that within the iTunes **Music Store**, the same gray arrow icons appear on all listed artists and albums—just like in your iTunes **Library**. Use these links to navigate to other work by the same artists within the music store.

▶ TIPS

iTunes must be able to match the song, artist, and album names exactly with the names in its own database to find useful matches for you. Be sure that your music is organized with the artist names spelled exactly as they are in the music store—if the store spells it **Emerson, Lake & Palmer** or **"Weird Al" Yankovic**, make sure that the quotes and commas and ampersands are in the same places on the songs in your local library! Refer to **61 Organize Your Songs** for more tips on organizing your music for maximum efficiency.

If you're a Mac user with Mac OS X Tiger and use iChat to communicate with your friends, you can set your status to **Current iTunes Track**; others viewing your status will see the name of your currently playing song, along with a QuickLink icon that leads them to the appropriate music store page in iTunes.

25 Publish a Playlist as an iMix

✔ BEFORE YOU BEGIN	→ SEE ALSO
9 Import a Music CD into iTunes	32 Create a Web Link to Your Favorite Music for Sale
20 Purchase Audio from the iTunes Music Store	36 Rate Your Music
34 Create a Playlist	

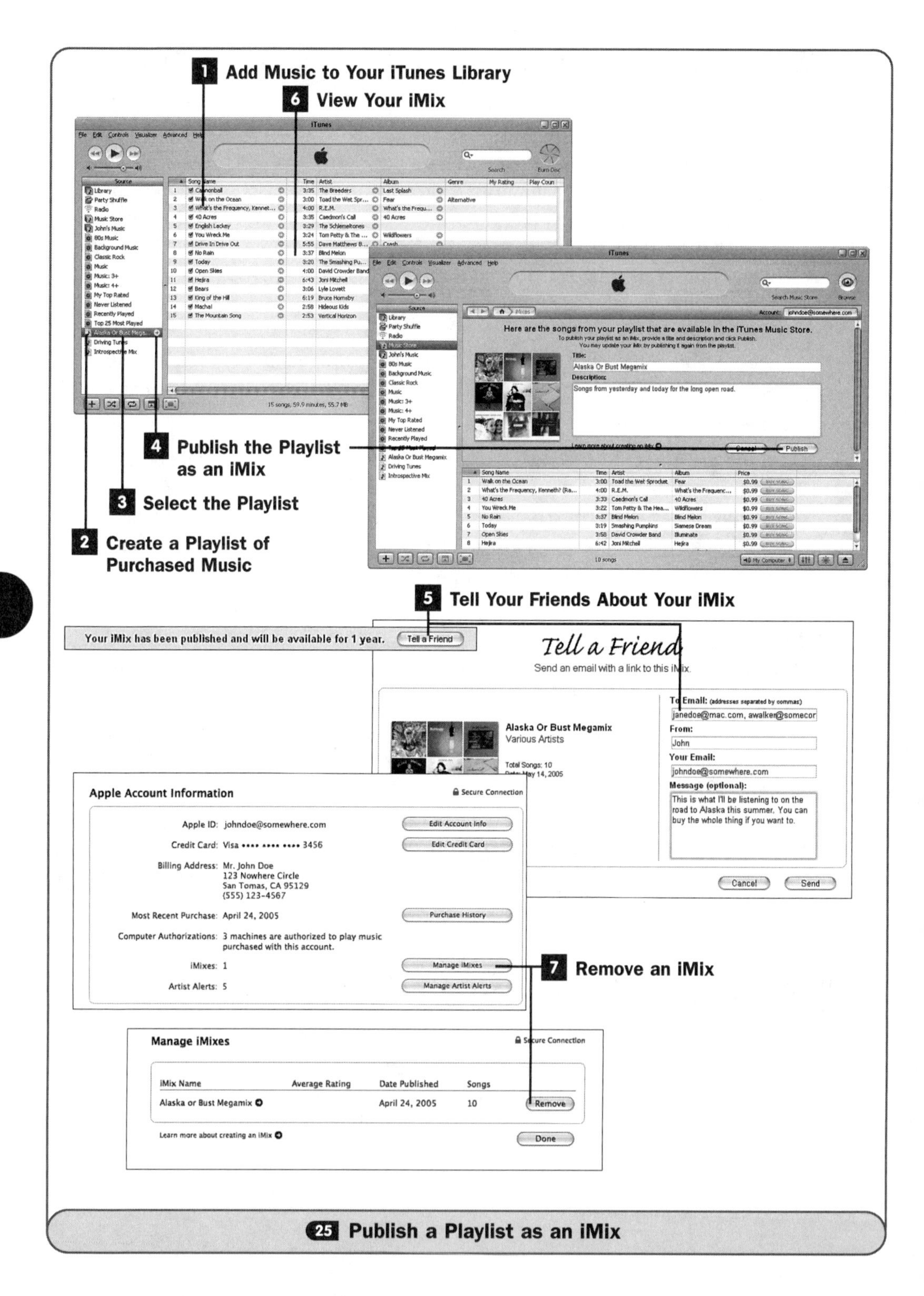

25 Publish a Playlist as an iMix

One of the nicest things about the interconnected, instant nature of the iTunes **Music Store** is its collaborative atmosphere. As customers buy music, artists' download pages are automatically updated with information about their most popular songs, the main genre pages are populated with hot links, and feedback to the store's employees is sent with the speed of email. Perhaps most fun of all, though, is a unique feature of the iTunes **Music Store** that's become wildly popular: ***iMixes***.

▶ KEY TERM

iMix—**A playlist of music from the music store that you create in iTunes and then publish to the music store's servers.**

After you publish your iMix to the iTunes **Music Store**, other customers can then find your iMix more or less accidentally by searching for artists and albums with music that's in your iMix. If they like your taste in tunes, they can purchase individual songs from the iMix or buy the entire iMix's song listing all at once. They can even cast a vote—one to five stars—rewarding your DJ skills by bumping it to the top of the list of available iMixes for more people to find. More than 300,000 iMixes have been published at the time of this writing, and it's no secret why: It's easy, fun, and free.

1 Add Music to Your iTunes Library

First build your iTunes **Library** by adding CDs to it (**9 Import a Music CD into iTunes**) or purchasing music from the music store.

2 Create a Playlist of Purchased Music

Create a ***playlist*** by clicking the **Add Playlist** button underneath the **Source** pane. Give the playlist a descriptive name and populate the playlist with songs from your library as discussed in detail in **34 Create a Playlist**.

3 Select the Playlist

Click the name of the playlist in the **Source** pane. A gray right-arrow icon appears next to it, as you've seen throughout the music store and your Library to indicate a ***QuickLink*** to a location in the store.

4 Publish the Playlist as an iMix

Click the arrow icon. A dialog box confirms that you really want to publish this playlist as a publicly visible iMix; click **Create** to proceed. You can suppress further warnings of this type by enabling the **Do not show this message again** check box.

iTunes connects to the music store (you must have an active Internet connection) and exchanges information with the server's database about the songs in your playlist. You are then shown a screen containing all the songs in your playlist that are in the iTunes **Music Store** (not all your songs will be available there, if you didn't buy them all through the music store). Next to a mocked-up piece of album art made up of the art from various songs in your playlist are text fields where you can enter a title (initially the same as the playlist name) and a description for the iMix. Make these fields as evocative as you can—they're what other music store customers will use when searching for interesting iMixes from which to buy music.

TIP

Don't use profanity in your iMix's title or description. For one thing, doing so is immature and rude, and for another, it can bring the music store's wrath down on you for abusing the inherent trust of the collaborative system and can result in the loss of your account.

Click **Publish** when you're ready to make your iMix public to the world.

5 Tell Your Friends About Your iMix

When your iMix is successfully published, you're shown its download page (as any other customer will see it) along with a banner along the top that tells you that the iMix will be available for one year, after which it will be deleted from the music store. There's also a **Tell a Friend** button; click this button to send an electronic postcard to one or more friends or family members letting them know about your new iMix. Fill in their email addresses (separated by commas), your name, your email address, and an optional message explaining what you're sending them. The message will contain the album art mock-up and a link to your iMix's page so that they can view it in their own copies of iTunes, and maybe buy the same songs you have if they like them. Click **Send** to deliver the message.

NOTE

An email notification is sent to you after you publish an iMix to confirm that the iMix was successfully published.

6 View Your iMix

After you leave your iMix's download page, there are several ways to get back to it in the future. The easiest is to click the gray right-arrow icon on the playlist name in the **Source** pane, which appears permanently after a playlist has been published as an iMix; in the dialog box that appears, click **View**.

Another way to view your iMix is to click the **iMix** link on the music store's Home page; there is a link on the following page labeled **Go to my iMixes**, which takes you to a list of all the iMixes you have published.

While you're there, browse other users' iMixes. You can give any iMix a star rating (from one to five stars) by selecting the appropriate radio button in the top area of the window and clicking **Submit**, just as any other user can do with your iMix. The cumulative rating for an iMix is noted in the **Average Rating** heading at the top of the window.

▶ TIP

You can update the contents of an iMix by simply publishing it again. Click the gray arrow icon on the playlist name and then click Update in the dialog box that appears.

7 Remove an iMix

To remove an iMix, click your Apple ID in the **Account** box and authenticate by entering your password when prompted; click the **View Account** button. In the account information screen, click **Manage iMixes**. This button takes you to a page where you can view all your iMixes and their average user ratings; you can delete individual iMixes from your account by clicking the **Remove** button. (Your local playlist is not affected if you remove an iMix.) Click **Done** when you're finished.

26 Buy a Gift Certificate for Someone Else

✔ BEFORE YOU BEGIN	→ SEE ALSO
18 Sign Up for the iTunes Music Store	27 Redeem a Gift Certificate 28 Create an iTunes Music Store Allowance

Once you've started buying music from the iTunes **Music Store**, it's hard to imagine a more welcome gift than $20 or $50 worth of free downloads. Gift certificates are a built-in part of the music store, and if you know anyone who enjoys iTunes as much as you do, there are many worse ideas for a birthday or the holiday season than to send one of these professionally printed, emailed, or home-printed certificates entitling the recipient to a musical shopping spree.

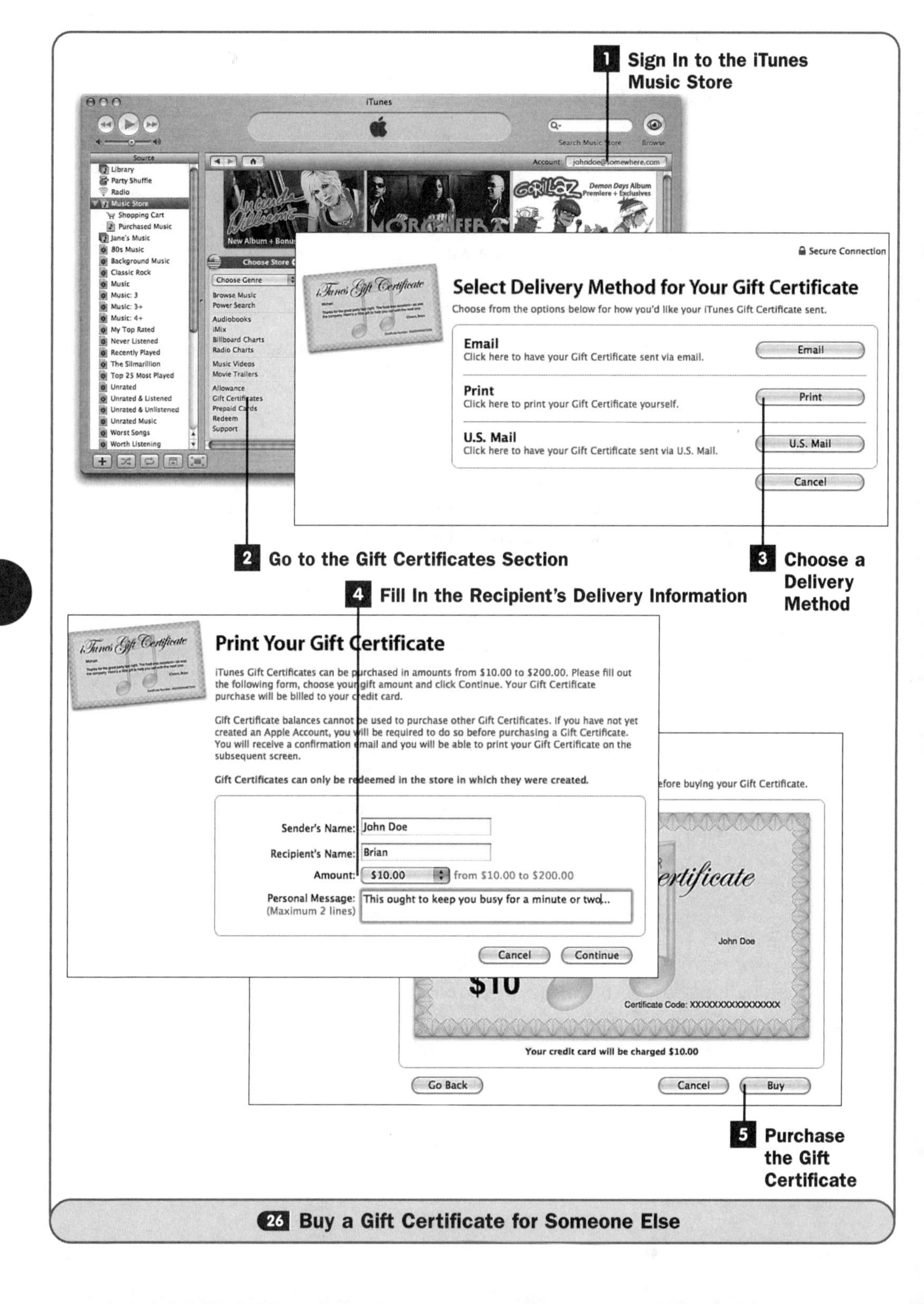
1 Sign In to the iTunes Music Store
Select Delivery Method for Your Gift Certificate
Choose from the options below for how you'd like your iTunes Gift Certificate sent.
Email
Click here to have your Gift Certificate sent via email.
Print
Click here to print your Gift Certificate yourself.
U.S. Mail
Click here to have your Gift Certificate sent via U.S. Mail.
Cancel
2 Go to the Gift Certificates Section
3 Choose a Delivery Method
4 Fill In the Recipient's Delivery Information
Print Your Gift Certificate
iTunes Gift Certificates can be purchased in amounts from $10.00 to $200.00. Please fill out the following form, choose your gift amount and click Continue. Your Gift Certificate purchase will be billed to your credit card.
Gift Certificate balances cannot be used to purchase other Gift Certificates. If you have not yet created an Apple Account, you will be required to do so before purchasing a Gift Certificate. You will receive a confirmation email and you will be able to print your Gift Certificate on the subsequent screen.
Gift Certificates can only be redeemed in the store in which they were created.
Sender's Name: John Doe
Recipient's Name: Brian
Amount: $10.00 from $10.00 to $200.00
Personal Message: (Maximum 2 lines) This ought to keep you busy for a minute or two...
Cancel Continue
Your credit card will be charged $10.00
Go Back Cancel Buy
5 Purchase the Gift Certificate

26

26 Buy a Gift Certificate for Someone Else

▶ TIP

You can also buy prepaid iTunes Music Store Gift Cards, available through the online Apple Store or at any Apple retail store, as well as in supermarket checkout lanes and other places where gift cards are sold. Redeem a prepaid gift card by clicking Prepaid Cards on the iTunes Music Store's Home page.

1 Sign In to the iTunes Music Store

Choose **Music Store** from the **Source** pane in the iTunes' window and connect to the store. If you are not already signed in, click the **Sign In** button in the upper-right corner and provide your Apple ID (or AOL screen name) and password to sign yourself in.

2 Go to the Gift Certificates Section

Click the **Gift Certificates** link on the music store's Home page. You are given a choice to redeem a certificate that was sent to you or to buy a new one; click **Buy Now**.

3 Choose a Delivery Method

A gift certificate can be delivered to the recipient in one of three ways: It can be sent through **Email**, with a confirmation code included in the message; it can be sent as a professionally printed card mailed through the **U.S. Mail**; or you can **Print** it yourself and hand it to the person in an envelope with a nice ribbon on it, or however you like to wrap your gifts. Choose the method that most appeals to you.

4 Fill In the Recipient's Delivery Information

Depending on the delivery method you chose, you now have to enter some basic information: For emailed certificates, enter your name, the recipient's name, and the recipient's email address (twice, to eliminate the possibility of typos), and select an amount from $10 to $200. Type a message to go with the gift—make sure that the recipient realizes that he must redeem this gift certificate by clicking the link in the message and that it's not just another piece of spam!

A printed gift certificate just requires you to fill in your name and the recipient's name, choose an amount, and fill in a brief personal message. When you buy the certificate, the certificate is sent to your printer, and the names and messages are printed as part of the certificate, which you can then fold and package however you like for gift giving.

If you chose the **U.S. Mail** option, your web browser launches and displays a page at the online Apple Store where you can purchase the card for delivery through the mail. The card printed in this way is on nice thick paper, with your name and personal message included on it. You'll have to use the online Apple Store's purchasing and billing system to complete the purchase. There is no extra charge, beyond the face value of the certificate, for a printed and delivered copy.

5 Purchase the Gift Certificate

Click **Continue** after filling in all the required information; after confirming your Apple ID and password, the next screen is a confirmation where you can preview your gift certificate and go back if you notice any errors. Click **Buy** when you're satisfied. Your credit card is billed, the same as if you had bought the music yourself in the specified amount. Depending on the selected delivery method, the certificate is emailed, prepared for physical delivery, or prepared for printing.

NOTE

If you chose to print the certificate yourself, you're given the opportunity to print it right now or to print it at any time in the future by going to your account information page (click your Apple ID in the **Account** box in the upper-right corner of the iTunes' window, enter your password when prompted, and click **View Account**). Click **Purchase History** to view everything you've ever bought through the music store, including the gift certificate you just purchased. Click the gray arrow icon to see the certificate in more detail, and then click **Print** to print out a new copy. Because a gift certificate can only be redeemed once, you can print as many copies of it as necessary.

27 Redeem a Gift Certificate

✔ BEFORE YOU BEGIN	→ SEE ALSO
18 Sign Up for the iTunes Music Store	26 Buy a Gift Certificate for Someone Else 31 Tell a Friend About the iTunes Music Store

If you're the lucky recipient of a gift certificate from a user of the iTunes **Music Store**, you can redeem it using a couple of quick steps, after which you'll have a bank of credit with which to buy free songs.

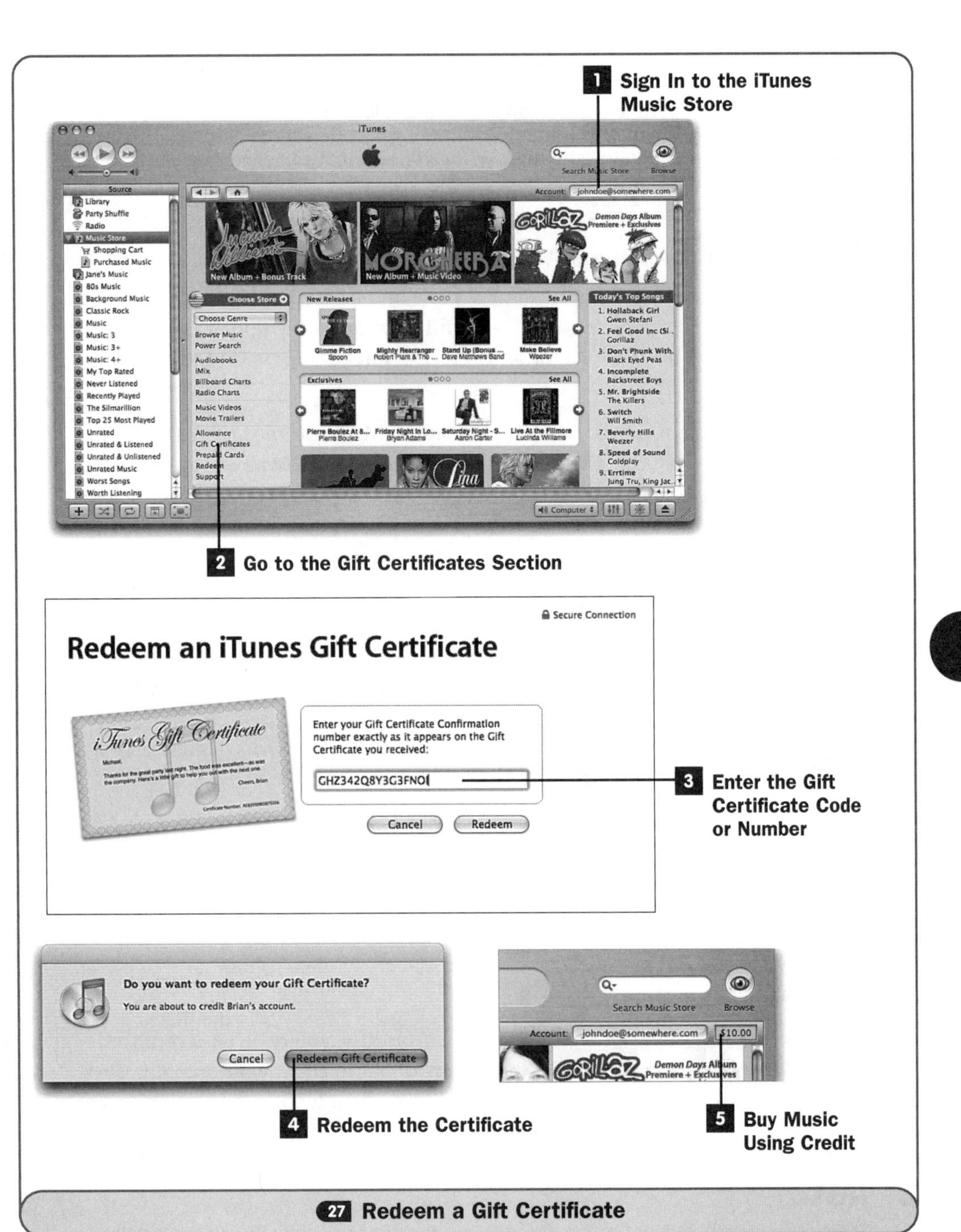
1 Sign In to the iTunes Music Store
2 Go to the Gift Certificates Section
Redeem an iTunes Gift Certificate
Secure Connection
Enter your Gift Certificate Confirmation number exactly as it appears on the Gift Certificate you received:
GHZ342Q8Y3G3FNO
Cancel
Redeem
3 Enter the Gift Certificate Code or Number
Do you want to redeem your Gift Certificate?
You are about to credit Brian's account.
Cancel
Redeem Gift Certificate
4 Redeem the Certificate
Search Music Store
Browse
Account: johndoe@somewhere.com
$10.00
5 Buy Music Using Credit
27 Redeem a Gift Certificate

27

NOTE

If you received a gift certificate in email, it contains a link that leads you to the proper place in the music store to redeem the certificate's value. Be sure to check your **Junk Mail** or **Spam** folders to make sure that a gift certificate that someone sent you didn't get dumped in there by mistake!

1 Sign In to the iTunes Music Store

Choose **Music Store** from the **Source** pane and connect to the store. If you are not already signed in, click the **Sign In** button in the upper-right corner and provide your Apple ID (or AOL screen name) and password to sign yourself in.

If you don't have an account with the iTunes **Music Store** yet, now's the time to create one—refer to 18 **Sign Up for the iTunes Music Store** for more information. (Although you're given the opportunity to create an account in Step 3 of these instructions after you enter the confirmation number, you may as well get the account-creation process out of the way now.)

2 Go to the Gift Certificates Section

Click the **Gift Certificates** link on the music store's Home page. You are given a choice to redeem a certificate that was sent to you or to buy a new one; click **Redeem**.

3 Enter the Gift Certificate Code or Number

Type in the code number printed on your gift certificate, whether you received it on paper or through email; this number might be called the **Certificate Code** or **Certificate Number**. It's a combination of letters and numbers 16 characters long. The number is case-insensitive; you don't need to worry about capitalization.

4 Redeem the Certificate

Click **Redeem**. If you entered the number correctly, you're given a confirmation dialog box informing you that you're about to credit your account. Click **Redeem Gift Certificate** to proceed. (If you made a typo, a red warning message asks you to try entering the number again.)

NOTE

There is no identity authentication encoded into the gift certificate; its value is applied to the account of whoever receives and enters the code.

5 Buy Music Using Credit

A new box appears next to your Apple ID in the upper-right corner; this box shows the amount of store credit you have. As you shop and buy music (see 20 **Purchase Audio from the iTunes Music Store**), that number (instead of your credit card or ***PayPal***) is debited until you've reduced it to zero, at which point it disappears and you're back to buying music under your own steam. It was fun while it lasted!

28 Create an iTunes Music Store Allowance

✔ BEFORE YOU BEGIN	→ SEE ALSO
18 Sign Up for the iTunes Music Store	26 Buy a Gift Certificate for Someone Else 27 Redeem a Gift Certificate

If you're a parent whose kids like to use the iTunes **Music Store** as much as you do, you might find that you're having to pay more for their music than you do even for your own. This can be especially worrisome if it turns out they're using your credit card to do it.

An allowance is a modified version of a gift certificate (see 26 **Buy a Gift Certificate for Someone Else**) that works on a periodic basis. The idea is that you set up a monthly amount of money to be charged against your own iTunes **Music Store** account, which is then applied as credit to the account of a recipient (for example, your music-loving son). The recipient of the allowance can buy as much music as the allowance will pay for; each month it's replenished. Best of all, it's legal—you're doing the actual purchasing, and you won't have to face the dilemmas of minors in your household using your credit cards.

1 Sign In to the iTunes Music Store

Choose **Music Store** from the **Source** pane and connect to the store. If you are not already signed in, click the **Sign In** button in the upper-right corner and provide your Apple ID (or AOL screen name) and password to sign yourself in.

2 Go to the Allowance Section

Click the **Allowances** link on the music store's Home page. The resulting screen explains the workings of an allowance and gives you a form to fill out that determines how the allowance is dispensed to its recipient.

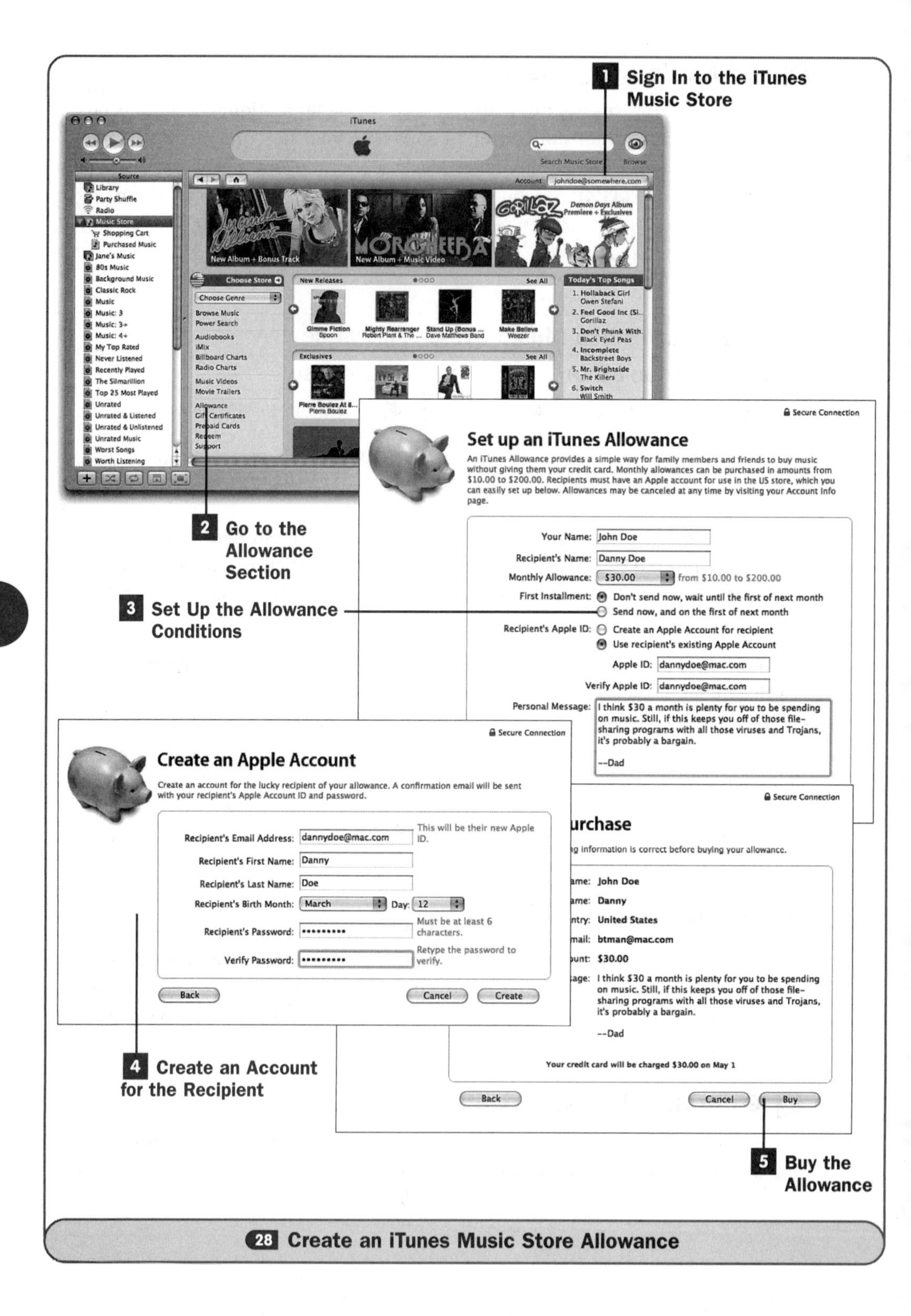

28 Create an iTunes Music Store Allowance

3 Set Up the Allowance Conditions

Fill in your name and the recipient's name. (These names are used in the notification email that's sent to the recipient.) Choose an amount of money to be charged automatically to your iTunes **Music Store** account; this amount can be anything from $10 to $200 (if you're a particularly generous parent).

Allowances are credited at the beginning of each month. If you're setting up the allowance in the middle of the month, you need to choose how the remainder of the current month should be handled—do you want to wait until the first of next month before funding the allowance, or do you want to start by fully funding the current month (even though it's partially over already)? Choose the option describing how you want to do it.

If the allowance's recipient has an Apple ID already, choose **Use recipient's existing Apple Account**, and fill in the Apple ID (twice, for safety) in the next two fields. If the recipient doesn't have an account already, choose **Create an Apple Account for recipient**. You'll be prompted to create a new Apple ID for the recipient in the next step.

▶ NOTE

An Apple ID does not have to be associated with a credit card or any personal information; thus a minor can legitimately have an Apple ID.

Finally, enter a personal message for the recipient. How you word this message is up to you—after all, this might be a new privilege for your kid, or a punishment!

Click **Continue** when you're ready to proceed. You're prompted to verify *your* Apple ID; enter *your password* and click **Setup**.

4 Create an Account for the Recipient

If you chose to create a new account for the recipient, the next screen must be filled out to create the new Apple ID. Fill in the recipient's email address, first and last name, and birth date. Choose a password and enter it twice. (More appropriately, you could have the recipient choose a password and enter it in the two fields provided.) As always, make sure that the password is hard to guess—a mixture of uppercase and lowercase letters, numbers, and special symbols.

Click **Create** when you're done; the recipient's Apple ID is ready to go.

▶ **TIP**

The owner of an Apple ID can change his password at any time. Go to the account information page (click the Apple ID in the **Account** box in the upper-right corner of the iTunes window; enter the password associated with that account when prompted, and click **View Account**). In the account information page, click **Edit Account Info** to change your password and update other security information.

5 Buy the Allowance

The final screen is a confirmation that summarizes the details of the allowance, including all the fields you filled out and options you chose. To make any changes, click **Back**; otherwise, click **Buy** to begin the allowance. From now on, the recipient will be able to log in to the iTunes **Music Store** using the account you set up for him, and buy music using credit as though he'd received a gift certificate.

You can cancel an allowance at any time by going to your account information page (click your Apple ID in the **Account** box; enter your password when prompted, and click **View Account**). When you cancel an allowance, future payments into the account are stopped, but any remaining balance is still usable until it's gone.

29 Request Music from the Music Store

✔ **BEFORE YOU BEGIN**

18 Sign Up for the iTunes Music Store

19 Browse the iTunes Music Store

➔ **SEE ALSO**

30 Watch for Newly Added Music Using an RSS Feed

31 Tell a Friend About the iTunes Music Store

Even though the iTunes **Music Store** has more than one and a half million songs in its catalog with thousands more being added every week, there's bound to be some music you'd love to buy in crisp clear AAC format but that just doesn't seem to be available in the store. Apple expends great effort in finding music not just from the big labels, but from small and obscure publishers as well. But there are simply far too many albums being produced every year for Apple to feature all of them (to say nothing of all the albums that have been published throughout music history). Furthermore, some big-name artists are conspicuously absent from the iTunes **Music Store**; these artists, such as Metallica or the Beatles, might have their own reasons for keeping their music out of the world's largest legal digital music downloading system, but for now there's nothing we—or Apple—can do but wait for the inevitability of progress to overtake them. (The Rolling Stones, originally missing from iTunes **Library**, are now prominently featured—perhaps a positive sign of things to come.)

▶ NOTE

The Beatles are unlikely to appear in the iTunes Music Store anytime soon because of a long-standing legal trademark battle between Apple Computer, Inc. and the Beatles' label, Apple Records. The two firms have clashed numerous times over the years, usually whenever Apple Computer decided to add more sound or music features to the Macintosh platform. Naturally, when Apple became a music publisher with the iTunes Music Store, Apple Records was far from pleased. We probably won't see any Beatles music in the store until Steve Jobs pays a handsome settlement to the Apple Records legal fund.

Nonetheless, the iTunes **Music Store** staff provides a mechanism for you to send them your requests for music that they simply haven't gotten around to adding yet. If they receive a lot of requests for a certain album or artist, that music is a lot more likely to show up soon than an album or artist that nobody's interested in. Communicate your interest and help make the iTunes **Music Store** as complete as it can be!

1 Search for Music

First, check to make sure that the music you want isn't actually in the store. Type the name of an artist, album, or track into the **Search Music Store** bar and press **Return** or **Enter**. If the desired music doesn't exist in the store, the search result page appears empty-handed (possibly with a suggestion of another artist name, if one with a similar spelling to what you typed exists).

2 Provide iTunes Feedback

On an unsuccessful search page, a message reads **Request music you can't find**; **Request** is a link. Click it to open the iTunes Feedback page at Apple's website. Another, more direct way to get to this page is to choose **iTunes, Provide iTunes Feedback** (Mac) or **Help, Provide iTunes Feedback** (Windows).

3 Enter Your Information

Fill out your name, email address, and as many of the rest of the fields as you want—they're all optional, but they help the Apple staff prioritize your request. Most importantly, select **Music Requests** from the **Feedback Type** drop-down list.

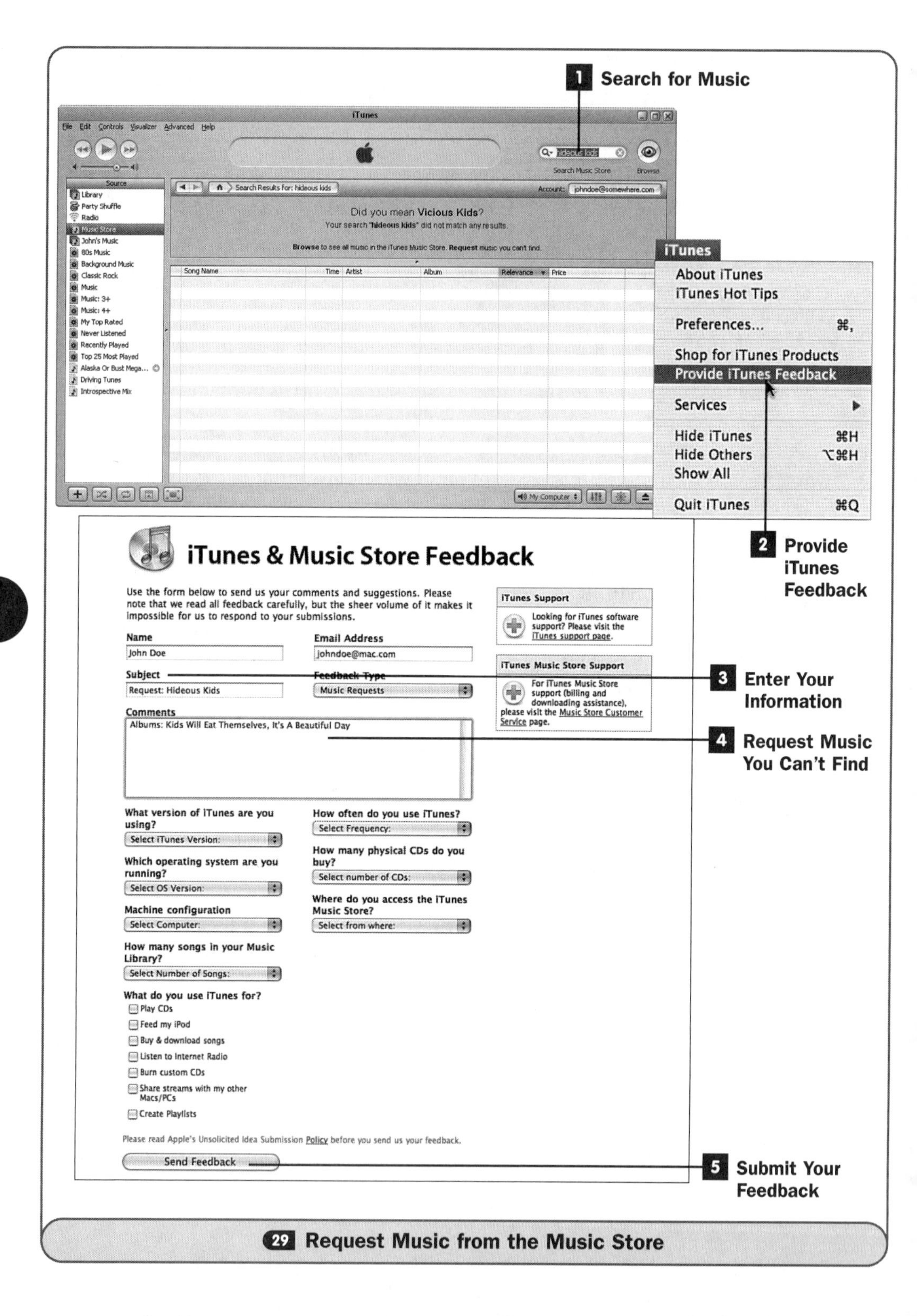

29 Request Music from the Music Store

4 Request Music You Can't Find

In the **Comments** box, describe the music you want; just list artist names and albums. You've already noted that this is a music request, so there's no need to be especially wordy. You may want to put a condensed version of your request into the **Subject** box as well, such as **Request: The Battlefield Band**.

5 Submit Your Feedback

Click the **Send Feedback** button. Your feedback is sent to Apple's support staff. Don't expect to hear anything back from Apple in response to your request; they've got their hands full. But be satisfied that you've made your request known, and watch the newly added music every Tuesday to see whether your requests have been acted on.

30 Watch for Newly Added Music Using an RSS Feed

✓ BEFORE YOU BEGIN	→ SEE ALSO
19 Browse the iTunes Music Store 29 Request Music from the Music Store	31 Tell a Friend About the iTunes Music Store 32 Create a Web Link to Your Favorite Music for Sale

The iTunes **Music Store** is certainly not without its share of obscure, technically esoteric features that the serious power user can enjoy. One of these, which is all but impossible to find within the music store interface itself, is the iTunes **Music Store** RSS Feed Generator.

RSS (Really Simple Syndication) is a mechanism by which you can "subscribe" to the URL (web address) of a dynamically updated list of pieces of information that you can browse using software usually known as an RSS reader or news reader. Software of this type exists for both Windows and the Mac; the top Windows RSS readers (NewzCrawler, FeedDemon, and NewsGator) sell for about $30 each. For Mac OS X, Shrook is a good choice, and free; if you have Mac OS X Tiger (10.4) or later, an RSS reader is built directly into the Safari browser, included as a part of the operating system.

▶ KEY TERM

Really Simple Syndication (RSS)—A mechanism for a dynamically updated series (or *feed*) of items, such as in a blog or "latest news" site, that are delivered to a specialized application for quick and easy perusal.

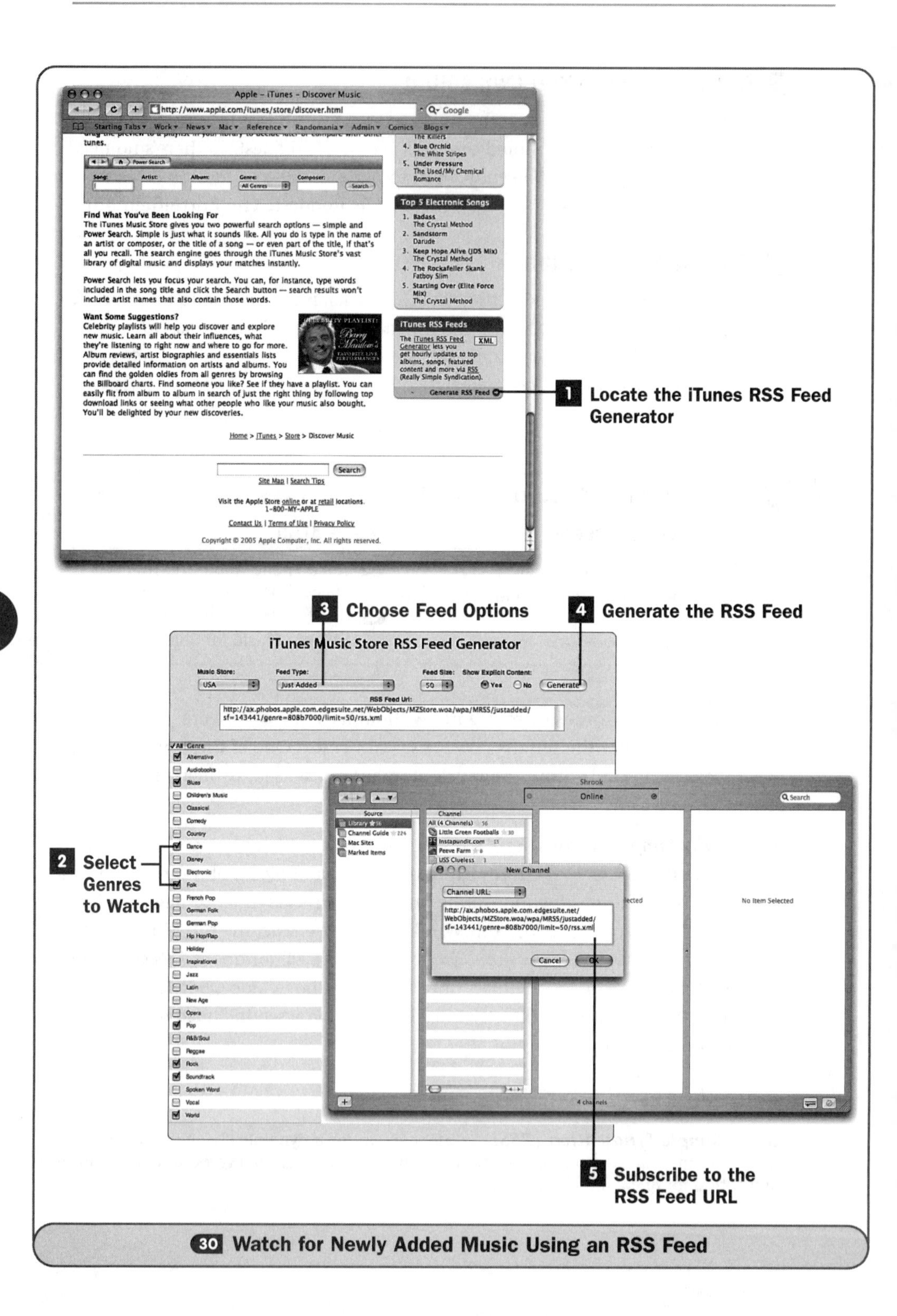

30 Watch for Newly Added Music Using an RSS Feed

RSS feeds, as the streams of information provided by an RSS subscription are known, are most popular as alternative methods of reading weblogs ("blogs"); RSS in combination with the iTunes **Music Store** means you get to keep a constant eye on all the new music being added to the store in any of the categories you want to watch.

▶ WEB RESOURCES

http://www.newzcrawler.com/

http://www.bradsoft.com/feeddemon/index.asp

http://www.newsgator.com/

NewzCrawler, FeedDemon, and NewsGator are three popular RSS readers for Windows.

http://www.fondantfancies.com/apps/shrook/

Shrook is the best-known RSS reader for the Mac (aside from Safari RSS).

1 Locate the iTunes RSS Feed Generator

The iTunes **Music Store** RSS Feed Generator used to be featured as part of the music store's Home page. Nowadays, the only way to reach it is to go through the iTunes' website. In your web browser, go to **http://www.apple.com/itunes/store/discover.html**, the "Discover Music" section of the iTunes' site. In the lower-right corner of the page is a box labeled **iTunes RSS Feeds**. Click the **Generate RSS Feed** link.

2 Select Genres to Watch

The **Generator** page features a long list of all the genres that are part of the music store. Enable and disable check boxes to indicate which genres you're interested in. Use the **Check All** header at the top left to select all the check boxes at once.

3 Choose Feed Options

At the top of the page, choose which country's version of the music store you want to follow; then pick from several options in the **Feed Type** drop-down list: **New Releases**, **Just Added**, **iTunes Top Albums**, and so on. Specify a size for the feed (the number of items shown in it) and whether explicit content should be hidden or shown. For example, you can create an RSS feed that shows you all the newly added music in the Rock, Pop, and Jazz genres in the USA store, with 50 entries per page and explicit content included. Adjust the options to match your needs.

4 Generate the RSS Feed

Click the **Generate** button. The header expands to show you an **RSS Feed URL**, which is what you need to use when subscribing your RSS reader software to the iTunes' feed. Select and copy this URL into memory.

5 Subscribe to the RSS Feed URL

Using the "subscribe" feature of your RSS reader (which varies depending on the application you use), paste in the RSS feed URL generated by the Apple website. Your reader now keeps track of all the music that matches your specified criteria, and you can watch for interesting music without having to browse the iTunes **Music Store** directly. Entries in the RSS feed are links that point directly to downloadable music in the store.

If at any point you want to change the characteristics of your iTunes **Music Store** feed, return to the Generator site (as described in step 1) and re-create the RSS feed URL. You can subscribe to multiple feeds created at different times and view them according to your tastes. Refer to the documentation of your RSS reader software for further instructions on how to get the most out of the software in tracking music releases this way.

▶ TIP

Another good way to watch for new music by a certain artist is to set up an Artist Alert. From any artist's discography page or album download page, click the **Add Artist Alert** link. From then on, whenever new music by that artist is added to the store, you will receive an email notifying you of the event. Turn off Artist Alerts in the account information page (click your Apple ID in the **Account** box in the upper-right corner of the iTunes' window; enter your password when prompted, and click **View Account**).

31 Tell a Friend About the iTunes Music Store

✓ BEFORE YOU BEGIN	→ SEE ALSO
18 Sign Up for the iTunes Music Store	25 Publish a Playlist as an iMix
19 Browse the iTunes Music Store	26 Buy a Gift Certificate for Someone Else

The iTunes **Music Store** provides a number of ways for you to spread the word about great music to download (and, naturally, to obtain more customers for itself). One of these methods is sending an "electronic postcard" about a particular album you'd like one or more friends to know about—perhaps as a hint for a gift idea, perhaps because you think your friend might like the music. It's all up to you.

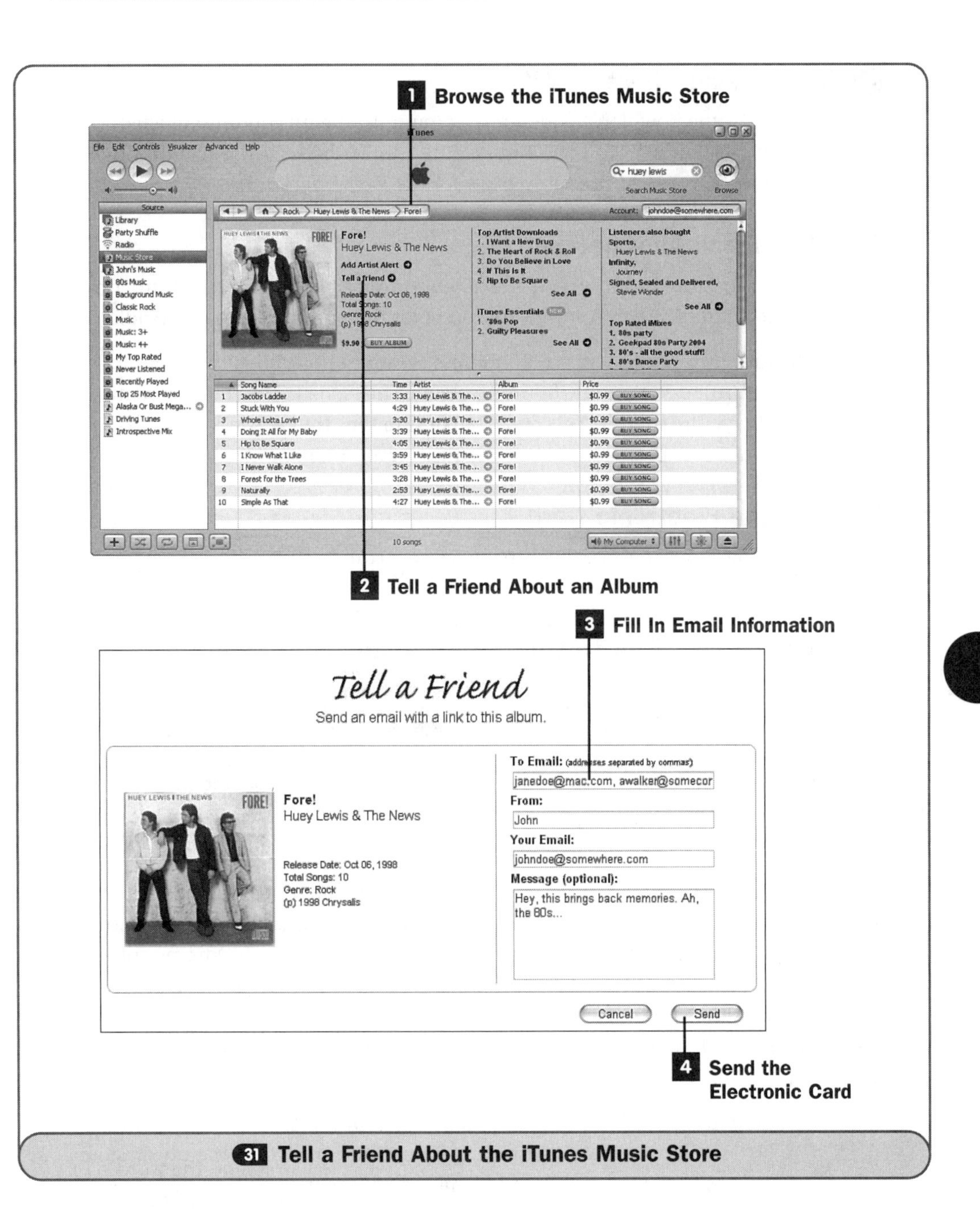

1 Browse the iTunes Music Store

Choose **Music Store** from the **Source** pane in the iTunes' window; browse the contents of the iTunes **Music Store** as described in **19 Browse the iTunes Music Store**. For this task, you don't even need to be signed in.

2 Tell a Friend About an Album

Navigate to the download page for an album. In the information block at the top of the screen, next to the album art, is a link labeled **Tell a friend**. Click this link to be taken to the setup page for the electronic card.

3 Fill In Email Information

You can send the card to a single recipient or multiple recipients; separate multiple addresses with commas as you enter them in the **To Email** field.

Fill in your own name and email address (so that the recipient can contact you in return); additionally, fill in a personal message letting the recipient know why you're sending this card. Make sure that the person knows this isn't just another piece of spam in their incoming mail!

4 Send the Electronic Card

Click the **Send** button to deliver the electronic card to the email recipient.

32 Create a Web Link to Your Favorite Music for Sale

✔ **BEFORE YOU BEGIN**

19 Browse the iTunes Music Store

➜ **SEE ALSO**

30 Watch for Newly Added Music Using an RSS Feed

31 Tell a Friend About the iTunes Music Store

If you're a little more experienced than the novice computer or Internet user, you might be familiar with how URLs (web addresses) work; this method of passing interesting links back and forth between friends has become fairly commonplace. Even though the iTunes **Music Store** is not a "website" in the traditional sense (being encapsulated entirely within a standalone application, iTunes), the individual pages within the store have their own web addresses you can exchange with your friends.

When you go to an iTunes **Music Store** URL, your browser handles the incoming data by redirecting it into iTunes, which launches and connects to the music store and then switches to the requested page. This way, you can send a standard web URL to a friend; when she clicks the link, her copy of iTunes pops up and shows her the album or artist you wanted her to see in the first place—with convenient purchasing links built right in.

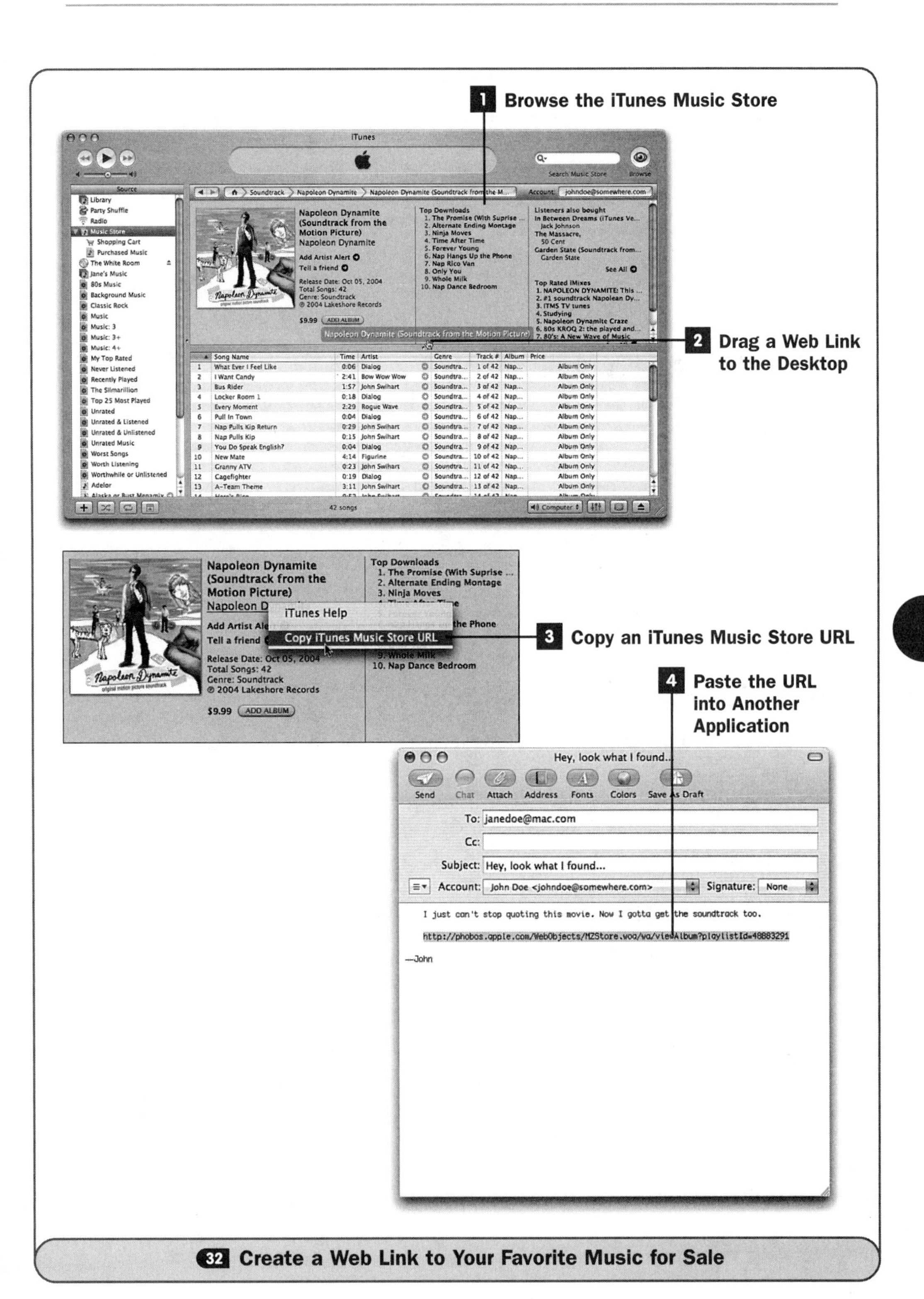
1 Browse the iTunes Music Store
2 Drag a Web Link to the Desktop
3 Copy an iTunes Music Store URL
4 Paste the URL into Another Application
Napoleon Dynamite (Soundtrack from the Motion Picture)
iTunes Help
Copy iTunes Music Store URL
Hey, look what I found...
To: janedoe@mac.com
Subject: Hey, look what I found...
Account: John Doe <johndoe@somewhere.com>
I just can't stop quoting this movie. Now I gotta get the soundtrack too.
http://phobos.apple.com/WebObjects/MZStore.woa/wa/viewAlbum?playlistId=48883291
—John
32 Create a Web Link to Your Favorite Music for Sale

1 Browse the iTunes Music Store

Choose **Music Store** from the **Source** pane in the iTunes' window; browse the contents of the iTunes **Music Store** as described in 19 **Browse the iTunes Music Store**. For this task, you don't even need to be signed in.

Navigate to the download page for an album. As you move your mouse over lines of text such as the artist name or album title, notice that the text becomes underlined. This indicates that the text is a live link, with a URL you can copy just as in a regular web browser.

2 Drag a Web Link to the Desktop

Click the highlighted text of an artist or album title and drag. A translucent label shows that the title and URL of the link is being copied. Drag the mouse pointer onto the Desktop and release; a web link or shortcut is created, which when opened leads back to the same download page from which you just dragged the link.

▶ TIP

Similarly, you can drag iTunes Music Store links directly from iTunes into other applications, such as into your email program.

3 Copy an iTunes Music Store URL

You can also use the more traditional copy-and-paste method to juggle URLs from within iTunes. Right-click (or, on the Mac, **Control**+click) the highlighted text of an artist or album title or on the album art for a given album. Choose **Copy iTunes Music Store URL** from the context menu to copy the web address of the page to your computer's Clipboard or temporary memory.

4 Paste the URL into Another Application

In another application, such as an email composition window, select **Edit, Paste** to insert the URL of the download page into the text. When the email recipient clicks the URL, she'll be taken straight to the page from which you copied the URL.

5

Enjoying Your Music in iTunes

IN THIS CHAPTER:

Now that you've got your iTunes **Library** packed full of the music you love, it's time to sit back and enjoy it—and to explore some of the ways iTunes takes advantage of the inherent versatility of the digital music medium to let you do more things with your music than you'd ever thought possible.

Finding a favorite album and playing it from beginning to end, as you're accustomed to doing with your CD collection, is a matter of two or three clicks to navigate to the album's location and start it playing. However, that's where the limitations of CDs start to kick in—and where iTunes starts to break free of them. Even with an expensive multi-disc changer, organizing lists of songs from various physical discs is a laborious and non-intuitive process. But with iTunes, creating a playlist of favorite tunes in a themed mix or carefully engineered progression is as simple as clicking and dragging. Randomizing (or "shuffling") tracks, something you can do in CD players, is something you can do in iTunes, too.

One thing no CD-player engineer ever dared dream, however, is the ability to generate a dynamically updated list of songs selected from your entire Library on the basis of certain specified criteria, such as the genre, release date, or a personal "star" rating you assign to each track. With ***Smart Playlists***, iTunes gives you this ability, making it not just possible to sift through your music to find exactly the right tunes for the right occasion, but automatic as well—as though you had your own private DJ.

Because of the versatility of software, several more features are available in iTunes to enhance the satisfaction you get from playing your music. You can ***crossfade*** songs, having one start playing while the previous one is fading out, like they do on the radio. You can have iTunes examine all your music with the **Sound Check** feature, ensuring that each album plays at the same relative volume level. And with the built-in **Visualizer**, iTunes turns your music enjoyment from a purely auditory pastime into a treat for the eyes as well.

33 Find and Play Music

✔ BEFORE YOU BEGIN	→ SEE ALSO
9 Import a Music CD into iTunes	34 Create a Playlist
20 Purchase Audio from the iTunes Music Store	46 Find and Play Music on the iPod
	60 AirTunes: Connect iTunes to a Stereo with AirPort Express

As a "jukebox" application, iTunes' primary function is to play music. Its controls for playing, pausing, and skipping forward and backward through your music are as straightforward as on any comparable piece of software or hardware.

Where iTunes differs from just about any other piece of software, to say nothing of a physical rack of CDs, is in navigating through your library to find the music you want by name and to play it through your computer's speakers.

Using the navigation lists in the **Library** view, you can select a single album, an artist (and all that artist's albums at once), or a whole genre (and all the artists and albums within it). The songs matching the selections you've made are listed according to the display columns you've highlighted, in a manner that's intended to make the most sense for the way you typically use the program. After you've chosen the music you want, just click **Play** and enjoy.

▶ TIP

An example of iTunes' intelligent sorting is that if you sort the songs in the listing by **Album** or **Year**, the tracks are secondarily sorted within each album in the order of their track number, making it a simple affair to listen to all of an artist's work from earliest release to latest in the artist's intended presentation.

1 Select the Library Source

Click **Library** in the **Source** pane of the iTunes' window. All your songs are shown in the listing area in the main body of the iTunes' window.

2 Choose a Genre, Artist, or Album

If the **Genre**, **Artist**, and **Album** lists at the top of the window are not shown, click the **Browse** button to display them. These lists work like filters, allowing you to make a selection from any list to limit the songs iTunes shows you to only the ones matching that selection.

▶ TIP

The **Genre** list is optional; you can hide or show it in the **General** pane of the iTunes **Preferences** window (choose **Edit, Preferences** in Windows or **iTunes, Preferences** on the Mac) by toggling the **Show genre when browsing** check box.

Suppose that you want to listen to some Paul Simon music. In the **Artist** list, scroll down until you see Paul Simon's name listed. Click his name. Notice that the **Album** list updates to show you only Paul Simon's albums, and all the tracks in all his albums are displayed in the listing below, hiding all the rest of your music. You can filter the listing further by selecting a single album from the **Album** list.

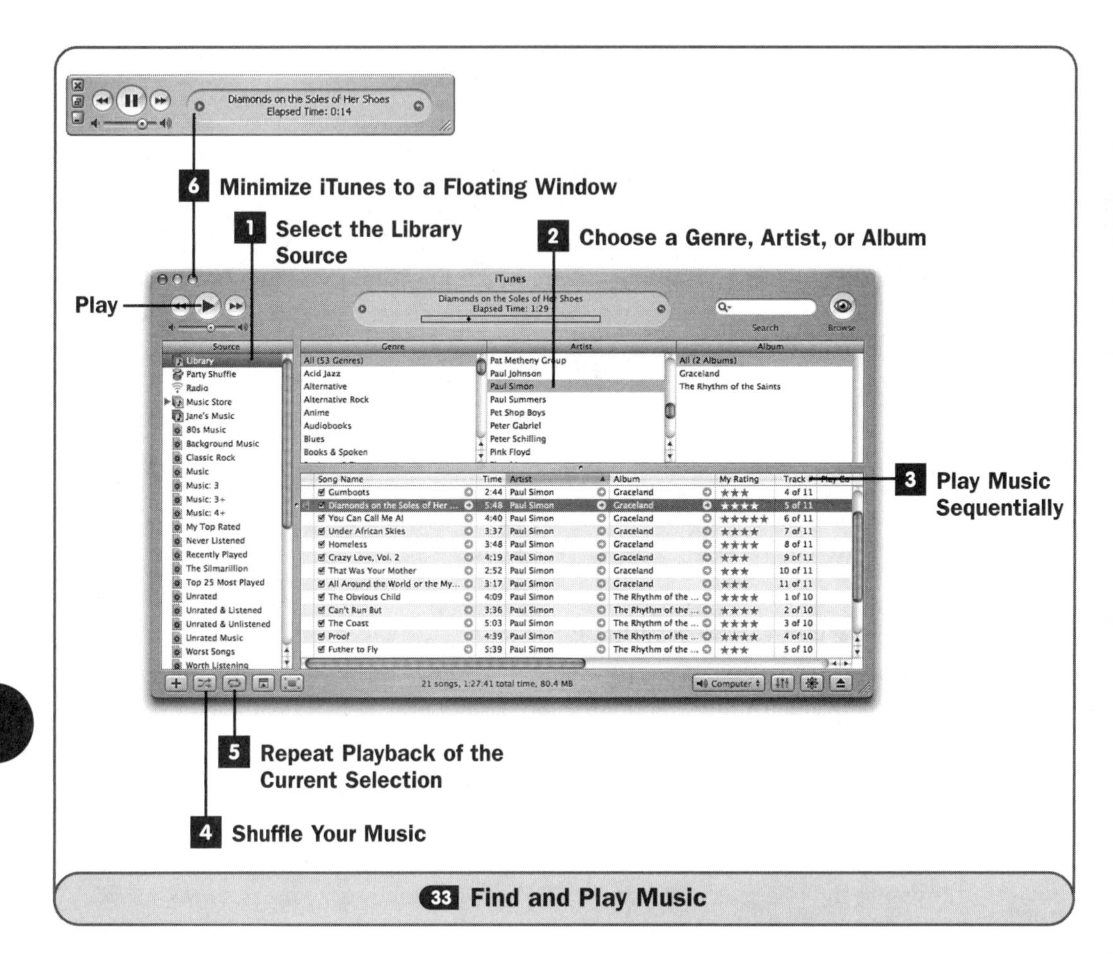

33 Find and Play Music

▶ NOTE

In the Artist list (and *only* in that list), artists whose names begin with *The* are sorted according to their name without the *The*; so to find music by The Romantics, look in the *R* part of the list.

To cancel your selections and return the song listing to showing the entire contents of your Library, scroll up to the first entry in a list where you selected an entry (it says **All**, followed by the number of entries in that list). Alternatively, click the header of the list to remove its filter and select the **All** option.

3 Play Music Sequentially

Click the **Play** button, and iTunes begins playing the first song in the list. Adjust the volume to your liking using the slider underneath the **Play** button (this slider doesn't affect the system volume, only iTunes' *relative* volume level).

▶ NOTE

When iTunes is playing, the Play button changes to a Pause button; click it to stop the music but retain your place, so that if you click Play again, iTunes resumes where it left off. However, if you select a different option in the Source pane (such as a *playlist*), the Play button changes to a Stop button, indicating that if you stop playback and then click Play again, iTunes will play using the currently selected source and not the original selection of music.

As iTunes plays each song, it moves automatically to the next one in the list as displayed. Skip to the next song or back to the previous one using the **Forward** and **Back** buttons; click and hold these buttons to fast-forward or rewind within a song.

When iTunes finishes playing a song, it updates the **Last Played** date/time field for that song and increments its **Play Count** field. Keep this in mind—it'll be important for when you create ***Smart Playlists***!

If you want to start playing in the middle of the song listing, click a song to select it and then click **Play** to begin playback with that song. Alternatively, double-click the song to play it.

33

4 Shuffle Your Music

Of course, you can play your music in its originally intended order as it appeared on the CD—but sometimes you're just not in the mood to listen to the tracks in someone else's recommended order. The **Shuffle** button, in conjunction with judicious use of the **Browse** lists, gives you plenty of new options for how to hear your music.

With an **Artist** or **Album** selected—or even if you're viewing the unfiltered **Library** with no selections—click the **Shuffle** button underneath the **Source** pane in the lower-left corner of the window; it lights up blue when **Shuffle** mode is activated. In this mode, iTunes skips randomly from song to song in the selection. The displayed list of songs is not rearranged accordingly (the songs are still shown according to which display column you've selected); you won't know which song iTunes will skip to next.

▶ TIP

iTunes automatically scrolls the display to show the currently playing song, indicated with a blue "speaker" icon next to its title. However, if you're scrolled far away from the playing song and want to jump to it without scrolling manually up and down in search of it, choose File, Show Current Song to skip directly to it.

If you're viewing a playlist (see 34 **Create a Playlist**), the **Shuffle** option actually rearranges the displayed songs based on the order in which they'll play. This reordering happens because playlists have a built-in play order, shown in the first column, which is the default column selected to sort the playlist.

5 Repeat Playback of the Current Selection

The **Repeat** button lets you choose what iTunes should do when it comes to the end of the selection of music. If the button is not selected, iTunes stops playing when it finishes the last song in the list. Click it to turn on **Repeat** mode; in this mode, the selected list of songs starts playing again from the beginning after it finishes. Click the button again to enter **Repeat Once** mode, indicated with a small **1** on the button's icon—this means iTunes keeps repeating the currently playing song over and over. Click **Repeat** once more to turn **Repeat** mode off.

6 Minimize iTunes to a Floating Window

You can get the iTunes' window out of the way while it's playing tunes by clicking the green **Zoom** button (on the Mac) or by choosing **Advanced, Switch to Mini Player** (on Windows); this command shrinks iTunes to a small floating controller known as the **Mini Player**. You can move this player anywhere on the screen that's convenient, play and pause the music, skip from track to track, adjust the volume, and see what song is currently playing.

▶ TIP

If you want, you can have the Mini Player float above everything else on your screen so that it's never hidden; select the Keep Mini Player on top of all other windows check box in the Advanced pane of the iTunes Preferences window (choose Edit, Preferences in Windows or iTunes, Preferences on the Mac to display the Preferences window).

34 Create a Playlist

✔ BEFORE YOU BEGIN	→ SEE ALSO
9 Import a Music CD into iTunes	35 Create a Smart Playlist
20 Purchase Audio from the iTunes Music Store	52 Create an Audio CD from a Playlist
33 Find and Play Music	

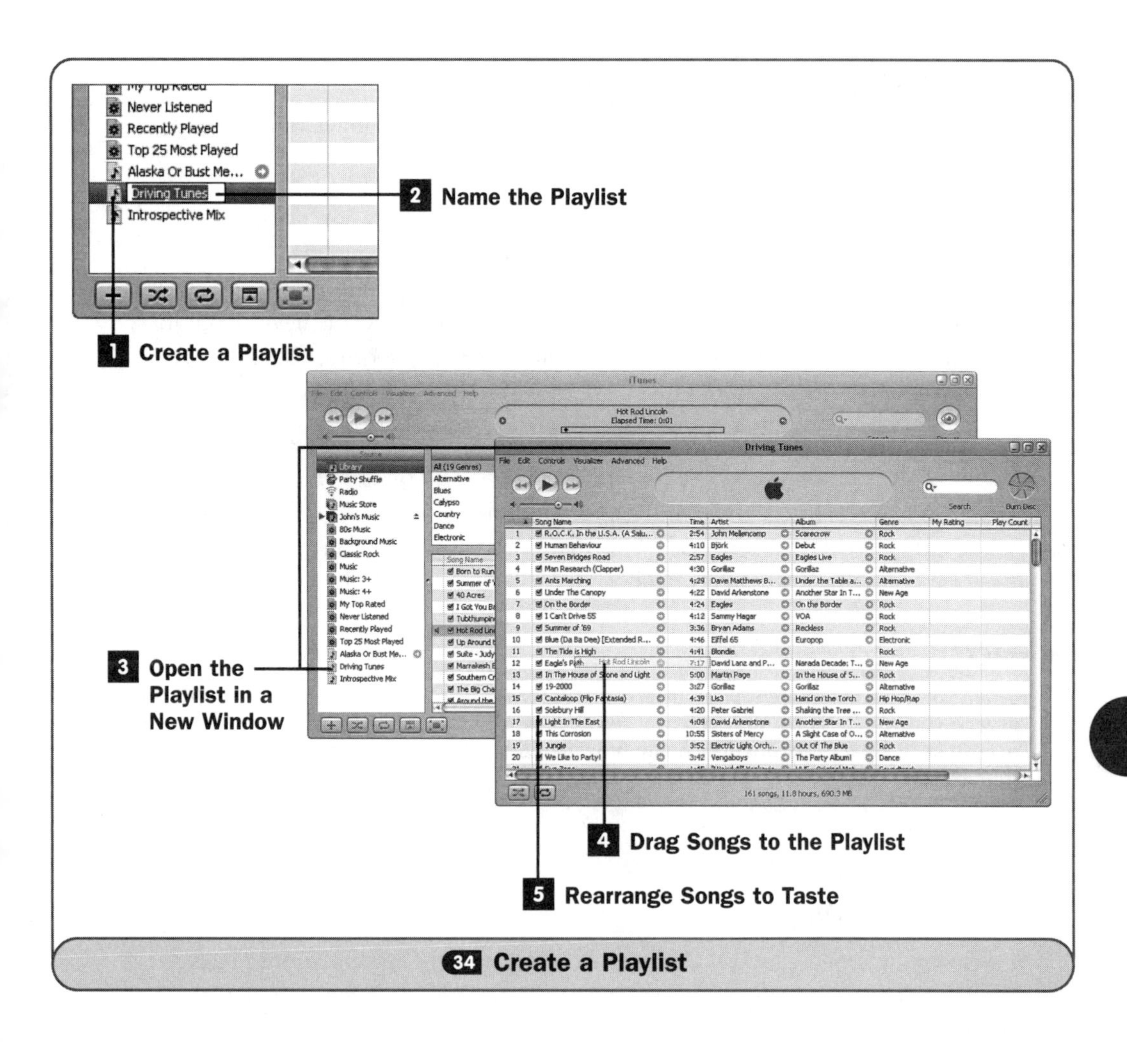

34 Create a Playlist

Although iTunes makes it easy to locate and play any individual song or album, sometimes you'll want to mix and match your music, pulling in one favorite song from here, another one from there—picking the best selections from different albums to make a progression of songs that fits a certain situation or mood. It's one thing to be able to select a single artist and simply play through all the songs that artist ever produced; it's quite another to compose a selection of your personal favorite 30 songs, a choice collection for working out at the gym, a soothing set of songs to fall asleep to, or your most highly rated rock songs from the '70s. These kinds of specialized, personalized groupings are what are known as ***playlists***.

▶ KEY TERM

***Playlist*—A collection of songs created by the user in a specific order, usually gathered according to a desired "theme" (such as "Driving Tunes" or "Workout Mix").**

You create a playlist by first specifying its name (which you can change later), then dragging songs one by one from your library into the playlist. You can rearrange a playlist's contents at any time, remove songs, add more songs as you buy them from the music store—whatever you like. A playlist is never fixed in form and can always be expanded or modified to suit your musical tastes, even while you're playing it.

Adding songs to playlists is like creating aliases or shortcuts to the original items—it doesn't take up any extra space on your disk or create any new files. Each song shown in a playlist is a representation of that song in the library. If you change or delete a song in the library, the song also changes in or disappears from any playlist in which it appears.

▶ NOTE

When you drag songs from your library into a playlist, you're not removing them from the library; you're merely creating a list of references to selected songs, and you can always access each song in its original location in the library. You can add the same song to multiple playlists, for example, or add the same song multiple times to the same playlist. If you delete a song from a playlist, the song isn't removed from iTunes altogether, just from the list.

1 Create a Playlist

To create a new playlist, click the + button underneath the **Source** pane, at the bottom left of the iTunes' window. (Alternatively, choose **File, New Playlist**.) A new playlist appears in the **Source** list, bearing the name **untitled playlist**.

▶ TIPS

Delete a playlist by selecting it in the **Source** pane and pressing **Delete** or **Del**. Remember, a playlist contains only *references* to the songs in it, not the songs themselves. Deleting a playlist or the individual songs in it doesn't affect anything in your library.

Another way to create a playlist is to first select a group of songs in the library, then choose **File, New Playlist From Selection**. A new playlist is created that includes the songs you'd selected.

2 Name the Playlist

The name of the new playlist is selected so that you can immediately type a new name, such as **Driving Tunes** or **Hair Band Classics**. Press **Return** or **Enter** after typing the perfect title for your collection.

3 Open the Playlist in a New Window

Optionally, you can open the playlist's contents in a separate window; this can be helpful if you want to see both the source and the destination as you drag songs into the playlist. Double-click the music note icon to the left of the playlist name to open the new window with the playlist's contents.

▶ TIP

When viewing a playlist in its own window or a separate window, a **Burn Disc** button appears in the upper-right corner instead of the usual **Browse** button. However, this icon doesn't prevent you from browsing a playlist using the navigation lists. Simply choose **Edit, Show Browser** to enable the lists.

4 Drag Songs to the Playlist

Click the **Library** option in the **Source** pane to view all the songs available in iTunes; navigate to each song you want to add to the playlist. Click to select a song (or a group of songs, by holding down **Shift** or **Ctrl/⌘** as you click) and drag the selection to the playlist in the **Source** pane, or into the separate window showing the playlist's contents.

If you drag songs to the playlist's name in the **Source** pane, each new addition is added to the end of the playlist. If you're using a separate window to build the playlist, you can drag songs directly to the place in the list where you want them to appear.

5 Rearrange Songs to Taste

Click the playlist in the **Source** pane to view its contents in the song list area, or switch to the separate window showing the playlist's contents. Click and drag individual songs to different places in the list to manually sort the playlist to your liking. You can also click any of the column headers to sort the playlist on that column; click the column header again to reverse the sort order. Click the first column, showing the play order numbers, to return the list to your manual sort order.

You can now play your playlist by simply clicking the **Play** button, just as you would in the **Library** view. Now you can immediately call up just the right playlist for the occasion—to relax as you read, to fire you up for an exercise routine, or to burn onto a CD for a long drive (see 52 **Create an Audio CD from a Playlist**).

35 Create a Smart Playlist

✔ BEFORE YOU BEGIN

9 Import a Music CD into iTunes
20 Purchase Audio from the iTunes Music Store
33 Find and Play Music

→ SEE ALSO

52 Create an Audio CD from a Playlist
36 Rate Your Music
73 Train iTunes to Play Your Favorite Music

iTunes can create two kinds of ***playlists***: standard ones, in which you simply make a new list and manually add songs to it, and ***Smart Playlists***, which are in fact sophisticated saved database queries that automatically select songs that match criteria you specify. Smart Playlists have near-infinite versatility; how they can be configured is limited only by your imagination.

▶ KEY TERM

***Smart Playlist*—A playlist automatically created from user-specified criteria that is updated to reflect new music you add that matches those criteria.**

You create a Smart Playlist in a somewhat different manner from a standard playlist. Instead of setting its name and then dragging songs to it manually, you set up the list of criteria at the time you create the playlist, and then name the playlist; the list is immediately populated with all the songs that match the criteria you set as soon as the Smart Playlist is created.

1 Create a Smart Playlist

To create a Smart Playlist, hold down the **Option** key (on Mac) or **Shift** key (in Windows) and click the + button; its icon changes from a + sign to a sprocket, indicating the automated mechanism underlying Smart Playlists. Alternatively, choose **File, New Smart Playlist**.

2 Define Criteria for the Smart Playlist

A **Smart Playlist** dialog box appears, giving you access to the specifications of the Smart Playlist query. Various check box options are available, such as limiting the list to a certain number of songs. You can add as many organizational criteria as you want by clicking the + button after any shown criterion. You can filter songs using any of the available info tags, as well as comparison operators such as **contains** or **starts with** for textual entries, **is** or **greater than** for numeric entries, or **is after** or **is in the range** for date entries.

You can, for instance, create a list composed of all songs in the **Rock** genre that were made in the years **1966–1974**, whose track number was **1**. You can even specify that songs in the playlist must also belong to another playlist, such as a Smart Playlist that contains all music by any of several selected artists. You can also achieve great control by limiting the playlist to a certain size or number of songs, and adjust the **selected by** criterion to any of several schemes, such as **highest rating**, **least often played**, or **random**. The details are all up to you.

▶ NOTES

By default, new Smart Playlists are created with the **Live updating** option enabled; this means that as you add new music to your iTunes **Library**, or change the ***info tags*** for songs so that they match the Smart Playlist's criteria, the playlist updates automatically to include them. Disable this option if you want the playlist to remain in the state it's in when you first create it, and not to automatically change as you add more music.

Songs shown in Smart Playlists are just references to the songs in your library, just as they are in regular playlists. However, you can't manually rearrange or remove individual songs from Smart Playlists because they're automatically selected according to your criteria.

Smart Playlists are especially useful in conjunction with the **My Rating** and **Play Count** fields. For instance, you can create a Smart Playlist that consists only of songs you've rated three stars or higher, or to which you've listened at least five times, or both conditions at once. (See 36 **Rate Your Music** for more information.) As you rate your songs and listen to the ones you like best, a Smart Playlist that you might have set up to include only highly rated or frequently played songs automatically becomes populated with your favorite music.

3 Name the Smart Playlist

Click **OK** when you're satisfied with the Smart Playlist's criteria. The playlist is created, with the name automatically set to the contents of the first criterion you set. The name is immediately editable, so you can type a more appropriate name (if you want) and press **Return** or **Enter**.

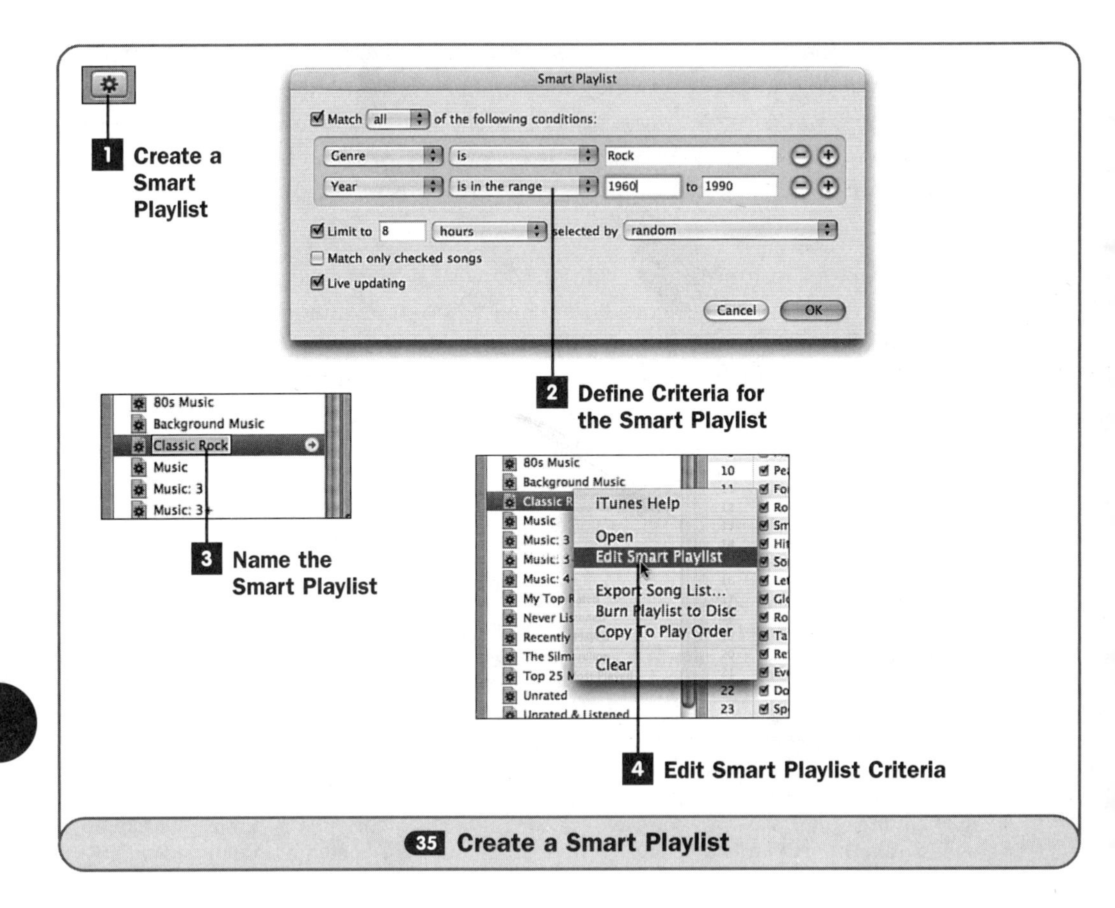

35 Create a Smart Playlist

4 Edit Smart Playlist Criteria

You can go back and edit the criteria on any Smart Playlist if you want to change its behavior. Select the playlist in the **Source** pane and choose **File, Edit Smart Playlist** or right-click the playlist and choose **Edit Smart Playlist** from the context menu. The same dialog box you used to define the playlist appears; make whatever changes you like and click **OK** to save them.

▶ TIP

If you create a randomized Smart Playlist (for example, one that chooses 4GB of music to fit into your iPod mini, as described in 43 Use a Large iTunes Library with a Small iPod), it can be difficult to get iTunes to re-shuffle the selection to pick new songs. One way to do it is to temporarily lower the Limit to number to something very small (such as 1 song), click OK, edit the criteria again, and raise the limit to the full 4GB size.

As you enter text in any of the criterion fields, such as the **Artist** name, iTunes tries to fill out the field with an existing info tag that matches what you've typed. This can both save you time and ensure that you set the field to exactly the spelling of info tags already in the database. See 69 **Examine and Modify Song Information** for more details.

36 Rate Your Music

✓ BEFORE YOU BEGIN

9 Import a Music CD into iTunes
20 Purchase Audio from the iTunes Music Store
33 Find and Play Music

→ SEE ALSO

35 Create a Smart Playlist
47 Rate Your Music on the iPod
73 Train iTunes to Play Your Favorite Music

iTunes isn't just a passive servant to your commands. It's also a trainable assistant that learns your preferences as you play your music and can serve up your favorites in place of those tracks you'd rather skip. All you have to do, as you play music in iTunes, is to set the **My Rating** field on your songs to anything between one and five stars, corresponding to your reaction to each track. For example, the meanings I use to interpret each star rating in my own library are as follows:

★★★★★	My absolute favorite tracks of all—musically superb and enjoyable in any circumstances.
★★★★	Music I actively enjoy listening to and would take the time to seek out.
★★★	Music to which I have no specific objection and don't mind listening to.
★★	Tracks that actively annoy me in some particular way.
★	Tracks I would prefer never to have to listen to, unless I specifically ask for them.

After you've set these ratings on most or all of the tracks in your library, it's a simple matter to set up a ***Smart Playlist*** that selects from your favorite tunes, automatically mixing up a batch of music you're guaranteed to enjoy.

▶ NOTE

The star rating is held within the iTunes database itself, not saved as a part of the song in its internal *info tags*. This means that if your iTunes Library database becomes lost or corrupted, your star ratings (along with your Last Played and Date Added fields) are lost. See 94 Back Up Your Music to CD or DVD for ways to keep yourself protected against data loss.

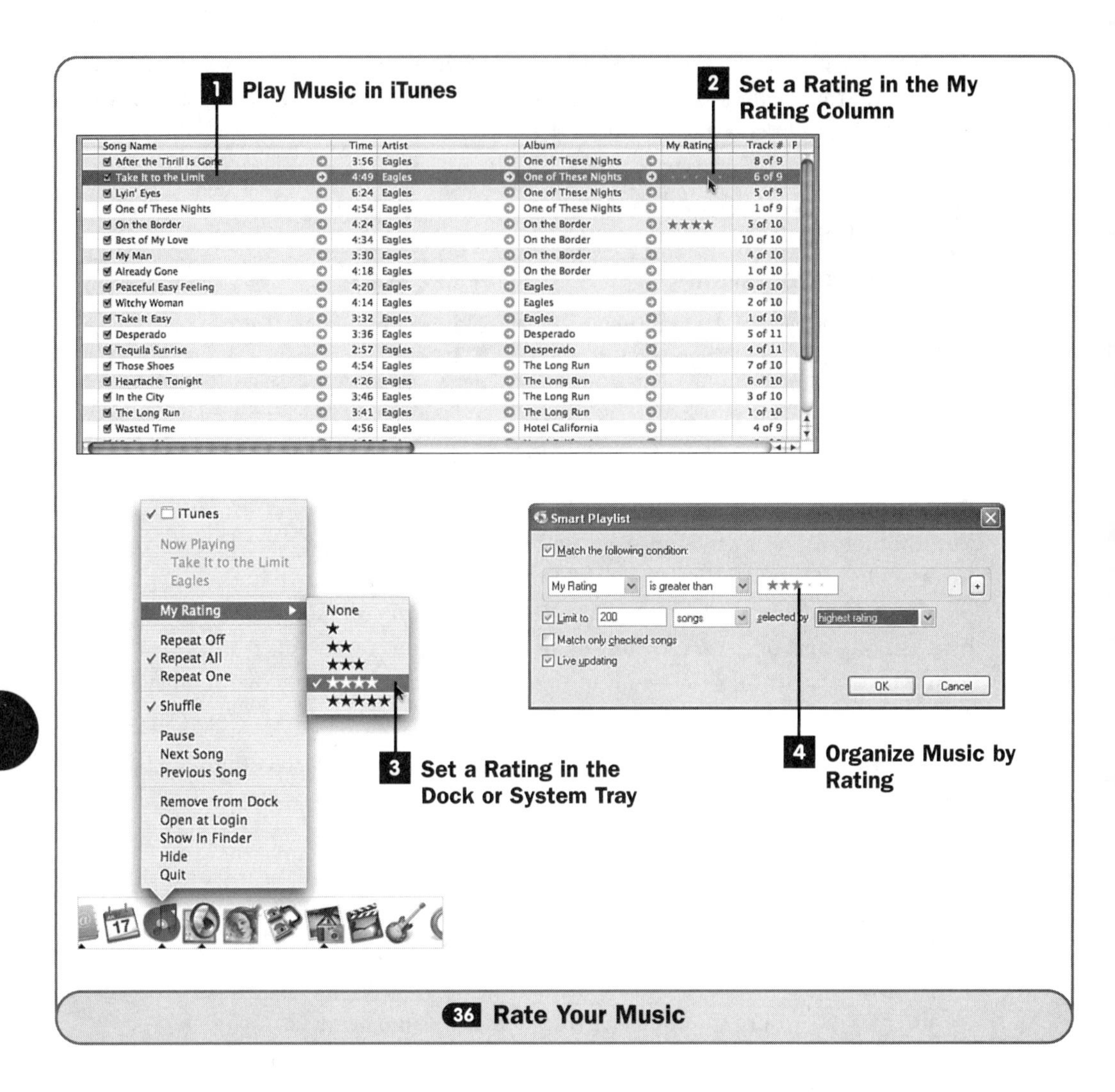

36

1 Play Music in iTunes

Using the **Library** view or a playlist, play your music as you normally would. As you listen, consider the five-star rating system and how you would categorize the songs you're hearing relative to each other. (You don't have to be playing a song to rate it in this way, but it helps to be hearing it as you consider its rating.)

2 Set a Rating in the My Rating Column

Select a song by clicking it. In the **My Rating** column, small dots appear indicating where the five stars would go. Click one of the dots to set that number of stars, or click and drag left and right to adjust the star rating. The rating is set as soon as you click the setting in the song listing.

▶ **NOTE**

Refer to 71 **Customize Which Information Columns Are Displayed** if the **My Rating** column is not visible.

3 Set a Rating in the Dock or System Tray

While a song is playing, you can set its rating through another, more direct method: using the System Tray (in Windows) or the Dock (in Mac OS X). In either case, right-click (or **Control**+click) the iTunes icon to display the context menu; from the **My Rating** submenu, choose the appropriate number of stars (choose **None** to clear the rating).

4 Organize Music by Rating

After you've set ratings on the bulk of the songs in your library, you can organize your music in a number of ways that are affected by the star ratings. Sort the music in the library on the **My Rating** column, in descending order, to see your favorite songs first. Create a Smart Playlist with a limited number of songs selected by **highest rating**. In the **Party Shuffle** playlist (39 **Use the Party Shuffle Playlist**), select **Play higher rated songs more often** to "weight" the appearance of songs according to their ratings.

37 Listen to an Internet Radio Station

✔ BEFORE YOU BEGIN	➜ SEE ALSO
2 Run iTunes for the First Time	33 Find and Play Music

Internet Radio, a mechanism by which "streams" of music are broadcast by amateur DJs over the Internet to anyone with a client program (such as iTunes), used to be a lot more prevalent than it is now. At the time of iTunes' introduction in 2001, many thousands of Internet Radio channels existed, served out of high-speed corporate networks and college dorm rooms alike. iTunes shipped with the capability to browse to any of these channels and tune in to listen for free. However, only a short time later, the record labels began to crack down on these illicit sources of music; only those channels that could afford to pay the new fees that the labels levied on them (usually by running ads) were able to stay on the air. Today, Internet Radio is only a shadow of what it once was—but it's still there, serving a die-hard cadre of loyal listeners, and iTunes still supports it the same way it always has. Internet Radio is still free and can prove to be a great source of enjoyment and music you might never otherwise hear.

1 Connect to the Internet

Make sure that you've got an active connection to the Internet; you can't connect to an Internet Radio station without being online. Dial your modem or connect your laptop to the wireless network, as necessary.

2 Select the Radio Source

Click **Radio** in the **Source** pane of the iTunes' window. The list of available Internet Radio genres appears in the song listing area.

3 Choose a Genre

Click the triangle next to any of the listed genres to reveal all the available Internet Radio channels within it. Some channels come and go over the course of the day, or from one day to the next; the central server to which iTunes connects gets an up-to-date listing of available channels when you select the **Radio** source, so each one listed should be available to connect.

The channels are listed by name along with their available bit rate (the speed at which the audio stream is delivered to you) and a description. The higher the bit rate, the better the audio quality will be. One caution: Do not choose a channel with a bit rate faster than your Internet connection. For example, a 56K modem connection (56 kilobits per second, or Kbps) won't be able to support a 64Kbps audio stream without the music stuttering and pausing to rebuffer. Choose a channel with a bit rate lower than the speed of your Internet connection (*much* lower, if you want to do other stuff online while you're listening).

4 Connect to an Internet Radio Channel

Double-click a listed channel to begin listening to it, or select the channel and click the **Play** button. iTunes connects to the server and downloads the channel's playlist of upcoming songs; this enables it to report to you the name of each song as the channel plays it, just like satellite radio.

▶ NOTE

Because Internet Radio channels are streamed, you can't fast-forward, rewind, or pause them. Holding down the Back and Forward buttons has no effect, and skipping forward and backward switches to different channels in the genre list rather than moving among individual songs.

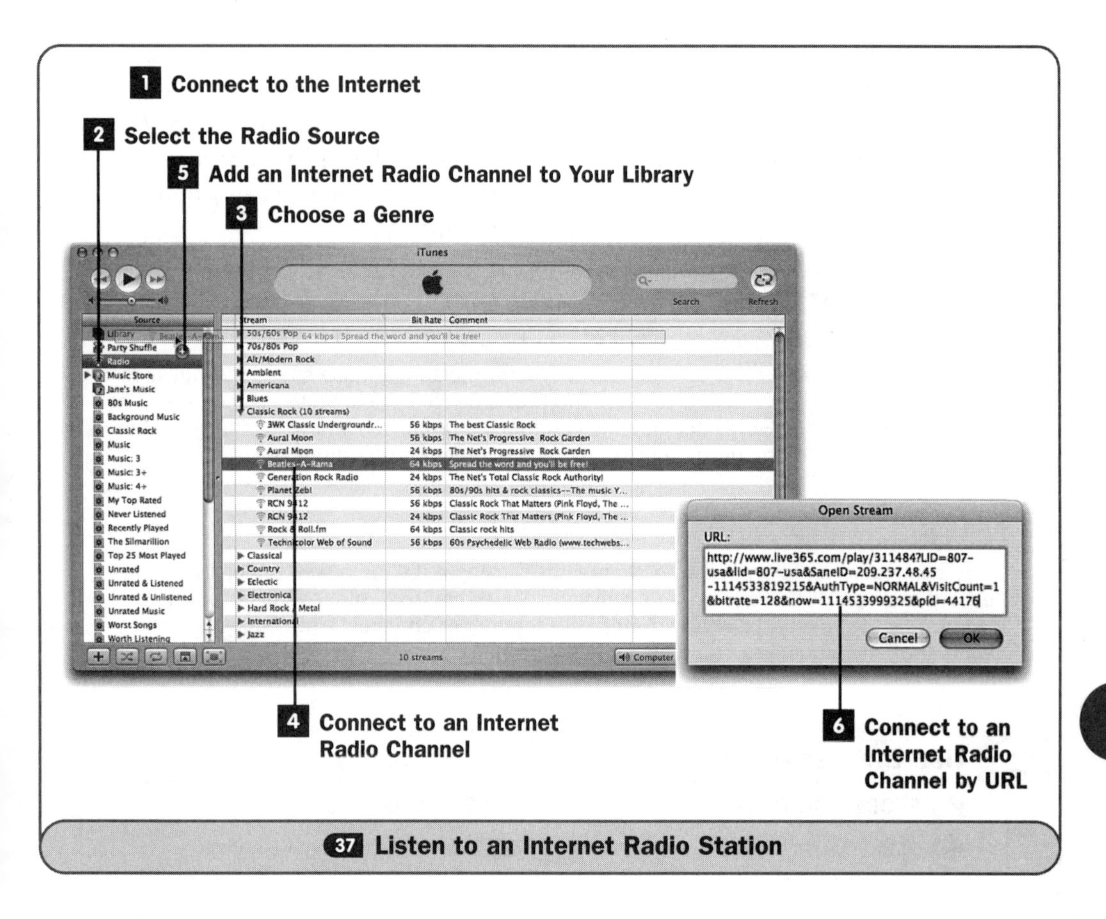

5 Add an Internet Radio Channel to Your Library

If you like a particular channel and want to be able to return to it easily in the future, you can add it to your library. Click and drag the channel from the **Radio** view to the **Library** option in the **Source** pane (the + icon on the mouse pointer indicates that the reference will be *added*). After you do this, you can navigate to the channel in the **Library** view by searching for its name or sorting the lists in a way that enables you to find it easily (for example, you can search by **Kind** and then locate the channels listed as **MPEG audio stream**, or you can sort on the **Date Added** field and scroll to the top or bottom where the newest entries appear).

6 Connect to an Internet Radio Channel by URL

Not every Internet Radio channel in the world is listed in iTunes' navigation system. Many more channels exist on the Web, organized onto websites that collect links to popular channels and make them available to listeners by simply clicking their links. You can connect to any of these channels using this method. Alternatively, you might find or be given the direct URL of a channel. You can connect directly to the channel by selecting **Advanced, Open Stream**, pasting in the URL of the channel in the **Open Stream** dialog box that appears, and clicking **OK**. Connecting to a channel directly in this way automatically adds the channel to your **Library**.

WEB RESOURCE

http://www.live365.com

Live365 is one of the largest and most widely known clearinghouse sites for thousands of freely available Internet Radio channels. The music on freely listenable audio streams are generally paid for by advertising, just like commercial radio. You'll have to choose **Other MP3 Player** when setting up the embedded player preferences on the site.

NOTE

If you connect to an Internet Radio channel by clicking a link on a web page, you might notice that a "playlist" file (with an extension such as **.m3u** or **.pls**) has been downloaded. This file is what launches iTunes with the proper channel. After iTunes has connected to the channel, you can delete the playlist file.

38 Use the iTunes Visualizer

✓ BEFORE YOU BEGIN	→ SEE ALSO
33 Find and Play Music	76 Add a Third-Party Visualizer

The idea certainly wasn't pioneered by iTunes, but it's where the art has really matured: the **Visualizer**, a program within iTunes that shows colorful graphical shapes swimming across the screen that jerk and jiggle and dance in response to the music that's playing, gives your music a whole new dimension in which you can enjoy it.

NOTE

The Visualizer built into iTunes is based on G-Force by SoundSpectrum. G-Force itself has continued to develop independently and can be added to iTunes as a third-party visualizer. See 76 **Add a Third-Party Visualizer** for more information.

It's difficult to describe what the ***Visualizer*** does—it's easier just to see it demonstrated. Fortunately, this is no more complex a task than clicking a button.

▶ KEY TERM

***Visualizer*—A program within iTunes that displays colorful patterns in a window or the full screen. The Visualizer responds visually to the playing music by creating agitated wave shapes in many different constantly changing forms.**

1 Turn On the Visualizer

As you're playing your music (or while it's stopped), click the **Visualizer** button in the lower-right corner of the iTunes' window or choose **Visualizer, Turn Visualizer On**. The contents of the entire iTunes' window are replaced by the swirling, colorful shapes of the Visualizer, shifting and reforming in response to the music.

▶ NOTE

The Visualizer responds to the waveform of the audio signal while music is playing by creating agitated wave shapes, and traces out smooth shapes when the music is paused. The amplitude of the wave shapes you see doesn't depend on the volume level of iTunes and won't get more spectacular if you crank the sound up all the way.

2 Switch to Full Screen Mode

To get the full psychedelic effect of the Visualizer, you really should run it in **Full Screen** mode (especially if you have a large monitor). Choose **Visualizer, Full Screen**, then turn on the Visualizer; the screen fades out and is replaced by the full-size Visualizer mode. Now you can turn off the lights and let your current playlist carry you away.

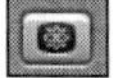

When the **Full Screen** option is enabled in the **Visualizer** menu, the computer switches to the **Full Screen Visualizer** mode whenever you invoke it; the **Visualizer** button in the lower-right corner of the iTunes window shows the **Visualizer** icon within a "TV screen" to indicate that it's in this mode. Choose **Visualizer, Full Screen** again to disable **Full Screen** mode and ensure that turning on the Visualizer won't take over your whole screen.

To exit the Full Screen Visualizer and return to your music listing, press **Esc**. Alternatively, press **Ctrl+F** (in Windows) or **⌘+F** (on the Mac) to switch out of Full Screen mode but keep the Visualizer running within the iTunes' window.

3 Adjust Visualizer Options for Better Performance

The Visualizer is a fairly processor-intensive feature, and the smoothness of its appearance depends a lot on how fast your computer is. If it looks choppy to you, there are a few things you can do to improve it.

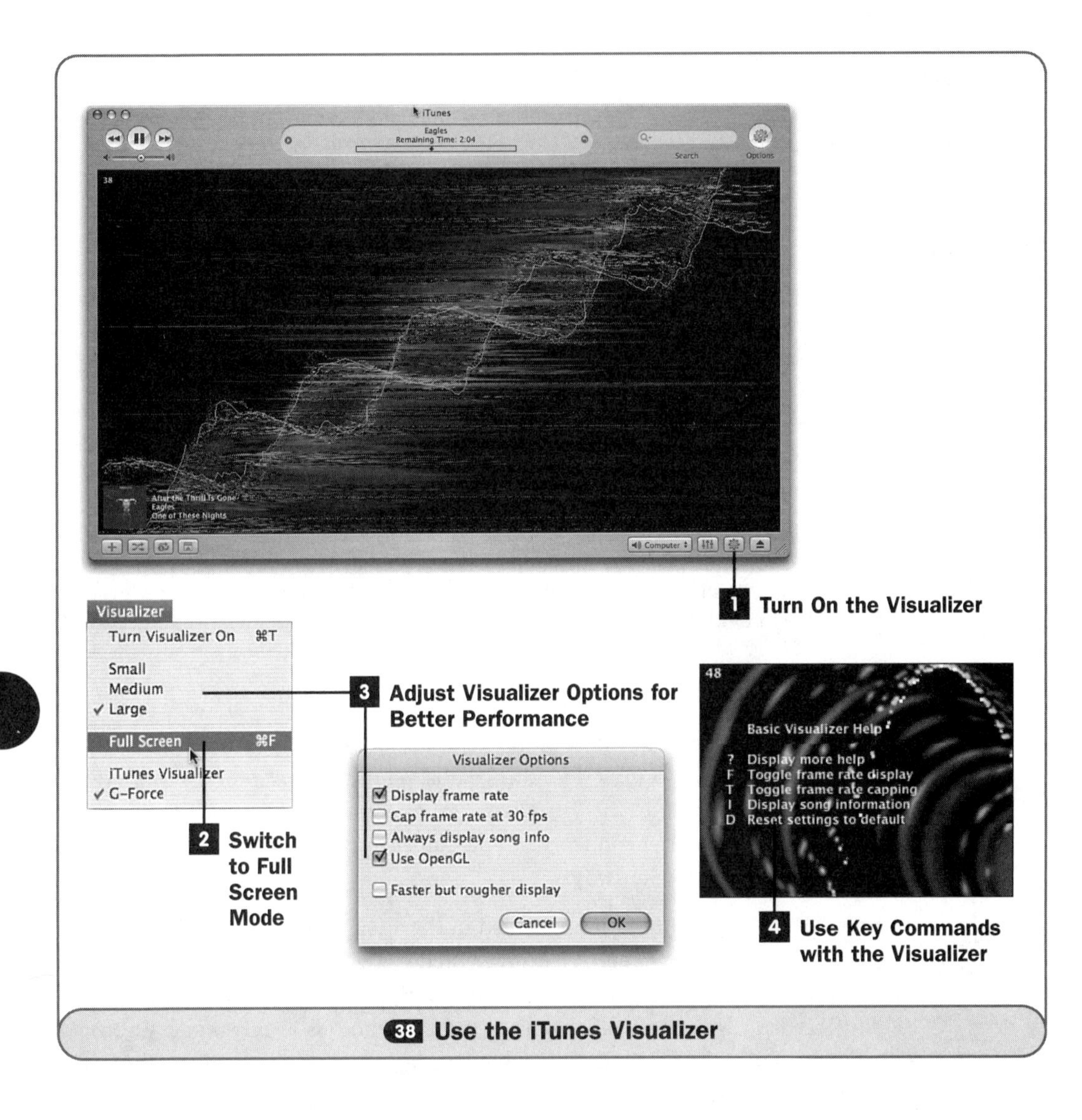

38 Use the iTunes Visualizer

First, try choosing **Medium** or **Small** from the **Visualizer** menu; these options shrink the image area of the Visualizer within the iTunes' window, reducing the amount of work the computer has to do.

If this doesn't help, or you don't like the smaller appearance, try reducing the resolution but not the size. Click the **Options** button in the upper-right corner of the iTunes window. In the dialog box that appears, enable the **Faster but rougher display** check box. The visual performance of the Visualizer should be greatly enhanced by this option, although the individual shapes look blockier. Also, on the Mac, make sure that the **Use OpenGL** option is selected if your computer has a video card capable of OpenGL instructions.

▶ TIP

The iTunes Visualizer can be a handy way to benchmark your computer's performance. Enable the Display frame rate option to see how many frames per second the Visualizer can draw, reflected in the upper-left corner of the display window. At 50 to 60 frames per second—faster than the human eye can effectively discern—your computer's pretty muscular indeed.

4 Use Key Commands with the Visualizer

For experts who really want to tweak their Visualizer experience, there are a number of keyboard commands available within the Visualizer. Press **?** while the Visualizer is running to see a list of basic key commands; press **?** again to see the second page of commands. Among the available commands are **R** to start a new visual style (or "config") at random, **C** to show the name of the current config, **0** through **9** to choose from among 10 popular configs, and **I** to show the current song information and album art. There are also key commands to turn on and off the frame rate display (**F**) and rate capping at 30 frames per second (**T**).

39 Use the Party Shuffle Playlist

39

✔ BEFORE YOU BEGIN	→ SEE ALSO
9 Import a Music CD into iTunes	41 Create Crossfades Between Songs
33 Find and Play Music	44 AutoFill Your iPod shuffle
	60 AirTunes: Connect iTunes to a Stereo with AirPort Express

iTunes and a well-stocked library are perfect for providing the background music at a party, particularly if you use an AirPort Express base station to broadcast your music wirelessly to your living room's big stereo system (see 60 **AirTunes: Connect iTunes to a Stereo with AirPort Express**).

However, you don't want to spend time putting together a manual ***playlist*** for an hours-long party, or trust the automatic ordering of a ***Smart Playlist***; in fact, you might want to be sure that certain songs show up at a certain time of the evening, or that certain pairs of songs flow into each other when the mood is just right. This need is answered by the **Party Shuffle** feature, which is like a specialized, dynamic playlist you can edit on the fly. **Party Shuffle** takes songs at random from a specified source (for instance, a playlist or Smart Playlist of your choice), shows you a certain number of upcoming songs and the last few songs it's played, and gives you the opportunity to fine-tune the random upcoming choices at any time by deleting selections, rearranging them, and adding new ones from the library. You can micromanage the **Party Shuffle** playlist during the party to make sure that it chooses all the right music, or leave it alone to pick its own random selections—it's up to you to be the perfect host by orchestrating the ideal musical atmosphere.

▶ NOTE

You can see a maximum of 100 upcoming songs in the Party Shuffle playlist, so that's the extent to which you can engineer the list before the party begins. Party Shuffle is intended to work from automatic random selections as it goes, but it gives you the option to change selections that are soon to be played.

1 Select the Party Shuffle Source

Click **Party Shuffle** in the **Source** pane of the iTunes' window. A random selection of 15 upcoming songs, randomly chosen from your library, is displayed in the track listing, with a shiny blue selection bar indicating the first song in the list.

2 Choose a Source Playlist

The first order of business is to pick the **Source** from which the music is going to come. You might want to pick a Smart Playlist that's designed to filter only the best songs of a certain genre, such as Reggae songs rated three stars or higher. See 35 **Create a Smart Playlist** for more information on creating such a playlist.

▶ TIP

Click the Refresh button in the upper-right corner of the window to discard the current list of upcoming songs and grab a fresh random lineup of songs from the selected source. Keep clicking until you're fairly satisfied with the list of upcoming tracks.

3 Choose to Weight Song Selections by Rating

If the **Play higher rated songs more often** check box is enabled, **Party Shuffle** gives a higher "weight" to songs with more stars when it's making its random selections—for example, a song rated five stars is five times as likely to appear in the list as a song with one star. Disable this check box if you want to give all your songs an equal chance of being heard, regardless of their rating.

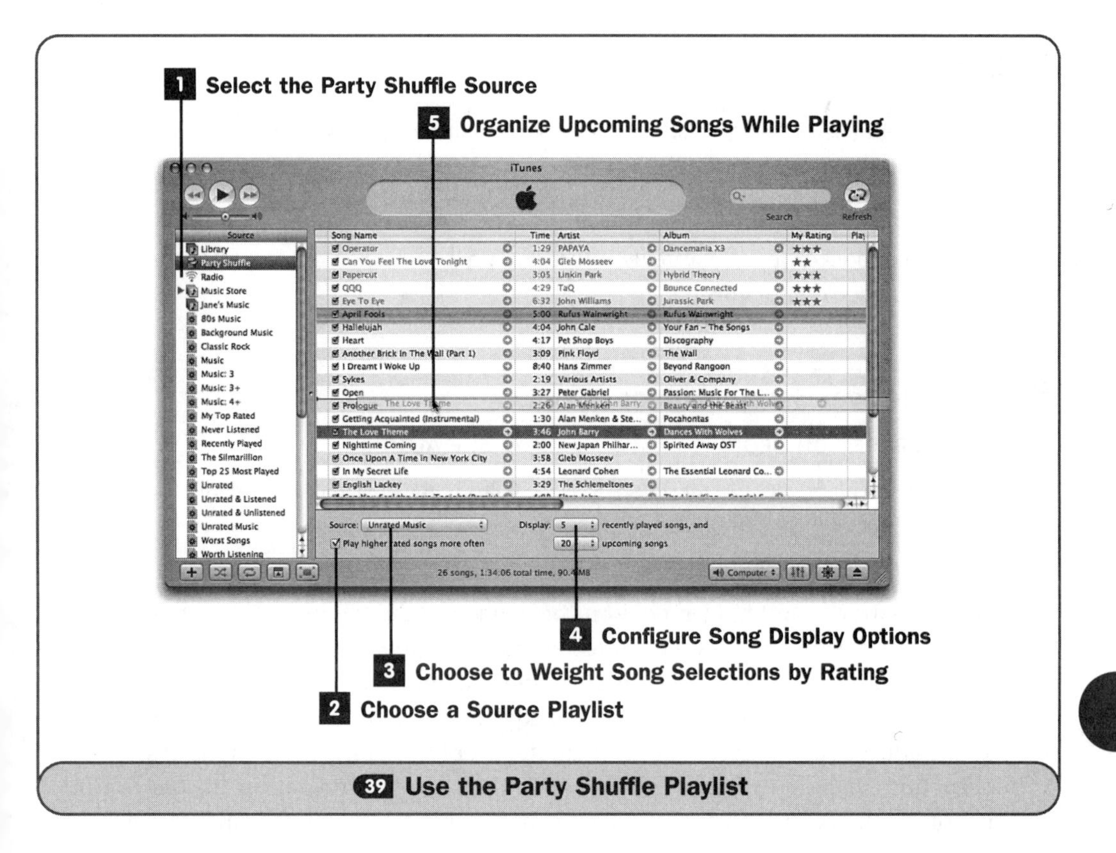

4 Configure Song Display Options

Use the drop-down menus to configure how many recently played and upcoming songs are shown. You can choose to show up to 100 of either one; if you show the maximum number of recently played songs, you can relive the evening after it's over by perusing the list of songs that iTunes played during the course of the party.

5 Organize Upcoming Songs While Playing

Click **Play** to begin playing songs from the **Party Shuffle** list. As the current song plays, you have plenty of time to fine-tune the upcoming music selection. Select a song and press **Delete** or **Del** to remove it from the list (this action doesn't delete it from the library). Click and drag songs into a more appropriate order, just as you would in a regular playlist, to make sure that songs flow naturally into each other. Add new songs to the list by selecting the **Library** option, navigating to the songs in question, and dragging them to the **Party Shuffle** option.

▶ TIP

To really impress your guests, be sure to turn on the *crossfade* effect (see 41 Create Crossfades Between Songs) and the full-screen Visualizer (38 Use the iTunes Visualizer).

With these options at your disposal, you can be sure you'll have the perfect musical backdrop for your event. Just don't get so carried away with it that you forget to serve hors d'oeuvres!

40 Auto-Level Song Volumes

✓ BEFORE YOU BEGIN	→ SEE ALSO
9 Import a Music CD into iTunes 33 Find and Play Music	41 Create Crossfades Between Songs

One of the most useful hidden fields in the headers of digital music files is the *preamp setting*, which is a level of correction to the volume of each individual song—either amplifying or quieting the audio signal in song files to compensate for the fact that every CD is mastered at a slightly different volume level. With a feature called **Sound Check**, iTunes evaluates every song in your library as it's added, finds its most extreme high and low volume levels, and adjusts the preamp setting for each song accordingly. Then, when iTunes plays the song file, the preamp setting is applied to the output volume to ensure that each song plays at approximately the same loudness. Never again will you have to turn up the volume to hear a quiet movement of a Beethoven symphony, only to have your ears blasted out by the Sisters of Mercy immediately afterward.

1 Open the Audio Preferences

Open the iTunes **Preferences** window (choose **iTunes, Preferences** on the Mac; choose **Edit, Preferences** in Windows). Click the **Audio** tab.

2 Enable Sound Check

If it's not checked already, enable the **Sound Check** check box. Click **OK**.

If the **Sound Check** option had not previously been enabled, iTunes now evaluates all the songs in your library to determine and apply a preamp setting to each one. This process can take a long time—several seconds for each track—because *every song* must be examined all the way through for extremes of volume. Be prepared to wait a while before the process is complete.

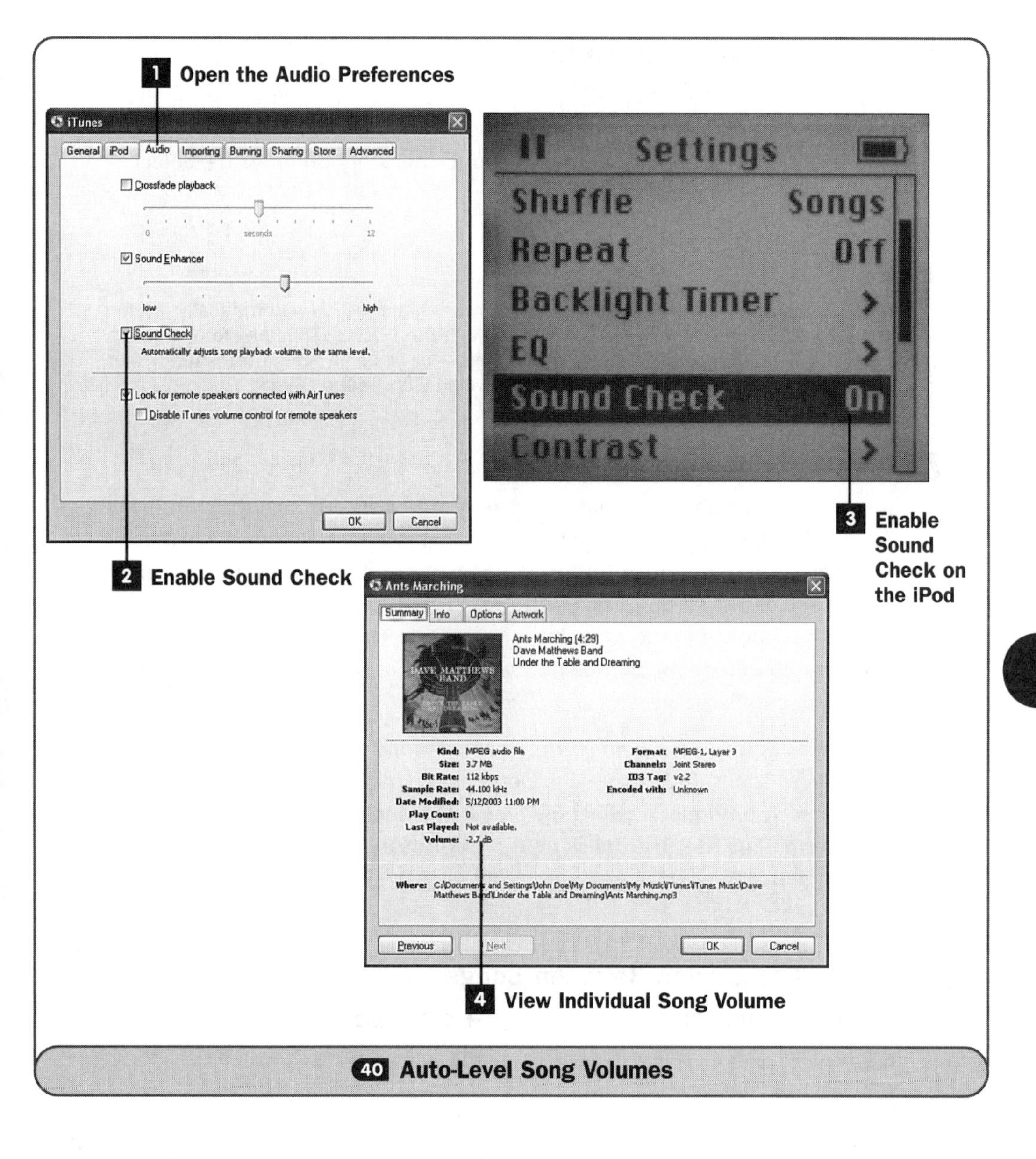

40 Auto-Level Song Volumes

From now on, whenever you play your music, each track is adjusted to match the volume level of the surrounding songs. As long as the **Sound Check** option is enabled, each new song you add to the library is evaluated for its preamp setting at the time you add it to the library.

3 Enable Sound Check on the iPod

You must enable the **Sound Check** feature on the iPod so that it can realize the same benefits as music played through iTunes. On the iPod, navigate to the **Settings** menu then scroll to the **Sound Check** option; press the **Select** button to toggle the setting **On**.

▶ NOTE

On the iPod, only the music played through the headphone jack is automatically leveled with the Sound Check option; music played through the Dock connector—for example, by connecting headphones to the back of the Dock—or by using an FM transmitter that connects through the Dock connector—is not leveled with Sound Check.

4 View Individual Song Volume

If you're curious about a song's preamp setting as determined through the **Sound Check** option, select the song and choose **File**, **Get Info**. Click the **Summary** tab of the **Information** dialog box. In the block of information in the middle of the window, the **Volume** field shows how many decibels of correction are applied to the song during playback. The higher the positive number, the quieter the music and the more it has to be turned up by **Sound Check**.

Sometimes **Sound Check** might apply an improper volume adjustment to one of your songs. If this happens, don't panic and turn off the whole feature—you can manually adjust the preamp setting for any individual song by choosing **File**, **Get Info**, clicking the **Options** tab, and moving the **Volume Adjustment** slider to a more appropriate setting.

41 Create Crossfades Between Songs

✔ BEFORE YOU BEGIN	→ SEE ALSO
9 Import a Music CD into iTunes	40 Auto-Level Song Volumes
33 Find and Play Music	

iTunes gives you access to certain audio effects that greatly enhance the atmosphere and professional sound of your music as you play it from your library or ***playlists***. One of these features is ***crossfading***. Crossfading eliminates the gap that's sometimes audible between tracks as iTunes reads the new file from the disk and—perhaps most importantly—crossfading simply sounds cool, like something you'd hear on the radio.

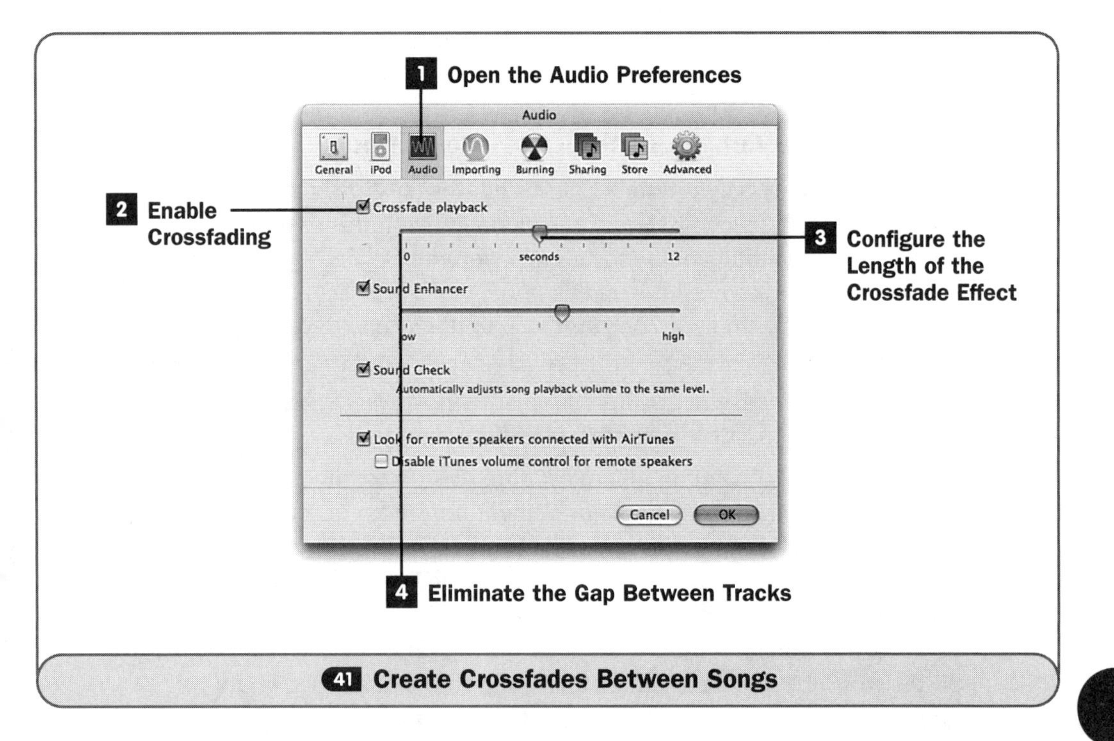

▶ KEY TERM

Crossfading—Having one track fade out at its end; the next track begins as the previous one is still fading.

You enable crossfading with a check box and use a slider that determines how long the fade-out should last. When it's active, crossfading applies to playback in any music source, including the library, playlists, or the **Party Shuffle** playlist.

▶ NOTE

Crossfading is not available on the iPod.

1 Open the Audio Preferences

Open the iTunes **Preferences** window (choose **iTunes**, **Preferences** on the Mac; choose **Edit**, **Preferences** in Windows). Click the **Audio** tab.

2 Enable Crossfading

Enable the **Crossfade playback** check box. This check box turns on the cross-fading feature, but leaves the crossfade length set at zero, so theoretically no change should be audible if you test the playback now (although in some cases, iTunes loads the upcoming track ahead of time, eliminating the pause between tracks that can sometimes result from slow disk access speeds).

3 Configure the Length of the Crossfade Effect

Use the slider to specify a number of seconds for the crossfade effect—anything from 0 to 12 seconds. You can experiment with this setting, trying a few different lengths until you see what's right for you. A good starting point is to set the slider to 6 seconds, the middle of the scale, and test it out by playing your music and letting one song give way to the next with a smooth fade-out and the next song's overlapping entry.

4 Eliminate the Gap Between Tracks

Particularly if your computer has slow hard disk access time, you might notice a brief gap between tracks as iTunes jumps from one song to the next during playback. You can mitigate this behavior using the crossfade feature. Simply move the slider almost all the way to the left—the slider slips into détentes at each full second, so try it at 1 second. This is probably enough to cover up any potential inter-track gaps. If so, try moving the slider back to 0—the crossfade feature is still enabled, and so the next track might be loaded ahead of time from the disk, which tends by itself to get rid of the gap.

6

iPod: iTunes to Go

IN THIS CHAPTER:

The first iPod was released within a year of iTunes itself, in November 2001, and it's been a smash hit since day one. It wasn't the first portable digital music player on the market—not by a long shot—and it wasn't even the first high-capacity, hard-drive-based player either. What made the iPod such a runaway success was a combination of its small size, its high capacity, and (perhaps most importantly) its groundbreaking user interface. With the navigation wheel enabling the user to scroll quickly through lists of hundreds or thousands of songs and zero-in immediately on the one she wanted, as well as to dig down into the hierarchical collection of music using the same implicit organizational methods as iTunes itself (instead of the arcane files and folders of contemporary players), the iPod truly was—as its original marketing described it—"iTunes to go."

The iPod was designed specifically so that the process of synchronizing it with your computer's music collection was a matter of simply plugging it in and waiting for the few seconds necessary for your music to be transferred to the iPod over the high-speed FireWire or USB 2.0 connection. Ideally, under the right conditions, that's all it involves: Just plug your iPod into its Dock whenever you return to your computer, and not only will its battery always remain fully charged, the music in your iTunes Library will always be synchronized with your iPod so that you can grab it and go, your newly purchased or imported music readily available right in your pocket.

However, there are some complicating factors to keep in mind. Your iPod, for instance, might not have enough capacity to contain all the music in your library; this is especially true of the budget, ultra-portable iPod shuffle with its comparatively tiny 1 gigabyte of capacity. Additionally, synchronizing your music carries with it some complexities regarding special kinds of audio files, such as ***audiobooks***, and the handling of unique features such as ***On-the-Go Playlists*** that you create on your iPod and sync back into iTunes.

▶ NOTE

Because every iPod model is of a slightly different thickness, the Dock must be specially fitted with a shell that has the right size slot for your iPod. If you're buying a Dock separately, be sure that it comes with the right snap-on shell for your particular iPod model.

42 Transfer Your Music to Your iPod

✔ BEFORE YOU BEGIN

4 Connect Your iPod for the First Time
9 Import a Music CD into iTunes
20 Purchase Audio from the iTunes Music Store

➜ SEE ALSO

43 Use a Large iTunes Library with a Small iPod
44 Autofill Your iPod Shuffle
46 Find and Play Music on the iPod

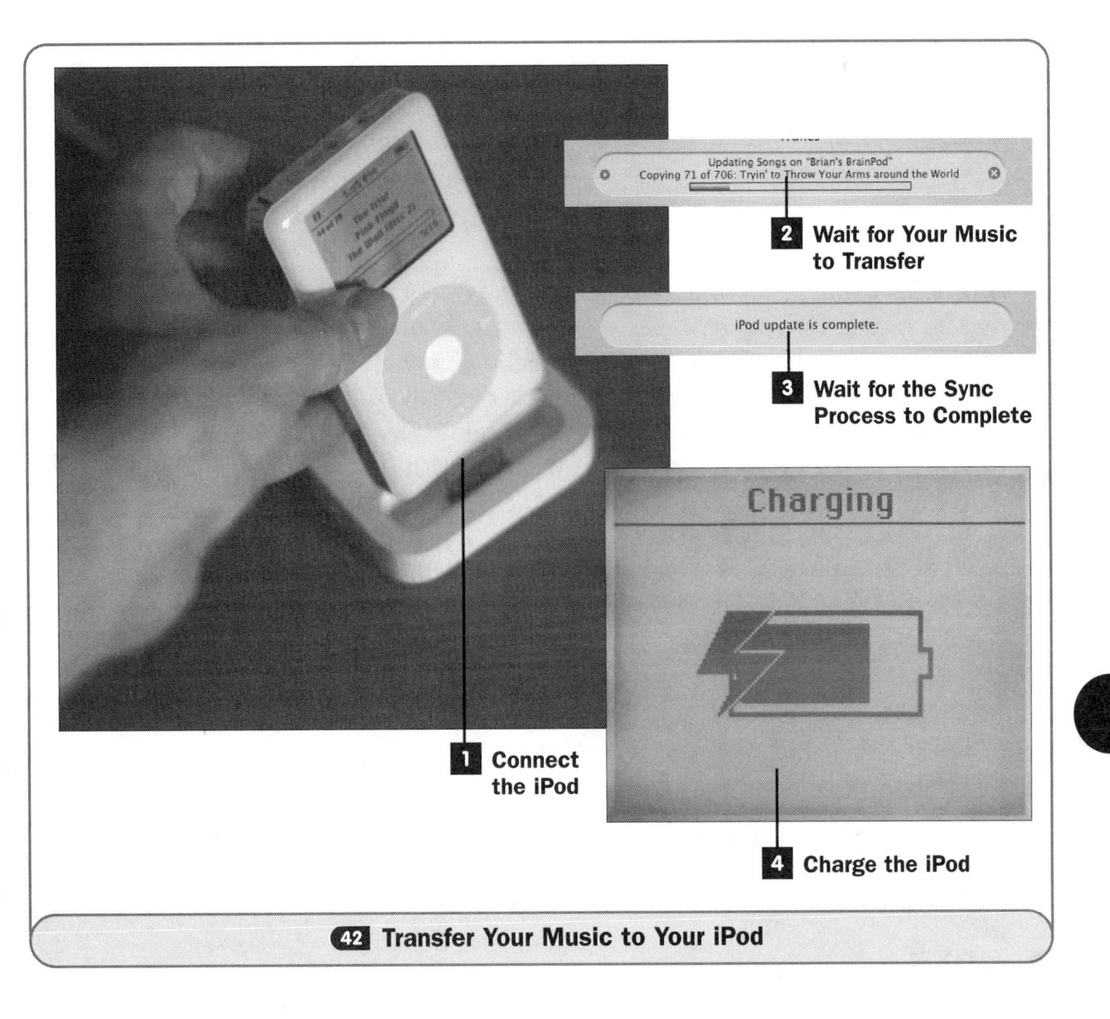

42 Transfer Your Music to Your iPod

Many iPod owners' first glimpse of iTunes comes when they unpack their new iPods and install iTunes for the first time on their Windows PCs. If this describes you, the first time you connect your iPod to your PC is as described in 4 **Connect Your iPod for the First Time**. After you name and register the iPod, you're free to disconnect it or let it sit in the Dock and charge its battery. Your iTunes **Library** starts out empty, and there's no synchronizing that takes place at the end of that process. However, if you've been using iTunes long enough to have added music to it, the act of interfacing the iPod with iTunes means something different: ***synchronizing*** your iPod's contents with those of the iTunes **Library**.

▶ KEY TERM

Synchronize—To connect your iPod to your computer so that the iPod is filled with all the music in your iTunes **Library**, with all the up-to-date info tags and playing history; iTunes is similarly updated to match the information on the iPod's songs.

Depending on your model of iPod, the process of connecting it to your computer can take any of several slightly different forms. The 1G and 2G iPods have a FireWire port on the top; you connect this to your Mac or PC using a double-ended, six-pin FireWire cable that either came with the iPod or that you purchased separately. 3G and later iPods (and the iPod mini) have a Dock connector on the bottom that contains both FireWire and USB 2.0 connections as well as audio output channels; this wide selection of data paths all located in the same connector means that you can connect the iPod to your computer using a FireWire or USB 2.0 cable (packaged with the iPod or sold as an iPod accessory by Apple) plugged into the Dock connector slot, or—if you have one—the iPod Dock itself. This Dock accessory, which comes standard with some models of iPod and can also be purchased separately, is a white rectangular pedestal with a slot for the iPod to stand up in. When you put the iPod into the Dock, the Dock connector engages with the protruding piece inside the Dock's slot and connects the iPod in the same way that the direct cable does, while allowing you to keep the iPod upright (making sure that its back doesn't get scuffed). Finally, the iPod shuffle has a standard USB connector built into its body; you plug this directly into any available USB port on your computer (or the keyboard of your Mac). There's even a small Dock available for the iPod shuffle, if you want it to have its own dedicated place to sit and charge.

▶ NOTE

When any iPod is connected to the computer, its internal battery is being recharged. It's best to leave your iPod charging at all times when you're not using it; see 51 **About the Care and Feeding of Your iPod** for more information.

The first thing that happens when you connect your iPod to the computer is that iTunes launches and begins synchronizing your music (an icon on the iPod's screen warns you not to disconnect it during the process). New songs you've added to your iTunes **Library** are copied to the iPod's internal disk. The number of times you've listened to songs on the iPod, and their **Last Played** dates, are read into iTunes, and your library is updated accordingly. Finally, when the sync process is complete, the iPod resets itself to show the Main Menu, and iTunes tells you that it's safe to disconnect the iPod at any time.

NOTE

It's important to be aware that an iPod can only be associated (or "linked") with a single copy of iTunes. If you synchronize your iPod with iTunes running on your home computer, and then you try to connect it to your PC at work, iTunes will tell you that the iPod is already linked to a different computer. iTunes then offers to delete the iPod's contents and replace them with those in the current copy of iTunes Library. This feature is obviously meant to inhibit piracy, as it would otherwise be a simple matter to use an iPod to ferry copies of music illegally from one computer to another. However, it's not too hard to imagine legitimate reasons to want to copy music from the iPod to iTunes, such as restoring your music after a crash. See 98 Copy Your Music from the iPod Back to iTunes for more information.

1 Connect the iPod

You should synchronize your iPod whenever you've made changes in iTunes that you want to be reflected on the iPod (such as adding more music), or whenever you've spent some time listening to music on the iPod and want the information in iTunes to reflect which songs you've played most recently and how you've rated them on the iPod.

NOTE

If your iPod is connected to the computer while you make changes to your iTunes Library, the changes are not automatically propagated to the iPod; the sync process occurs only when you plug in the iPod or launch iTunes while the iPod is connected. To make sure that later changes to your iTunes' music are synchronized with the iPod, quit iTunes and restart it—a new sync process takes place when iTunes restarts. Alternatively, choose File, Update iPod.

For iPods with a Dock connector (3G and later models), place the iPod into the Dock's slot until you hear the soft chime indicating that the iPod has awakened and is ready to synchronize. If you don't have a Dock, or if your iPod is a 1G or 2G model, plug in the FireWire or USB 2.0 cable directly to the iPod. If you have an iPod shuffle, plug it directly into an available USB port.

2 Wait for Your Music to Transfer

iTunes automatically launches, if it is not already running. The selection in the **Source** pane in the iTunes' window switches to the iPod, which is listed by the name you gave it during the initial setup procedure.

In the music listing pane, all the music on the iPod is shown in one long list, with the text in gray (indicating that it can't be played). iTunes displays a readout showing how much space is available on the iPod and how much is being used. If there's new music in iTunes that isn't on the iPod, or songs whose ***info tags*** have changed, that music immediately begins transferring; the "progress" icons to the left of every new or updated song show you iTunes' progress as the files are transferred.

iTunes does not transfer songs that the iPod cannot play. These kinds of files include MIDI files, QuickTime movies, and Internet Radio streams, among others. A dialog box warns you that some of the songs can't be transferred; you can opt not to get that same warning again by enabling the check box before dismissing the warning.

▶ NOTE

FireWire transfers data at a rate of 400 megabits per second; USB 2.0 transfers at 480 megabits per second (although technical limitations place it at about the same speed as FireWire). This means that a single album can be transferred to the iPod in about 10 seconds, and a single song takes a fraction of a second to transfer. A 40-gigabyte iPod can be completely filled in less than half an hour. You can't use USB 1.1 to fill any iPod other than the iPod shuffle; USB 1.1 transfers data at a rate of only 12 megabits per second, meaning that a 40GB iPod would take almost 10 hours to fill.

3 Wait for the Sync Process to Complete

Don't unplug the iPod while the sync process is underway; warning messages on the iPod's screen and iTunes' status readout both remind you that doing so can cause data loss on either your iPod or your computer (remember, the iPod is essentially an external hard drive; like all hard drives, it must be unmounted properly by its software—in this case, iTunes—before it can be disconnected). When the process is finished, the iPod's Main Menu appears on its screen, and iTunes reports **iPod update is complete**.

42

▶ NOTE

Early iPod models (1G and 2G) show a check mark and an **OK to disconnect** message when the sync process is done rather than returning to the Main Menu.

4 Charge the iPod

Leave your iPod in its Dock, or connected with its FireWire cable, to charge its battery. Because of the characteristics of the lithium-polymer battery in the iPod, it's better to recharge it even after short uses than to let the battery run down all the way (as you would with nickel-cadmium batteries). See 51 **About the Care and Feeding of Your iPod** for more information.

When the iPod is done charging and its display shows *Charged*—or any time after the sync process has completed—you can grab it out of its Dock or disconnect its cable and take it on the go again.

43 Use a Large iTunes Library with a Small iPod

✔ BEFORE YOU BEGIN	➜ SEE ALSO
4 Connect Your iPod for the First Time	44 Autofill Your iPod Shuffle
42 Transfer Your Music to Your iPod	48 Transfer Only Preferred Music to the iPod

Your iTunes **Library** increases in size as you acquire more music; your iPod, however, is a fixed size and can hold only a certain maximum amount of music. There might come a time, either because your iPod is an older model or because you've got a truly vast collection of music, that you won't be able to fit all the music you own onto the iPod using the automatic, zero-effort sync process. Perhaps that day is today.

You have several options for dealing with a situation in which your iTunes **Library** has outgrown your iPod. One is to do it all manually—instead of iTunes synchronizing all your music by itself, it shows the iPod as another item in the **Source** pane to which you can drag choice tracks from the library, just as though the iPod were a ***playlist***. Another, more versatile method is to choose certain playlists that you want to ***synchronize***; with the clever use of ***Smart Playlists***, you can use fill up the iPod with just enough automatically chosen music to suit your tastes.

43

▶ NOTE

This task is intended for owners of hard-disk-based iPods; if you have an iPod shuffle, skip to 44 Autofill Your iPod Shuffle.

1 Connect the iPod

For iPods with a Dock connector (3G and later models), place the iPod into the Dock's slot until you hear the soft chime that indicates the iPod has awakened and is ready to synchronize. If you don't have a Dock, or if your iPod is a 1G or 2G model, plug in the FireWire or USB 2.0 cable directly to the iPod.

2 Open the iTunes Preferences

Instead of automatically copying your music, iTunes displays a dialog box warning you that the iPod is too small for your entire library to fit. Dismiss this message and open the iTunes **Preferences** window (choose **iTunes, Preferences** on the Mac, or **Edit, Preferences** on Windows). Click the **iPod** tab.

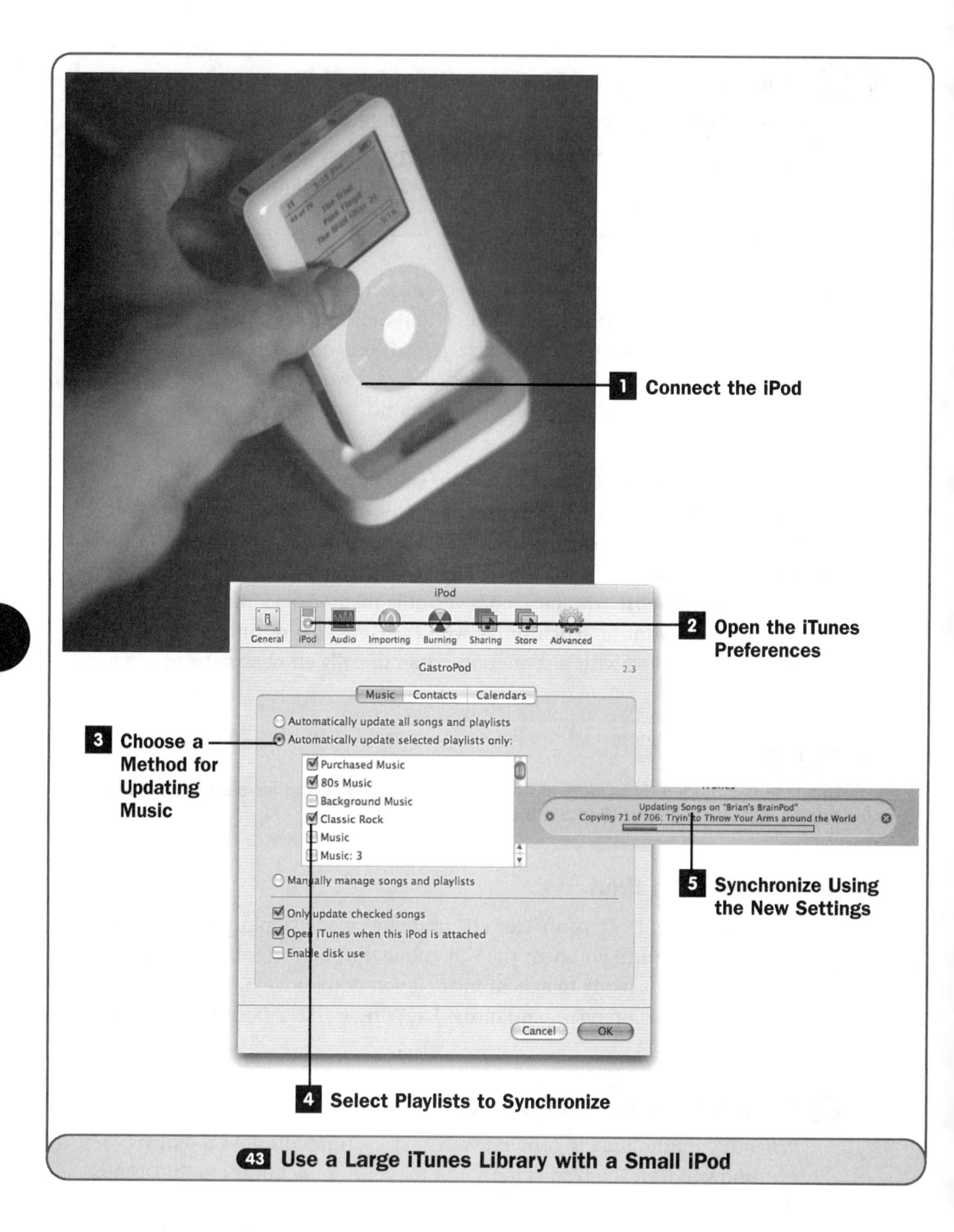

43 Use a Large iTunes Library with a Small iPod

3 Choose a Method for Updating Music

There are three radio buttons describing the three ways iTunes can synchronize its music with your iPod. If your iPod is too small for your library, the first option—**Automatically update all songs and playlists**—is unavailable. You must pick one of the two remaining options.

If you like having a lot of control over the music on your iPod, choose the third option (**Manually manage songs and playlists**). With this option selected, the iPod appears as a mounted external hard disk on your computer. Within iTunes, you can drag exactly the music you want onto the iPod and remove music from the iPod to make room for other songs. When it's time to disconnect the iPod and go, you must first eject (or unmount) the iPod from the computer, using your operating system's "eject" command, or the **Eject** button next to the iPod's icon in the **Source** pane.

A more versatile and less painstaking way to fill your iPod is to pick the second option, **Automatically update selected playlists only**. This option lets you select from among the playlists you've created to define which tracks are transferred to the iPod. Because this list includes Smart Playlists, you can combine some of iTunes' best features to make sure that your iPod is always full of music without the everyday sync process being any more complicated than what's described in 42 **Transfer Your Music to Your iPod**.

4 Select Playlists to Synchronize

Choose the second option. From the list box below it, enable the check boxes for the playlists whose contents you want transferred to your iPod. Any music that is not in any of the selected playlists is not copied to the iPod, and iTunes deletes any music from the iPod that you don't say should be there, clearing off room for only the selected playlists' music. Remember that the iPod's primary navigation method is the same as the **Browse** lists of iTunes; the playlists are only logical groupings of tracks that might appear in more than one playlist. Regardless of how many playlists a song appears in, no track is copied to the iPod more than once.

See 48 **Transfer Only Preferred Music to the iPod** for an example of how to use Smart Playlists to efficiently fill your iPod with choice selections.

▶ NOTE

Unfortunately, iTunes doesn't show you how much space each playlist takes up, which would allow you to calculate the total space a given selection of playlists consumes; you have to go by trial and error until you've filled up the iPod and no more playlists will fit.

5 Synchronize Using the New Settings

Click **OK** to save the new settings for your iPod. If you chose to synchronize selected playlists, iTunes begins transferring the music in these playlists over the FireWire or USB connection (or tells you that your selected playlists take up too much space, if you went over the limit).

If you chose to manually update your songs and playlists, the iPod's icon becomes fixed in the **Source** pane (for as long as it's connected); it's now mounted on your computer as an external hard disk. Select library and navigate to music you want to copy to your iPod. You can drag individual tracks, or you can select items from the **Genre**, **Artist**, or **Album** lists and drag them to the iPod's icon. You can also drag playlists from their positions in the **Source** pane to the iPod's icon also in the **Source** pane; click the triangle next to the iPod's icon to see the playlists that have already been copied to the iPod. Click the iPod in the **Source** pane to view its current contents, which now appear in black text just like any other playlist. Select any song or group of songs and press **Delete** or **Del** to remove them from the iPod. Similarly, you can select and delete playlists from below the iPod's icon if you want to remove them from the iPod. The readout at the bottom of the screen indicates how much space is left on the iPod's internal disk.

▶ TIP

Because no track is copied to the iPod more than once, don't worry if you can't remember whether you already copied a track; just try copying it again. iTunes ignores any tracks that have already been transferred.

When you're ready to disconnect the iPod, be sure to click the **Eject** icon next to the iPod's name in the **Source** pane; this action disconnects the iPod as an external hard drive from your computer and prevents data corruption or loss. You can now unplug the iPod or remove it from the Dock.

As you experiment with configuration options, iTunes can become confused about whether the iPod is connected (mounted) or not; if its icon appears in the **Source** pane and you've configured iTunes to synchronize automatically, try ejecting it by clicking the **Eject** icon next to the iPod's name, or by quitting and restarting iTunes. Make sure that the **Enable disk use** option is not selected in the **Music** pane of the **iPod** tab in the iTunes **Preferences** window; that option prevents the iPod from being unmounted after synchronization.

44 Autofill Your iPod Shuffle

✔ **BEFORE YOU BEGIN**

- 4 Connect Your iPod for the First Time
- 9 Import a Music CD into iTunes
- 20 Purchase Audio from the iTunes Music Store

→ **SEE ALSO**

- 39 Use the Party Shuffle Playlist
- 43 Use a Large iTunes Library with a Small iPod
- 48 Transfer Only Preferred Music to the iPod

The Flash-based iPod shuffle, available in 512MB or 1GB varieties, is a much simpler device than the rest of the iPod line—lacking a display, it gives its owner a lower-cost alternative to the iPods whose high level of portable playback control is offset by their higher prices. With the iPod shuffle, you can't directly select a ***playlist*** or artist as you can with a regular iPod; instead, you get the (perhaps dubious) enjoyment of letting the iPod shuffle pick a song at random from the list of only several dozen that its internal Flash disk can hold. That's the value proposition of this member of the iPod family: For a much lower price than a regular iPod, you get a tiny, fun player whose shuffled (random) playback characteristics give it personality. Certainly, when compared to its competition (other Flash players whose tiny screens barely justify their extra cost), the iPod shuffle's price-to-feature-set balance seems like a sensible one.

44

Even if you can see past the iPod shuffle's limitations and teach yourself to love it for them, it's hard to deny that without a good way to control the music that gets put on the device, the iPod shuffle—whose 512MB or 1GB capacity is virtually guaranteed to be much smaller than your iTunes **Library**—barely has a chance. Fortunately, iTunes provides just such a feature: ***Autofill***. The Autofill feature is similar to the **Party Shuffle** playlist (see **39 Use the Party Shuffle Playlist**) in that you configure it by selecting a source (the library or a selected playlist), and then fill the iPod shuffle by telling iTunes to grab a random selection of songs from that source and matching a few criteria that you define.

▶ KEY TERM

***Autofill*—A technique for selecting just enough songs at random from a specified source to fill your iPod shuffle to capacity. With one button click, you can copy a whole new set of music to the device.**

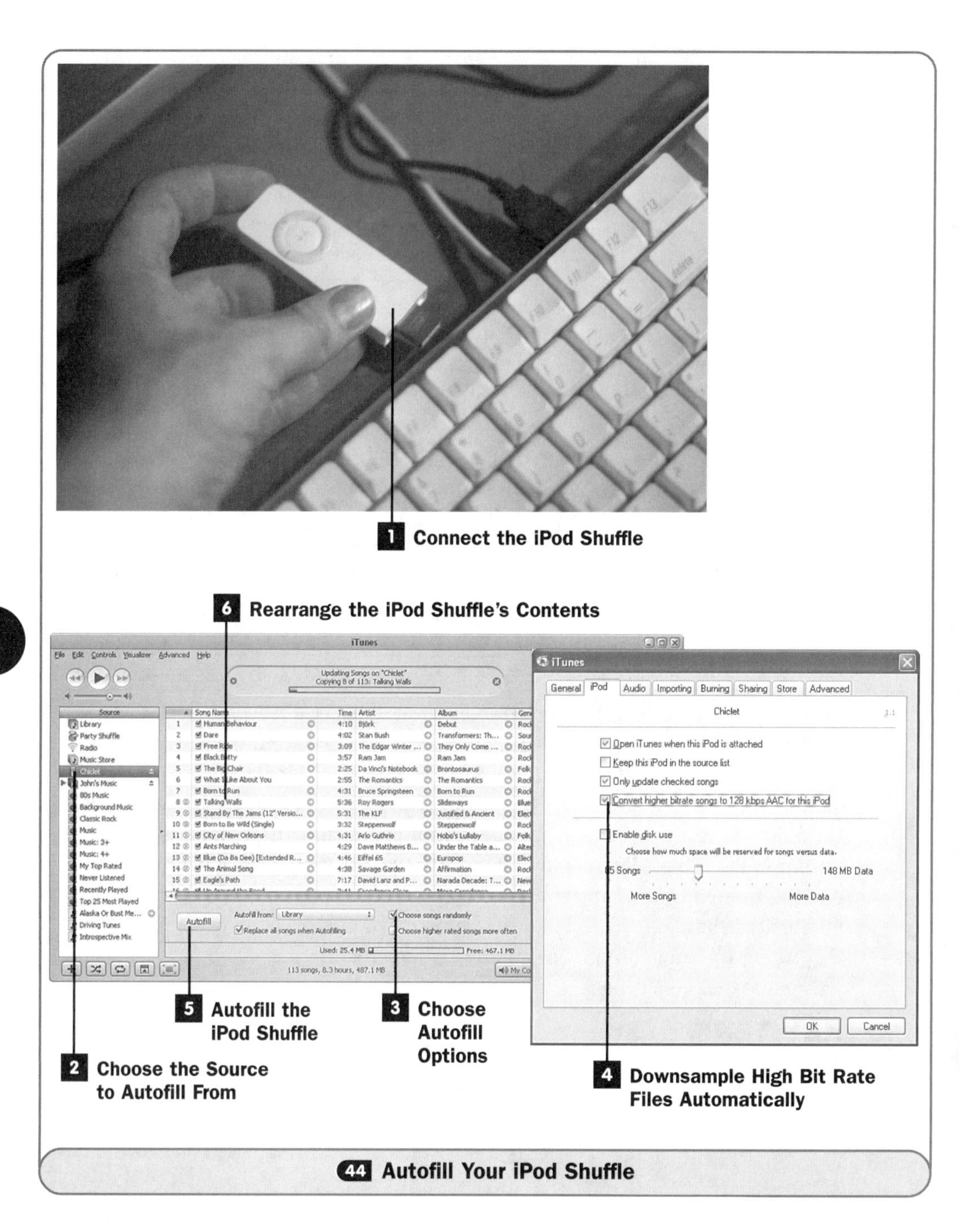

44 Autofill Your iPod Shuffle

Autofill works in tandem with manual updating of the iPod shuffle; you can fill the device with songs you drag in manually from the library, or you can Autofill it and then replace songs you don't like with other ones you do (just as you can with the **Party Shuffle** playlist). In essence, the loss of control over your music that's inherent in the iPod shuffle's lack of a display isn't so much of a loss at all—the control of the flow of your music has merely been moved back into iTunes.

1 Connect the iPod Shuffle

Remove the protective cap from the iPod shuffle's USB connector and plug the device into any available USB port on your computer (on the Mac, a convenient port is on the back or side of the keyboard). The iPod shuffle appears in the **Source** pane in the iTunes' window, listed by the name you gave it when you first connected it to your computer (see 4 **Connect Your iPod for the First Time**). Click its name to view the iPod shuffle's contents.

2 Choose the Source to Autofill From

At the bottom of the screen is a gray bar, specific to the iPod shuffle, with several buttons and options to help you pick the music with which to fill your iPod shuffle. First, choose a source from the **Autofill from** drop-down list. This source can be your entire library, a playlist, or a ***Smart Playlist*** of your choice. The source you choose can be especially useful if you want to limit your iPod shuffle's repertoire to only a certain genre, or to songs rated three stars or higher. See 35 **Create a Smart Playlist** for more information on making useful Smart Playlists.

3 Choose Autofill Options

The **Replace all songs when Autofilling** check box determines whether songs you've manually dragged to the iPod shuffle are replaced when you click the **Autofill** button to copy a new selection of music to the device. Disable this check box if you want the flexibility of filling the iPod shuffle partway with manually selected songs and then Autofilling the rest. If you leave this option enabled, clicking **Autofill** deletes all songs from the iPod shuffle and replaces them all with new random selections.

The **Choose songs randomly** check box ensures that music is chosen arbitrarily from throughout the selected music source rather than from the top of the list as it's currently sorted.

Finally, the **Choose higher rated songs more often** option uses the **My Rating** field to "weight" selected songs—as is true in the **Party Shuffle** feature, a song rated with 5 stars stands a five times better chance of being chosen for Autofill than a song rated with 1 star.

4 Downsample High Bit Rate Files Automatically

Open the iTunes **Preferences** window (choose **iTunes, Preferences** on the Mac or **Edit, Preferences** in Windows). On the **iPod** tab are several options for the iPod shuffle, considerably different from the ones available for disk-based iPods. One of these options is **Convert higher bit rate songs to 128 kbps AAC for this iPod**. If you enable this option, iTunes saves space on your iPod shuffle by downsampling songs that are recorded at a ***bit rate*** higher than 128 kilobits per second—that is, it re-encodes them into AAC format at that bit rate. This option does not affect the saved format of these files within your iTunes **Library**, and 128Kbps AAC files generally sound pretty good—so this might be a good option to turn on. Every little bit of Flash space you can save helps!

Click **OK** to save your settings and close the **Preferences** window.

5 Autofill the iPod Shuffle

Back in the iTunes' window, click the **Autofill** button. iTunes selects enough songs from your selected music source to fill the iPod shuffle completely, and immediately begins transferring them to the device.

▶ NOTE

The iPod shuffle uses a USB 1.1 (a.k.a. USB Full-speed) interface, so the transfer of all the selected songs can take 10 minutes or more at the interface's full 12Mbps speed.

6 Rearrange the iPod Shuffle's Contents

When the transfer of songs to the iPod shuffle is complete, all the songs now on the iPod shuffle appear in the listing window. As you can with any playlist, click and drag to rearrange the order of the songs as they appear on the iPod shuffle. The randomized playback—the vaunted "shuffle"—takes effect only if the slider switch on the back of the iPod shuffle is switched to the "shuffle" position; if it's in the straight-playback position (the middle), playback occurs according to the play order you specify in iTunes by dragging songs into position according to your taste.

▶ TIP

There's no need to wait for iTunes to finish transferring songs to the iPod shuffle before you start rearranging them; even while iTunes and the iPod shuffle are synchronizing, you can reorder or delete songs, and your changes are immediately reflected on the device.

Select a song and press **Delete** or **Del** to remove it from the iPod shuffle; switch to the library source and drag songs from it to the iPod shuffle to fill in the gaps created by your deletions. If you disabled the **Replace all songs when Autofilling** option, you can simply click **Autofill** again to pick enough randomly selected songs to fill the rest of the device, leaving the existing songs alone.

As soon as the data transfer is finished and iTunes displays **iPod update is complete**, you can unplug the iPod shuffle from your computer. If you had selected **Enable disk use** in the **Preferences** window, you must eject (unmount) the device first by clicking the **Eject** icon next to the iPod shuffle's name in the **Source** pane; otherwise you risk data loss or corruption.

45 Transfer Your Music to a Mobile Device

✓ BEFORE YOU BEGIN

9 Import a Music CD into iTunes
42 Transfer Your Music to Your iPod

→ SEE ALSO

83 Transfer and View Contacts
84 Transfer and View iCal Calendar Items (Mac only)

After you've filled your iTunes **Library** with music from your CDs, you'll want a way to carry them with you. Although Apple wants everyone to buy an iPod for that task, not everyone has jumped on board that bandwagon yet. In particular, people who already own Portable Digital Assistants—those devices can be powered by Palm OS or be of Microsoft's Pocket PC persuasion—might be reluctant to add yet another geek toy to their utility belts just to listen to music. Although the iPod has PDA-like functionality—such as the ability to view contacts, calendar items, and text notes, and to take voice notes using third-party add-on software—that doesn't make it a PDA. In this day and age, when your PDA might also be your cell phone and your digital camera, it seems sensible to want to use it to play your iTunes' music as well.

Copying your iTunes' music to your Palm PDA, Pocket PC, or Microsoft Smartphone is not a function that's built into iTunes—you must purchase and install third-party software for this. You also cannot transfer copy-protected ***AAC*** songs (purchased from the iTunes **Music Store**) to the device; to play copy-protected AAC songs, you need an iPod. Playing unprotected AAC files is also often not supported on devices without special software, and you'll have to restrict yourself to MP3s (or uncompressed formats such as WAV). With these caveats, however, loading iTunes' music onto your PDA can be as seamless a process as it is with an iPod.

45

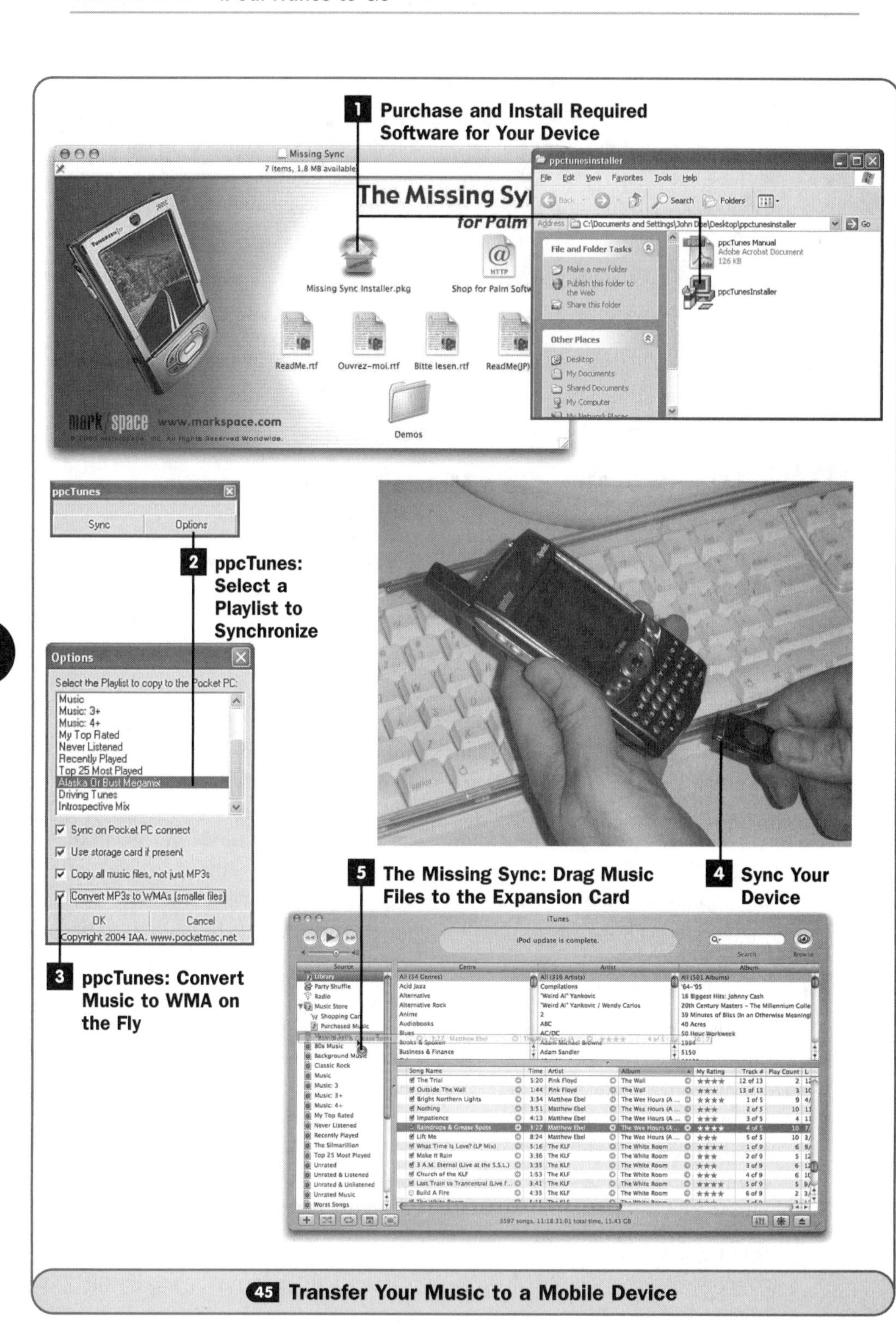

45 Transfer Your Music to a Mobile Device

1 Purchase and Install Required Software for Your Device

The first step is to determine what kind of device you have and, by extension, what software you must acquire before you can sync your music with it. This decision also, naturally, depends on what kind of computer you have.

On Windows: PocketMac produces a utility called **ppcTunes**, which integrates into Microsoft ActiveSync and lets you pick your iTunes' music by ***playlist***. It can (optionally) convert your ***MP3*** files to higher-compression ***WMA format*** as you sync it to save space. ppcTunes is available for $9.95 at **http://www.pocketmac.net/products/ppctunes/**. (If you have a Palm PDA, unfortunately, it does not appear that syncing your iTunes' music with it is currently possible from Windows.)

On the Mac: Whether you have a Palm OS or Pocket PC handheld device, the best software for the job is **The Missing Sync** by Mark/Space, Inc. This software enhances your Mac's ability to synchronize not just your iTunes' music, but all the rest of your computer's relevant information to your PDA, whether it's a Palm, Pocket PC, or even a T-Mobile Sidekick ("hiptop"). If you have a Pocket PC device, the Missing Sync is the only way to sync it with your Mac. If you have a Palm PDA, the Missing Sync actually does a better job than the official Palm Desktop software integrated with iSync. The Missing Sync sells for $39.95 at **http://www.missingsync.com**.

▶ NOTE

Most PDAs don't have enough built-in storage space to carry more than a few songs at once. Even with an expansion card, you'll have no more than 512MB or 1GB of space, the same as an iPod shuffle.

Purchase and download the appropriate software for your platform and PDA type; install it according to the procedures outlined in its included documentation. Be sure to read the instructions carefully—the various kinds of sync software differ from each other significantly, and they're changing rapidly as the needs of consumers develop—what you see may be nothing like what's described in this book.

2 ppcTunes: Select a Playlist to Synchronize

On Windows, run the ppcTunes program (it should be available in the **All Programs** menu after you install it). Register the program using the serial number you received when you purchased it. When you see the small two-button ppcTunes window, click **Options**.

Select a single playlist to copy to your Pocket PC device. ppcTunes will copy as many songs from this playlist as will fit on the device when you sync it.

▶ TIP

Enable the Use storage card if present option to indicate that the transferred music should go to the expansion card rather than the device's internal memory. This option usually enables you to put much more music on the device.

Enable **Sync on Pocket PC connect** if you want ppcTunes to sync the selected playlist each time you connect the device to your iTunes' computer.

3 ppcTunes: Convert Music to WMA on the Fly

To save as much space as possible (at the expense of some audio quality), enable the **Convert MP3s to WMAs (smaller files)** check box. This option re-encodes the selected songs during transfer, resulting in files about half the size of the original MP3s. The original songs in iTunes are not changed by this option.

Click **OK** and quit ppcTunes.

4 Sync Your Device

Connect your device (the Pocket PC or Palm) to your computer and press the **Sync** button on the cradle or cable if necessary. If you're using a Pocket PC with Windows, ppcTunes launches during the normal sync process and copies your selected playlist's songs to the device. After you disconnect the device, you can use the mobile version of Windows Media Player on the device to play your transferred songs.

5 The Missing Sync: Drag Music Files to the Expansion Card

On the Mac, with the Pocket PC or Palm device connected, look in the **Source** pane in the iTunes' window; you should see a new item labeled **Missing Sync** (or a similar label that indicates your device's brand). This item is a representation of your device's storage medium. You can now load songs onto the device by dragging them from the library view to the **Missing Sync** item, just as though it were an iPod mounted in manual mode. After you disconnect the device, you can play your transferred songs using Windows Media Player (on Pocket PC devices) or any available Palm music-player application, such as Pocket Tunes (available from **http://www.pocket-tunes.com/**).

46 Find and Play Music on the iPod

✔ BEFORE YOU BEGIN	→ SEE ALSO
36 Rate Your Music	48 Transfer Only Preferred Music to the iPod
42 Transfer Your Music to Your iPod	49 Create an On-the-Go Playlist

After your iPod is full of music, it's finally time to get down to what you really bought it for: listening to it wherever you go.

The iPod interface is designed to be a physical manifestation of iTunes' controls and navigation system. It doesn't work exactly the same way—controls such as sliders for volume control and mouse navigation just aren't possible on a device the size and shape of the iPod. Instead, the iPod's navigation wheel takes the place of your mouse's control of iTunes' scroll bars and volume slider, and the **Select** button in the center of the wheel takes the place of the mouse button. The **Play/Pause** button works the same as in iTunes, as do the **Forward** and **Back** buttons. The remaining button, **Menu**, takes care of navigating back up through the menu system after you've drilled down to a particular screen.

With these control mappings in mind, think about how you'd navigate iTunes itself: You play music either by selecting a ***playlist*** and clicking **Play**, or by navigating through the **Browse** lists to find the music you want and then double-clicking a song or pressing **Play**. How you'd navigate in iTunes tells you how to navigate the iPod to get to the same selection of music.

1 Start at the Main Menu

First make sure that the **Hold** switch (on the top of the unit) is not engaged; if the iPod's screen is blank, press any button to wake up the iPod from sleep. It's possible that what appears on the display is a deeply buried menu such as **Songs** or **Settings**, or the **Now Playing** screen; to return to the Main Menu, press **Menu** several times until you see the top-level options (**Music**, **Extras**, **Settings**, and so on) and the iPod can't back up any further.

2 Shuffle Songs

The easiest way to start your iPod playing, and perhaps the one you'll use most often, is **Shuffle Songs**. This option, with a single touch of the **Select** button, makes a single huge playlist out of all the songs on the iPod, shuffles them into a random order, and then begins playing them.

46 Find and Play Music on the iPod

▶ TIP

If you don't like a song that comes up in **Shuffle Songs** mode, just press the **Forward** button to skip to the next one. Remember that the **Last Played** count is incremented at the end of the song, so unless you listen to a song all the way through, iTunes won't count it as having been listened to.

After the iPod has been playing music for several seconds, it switches to the **Now Playing** screen. This screen shows you the name of the current song as well as its artist and album information; it also shows the progress bar indicating how far through the song it's played, and (if you have an iPod photo) the song's album art. Press **Menu** to return to the Main Menu, where the **Now Playing** option is an extra entry at the bottom of the list; if you don't do anything for a few seconds, the iPod reverts to the **Now Playing** screen.

▶ **NOTE**

To display album art on your iPod photo, you must enable the **Display album artwork on your iPod** check box on the **Music** tab in the **iPod** pane of the iTunes **Preferences** window.

3 Play a Playlist

To play a playlist, first start at the Main Menu as in step 1; then select the **Music** option and press **Select**. Roll the wheel to highlight the **Playlists** option in the **Music** menu; press **Select** again. All your iTunes' playlists are shown in the next screen.

▶ **TIP**

While a song is playing and the **Now Playing** screen is showing, you can control the iPod's sound volume simply by rolling the navigation wheel back and forth.

Roll the wheel to move the cursor to the playlist you want to play. To begin playing the playlist from the beginning, press the **Play/Pause** button, not the **Select** button—press **Select** to open the playlist so that you can browse its contents. If you want to start the playlist at a specific song, press **Select** to browse the playlist, scroll using the wheel until you highlight the song you want, and then press **Select** one final time (alternatively, press **Play/Pause**).

Choose **Settings** from the Main Menu and turn on **Shuffle** (by toggling the **Shuffle** option to **Songs** or **Albums** mode, which proceeds through random selections of songs or whole randomly selected albums, respectively), to make the iPod skip randomly to another song in the selected category (artist, album, genre, playlist, and so on) after it finishes playing any song.

4 Play an Entire Genre, Artist, or Album

Press **Menu** repeatedly to return to the Main Menu. Select the **Music** option again, as you did in step 3; this time, choose an option such as **Artists**, **Albums**, or **Genres**. When you select one of these options, all the entries within that category are selected: for example, all the albums represented by the music copied to your iPod from your iTunes **Library** are listed alphabetically in the **Albums** menu.

Scroll to select an album name, then press **Play/Pause** to play that album from the beginning. Alternatively, open the album by pressing **Select**, scroll to a specific song you want to hear, and press **Select** or **Play/Pause**. The album plays starting with the selected song.

You can play the entire contents of any category by selecting that category name and pressing **Play/Pause**; for example, if you navigate into the **Artists** menu and scroll to highlight the Eagles, pressing **Play/Pause** plays all the Eagles' songs in all their albums from beginning to end, just as they're sorted in iTunes itself according to the inherent cascading sort behaviors defined by the songs' ***info tags***.

▶ **TIP**

The iPod's navigation wheel features *acceleration*, a term that describes faster perceived motion of the cursor in response to fast or sustained motion of the input device. In other words, in the case of the iPod, the longer you continuously rotate the wheel, the faster it scrolls through the options on the screen. If you have hundreds or thousands of songs or albums on your iPod, this feature makes it possible to zero in on a particular entry in the alphabetical list without having to roll and roll the wheel for minutes on end. Learning to control the wheel's acceleration takes a little bit of practice, but before long, it comes naturally.

5 Play a Specific Song

To play a specific song, start at the Main Menu (press **Menu** repeatedly until the iPod can back up no further). Navigate into **Music** once more, and then into the **Songs** submenu. All the songs on the iPod are listed in alphabetical order here. Scroll through them using the wheel, taking advantage of the wheel's acceleration to zoom in on the song you want. Press **Select** or **Play/Pause** to begin playing that song. When the song is over, the iPod proceeds to the next song in the list.

▶ **TIP**

To scan through a playing song to a particular point, first go to the **Now Playing** screen (either by navigating to it from the Main Menu, or by simply waiting a few seconds for the iPod to switch to it automatically); then press **Select** to switch to scan mode. Use the wheel to move the playhead back and forth through the song. When you stop moving the playhead, the iPod resumes normal playback at the point where you put the playhead.

47 Rate Your Music on the iPod

✔ BEFORE YOU BEGIN

42 Transfer Your Music to Your iPod
46 Find and Play Music on the iPod

➔ SEE ALSO

36 Rate Your Music
48 Transfer Only Preferred Music to the iPod
73 Train iTunes to Play Your Favorite Music

It's important to let iTunes know what music you like and what music you'd rather avoid. You saw how to set star ratings on your songs in iTunes in 36 **Rate Your Music**; you can do the same thing on the iPod as well, setting star ratings on each song as you listen to it. When you synchronize the iPod with your iTunes **Library**, the star ratings you set on the iPod are incorporated back into the ***info tags*** of your songs in iTunes. Any ***Smart Playlists*** you might have defined using the **My Rating** field are updated to reflect your new settings. By diligently tagging each song you play with an appropriate rating, iTunes and the iPod both gain the ability to present music you'll like, making your listening experience better and better the more you use them.

47

1 Play Music on the iPod

As described in 46 **Find and Play Music** on the iPod, navigate to any playlist or other music source on the iPod and start the music playing with the **Play/Pause** or **Select** button.

2 Switch to Rating Mode

While a song is playing, and after you've decided how many stars it's worth (from 1 to 5, the more the better), press the **Select** button twice. The first press puts the iPod into scan mode, which lets you skip immediately to an arbitrary point in the song by rotating the wheel. The second press, however, puts the iPod into rating mode, where the song's star rating (if set) is shown below the track, artist, and album names.

3 Set a Rating

Use the wheel to set the number of stars you want to assign the song. If a rating has already been set, the wheel adjusts the number of stars up or down; otherwise, it begins at the default of zero stars and increases the number of stars as you rotate the wheel clockwise.

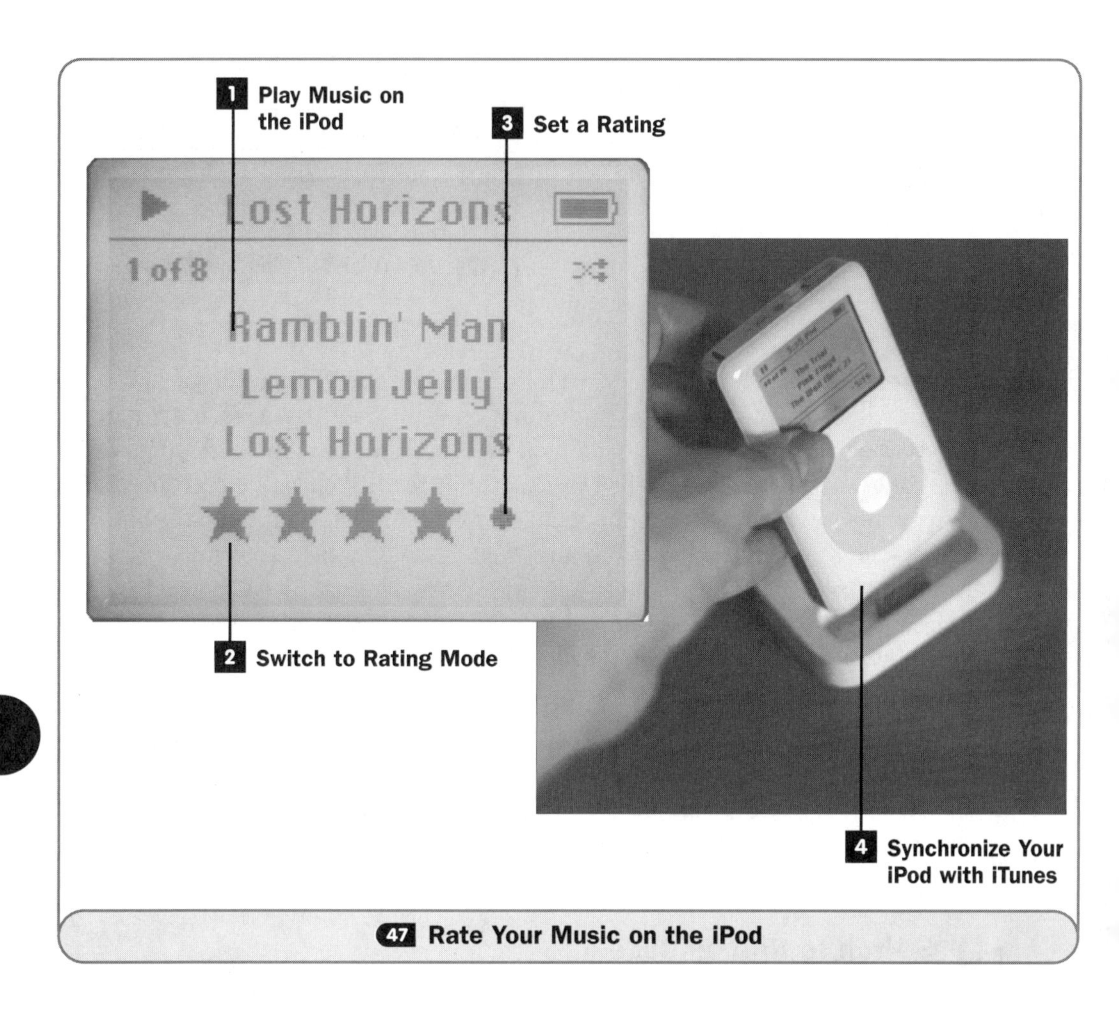

47 Rate Your Music on the iPod

Press the **Select** button to set the star rating, or just wait a few seconds to let the iPod automatically go back to the ordinary **Now Playing** screen that shows the progress through the song. The rating is set.

Repeat this process for every unrated song the iPod plays for you.

▶ NOTE

The iPod saves information about the songs it's played (such as the star rating you've set and the **Last Played** field) on its internal disk as it plays; however, it only writes this information to the disk after every set of about five songs (the iPod has 32 megabytes of internal RAM, or temporary memory, which it fills with about five songs at a time to avoid accessing the disk too frequently). If you play a lot of music and set a lot of ratings, and then the iPod runs out of battery power and shuts down before you have a chance to synchronize it with iTunes, that information might be lost and won't be synchronized into your iTunes **Library**. Always be sure to sync your iPod after use!

4 Synchronize Your iPod with iTunes

Connect your iPod to your computer using the Dock or included cable as described in 42 **Transfer Your Music to Your iPod**. When iTunes has finished exchanging information with the iPod—transferring newly added music to it and downloading the changes you've made while on the go—you'll be able to view the songs you listened to on the iPod using the **Recently Played** Smart Playlist, or by sorting the library using the **Last Played** column; the ratings you set on these songs on the iPod should be reflected in your iTunes' window.

48 Transfer Only Preferred Music to the iPod

✔ BEFORE YOU BEGIN	➜ SEE ALSO
43 Use a Large iTunes Library with a Small iPod	36 Rate Your Music
35 Create a Smart Playlist	47 Rate Your Music on the iPod

Now that you know how to use a few of iTunes' more intricate features—***Smart Playlists***, the **My Rating** field, and iPod ***synchronization*** by ***playlist***—you can put them all together to help you use even a small-capacity iPod to its fullest potential. By using a Smart Playlist defined on the basis of the star ratings you've set on all the music in your library, you can fill the iPod to bursting with music that's defined automatically to be culled from among your favorite tunes, ensuring that although you might not have every piece of music you own in your pocket at all times, at least you'll always have the good stuff.

1 Connect the iPod

Connect the iPod to your computer using the Dock or the included cable, as described in 42 **Transfer Your Music to Your iPod**. Wait for the synchronization process to complete.

2 Determine Your iPod's Actual Capacity

With the iPod selected in the **Source** pane of the iTunes' window, use the capacity readout at the bottom of the song listing area to tell you what your iPod's practical disk capacity is. Add up the **Used** and **Free** numbers to get this figure. Don't just use the capacity printed on the back of your iPod—this latter number can be an inaccurate reflection of the actual formatted capacity of the iPod's disk. For instance, if you have a 20GB iPod, the actual capacity is about 18.6 gigabytes, or 19,046 megabytes (a gigabyte is 1024 megabytes).

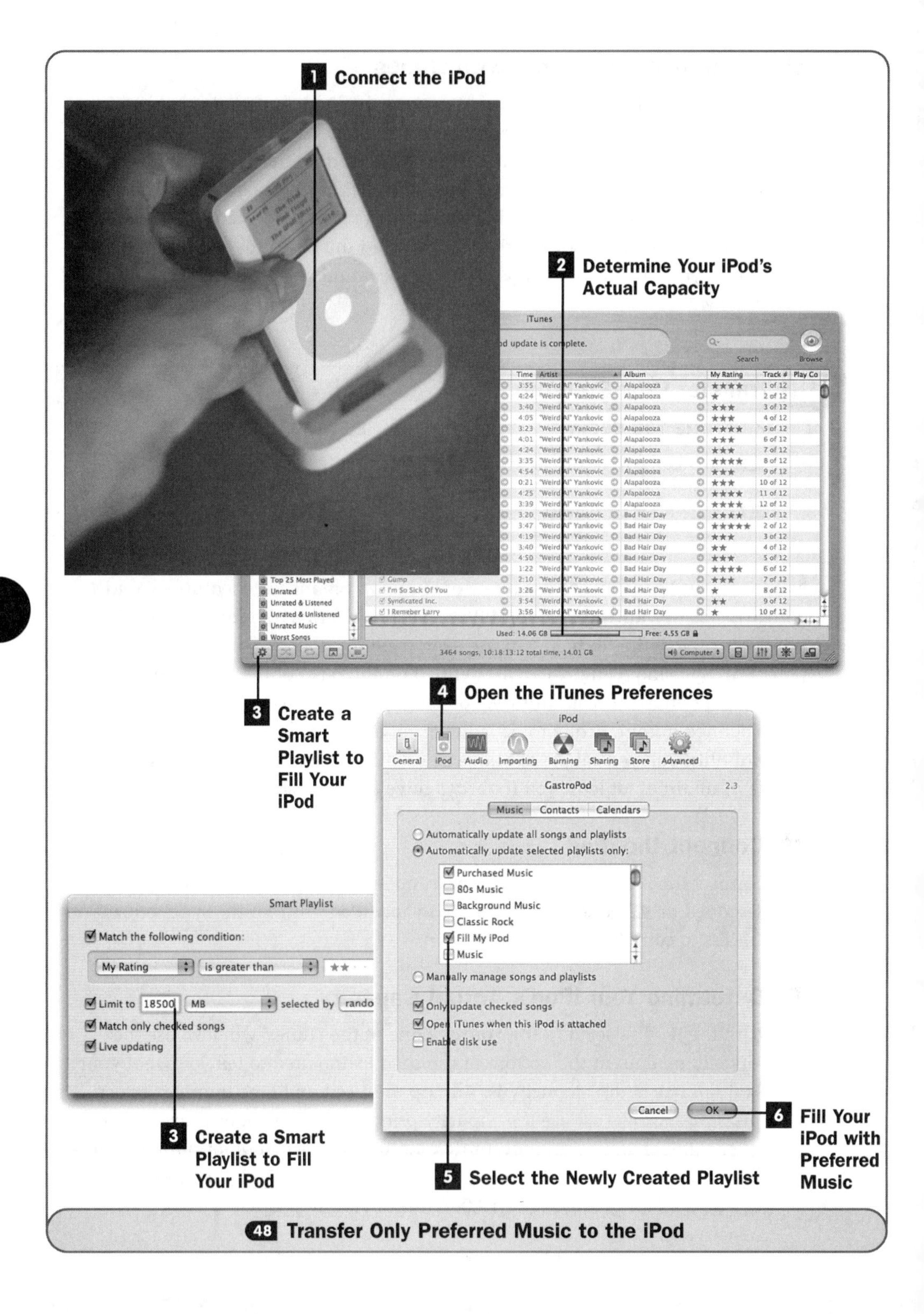

48 Transfer Only Preferred Music to the iPod

3 Create a Smart Playlist to Fill Your iPod

Create the Smart Playlist as described in 35 **Create a Smart Playlist**. Specify criteria according to your taste; you might want to choose only music rated three stars or higher, or you might opt for music from another Smart Playlist that only contains certain genres, or you might allow the playlist to include music from your entire library. The important part is the **Limit to** option.

Enable the **Limit to** check box; then, using the text input field and drop-down menu, specify the capacity of your iPod in megabytes (MB) rather than gigabytes (GB)—this approach allows you to define a playlist that's just a little bit less than the capacity of your iPod, which allows for some leeway in case you want to add a couple of other playlists as well. For example, if you have a 20GB iPod (whose physical capacity is 18.6 gigabytes or 19,046 megabytes), set up your Smart Playlist to be limited to **18,500** megabytes to ensure that there's extra space for other playlists of cool songs you want to make sure are always available on the iPod. (Adjust these numbers according to your tastes and needs.)

▶ TIP

You can avoid putting songs on the iPod that you've deemed unworthy of listening by disabling the check boxes next to their names in the iTunes Library. The first way is by enabling the Only update checked songs option in the iTunes Preferences window, on the General page of the iPod tab. When you're defining a Smart Playlist as in this step, the second way to avoid songs you don't like is to enable the Match only checked songs check box in the Smart Playlist's definition.

Finally, choose an appropriate policy from the **selected by** drop-down menu. You might choose to select songs with the **highest rating**, or that are the **most often played** or the **least recently played**. If you choose **random**, you get a broad cross-section of the music defined by the Smart Playlist's other criteria.

If you're selecting music by **random** and you want to get a different randomized selection of music, first lower the Smart Playlist's size to almost nothing (enter **1** in the text input field) and save the Smart Playlist; then edit it again to return it to its former size. This approach forces iTunes to rebuild the playlist from new random selections.

Click **OK** to save the Smart Playlist; give it a name such as **Fill My iPod**.

4 Open the iTunes Preferences

Open the iTunes **Preferences** window (choose **iTunes, Preferences** on the Mac, or **Edit, Preferences** in Windows). Click the **iPod** tab.

5 Select the Newly Created Playlist

In the box that appears under the second synchronization option (**Automatically update selected playlists only**), select the Smart Playlist you created in step 4 (**Fill My iPod** in this example) as one of the playlists to synchronize to your iPod. You can select other playlists too, as long as their contents overlap the new Smart Playlist's; any songs they contain that aren't in the **Fill My iPod** playlist will take up additional space on the iPod, and you'll have to adjust your playlist's settings accordingly.

6 Fill Your iPod with Preferred Music

Click **OK** to save the settings. iTunes synchronizes with your iPod, transferring onto it all the music in the Smart Playlist you defined. If you calculated the size of the Smart Playlist correctly, it should fill the iPod almost to its full capacity with music selected on the basis of your criteria. (If you went over the limit, iTunes tells you so in an error dialog box; simply edit the Smart Playlist and lower its **Limit** size slightly, then repeat steps 3 and 4.)

As you use the iPod, you can still navigate your music using the **Artists**, **Albums**, **Genres**, and other grouping options. The iPod just won't have all the songs that are in your iTunes **Library**—it will be missing songs that didn't match your criteria (for example, by not having a high enough rating). Thus, you can select and play an entire album straight through on the iPod without having to listen to the songs you don't like—they won't be on the iPod in the first place!

▶ TIP

Enable the Only update checked songs check box in the iPod tab of the iTunes Preferences window to exclude songs whose check box has been disabled. This approach lets you omit songs from the iPod on a piecemeal basis. See **70 Eliminate Duplicate Tracks** **for a further application of this technique.**

49 Create an On-The-Go Playlist

✔ BEFORE YOU BEGIN	→ SEE ALSO
46 Find and Play Music on the iPod	34 Create a Playlist

The iPod is primarily designed as a device whose content is loaded onto it in a one-way direction from iTunes, where you do all your music organization. You make all your changes in iTunes and then sync them to the iPod where you don't do much but passively enjoy the music. Aside from setting star ratings and having the iPod report **Last Played** dates back to iTunes, there doesn't seem to be much you can do with the iPod that's then reflected back into iTunes the way iTunes information is loaded onto the iPod.

That, however, is true only if you don't know about On-The-Go ***playlists***. This feature, well-hidden in the iPod interface, is a useful way to organize music as you listen to it on the road. If you decide you want to make a manual grouping of certain songs while you're thinking about it, no matter where you are, you can do so in the iPod itself instead of waiting until you're back at your computer with iTunes. The playlists you create on the iPod using this feature are then ***synchronized*** back into iTunes when you return the iPod to its Dock.

1 Navigate to Music on the iPod

As described in 46 **Find and Play Music on the iPod**, navigate through the music on your iPod using the various subcategories of the **Music** screen. Drill down through **Artists**, **Albums**, **Genres**, **Songs**, or other options to reach the music you want to organize into a playlist.

2 Add Songs to the On-The-Go Playlist

Use the wheel to scroll to each appropriate item you want to add to a newly created playlist. This can be a single song, a whole album, an entire artist's work, or any other listed item in any of the navigation listings. Place the highlight over the item using the wheel, and then press and hold the **Select** button. After about a second, the highlight blinks a few times; this means that the item has been added to a new On-The-Go playlist. Repeat this process by navigating to further songs or other items; hold down the **Select** button to add each one to the new playlist. The songs appear in the playlist in the sequence that you add them.

▶ NOTE

You can create new playlists using the On-The-Go mechanism, but you can't sort them manually or rename them. To do this, you must synchronize the iPod with your computer and then edit the playlists in iTunes. See step 6.

3 View or Play the On-The-Go Playlist

At any time, you can go back and view the songs you've added to the playlist. To do this, first return to the Main Menu (press **Menu** several times until **Main Menu** appears at the top of the screen). Then choose **Music**, then **Playlists**. Scroll to the bottom of the **Playlists** screen. The option at the very bottom is **On-The-Go**. Highlight this option and press **Select**.

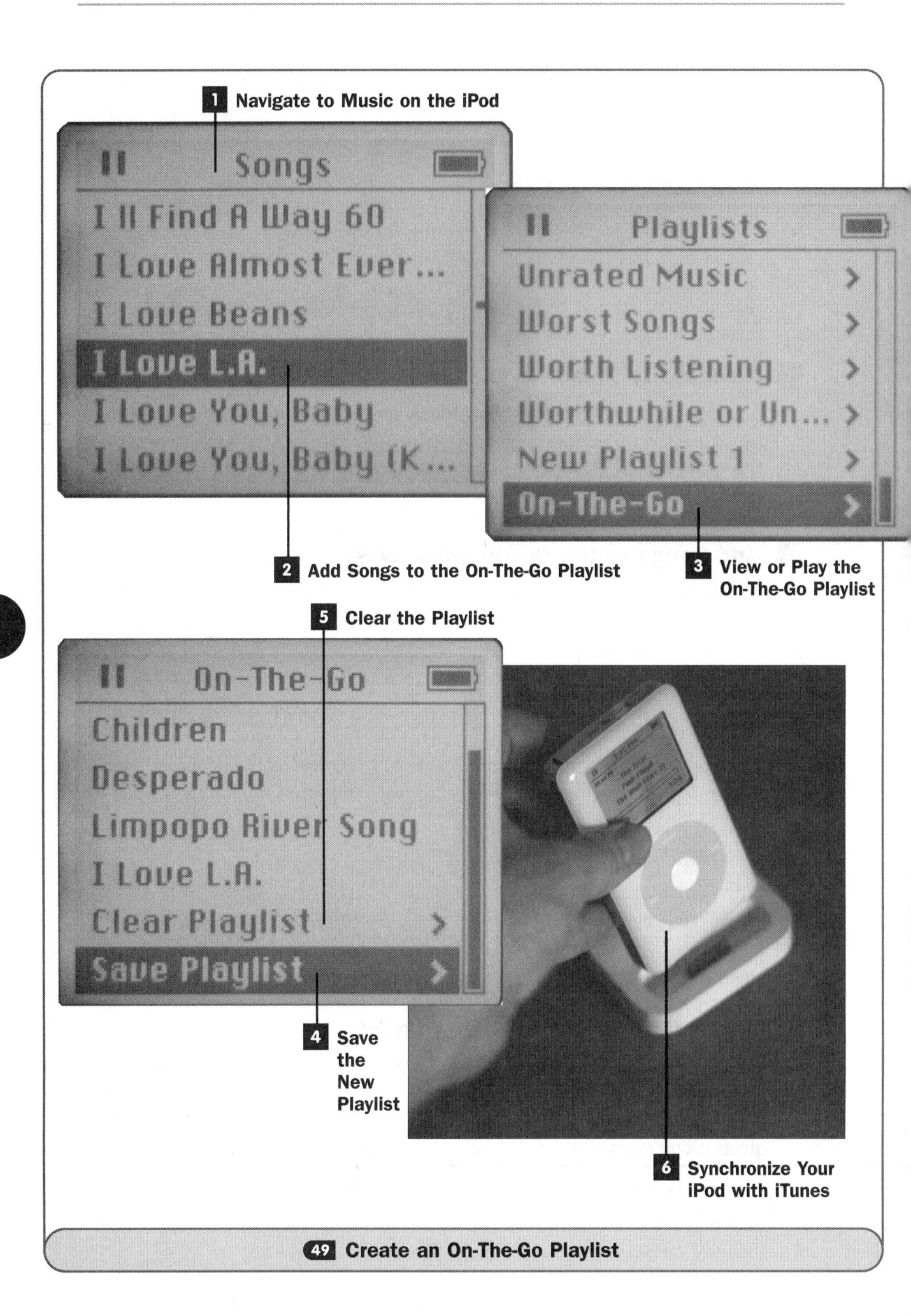

49 Create an On-The-Go Playlist

All the songs you added in steps 1 and 2 are listed in order in this screen. If you added groups of songs, such as entire albums, the songs in those groups are added in the order they're listed in the iPod's navigation lists.

Press **Play/Pause** to play the contents of the On-The-Go playlist as it stands.

4 Save the New Playlist

If you want to close off an On-The-Go playlist you've been building and begin creating a new one from scratch, you can do so by saving the first playlist. Scroll to the very bottom of the On-The-Go playlist screen. There are two options available: **Clear Playlist** and **Save Playlist**. Choose **Save Playlist** and press **Select**. In the next screen, you can either choose **Save Playlist** or **Cancel**; choose **Save Playlist**.

The On-The-Go playlist is saved as a new playlist with the name **New Playlist 1**. The new playlist appears right above the original On-The-Go playlist in the **Playlists** screen; the original On-The-Go playlist's contents are cleared.

You can now go back to your music and add more songs to the original On-The-Go playlist. If you save this new playlist, its name becomes **New Playlist 2**, and so on.

5 Clear the Playlist

To clear the contents of the current On-The-Go playlist without saving it, choose **Clear Playlist** from the On-the-Go playlist screen. Choose **Clear Playlist** in the confirmation screen. The accumulated songs are removed from the list and you can start over from scratch.

6 Synchronize Your iPod with iTunes

When you connect your iPod to your computer using the Dock or cable—transferring newly added music to it and downloading the changes you've made while on the go—you'll notice that one or more new playlists have been added to the **Source** pane in the iTunes' window: **On-The-Go 1**, **On-The-Go 2**, and so on. The numbers in these playlists correspond to the numbers of the On-The-Go playlists you created on the iPod; for instance, **New Playlist 1** on the iPod becomes **On-The-Go 1** in iTunes. Even if you did not save the current On-The-Go playlist, its contents are copied into a new playlist in iTunes with a number reflecting what number it would have been given if you'd saved it.

During the sync process, the newly renamed **On-The-Go #** playlists are copied back to the iPod, the iPod's **New Playlist #** entries are removed, and the active On-The-Go playlist is cleared.

You can now rename the **On-The-Go #** playlists within iTunes, rearrange the songs in them, and delete the ones you don't want (see **34 Create a Playlist** for more). The next time you sync your iPod, the changes are transferred back to it to match the newly edited playlists in iTunes.

50 Listen to an Audiobook

✔ **BEFORE YOU BEGIN**

20 Purchase Audio from the iTunes Music Store
33 Find and Play Music
46 Find and Play Music on the iPod

An ***audiobook*** is a special kind of digital music file that has some interesting and unique properties: namely, iTunes and the iPod both know how to keep track of where you stop listening to one. This is pretty important, considering that audiobooks—which are essentially the digital music equivalent of books on tape, and thus have an entire spoken-word version of a full-length book encoded into a single digital audio file—are typically very long, often several hours in length. (Leo Tolstoy's *War and Peace* is almost 61 hours long.) You aren't going to be able to listen to an entire audiobook all in one sitting, and you don't want to have to seek your way back to the point where you last stopped it every time you want to resume. You might even want to pause the audiobook in iTunes, resume listening to it on the iPod, and then switch back to iTunes for the remainder—and you particularly don't want to have to try to find your place in the file while you're jogging or driving.

▶ NOTE

Audiobooks are a little more specialized than simply being ***AAC*** or ***MP3*** files whose **Genre** is set to **Audiobooks**. Automatic resuming is only possible on audiobooks you purchase through the iTunes **Music Store** or through Audible (**http://www.audible.com**), a service that sells audiobooks in a manner similar to the iTunes **Music Store**. If you have an Audible account, audiobooks you purchase from Audible can be played in iTunes. Click the **Set** button next to **Use iTunes for Internet Music Playback** in the **General** tab of the iTunes **Preferences** window to ensure that iTunes can accept Audible's streamed content.

With iTunes and the iPod, it's easy to keep your place in an audiobook—in fact, it's automatic. Every time you stop playing the file, iTunes saves your place. When you want to start "reading" again, just select the file and press **Play**, and iTunes picks up again right where you left off. The same goes for the iPod—it remembers where you stopped playback last time (even if that was in iTunes) and resumes at that point. Synchronizing the iPod with iTunes ensures that the stopping point is always preserved regardless of where you want to pick up the audiobook again.

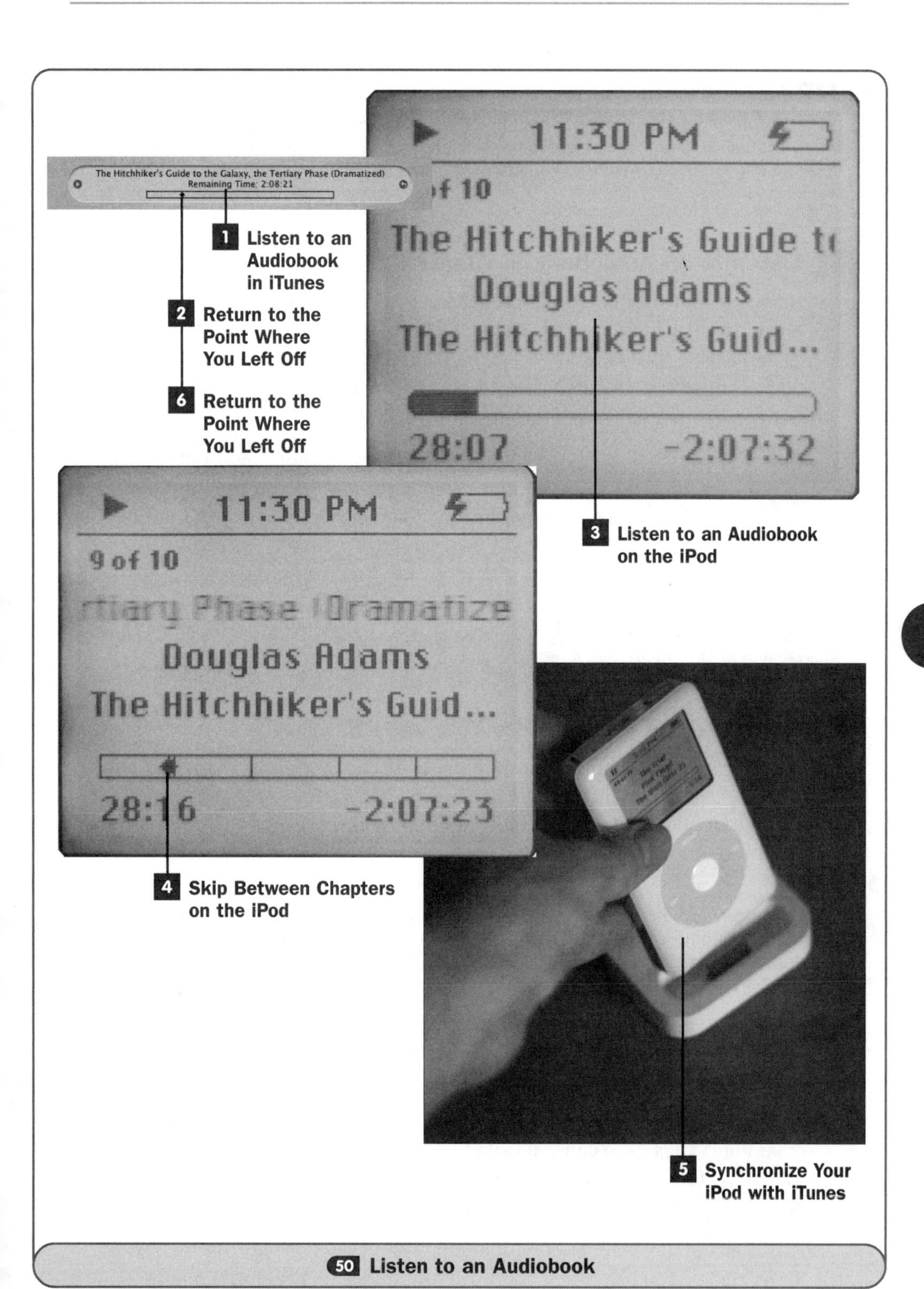

The Hitchhiker's Guide to the Galaxy, the Tertiary Phase (Dramatized)
Remaining Time: 2:08:21
1 Listen to an Audiobook in iTunes
2 Return to the Point Where You Left Off
6 Return to the Point Where You Left Off
11:30 PM
The Hitchhiker's Guide t
Douglas Adams
The Hitchhiker's Guid...
28:07
-2:07:32
3 Listen to an Audiobook on the iPod
11:30 PM
9 of 10
Douglas Adams
The Hitchhiker's Guid...
28:16
-2:07:23
4 Skip Between Chapters on the iPod
5 Synchronize Your iPod with iTunes
50 Listen to an Audiobook

▶ TIP

Owners of 4G iPods (including the iPod photo) have the option to play back audiobooks at any of three different pitch-adjusted speeds: **Normal**, **Slower**, or **Faster**. Choose one of these settings from the **Audiobooks** submenu of the **Settings** menu (under the Main Menu screen).

1 Listen to an Audiobook in iTunes

Navigate to the location of an audiobook you purchased from the iTunes **Music Store** or from Audible. These audiobooks can be anything from novels or non-fiction texts to radio shows, political speeches, or magazine articles, and are most easily found by navigating to the **Audiobooks** option in the **Genre** list.

Play the audiobook as you would any other song or music file: Double-click its name or select it and click **Play**. Listen for as long as you like, and then stop playback by clicking **Pause**, starting another song playing, or quitting iTunes.

50

▶ NOTE

An audiobook works the same way if you first start listening to it on the iPod: just press **Play/Pause** or skip to another song, and your place is saved.

2 Return to the Point Where You Left Off

The next time you want to return to the audiobook, simply select it and play it again; instead of starting over at the beginning, iTunes remembers where you last stopped and resumes playback at that exact point.

▶ TIP

To give yourself some context and a refresher about where you were in the audio stream, click and hold the **Back** button for several seconds to rewind the track. You can also drag the playhead all the way to the left in the ***scrub bar*** to start the audiobook over from the beginning.

3 Listen to an Audiobook on the iPod

Synchronize your iTunes **Library** with your iPod as discussed in 42 **Transfer Your Music to Your iPod** On the iPod, an audiobook behaves just like any other audio track: You can navigate to it by its artist (usually the author, but sometimes the person narrating the book) or by the title (found in the **Songs** listing). The album name is usually set to the same text as the title.

Play the audiobook by selecting it and pressing **Select** or **Play/Pause**. Listen for as long as you like; when you want to stop, press **Play/Pause** again.

4 Skip Between Chapters on the iPod

On the iPod, you can skip between internal chapter marks within the audiobook track. While the track is playing, press the **Select** button to change to scrub mode; the chapter marks are visible in the scrub bar. You can scrub manually to a specific point as you can with a regular track, or use the **Forward** and **Back** buttons to move directly to a chapter break point.

5 Synchronize Your iPod with iTunes

Connect your iPod to your computer using the Dock or included cable, as described in **42 Transfer Your Music to Your iPod**. During this process, the point at which you last stopped listening to the audiobook is synchronized with iTunes and saved as part of the information about the audiobook file.

▶ NOTE

If you listened to the audiobook on the iPod as well as in iTunes, the stopping point that "wins" is the one that occurred more recently.

6 Return to the Point Where You Left Off

Play the audiobook in iTunes. The audio track resumes where you left off listening on the iPod, just as though you'd done so in iTunes.

When you reach the end of the audiobook, the next time you play it, it begins at the beginning.

51 About the Care and Feeding of Your iPod

✔ BEFORE YOU BEGIN

Just jump right in!

The iPod is arguably the most desirable piece of consumer electronics in the world today; millions of people own them, and millions more pine for them. People who would never otherwise have considered buying an Apple product are discovering that there's simply no arguing with the iPod's ease of use, quality of production, or the ineffable "cool factor" of those white headphone cords and the device's iconic shape.

Yet reality sometimes doesn't mirror the fantasy created by the hype. The iPod is a piece of technology with electronic and mechanical components just like any computer accessory; likewise, it's prone to failures and degradation over time. Apple even engineered the iPod with several assumptions in mind, namely that people's music collections would grow fast enough to obligate them to buy new and larger iPods within a few years. This assumption permitted the Apple engineers to make design decisions that some people find controversial, such as making the battery non-replaceable, and using that great-looking (but scratch-prone) stainless-steel rear cover. The idea is that you'll want a bigger iPod before your battery becomes unusable or your iPod's back cover becomes too scratched up.

These observations perhaps betray a cynical outlook toward Apple's motives in designing the iPod, and more recent generations of the iPod show improvements in the technology that indicate that there's no malice aforethought in Apple's design decisions. The iPod is consistently rated very high in consumer reports that rank its initial quality and support; the company provides service that often goes above and beyond what the basic warranty would seem to guarantee, such as replacing iPods in-store with brand new units with no questions asked. Some original-generation iPods that were sold in the fall of 2001 are still going strong. Yet there's always the possibility of units that degrade faster than you think they ought to do, and it's hard under those circumstances to keep from wondering what—if anything—you did wrong.

If you've spent hundreds of dollars on an iPod, you're going to want to make sure you get your money's worth—you'll still look cool if you carry around an iPod that doesn't work, but obviously looks aren't everything. You want to ensure that your iPod will last as long as your interest in digital music does, even if that means keeping it in action for years and years, outliving Apple's own predictions for how long it should survive.

The following set of tips should help ensure that your iPod remains in top working order for a long time.

- **Keep the iPod's battery charged to its maximum capacity at all times.** The iPod uses a lithium-polymer or lithium-ion (Li-ion) battery that has somewhat different characteristics from the nickel-cadmium (NiCd) batteries you might be accustomed to in camera or laptop devices. Whereas NiCd batteries last longest if you discharge them completely (running them down to the point where they're completely out of juice) before recharging them, lithium-polymer and lithium-ion batteries (such as those used in the iPod) last longer if you keep them topped up as much as possible. These are known as ***shallow discharge*** characteristics, as opposed to the ***deep discharge*** characteristics of nickel-cadmium batteries.

▶ KEY TERM

Deep discharge—**Battery characteristics where optimum longevity and performance result from discharging the battery completely before recharging it.**

Shallow discharge—**Battery characteristics where optimum longevity and performance result from keeping the battery's charge "topped up" at all times and preventing the charge from running down all the way.**

Don't allow the iPod's charge to dip below 50% if you can help it. Whenever the iPod is not in use, keep it in its Dock or connected to a power source such as a computer or the external power supply. If you use the iPod in the car, try to use a power adapter that connects the iPod to the car's cigarette lighter or power outlet, thus ensuring that the batteries aren't being drained during normal use.

Use additional common-sense precautions such as making sure that the iPod isn't playing music endlessly when you leave it unattended (use the **Hold** switch to ensure that the iPod doesn't wake up and start playing music in response to a jostle while it's in your backpack). Make sure that the backlight isn't on all the time (the backlight can use a lot of power). The same is true of any operations that cause frequent hard drive access, such as skipping songs randomly or playing the **Music Quiz** game (see 81 **Play iPod Games**).

▶ WEB RESOURCE

http://www.ipodbatteryfaq.com

The iPod Battery FAQ (Frequently Asked Questions list) is an excellent source of answers to any questions you might have about how to improve your iPod's battery life. The site also has links to resources that will help you replace a dead battery for a small cost, as well as news on class-action lawsuits that Apple has settled with owners of older iPods with defective batteries.

- **Purchase an AppleCare extended warranty for your iPod.** You get 90 days of free tech support and a year of free service with your iPod purchase, but those months go by fast. For an extra $59, you can extend both service and support coverage to two years from the purchase date. This coverage protects not just your iPod, but any accessories that come with it—the headphones or earbuds, the Dock, the battery, and so on. You can pick up the AppleCare plan anytime within the iPod's first complimentary year of service coverage. With the service coverage in effect, if anything goes wrong with your iPod—a battery that runs down too fast, a headphone jack or Dock connector that becomes loose, an LCD screen that flickers, or even a back cover that doesn't quite fit right—just bring it in to any Apple Store, and you'll walk out the door with a brand-new unit. You can also call the AppleCare number to set up an exchange through the mail. It's quite a bargain—especially considering that any replacement unit you get comes with its own fresh year of coverage. Taking advantage of these warranty options means that the only reason you ever have to buy a new iPod is if your music collection outgrows it.

▶ WEB RESOURCE

http://store.apple.com

Visit the online Apple Store at this URL or go into any Apple Store to buy an AppleCare plan.

- **Invest in some protective gear for your iPod.** It might be tempting to keep your iPod loose in your shirt pocket or hold it in your hand so that everyone can see it, but that's just asking for trouble—microscopic dust can wreak havoc on the iPod's polished back surface, and before you know it, it'll be scuffed and ugly. Prevent this problem by getting a good belt clip or carrying pouch that has a soft backing surface without any protruding edges or creases that can trap dust. Apple also sells "iPod socks" through the online Apple Store or retail locations. These little multicolored fabric sleeves might look silly, but they get the job done: They keep the back from getting scuffed and also cushion the iPod in case of a fall.

51

If your iPod's back cover becomes scuffed or scratched, all is not lost: see 101 **Turn a Scratched iPod into a Brushed Metal iPod** for an idea that might help make it look nice again.

iPod socks come in a variety of colors. Don't laugh—they work!

7

Sharing Your Music with Others

IN THIS CHAPTER:

The iPod isn't the only way to take your iTunes' music with you away from your computer—it's just the most personal. iTunes was originally released into a world in which the most popular legitimate way to enjoy digital music was to create "mix" CDs of the music you own, which you could then share with your friends by playing the CDs at parties or in the car. Today, the digital music industry has evolved in a number of significant ways, as have the number of ways to let your friends and family enjoy your music; but the ability to burn custom CDs still remains as fundamental a part of iTunes as ever. It's even attained its own supporting features, such as the ability to print attractive custom CD jewel case inserts based on the album art in your music, or to create MP3 data CDs that contain hundreds of songs instead of just a couple dozen, and that play in any of the popular car stereo units or home DVD players that read MP3 discs.

In the age of the wireless home network, Apple has enhanced iTunes to take advantage of emerging technology to give you even more music-sharing options. The modern home has more than one computer in it, which implies more than one copy of iTunes under the same roof; these copies of iTunes can "see" each other on the network and play each other's music, just as your daughter might borrow your CDs to play in her room. With ***AirTunes*** technology as part of the AirPort Express wireless base station, you can even hook up your computer to the big A/V system in the den—no wires needed—and play your iTunes' music over the best speaker system in the house. This technology is all built into iTunes, just waiting for you to discover its potential.

52 Create an Audio CD from a Playlist

✓ BEFORE YOU BEGIN

9 Import a Music CD into iTunes
20 Purchase Audio from the iTunes Music Store
34 Create a Playlist

→ SEE ALSO

53 Customize CD Burning Options
55 Print a CD Jewel Case Insert with Album Art

"Rip, Mix, Burn," exhorted Apple's ad when iTunes was released. The whole idea of digital music management is that you can take the music you already own, import it into your computer, organize it according to your own likes and dislikes, and then make your own "mix" CDs of your favorite music arranged just the way you want it.

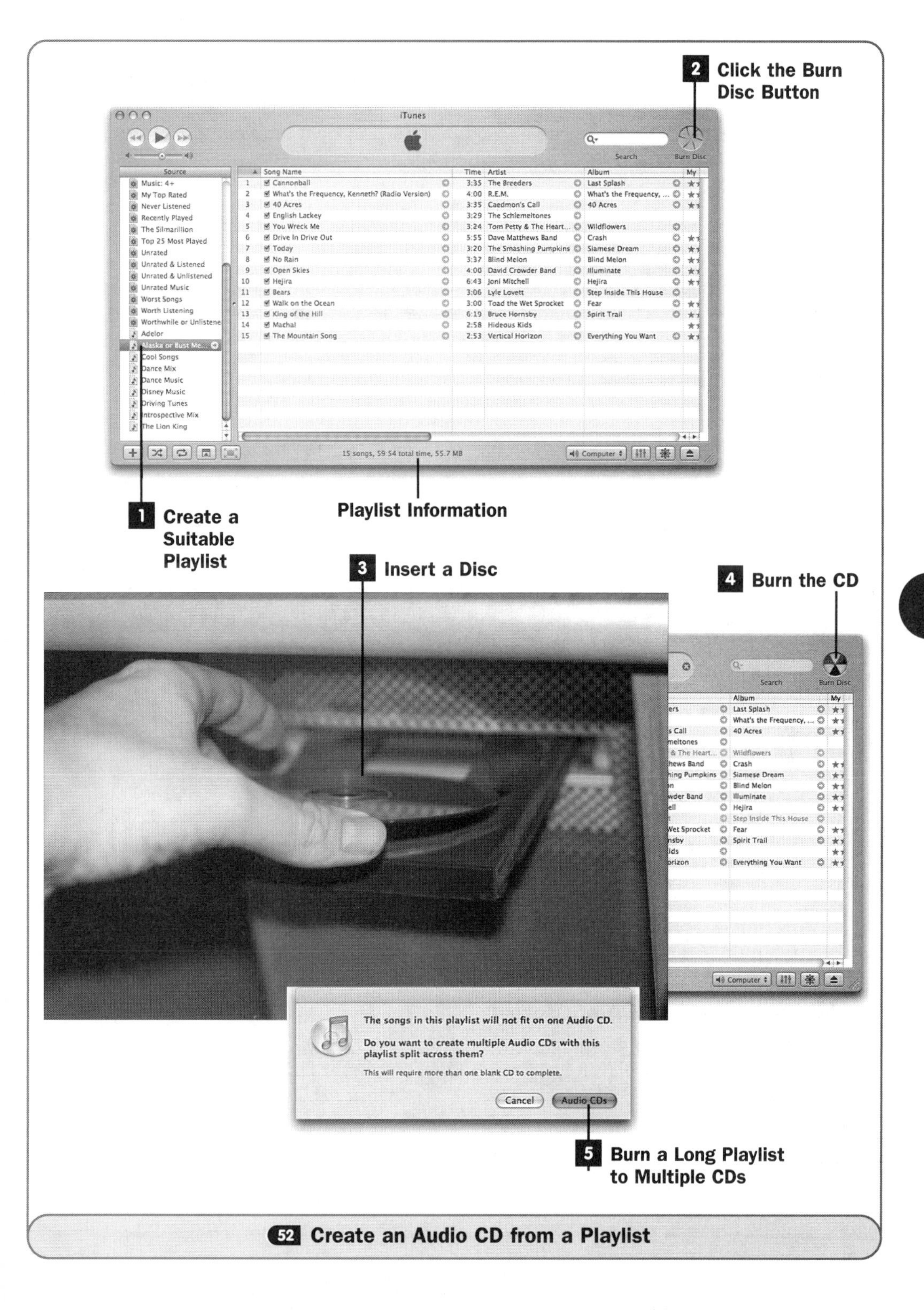
2 Click the Burn Disc Button
1 Create a Suitable Playlist
Playlist Information
3 Insert a Disc
4 Burn the CD
The songs in this playlist will not fit on one Audio CD.
Do you want to create multiple Audio CDs with this playlist split across them?
This will require more than one blank CD to complete.
Cancel
Audio CDs
5 Burn a Long Playlist to Multiple CDs

52 Create an Audio CD from a Playlist

52

iTunes makes creating your own mix CDs nearly as simple as importing the music in the first place. Simply create a ***playlist*** containing the music you want to burn onto a CD; then insert a blank writable CD into the CD-ROM drive, and let iTunes do the rest. The tracks are burned to the CD in their native audio format (***CDDA***) in the order you specify. You can then play the CD in your car, on your portable stereo, at a dance, or wherever your fancy strikes.

▶ KEY TERM

Compact Disc Digital Audio (CDDA)**—The standard specification for mastering compact discs, which includes a specific format for the uncompressed audio data in each track.**

1 Create a Suitable Playlist

The first step in creating a custom mix CD is to make a playlist containing the songs you want on the disc. As discussed in **34 Create a Playlist**, navigate into the library and drag songs from it into the playlist, keeping in mind that typical CD-R discs can hold up to either 71 or 74 minutes of music. Don't make the playlist any longer than this! Use the statistics shown at the bottom of the iTunes' window to determine how many minutes your playlist will last. (Don't pay attention to the number of megabytes, or MB, that is reported for the playlist; the files become much larger when they're written in uncompressed CDDA format on the disc. The important thing for this task is the **total time** number.)

▶ TIPS

iTunes can burn playlists that are longer than what will fit on a single CD, if you have multiple blank CDs to use. See step 5 for details.

Hold down Ctrl or ⌘ while clicking a check box next to a song name to enable or disable *all* the check boxes in the current listing.

To skip burning certain songs in the playlist, disable the check boxes next to the names of those songs in the list.

2 Click the Burn Disc Button

When you're viewing the playlist, the **Browse** button in the top-right corner of the iTunes' window becomes a **Burn Disc** button; click it to begin the creation of the new disc.

3 Insert a Disc

In its display oval at the top of the window, iTunes prompts you to insert a blank disc and tells you the total burned capacity and playing time of the selected playlist (this can differ from the reported length of the playlist at the bottom of the iTunes' window if you disabled any of the songs' check boxes). If your computer has a CD tray, it is automatically ejected so that you can insert the blank disc. Otherwise, insert the disc into the drive slot until the drive pulls it in.

When the disc is inserted, iTunes recognizes the blank media and automatically changes the message in the display oval to a prompt telling you to click the **Burn Disc** button again (it is now throbbing gently) to begin burning the playlist to the disc.

If you don't click **Burn Disc** within about 10 seconds, iTunes cancels the operation and ejects the disc.

▶ TIP

On the Mac, you can also insert the CD before you click the Burn Disc button the first time; if you do, Mac OS X prompts you whether it should prepare the disc for use as an audio CD (by switching to iTunes) or a data CD (by mounting it in the Finder). If you choose to open iTunes, iTunes can then burn a playlist immediately without prompting you to insert a disc.

4 Burn the CD

Click the **Burn Disc** button the second time to begin the burn process. When the process is complete, the CD appears in the **Source** pane in the iTunes window to show the tracks you've just burned.

You can now eject the disc from your computer; its contents are written as standard uncompressed CDDA audio, which means that any CD player can play it—even old ones from the 80s.

5 Burn a Long Playlist to Multiple CDs

When you insert the blank disc (as in step 3), iTunes checks its capacity and compares it to the length of the playlist you're trying to burn. If the playlist contains too much music to fit on the disc, iTunes asks whether you want to burn the entire playlist to multiple CDs, or to cancel the burn process so that you can trim the playlist down to fit on a single disc.

If you choose to burn the playlist to multiple discs, iTunes burns as many tracks as will fit onto the first disc, and then prompts you to insert another blank disc to continue. This process continues until all the tracks in the playlist have been burned onto discs. Be sure to label the discs appropriately so that you don't forget their sequence!

▶ NOTE

iTunes will remember the track names of the burned discs if you insert them again into your computer; but other CD players don't have that ability. It's easy to lose track of what's on your mix CDs, especially if you burned a long playlist onto several discs. See **55 Print a CD Jewel Case Insert with Album Art** **for a way to ensure that these burned CDs don't become unlabeled mystery discs floating uselessly around the house.**

53 Customize CD Burning Options

✔ BEFORE YOU BEGIN	→ SEE ALSO
52 Create an Audio CD from a Playlist	54 Create an MP3 CD 64 Customize Importing Options 94 Back Up Your Music to CD or DVD

One of the biggest challenges faced by Apple in bringing iTunes to Windows has been supporting all the different kinds of CD ***burners*** (drives capable of writing data to optical discs such as ***CD-R***, ***CD-RW***, and ***DVD-R***) found in Windows PCs. Apple's Macintosh computers have traditionally used drives from known manufacturers with drivers written in-house and built into the operating system; thus it has been easy for Apple to design iTunes to support the drives used by Macs. But in taking iTunes to Windows, Apple had to develop support for dozens more drive manufacturers and models than they'd ever used before. This support is good, but not perfect; Apple can't test every possible hardware configuration to ensure that it'll work with your particular PC. You might find that your computer can produce only audio CDs that have frequent errors or that can't be read at all.

52

▶ KEY TERMS

Burner—A CD or DVD drive capable of creating written, or *burned*, discs as well as reading them. Most modern computers are sold with CD burners, and many come with DVD burners as well.

CD-R—Writable compact disc. A CD-R can be burned once, and after that its contents cannot be changed. A CD-R or CD-RW can hold 650 or 700 megabytes of data, depending on the format.

CD-RW—Rewritable compact disc. A CD-RW can be burned multiple times, usually up to a few dozen times.

DVD-R—Writable digital versatile disc. A DVD can hold 4.7 gigabytes of data and generally costs significantly more than a writable CD. Data on a DVD is heavily compressed, making the format much more complex than that of a CD. Some DVD formats, such as DVD+RW and DVD-RW, can be written to more than once. "Dual-layer" discs cost more and can store twice as much data.

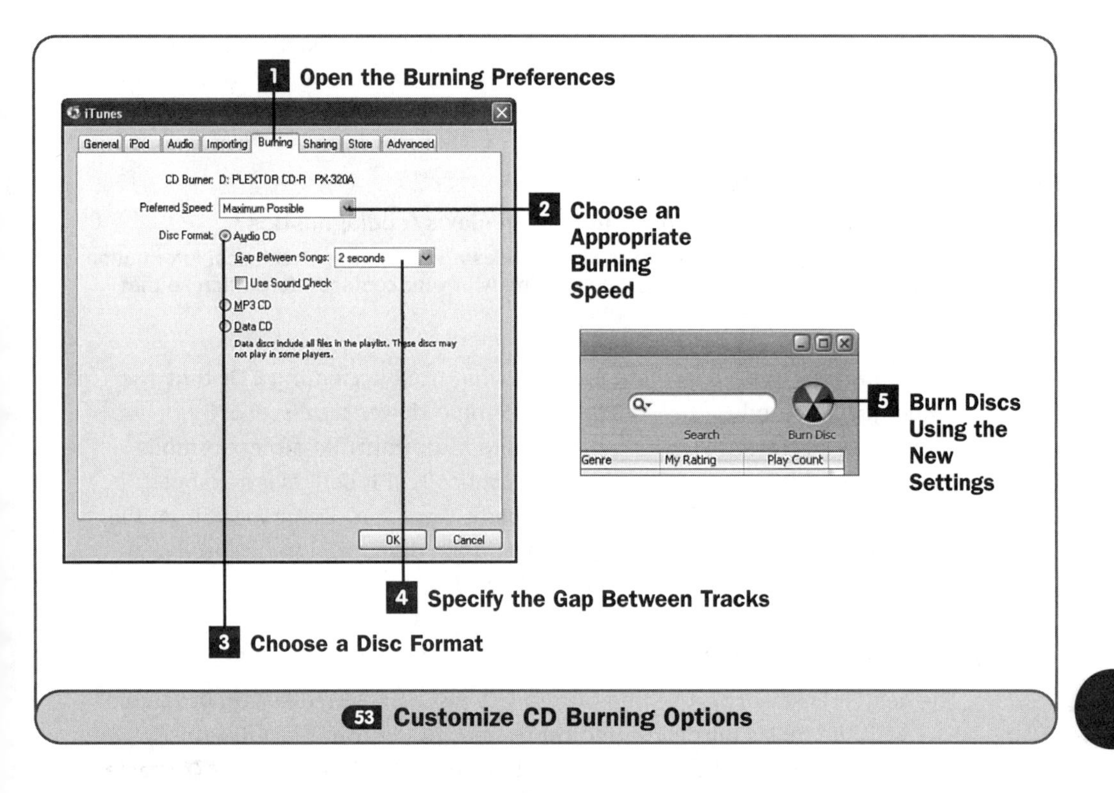

53 Customize CD Burning Options

This task describes some ways to adjust your disc-burning settings in ways that might help the quality of your burned discs; it also discusses some settings you can adjust to control the structure of the discs you create and how they sound when played.

1 Open the Burning Preferences

Open the iTunes **Preferences** window (choose **iTunes, Preferences** on the Mac or **Edit, Preferences** in Windows). Click the **Burning** tab to display the options for burning discs.

2 Choose an Appropriate Burning Speed

First, verify that iTunes recognizes your burner. Following the **CD Burner** entry should be the name and model of your CD/DVD drive. If you instead see a message such as **Burner or software not found**, either you don't have a burner or iTunes doesn't recognize the one you have. The good news is that you're probably not alone; you can sign in at the iTunes Discussions boards (available from **http://www.apple.com/support/itunes/**, or by choosing **Help, iTunes and Music Store Service and Support** or **Help, Music Store**

Customer Service from the menu) and post a question regarding your burning hardware. Chances are that someone else uses the same hardware and might have tips for you.

▶ WEB RESOURCE

http://www.apple.com/support/itunes/windows/cddiagnostics/

The iTunes for Windows CD Diagnostics site provides a way to gather technical information about your CD drive and submit it to Apple, along with your contact information so that they can get back to you with an answer.

If your burner is recognized but you're having trouble creating CDs that sound good, you might benefit from choosing a slower burn speed. By default, the **Preferred Speed** option is set to **Maximum Possible**; normally iTunes slows down the burn process automatically if it detects errors, but sometimes this process doesn't work properly. Choose a slower speed from the drop-down menu (**1x** is the slowest, burning the disc at the same speed as it would be played).

3 Choose a Disc Format

The default **Disc Format** setting, **Audio CD**, lets iTunes create standard audio CDs with the music burned in uncompressed CDDA format just like an album you'd buy off the shelf. Other options include **MP3 CD** (see 54 **Create an MP3 CD**) or **Data CD or DVD** (see 94 **Back Up Your Music to CD or DVD**). An MP3 CD lets you put much more music on a single disc than an audio CD, but the player must be able to read MP3 CDs. Not all CD players do.

4 Specify the Gap Between Tracks

The **Audio CD** option has a couple of settings you can adjust. By default, the **Gap Between Songs** is set to **2 seconds**; you can change this to anything from no gap at all (**none**) to **5 seconds**, if you prefer the way a longer pause sounds. Choose **none** if you want to burn a copy of a live performance where the gap between tracks would be distracting and interrupt the flow of applause from one track to the next.

Enable the **Use Sound Check** check box to make the audio output on the disc adhere to the automatic leveling discussed in 40 **Auto-Level Song Volumes**. If this box is not enabled, all tracks on the disc are burned at the original levels of the CDs they came from, which might lead to variable volume levels from track to track on a mix CD. However, if the check box is enabled and you're burning a copy of a single CD (such as a comedy routine or live performance), iTunes might auto-level the individual tracks differently, which can be just as distracting.

5 Burn Discs Using the New Settings

Click **OK** to save the new burn settings. The next disc you burn, whether an audio CD, an MP3 CD, or a CD or DVD backup disc, will be created according to the settings you defined here.

54 Create an MP3 CD

✔ BEFORE YOU BEGIN	→ SEE ALSO
52 Create an Audio CD from a Playlist	56 Create an MP3 CD from Purchased AAC Music
53 Customize CD Burning Options	94 Back Up Your Music to CD or DVD

These days, the mix CD is starting to fall from favor as the preeminent way to create discs of your digital music. Without any inherent way to identify the track names or artists, and with the capacity to hold only about 75 minutes of music when you use uncompressed CDDA audio ***format***, you're stuck with burning dozens of discs if you want enough to keep you entertained on a long road trip.

The answer has come in the form of the ***MP3*** CD, which is a standard data compact disc whose contents—instead of a couple of dozen uncompressed CDDA files—are hundreds of much smaller MP3 files, which sound almost as good. Whereas the music on a standard audio CD lasts only a little more than an hour, an MP3 CD can hold up to 12 hours of music; what's more, the MP3 files retain all their info tags, such as each track's song name, artist, album, and genre, which can be read and displayed during normal playback by devices that can read MP3 CDs. More and more car audio systems entering the market today support MP3 CDs, and just about all commercial DVD players do as well—it's become a ubiquitous technology. Fortunately, iTunes makes it just as easy to create MP3 CDs as it does to burn standard audio discs.

▶ NOTE

The music on an MP3 CD will sound just as good as any mix CD you create from songs in iTunes, because those songs are compressed to begin with; uncompressing them to burn them to a disc doesn't increase their sound quality in comparison with how they sounded on the original source discs. Fortunately, it's difficult to tell the difference unless you're a real hard-core audiophile.

iTunes does not convert tracks to MP3 format on the fly as it burns, so you can create an MP3 CD only from tracks that are already in MP3 format. If you plan on burning a lot of MP3 CDs, consider importing your CDs' music in MP3 format instead of in AAC format (which cannot be burned directly to an MP3 CD). See **64 Customize Importing Options** for details or **56 Create an MP3 CD from Purchased AAC Music** for instructions on how to create an MP3 CD using existing music in formats other than MP3.

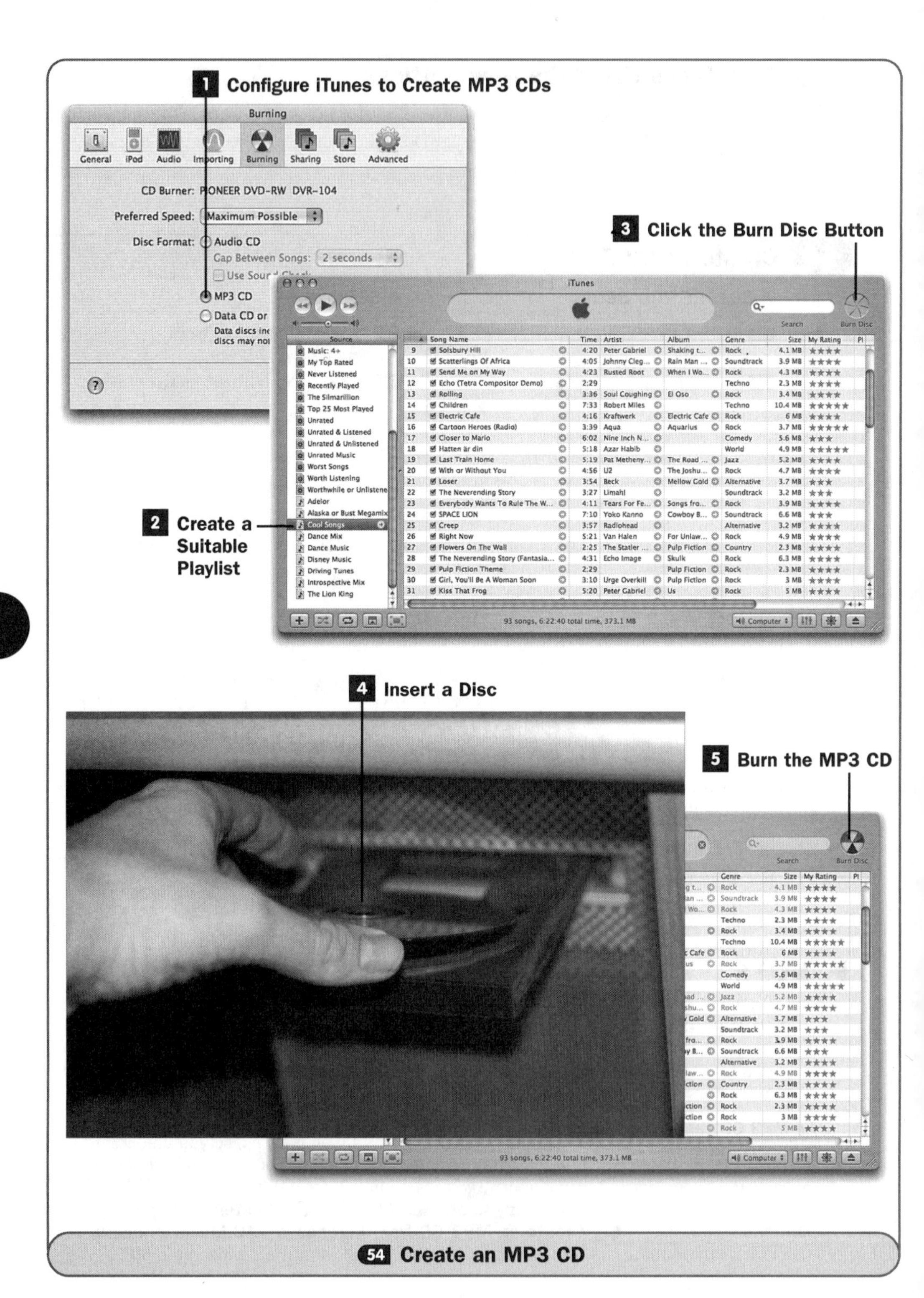

54 Create an MP3 CD

1 Configure iTunes to Create MP3 CDs

Before you can burn an MP3 disc, you must set up iTunes' **Preferences** to do that. As described in 53 **Customize CD Burning Options**, set the **Disc Format** option on the **Burning** tab of the iTunes **Preferences** window to **MP3 CD**. Click **OK**. Each disc you create from now on will be an MP3 CD, until you go back into the **Preferences** window and change the **Disc Format** back to **Audio CD**.

2 Create a Suitable Playlist

Make a ***playlist*** containing the songs you want on the disc. As discussed in 34 **Create a Playlist**, navigate into the library and drag songs from it into the playlist, keeping in mind that typical CD-R discs can hold up to 650 or 700 megabytes (MB) of music data (depending on the type of disc; the disc packaging will note the exact capacity). Use the statistics shown at the bottom of the iTunes' window to determine how large (in megabytes) your playlist will be. (For MP3 CDs, the total file size of the playlist is a more important consideration than the playback duration, which you used in 52 **Create an Audio CD from a Playlist**.)

▶ NOTE

If you create a playlist that's larger than the capacity of the disc, iTunes presents a warning at the time you burn the disc, telling you that only a portion of the playlist will be burned. You can choose to burn as much of the playlist as will fit on a single disc, or cancel the operation so that you can reduce the playlist's size yourself. iTunes won't burn a playlist to multiple MP3 CDs because Apple figures that 12 hours of listening time should be enough for any playlist you've constructed.

The playlist name becomes the volume name for the burned disc; be sure to use a short, simple name (15 characters or less) that doesn't contain any special characters because the standard ISO 9660 CD-ROM format that iTunes creates doesn't support long or complex volume names.

To skip burning certain songs in the playlist, disable the check boxes next to the song names in the list.

▶ NOTE

An MP3 CD can only contain MP3 files, so tracks in the playlist that are not in MP3 format become grayed out and their check boxes are disabled during the burn.

3 Click the Burn Disc Button

When you're viewing the playlist, the **Browse** button in the top-right corner of the iTunes window becomes a **Burn Disc** button; click it to begin the creation of the new disc.

4 Insert a Disc

In the display oval at the top of the window, iTunes prompts you to insert a blank disc and tells you the total burned capacity and playing time of the selected playlist (this can differ from the reported length of the playlist at the bottom of the iTunes' window if you disabled any of the songs' check boxes). If your computer has a CD tray, it is automatically ejected so that you can insert the disc. Otherwise, insert the disc into the drive slot until the drive pulls it in.

▶ NOTE

You can use a burnable DVD (*DVD-R*, DVD-RW, DVD+RW) disc instead of a CD in this task to create a data disc with up to 4.7GB of music files on it; however, be aware that hardly any players on the market will be able to read it (it won't play in a car stereo, even if your car player supports MP3 CDs). An MP3 DVD can be used only in computers.

When the disc is inserted, iTunes recognizes the blank media and automatically changes the message in the display oval to a prompt telling you to click the **Burn Disc** button again (it is now throbbing gently) to begin burning the playlist to the disc.

If you don't click **Burn Disc** within about 10 seconds, iTunes cancels the operation and ejects the disc.

5 Burn the MP3 CD

Click **Burn Disc** for the second time to begin the burn process. When the process is complete, the MP3 CD appears in the **Source** pane in the iTunes' window to show the tracks you've just burned.

Eject the disc from your computer; it's formatted as a data CD-ROM (with a volume name equal to the name of the playlist) that you can mount in any PC or Mac and can play in any CD player that is capable of reading MP3 CDs.

55 Print a CD Jewel Case Insert with Album Art

✓ BEFORE YOU BEGIN	→ SEE ALSO
13 Add Album Art to Songs 52 Create an Audio CD from a Playlist	57 Export a Song List

After you've burned a custom mix audio CD or ***MP3*** CD, what do you do with it? Do you get out a sheet of paper, or pull out the generic insert in the CD's jewel case, and painstakingly write down each of the track names along with the artist names and track lengths so that you don't forget what's on the disc? Do you scrawl the track names on the CD's surface with a permanent marker? Or do you throw it unmarked into a pile with dozens of other anonymous burned CDs, its contents to remain forever a mystery unless you stick it back in the computer to see what's on it?

We might like to think we're organized enough to keep track of all our burned music, but the fact is that as CD media becomes cheaper, and computers and burners become faster, there's less and less pressure on us to treat the process of burning music discs with delicacy and respect. CDs become disposable items, and we're unlikely to take the time to make sure that they'll last and their contents will stay known.

That's the benefit of iTunes' ability to print custom jewel cases from the ***playlists*** you used to create the custom music CDs. After you burn a disc, simply choose **File**, **Print** to have iTunes automatically print an attractive, professional-looking paper insert you can cut out, fold in half, and stick into the jewel case along with the CD so that it looks like something you spent real money on. This insert contains not only the list of tracks on the disc, but (optionally) an attractive mosaic made up of the album art from each track. You can also print track lists in other formats, such as complete tabular listings on full-size sheets of paper or tracks grouped by album.

1 Burn an Audio or MP3 CD

As discussed in **52 Create an Audio CD from a Playlist** and **54 Create an MP3 CD**, create a playlist and burn a CD or MP3 CD from it. Remove the CD from the drive.

▶ NOTE

If you deselected some of the songs in the playlist to exempt them from being burned, they'll also be left out of the track listing printed on the jewel case insert. For best results, be sure to print the insert at the same time you burn the disc to ensure that the contents of the disc and the printed track listing are the same.

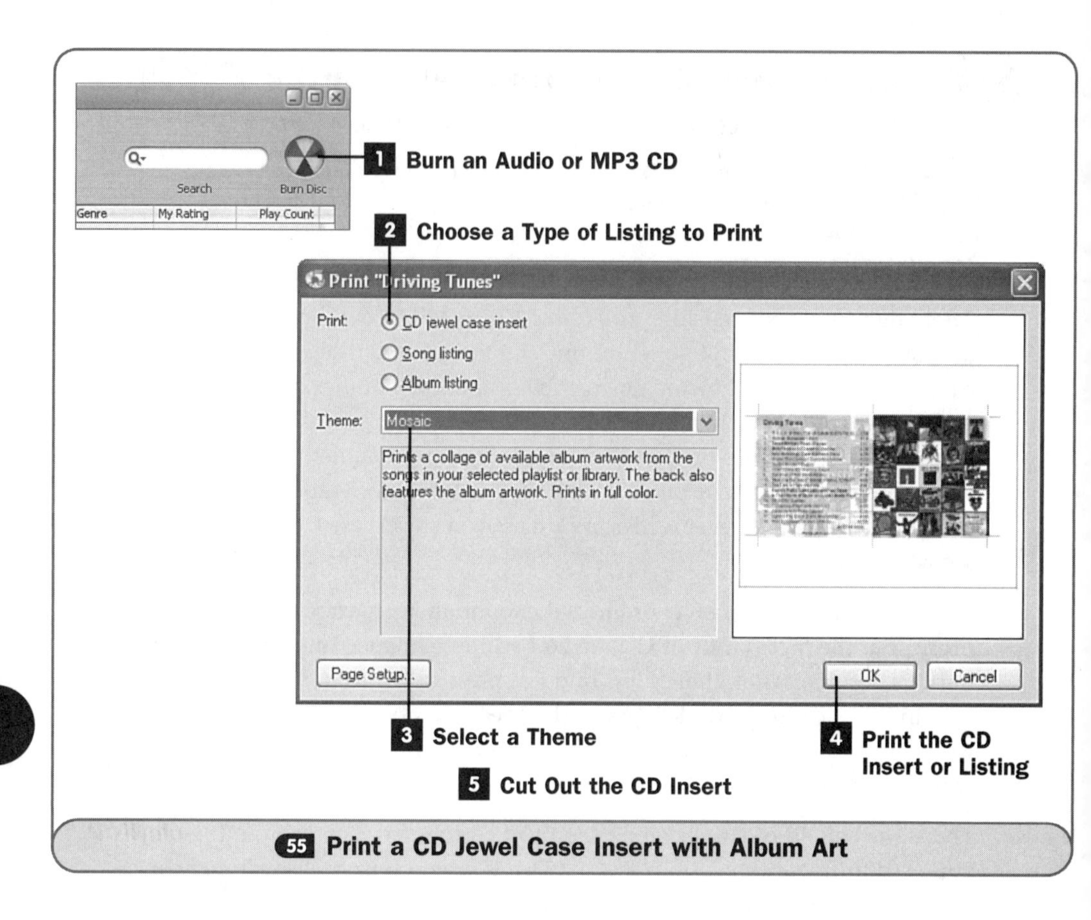

55 Print a CD Jewel Case Insert with Album Art

2 Choose a Type of Listing to Print

While you're still viewing the same playlist from which you burned the CD, choose **File**, **Print**. This command brings up the **Print** dialog box, in which you choose what kind of track listing to print. There are three options: **CD jewel case insert**, which is the right size and shape to be folded in half and slipped into a standard CD jewel case, and can be printed with mosaic art composed automatically from the album art in the playlist's songs; **Song listing**, which prints the list of the playlist's songs and certain predefined info fields in one of several predefined tabular formats on a standard-sized sheet of paper; or **Album listing**, which prints a list of each album represented in the playlist, along with the included tracks from each album.

Feel free to experiment with the options in **Song listing** or **Album listing**, which can be just as useful as the **CD jewel case insert** option, but contain fewer possible configurations. For this example, select **CD jewel case insert**.

3 Select a Theme

iTunes can print several different styles of jewel case inserts, selectable using the **Theme** drop-down list. There are four distinct styles (**Text only**, **Mosaic**, **White mosaic**, and **Single cover**), available in either full color or black & white modes, for a total of eight different themes. First note whether your printer is capable of printing color. If it is, use a full-color theme; otherwise, use one of the black & white themes.

▶ NOTE

Whether the track listing is printed in black on a light background or white on a dark background depends on how light or dark the selected album art or the composed mosaic of album art is. If it turns out dark, the track listing is printed in white on a dimmed version of the album art; if it's lighter than medium tone, the background is washed out and the text is printed in black over it.

Use the preview pane on the right side of the **Print** dialog box to get an idea of what the finished product will look like:

- The **Text only** theme prints only a simple text listing of the songs on a solid-color background. The playlist name is printed on the outward-facing leaf, and the track names are listed on the inward-facing leaf.
- **Mosaic** gathers together all the distinct pieces of album art from all the tracks in the playlist and chooses a square number (1, 4, 9, 16, or 25, whichever is highest without exceeding the number of songs in the playlist) of these pictures at random. The pictures are then arranged into a square and used both for the outward-facing leaf of the insert and (in a dimmed form) for the background of the leaf on which the track names are printed.
- The **White mosaic** mode is similar to **Mosaic**, except that the inward-facing leaf features the track names printed in black on a white background, which can be easier to read; the arrangement of album art on the cover also shows thin white lines between each of the rows of pictures.
- **Single cover** works like **Mosaic**, except that instead of a random selection of album art composed into a square mosaic, only a single piece of cover art at full size—the art from the currently selected song—is used. For this mode, select a song in the playlist you just burned before choosing the **Print** option.

4 Print the CD Insert or Listing

Click **Print** when you're satisfied with the layout of the jewel case insert (or, if you chose one of the other layout options, the track listing).

Depending on your operating system, you'll next see the default print options for your system. Click **Preview** to see a full-size preview of the printed project before you send it to the printer. If you want (and if your printer supports it), take the opportunity to load heavy-duty or glossy paper or otherwise set up your printer to produce a printout that will stand the test of time.

When you're satisfied, click **Print** to begin printing.

5 Cut Out the CD Insert

The jewel case insert is printed in the middle of the sheet of paper, with registration lines in each corner indicating where you must cut the sheet to fit a jewel case correctly. Lay a ruler or straightedge along these registration marks and cut along the edge using a razor knife. Because the artwork is printed in "full bleed" mode, with the color spilling past the cut line, the finished cutout piece should look quite professional.

Fold the sheet in half, with the printed surfaces facing outward, and insert it into the CD jewel case with the track listing facing in. Now make sure to mark your CD (use a permanent marker for this chore) with the name of the playlist as indicated on the outside of the insert. Now you hardly have any excuse for losing track of what's on your burned discs!

56 Create an MP3 CD from Purchased AAC Music

✔ BEFORE YOU BEGIN	→ SEE ALSO
20 Purchase Audio from the iTunes Music Store	64 Customize Importing Options
54 Create an MP3 CD	94 Back Up Your Music to CD or DVD

This task's subject is a touchy one. Apple intends for you to build your music library using the ***AAC format*** to import your CDs, and using the protected AAC format to purchase music from the iTunes **Music Store**. Yet with the proliferation of in-dash and portable CD players that read the MP3 CD format, it's hard to ignore the fact that music acquired this way won't play in these players. You own the music rightfully; why, then, shouldn't you be able to create CDs that let you play your own legitimately purchased music with the convenience your MP3 CD player affords you? Apple's recommendation that you buy an iPod to play your AAC music is small consolation when your choice is between using your iPod with a clunky tape adapter or FM transmitter in the car, or burning a nice crisp MP3 CD with a professional-looking jewel case insert to play in your cutting-edge in-dash MP3 CD player.

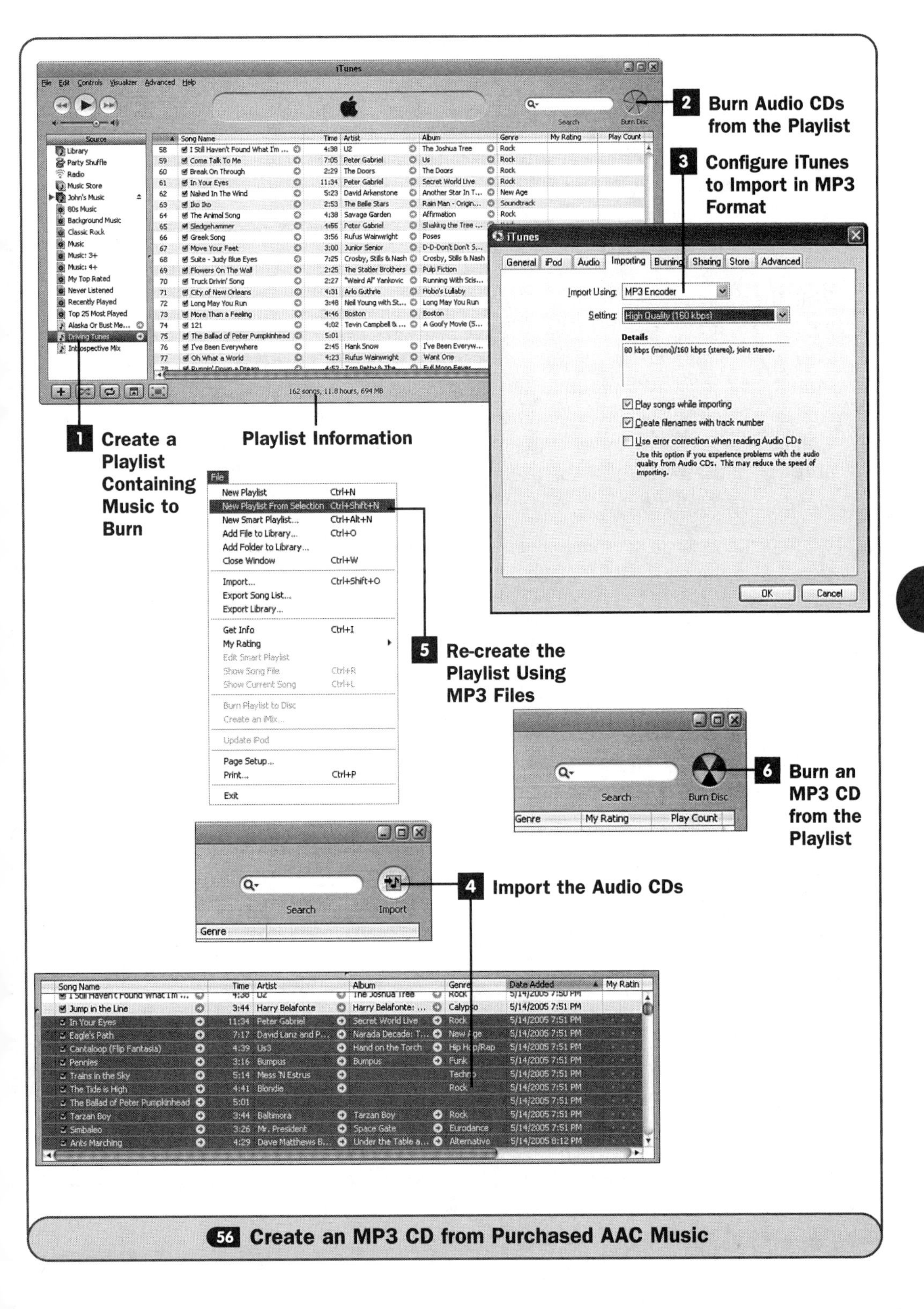

56 Create an MP3 CD from Purchased AAC Music

It should be fairly clear that Apple would be foolish to allow users to create unprotected MP3 CDs directly from purchased AAC music; such a feature would essentially be an invitation to piracy. All a user would have to do would be to burn one of these data discs, and he'd have an instant selection of high-quality MP3 files ready to transmit over the file-sharing networks. The record labels would never have signed on with iTunes if it had contained such a feature.

Yet you *can* create regular music CDs (using songs in uncompressed ***CDDA*** format) from your purchased AAC music. Why is that?

Well, the difference is that burning an uncompressed music CD creates unprotected music at a much slower pace than converting AAC files directly to MP3 would. A would-be pirate has to burn the music CD, re-import the dozen or so songs from it, and repeat the process 12 times just to get the same number of freely copy-able songs he would have if he'd been able to directly create an MP3 CD with one click. This inconvenience, Apple has gambled, is a sufficient barrier to piracy to make the iTunes **Music Store** a viable business proposition while remaining friendly to law-abiding users like yourself.

But you still want to be able to burn those purchased songs to an MP3 CD you can play in the car.

This task describes how to accomplish that goal. However, use it with caution; remember that you're treading the ragged edge of what's allowable under the "Terms of Sale" of the iTunes **Music Store** to which you agreed. These terms read in part, "Any burning or exporting capabilities are solely an accommodation to you and shall not constitute a grant or waiver (or other limitation or implication) of any rights of the copyright owners of any content, sound recording, underlying musical composition or artwork embodied in any Product." In other words, it was hard enough for Apple to get the labels to agree to let you burn even regular audio CDs. Don't abuse their trust by using these instructions to create unprotected music for anyone's use but your own. If you do, remember that it's not just your iTunes **Music Store** account that's at stake—it's the still uncertain future of the legal music download industry. Help keep it viable by following the rules!

In this task, you'll convert your purchased AAC files to unprotected MP3 files by first burning them to uncompressed audio CDs in CDDA format and then re-importing them into iTunes in MP3 format. Then you can burn the MP3 CDs freely as described in 54 **Create an MP3 CD**. For this task, you'll need enough blank writable CD discs to hold all the AAC files you want to convert, written in uncompressed CDDA format with approximately 20 tracks to each disc, which you'll eventually discard. It's a wasteful process, but it's the only way to do it.

▶ WEB RESOURCE

http://www.apple.com/support/itunes/legal/policies.html

The iTunes Music Store "Terms of Sale" are available at this direct URL—as well as by clicking the **Terms and Conditions** button in your account information page at the iTunes Music Store.

1 Create a Playlist Containing Music to Burn

Make a ***playlist*** containing the protected AAC songs you want to put on the disc. As discussed in 34 **Create a Playlist**, navigate into the library and drag songs from it into the playlist. Make the playlist as long as you want, up to a maximum of about 12 hours of total play length (as indicated by the readout at the bottom of the iTunes' window); if the playlist contains more than about 75 minutes of music, iTunes will allow you to burn the playlist across multiple discs. Be sure you have enough blank CD media to contain all the playlist's music in uncompressed CDDA form!

You can determine which of your tracks are in which format by displaying the **Kind** column in the track listing. See 71 **Customize Which Information Columns Are Displayed** for more information.

▶ NOTE

There's no need to go through this burning process for songs in any format other than Protected AAC; if your songs are in regular (unprotected) AAC format or another format without ***DRM*** restrictions, see 66 **Convert Audio Files to Other Formats** for instructions on converting them to MP3 format within iTunes itself.

2 Burn Audio CDs from the Playlist

Be sure iTunes is set up to burn audio CDs; to check this, open the iTunes' **Preferences** window (choose **iTunes, Preferences** on the Mac or **Edit, Preferences** in Windows) and click the **Burning** tab. Set the **Disc Format** option to **Audio CD** and click **OK**.

With the playlist selected, click the **Burn** button; insert a writable CD when prompted, and click **Burn** again to begin burning the playlist to the disc in uncompressed CDDA audio format. Insert more discs when prompted until the entire playlist is burned to CDs.

3 Configure iTunes to Import in MP3 Format

The next step is to import the music back into iTunes, this time as unprotected MP3 files. Open the iTunes' **Preferences** window again. Click the **Importing** tab. Set the **Import Using** option to **MP3 Encoder**. From the

Setting drop-down menu, choose an audio quality level for the imported files; the default, **High Quality (160 kbps)**, is generally sufficient, although you might want to choose a different quality level depending on your needs. Use the **Custom** setting to enable certain options such as Variable ***Bit Rate*** (VBR) recording. Click **OK**.

4 Import the Audio CDs

One by one, insert the audio CDs that you just burned and import them by clicking the **Import** button (see 9 **Import a Music CD into iTunes**). The track names should be filled in automatically by iTunes, because it remembers each disc that it burned by its unique combination of track lengths. Make sure that you import the CDs in the correct order in which you burned them; doing so makes the next step easier.

The newly imported songs are added to your library in parallel with the protected AAC versions of the same songs that already exist.

5 Re-create the Playlist Using MP3 Files

Create a new playlist containing the MP3 files you just imported. An easy way to do this is as follows: in the **Library** view, scroll horizontally to the **Date Added** column and sort on that column by clicking its header. Click it again if necessary to sort the tracks in ascending order (earliest to latest). Scroll to the bottom of the song listing. Locate the selection of songs you just imported; the block of newly imported songs should be easily identifiable as all having been added within the last half-hour or so. Select all these songs by clicking the first one in the list (the earliest one you imported), scrolling to the end of the list, and holding down **Shift** as you click the last song in the listing.

Next, choose **File, New Playlist From Selection**. A new playlist appears in the **Source** pane, with the name **untitled playlist**. This name is selected so that you can type a new one. Enter a simple and short name for the new playlist; the name you type will become the volume name for the new MP3 CD you'll create. Press **Return** or **Enter**.

6 Burn an MP3 CD from the Playlist

Select the newly created playlist and verify that its contents are the way you want them—all MP3 files (identified in the **Kind** column as **MPEG audio file**), not missing any songs you want, and arranged in the right order. If they're not, move songs around until they're sorted in the order you want them.

Open the iTunes **Preferences** window again and click the **Burning** tab. Set the **Disc Format** option to **MP3 CD**. Click **OK**.

Now burn the MP3 CD by clicking **Burn**. Insert a disc when prompted. The playlist is burned to the disc in unprotected MP3 format, suitable for playing in your car's MP3 CD unit or your portable disc player—any device that reads MP3 CDs. Just don't tell anybody where you heard how to do this....

▶ NOTE

If the playlist is too long to fit on a single MP3 CD, iTunes offers to burn only the portion of the playlist that will fit or to allow you to cancel the operation and trim down the playlist yourself before burning it again. Make sure that the playlist doesn't exceed the 650 or 700 megabytes that your disc will hold.

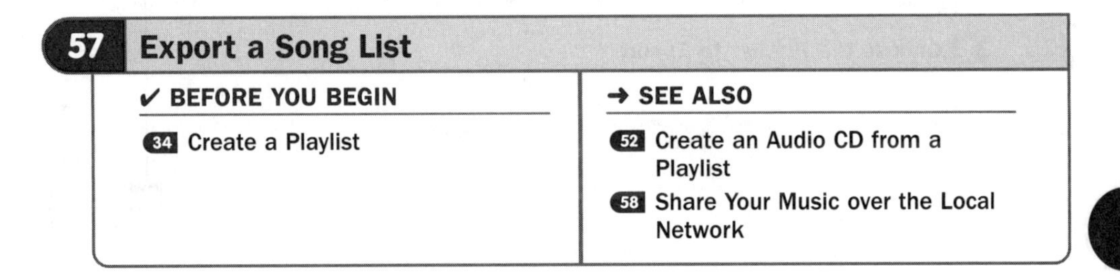

57 Export a Song List

✔ BEFORE YOU BEGIN

34 Create a Playlist

➔ SEE ALSO

52 Create an Audio CD from a Playlist

58 Share Your Music over the Local Network

You can use iTunes to save a list of songs in a portable text format. The reasons for doing this might not be immediately clear, but if the need ever does arise, you'll be thankful for the ability. One example might be that someone wants to know what songs you're burning onto a CD for a mutual friend's birthday party; exporting the song list to a plain text file is a great way to make this information available without having to copy every track name down manually. No doubt you can imagine many other sets of circumstances in which you'd be quite glad not to have to recite track names over the phone or scribble them down on a piece of paper.

1 Choose the Playlist to Export

Choose a ***playlist***, a CD, the library, or any other aggregation of music from the **Source** pane in the iTunes' window. Organize the song listing in the way you want it to be exported—sort the songs on the column of your choice, or drag them manually into the order you want them in.

2 Export the Song List

Choose **File, Export Song List**. This command brings up the **Save** dialog box.

57 Export a Song List

Navigate to the location on the disk where you want to save the output file (the format of the navigator depends on your operating system) and specify a filename. This name is initially set to match the name of the playlist or the music source you selected in step 1, but you can type a new name to replace it.

3 Choose an Output Format

You can export the song list in **Plain Text** or **XML** format; on the Mac, you can additionally use **Unicode Text** format, which is useful for song names written in non-Western character sets (such as Japanese, Russian, or Hebrew). Choose the format appropriate to your needs.

4 Save the Song List File

Click **Save**. The exported song list is saved to your selected location in the format of your choice. If you saved in **Plain Text** mode, the contents are tabular, with cells representing every info tag in every file in the listing, each separated by tab characters. If you saved in **XML** format, the fields are all delineated in standard XML data containers which can be imported using any database application that can read XML format.

▶ NOTE

Saving a song listing in XML format is a good way to back up your song information. Another, more comprehensive, method is to choose File, Export Library; this command saves the contents of your entire iTunes Library database (not the music itself!) in XML format, in much the same way as this task describes. Be sure to save your Library.xml file in a safe place—you might need it! See 97 Restore Your Music Library Database from a Backup Copy for more.

58 Share Your Music over the Local Network

✔ BEFORE YOU BEGIN	→ SEE ALSO
2 Run iTunes for the First Time	23 Authorize a Computer to Play Purchased Music
	59 Listen to Shared Music on the Local Network
	60 AirTunes: Connect iTunes to a Stereo with AirPort Express

iTunes isn't just a single person's private jukebox; it's designed to give digital music the same versatility within a household as physical CDs have done, within the reasonable limits imposed by ***Digital Rights Management***. This means that just as you might have a big organizer of CDs in your den that anyone in the family can borrow from and take into his or her own room to enjoy, iTunes lets you connect to another computer on the same home network and browse that computer's iTunes' music collection. In a household with three or four members, each with his or her own computer, the music that's stored on one computer can be easily broadcast to any other computer and enjoyed on demand. In the same way, one computer's music collection on a corporate LAN can be enjoyed by anyone else on the network who has a copy of iTunes.

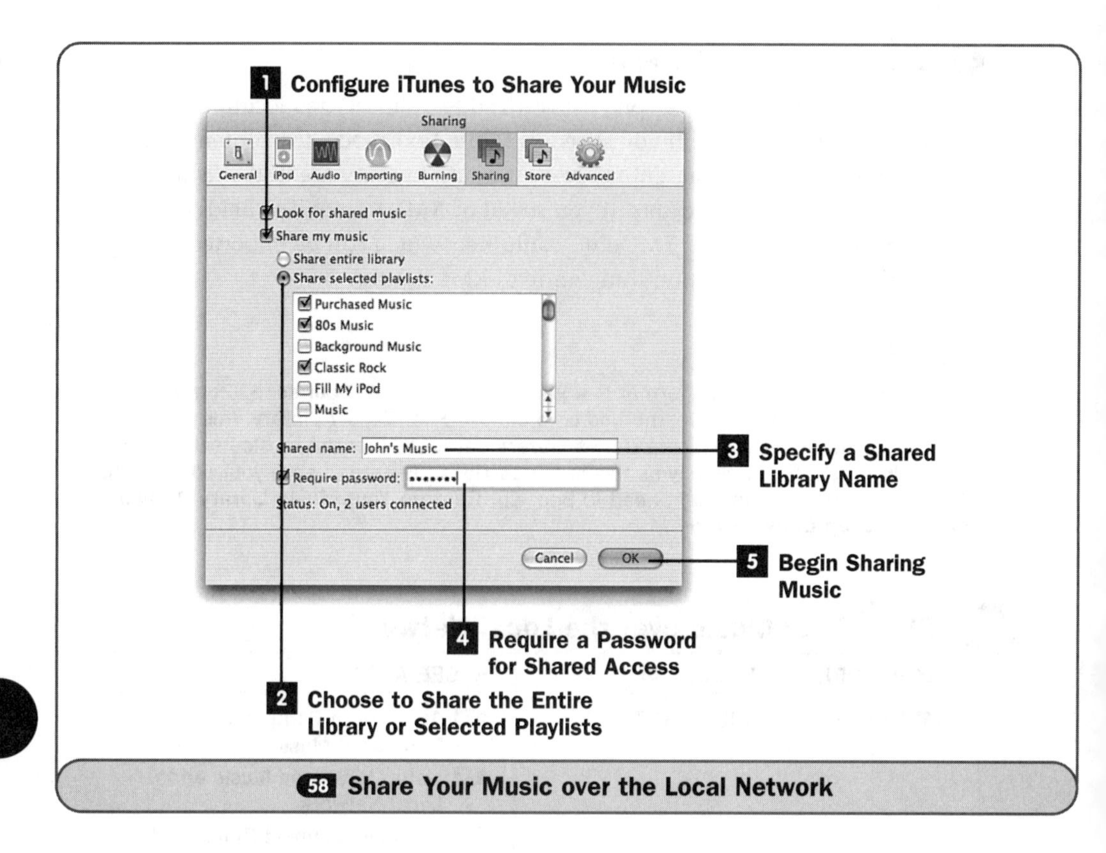

58 Share Your Music over the Local Network

58

NOTE

Listening to someone else's purchased ***AAC*** music requires that your computer be *authorized* to play that person's music. Because each person has his or her own iTunes **Music Store** account and five authorizations to deploy, that person can log in to and authorize every other computer in the house to access his or her own music. See 23 **Authorize a Computer to Play Purchased Music** for details.

Each computer must first be set up to share its music. This task describes how to enable music sharing, as well as how to restrict your sharing to certain ***playlists*** and to protect it with a password in case you don't want others snooping around in your music collection.

1 Configure iTunes to Share Your Music

Open the iTunes **Preferences** window (choose **Edit, Preferences** in Windows or **iTunes, Preferences** on the Mac). Click the **Sharing** tab.

Enable the **Share my music** check box to turn on music sharing for this particular computer.

2 Choose to Share the Entire Library or Selected Playlists

You can share your entire library and all its playlists with other iTunes' users on the local network (within your household or corporate LAN), or you can choose instead to limit your music sharing to certain playlists. Choose the option that best suits your needs.

If you choose to share only selected playlists, use the check boxes in the list under the radio buttons to define which playlists you want to share.

▶ NOTE

If you're running a personal firewall on your computer, you might have to "poke a hole" (create an exception rule) in the firewall to allow iTunes' music-sharing traffic to get through. Define the rule to allow traffic on TCP port 3689. (In Mac OS X, a predefined rule is available in the system firewall for this port; select the Firewall tab on the Sharing pane in the System Preferences application and enable the check box for iTunes Music Sharing.) If you want to selectively restrict access to your shared music, consider setting a password as explained in step 4.

3 Specify a Shared Library Name

When others connect to your shared iTunes' music, your music list appears in their **Source** panes under a name that you specify. By default, this name is set to ***John's* Music**, where ***John*** is your own name as set in your operating system's user account system. You can change this to something more evocative if you like—**House Music Server**, for example, or **BriTunes**.

4 Require a Password for Shared Access

Perhaps you don't want your inquisitive siblings rummaging around in your music collection, but you don't mind if your live-in uncle accesses your music. You can protect your shared music with a password; everyone on the network will see your shared music in their **Source** panes, but they won't be able to connect or browse your music without entering a valid password.

Enable the **Require password** check box and type the password you want to use. The password is hidden as you enter it, so be sure to enter it correctly. Give this password to only those people you want to be able to access your shared music.

5 Begin Sharing Music

Click **OK** to start sharing your music. At any time after this, you can return to the **Sharing** tab of the **Preferences** window to view the **Status** readout, which reports how many users are currently connected to your iTunes **Library**. If anyone is connected and listening to your music, you'll get a warning message if you try to quit iTunes, letting you know that you'll be interrupting these other users' musical enjoyment. You'll have to confirm that you really want to quit regardless of who's using your iTunes' music at the moment.

▶ NOTE

iTunes has a restriction that limits the number of new connections to your shared music to five within a given 24-hour time period. If more than five users try to connect to your iTunes **Library**, they'll be told that the connection was refused. This restriction was recently imposed as a result of contract renegotiations between Apple and the labels, the positive upshot of which was that you get five authorization spots to use instead of the original three.

59 Listen to Shared Music on the Local Network

✓ BEFORE YOU BEGIN

- 2 Run iTunes for the First Time
- 58 Share Your Music over the Local Network

➜ SEE ALSO

- 23 Authorize a Computer to Play Purchased Music
- 60 AirTunes: Connect iTunes to a Stereo with AirPort Express

58

If someone else in your household, with his computer connected to the house network, has iTunes installed and set up to share music (see 58 **Share Your Music over the Local Network**), you can connect to that shared music library using your own copy of iTunes and stream his music to your computer just as though it were stored on your local machine. This arrangement enables music stored on any computer within a household or corporate network to be essentially "borrowed" and played on other computers under the same roof, just as a physical CD could be borrowed and played.

▶ NOTE

Listening to someone else's purchased AAC music requires that your computer be authorized to play that person's music. Because each person has his or her own iTunes **Music Store** account and five authorizations to deploy, that person can log in and authorize another computer in the house to access his or her own music. See 23 **Authorize a Computer to Play Purchased Music** for details.

iTunes is not a file-sharing application—when you listen to shared music over the network, you're merely streaming the music from the remote iTunes to your speakers, not copying the other person's music files to your computer. You can only listen to another person's iTunes' music if their copy of iTunes is running.

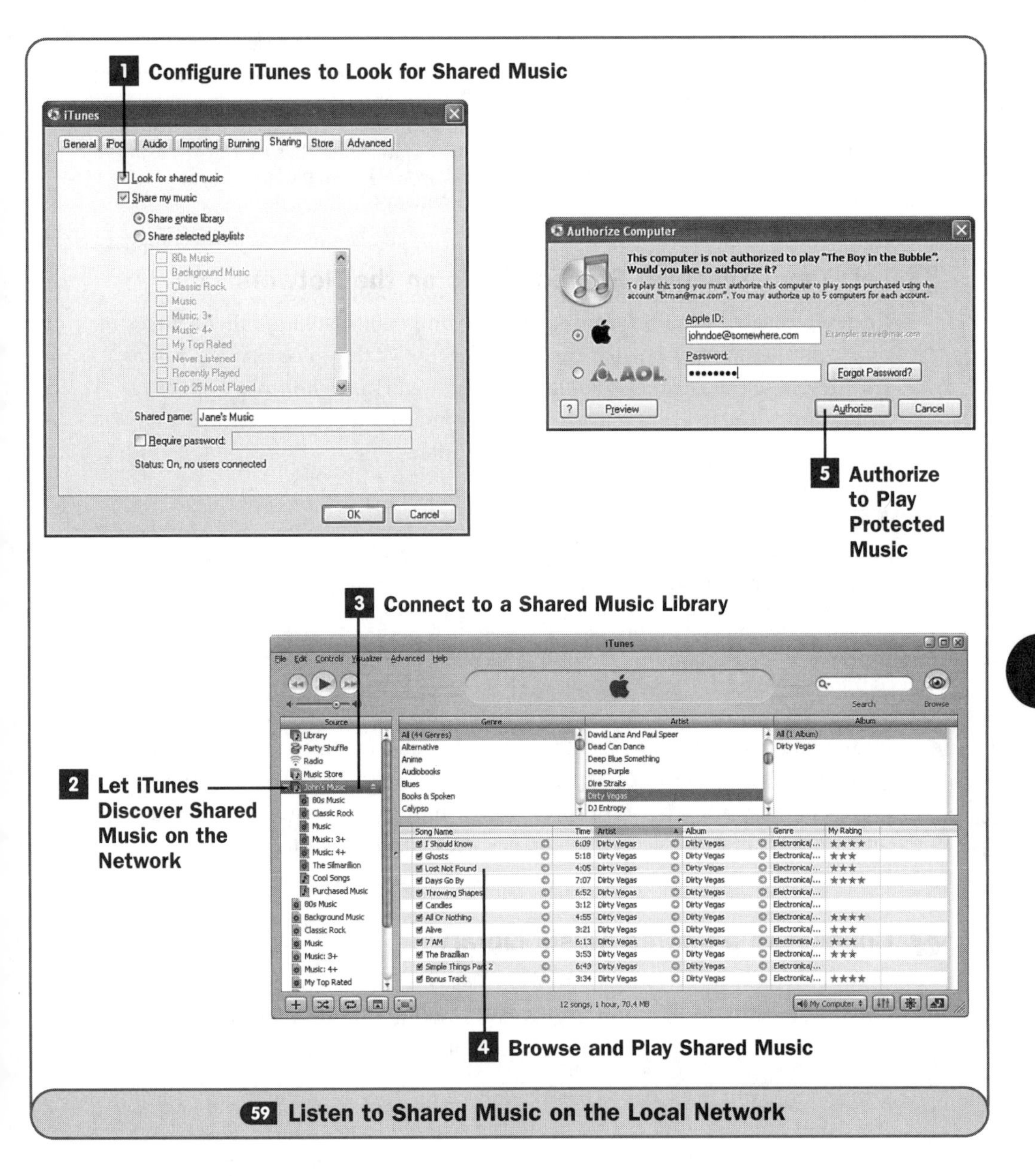

1 Configure iTunes to Look for Shared Music

Open the iTunes' **Preferences** window (choose **Edit, Preferences** in Windows or **iTunes, Preferences** on the Mac). Click the **Sharing** tab.

Enable the **Look for shared music** check box to cause your copy of iTunes to start watching the network for other copies of iTunes.

► **NOTE**

iTunes uses a technology called **Bonjour**, Apple's implementation of an open-source protocol called ZeroConf, to discover services on the local network such as shared iTunes music. **Bonjour** is built into many other applications in Mac OS X, but isn't in widespread use on Windows. Nonetheless, music sharing can flawlessly take place between Windows and Mac versions of iTunes on the same network.

2 Let iTunes Discover Shared Music on the Network

Click **OK** to close the **Preferences** window and begin seeking other sources of music on the network. Watch the **Source** pane. Within a couple of seconds, you should see the names of other users' shared iTunes libraries appearing beneath the **Music Store** entry and any connected iPods or mounted CDs that are physically available to your computer.

► **NOTE**

If you're running a personal firewall on your computer, you might have to "poke a hole" (create an exception rule) in the firewall to allow iTunes' music-sharing traffic to get through. Define the rule to allow traffic on **TCP** port **3689**. (In Mac OS X, a predefined rule is available in the system firewall for this port; select the **Firewall** tab on the **Sharing** pane in the **System Preferences** application, and enable the check box for **iTunes Music Sharing**.)

If only one other person currently running iTunes is present on the network, that person's shared music appears by name directly in the **Source** pane; if more than one other person is present, the multiple sources are grouped under the **Shared Music** heading. Click the triangle next to this option's icon to expand the category and see all the shared music libraries inside it.

3 Connect to a Shared Music Library

Click once on a shared music library to select it. Immediately, iTunes attempts to connect to it and begins downloading information about the music tracks and playlists that are available.

If the shared music library is protected by a password, you're prompted to enter that password to gain access to the selected music source. If you don't enter the password correctly, you're returned to the main **Library** view.

► **NOTE**

You can recognize password-protected shared music collections by the "lock" icon that appears next to their names under the **Shared Music** heading in the **Source** pane.

When all the information about the shared music library is downloaded (which should take no more than a few seconds), an expansion triangle appears to the left of the shared music library's name, and an **Eject** icon appears to its right; this second icon is used to disconnect you from the shared music library. Disconnecting is a good idea when you're done listening to a remote shared music library because it prevents unnecessary network traffic while you're not using iTunes.

4 Browse and Play Shared Music

If you select the entire shared music library, you can browse the whole thing just as though it were on your local computer. The **Browse** lists (**Genre**, **Artist**, and **Album**) work the same as in your own **Library** view. Navigate to an artist or album you want to hear and double-click to start playing the music.

You can also view the remote user's shared playlists. Click the expansion triangle to the left of the shared library's name; all the playlists on the remote user's computer are listed under the name of the shared library. Select a playlist to view it, and click **Play** to start it playing.

▶ NOTE

Because you can't burn a remote playlist to a CD, the button in the upper-right corner of the iTunes' window—which normally is a Burn button when you're viewing a playlist—is a Browse button in this case. You can use the Browse view on playlists even in your local copy of iTunes, too—just select Edit, Show Browser.

5 Authorize to Play Protected Music

You can freely listen to any music in the remote user's library—with the exception of protected AAC files purchased from the iTunes **Music Store**. Your computer must be authorized for the remote user's iTunes **Music Store** account before her purchased music can play on your computer.

Select and attempt to play a protected file by double-clicking its name or by clicking the **Play** button. A dialog box pops up that challenges you for the iTunes **Music Store** account password matching the account that was used to buy the music. Unless the remote user has shared her password with you, you essentially have two options: either cancel the attempt and don't try to listen to any more of the person's purchased songs, or get the person to come into your room and authorize your computer by typing her password and clicking **Authorize**. When the iTunes **Music Store** account for that song has been validated (by connecting to the central iTunes **Music Store** server), you're free to play any other music that was bought using that same account.

▶ TIP

Remember that there are only five authorization spots available for a given iTunes **Music Store** account. If the other person has to regain the authorization she's given to you, she must deauthorize your computer as described in **23 Authorize a Computer to Play Purchased Music**; afterwards, you will no longer be able to play her purchased music files.

60 AirTunes: Connect iTunes to a Stereo with AirPort Express

✓ BEFORE YOU BEGIN	→ SEE ALSO
9 Import a Music CD into iTunes	58 Share Your Music over the Local Network
20 Purchase Audio from the iTunes Music Store	59 Listen to Shared Music on the Local Network

It's all well and good to play your music using iTunes on your computer; but there's still something missing, something that's keeping your digital music separate from the CDs in your main collection: a good set of amplified speakers and a way to get your music to them. Chances are that the speakers hooked up to your computer aren't the best audio reproduction system in your household, and without a way to play your computer's music through your main A/V system, it's just not quite the same experience. Fortunately, Apple's got that base covered, too.

Available for Mac or PC (just like everything else in the Apple digital music product line), ***AirPort Express*** is a device that lets you connect your computer running iTunes to any set of speakers elsewhere in the house and play your music through those remote speakers. iTunes does it all without wires, because AirPort Express is actually a ***wireless base station***—a device variously known throughout the industry as a wireless access point, an 802.11 base station, a Wi-Fi hub, or any of several other such names. AirPort Express is a small wireless access point in the shape and size of a small AC adapter that plugs directly into a wall outlet and allows all the computers in your house to connect over the airwaves, without any wires or cables. The device also has an audio out port; this port, and the software in the base station that controls it (known as AirTunes), is a combined analog and digital (optical) audio port that can connect to any stereo system, high-end or low-end. The upshot is that AirPort Express provides the last link in the chain between the digital music stored on your computer and the good stereo system where you're accustomed to playing your music.

The software in AirPort Express is designed so that you can add its wireless hub capabilities to those of an existing wireless network you might already have set up in your house, or to act as its own standalone base station. To set it up, you simply plug it into the wall and turn it on, optionally connecting an ***Ethernet*** cable to it, and run a setup assistant utility on another computer (Mac or PC). This utility lets you set up the AirPort Express unit by assigning it a name and connecting it to your existing wireless network, if you have one, or configuring its TCP/IP settings to act as its own wireless router. Finally, when it's all set up, its light goes green and a new menu appears in your iTunes' window: a drop-down list from which you choose which set of speakers you want to use for your music output. Just pick one and start playing! The music is streamed from your computer to AirPort Express in uncompressed digital format, and particularly if you have an optical audio input port on your stereo system, the sound quality is thus just as good as on your own computer, without any signal loss from the transmission.

▶ KEY TERMS

AirPort Express—One of Apple's brand of wireless Internet connectivity devices, a wireless base station that provides not just wireless (802.11g) connectivity but also an audio connection between iTunes and a set of speakers to which it's connected.

Wireless base station—A networking device that enables you to share a broadband connection within a household by allowing computers with wireless capabilities to connect to it and share its connection.

AirTunes—A feature of AirPort Express that broadcasts the capability to route music to a set of externally connected speakers to any copy of iTunes running on the network; any of these iTunes computers can choose the AirTunes speakers and play music through them wirelessly.

Ethernet—A physical connection to a LAN is done using Ethernet, a low-level communication protocol that involves cables that end in RJ-45 jacks, which resemble large phone jacks. All modern Macs have an Ethernet port, which runs at 10, 100, or (on top-end models) 1000 megabits per second.

AirPort Express is available from Apple for $129.

1 Install and Set Up the AirPort Express Base Station

Unpack your new AirPort Express base station and plug it into the wall. You can use either the standard wall prongs (which allow you to plug the unit directly into an outlet as you would an AC adapter), or you can snap it out and replace it with the longer power cord that comes with the unit to gain better placement options.

If you don't already have a wireless network in place, you must connect the AirPort Express unit to your broadband router using an Ethernet cable.

The light on the AirPort Express unit begins flashing orange. It's now ready to configure.

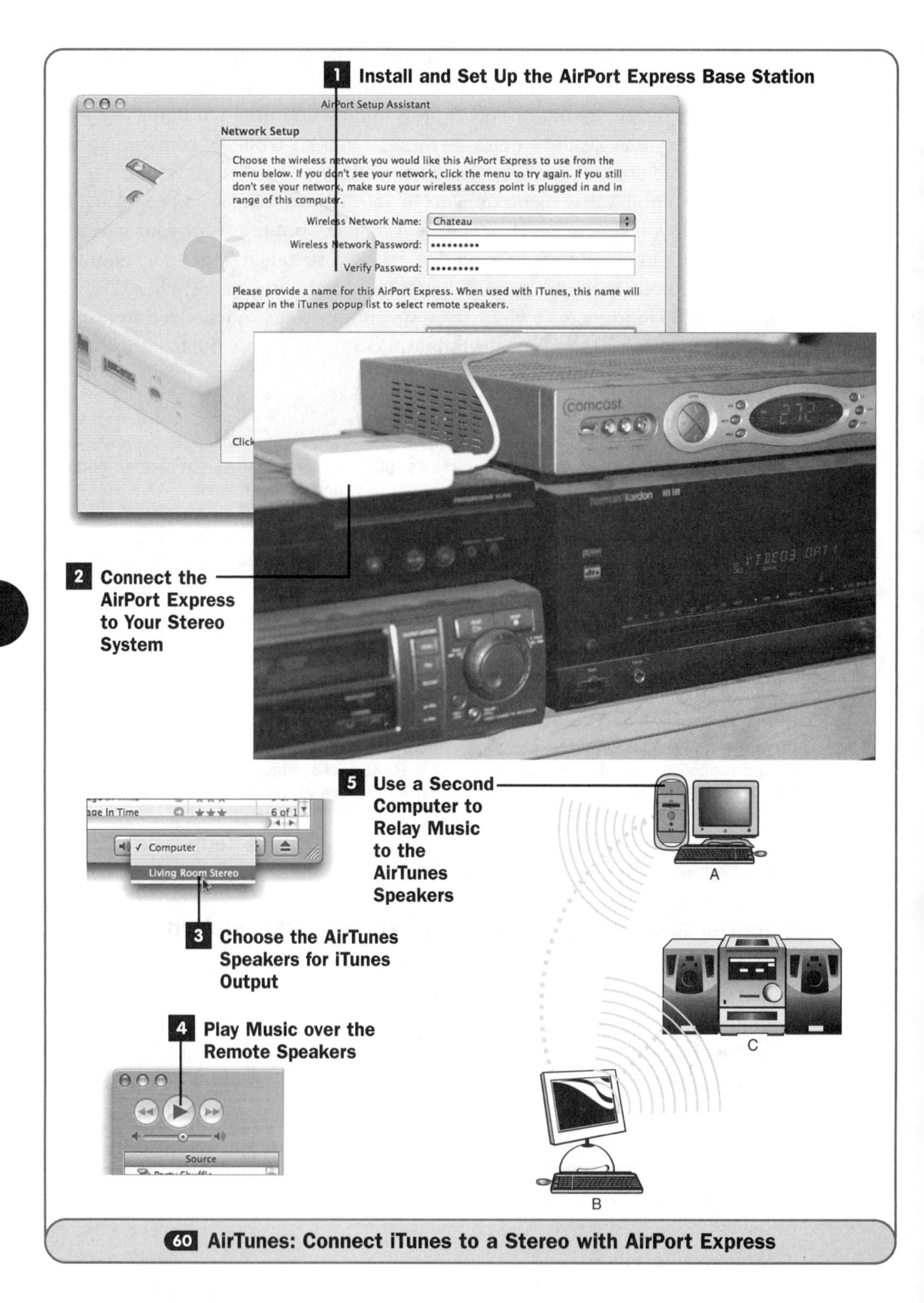
1 Install and Set Up the AirPort Express Base Station
AirPort Setup Assistant
Network Setup
Choose the wireless network you would like this AirPort Express to use from the menu below. If you don't see your network, click the menu to try again. If you still don't see your network, make sure your wireless access point is plugged in and in range of this computer.
Wireless Network Name: Chateau
Wireless Network Password:
Verify Password:
Please provide a name for this AirPort Express. When used with iTunes, this name will appear in the iTunes popup list to select remote speakers.
2 Connect the AirPort Express to Your Stereo System
5 Use a Second Computer to Relay Music to the AirTunes Speakers
Computer
Living Room Stereo
3 Choose the AirTunes Speakers for iTunes Output
4 Play Music over the Remote Speakers
Source
A
B
C

60

60 AirTunes: Connect iTunes to a Stereo with AirPort Express

On any computer on the local network (Mac or PC), install the included Airport Express software; this includes a utility called AirPort Setup Assistant. Run this program. It walks you through the several steps of the setup process, allowing you to make several choices along the way:

- Do you want to set up a new AirPort base station, or configure an existing one—first-time users specify that you want to set up a new base station.
- Do you want to join the AirPort Express unit to an existing wireless network as a plain client (like any computer), or do you want to use AirPort Express' own wireless base station capabilities to extend the main base station's wireless range? Either option lets you use AirTunes to connect stereo speakers, but extending the network's wireless range by adding AirPort Express' range can mean a somewhat more complex setup procedure (depending on your main base station's configuration).
- What name do you want to assign to the new AirPort Express unit? This name is also the name associated with AirTunes, so you should pick a name that describes the speaker system to which the Airport Express unit will be connected, such as **Living Room Stereo**.

Refer to the manual that comes with AirPort Express for further details on the setup process. When you're done with the configuration, click **Update** on the final screen of the setup utility to reset the AirPort Express unit. When it becomes available again (in about 30 seconds), the light on the unit goes green, and you're ready to use it to stream your iTunes music to your stereo.

2 Connect the AirPort Express to Your Stereo System

Using a separately purchased mini-optical audio cable, or any standard analog 1/8" stereo cable, connect the AirPort Express unit to an audio input port on your stereo system. Optical input is certainly the best choice if you have it because there's no possibility of signal loss between the AirPort Express unit and the stereo itself; an analog connector should work fine in a pinch, or if you don't have an optical input jack on your stereo system.

3 Choose the AirTunes Speakers for iTunes Output

On any computer on the network with iTunes installed, look in the lower-right corner of the iTunes' window; next to the Equalizer and Visualizer control buttons is a new drop-down menu with a speaker icon. By default, the menu is set to **Computer**, which means that your iTunes' music is played through your computer's own speakers. However, if you open the menu, it should now contain the name of the AirPort Express unit you just set up: in this example, **Living Room Stereo**. Select this new option.

4 Play Music over the Remote Speakers

Now when you play your iTunes' music, the audio stream no longer plays through your computer's speakers at all, but is instead broadcast over the wireless network to the AirPort Express base station. The base station then routes the music through AirTunes into the audio input port of the stereo system.

Make sure that your stereo is set to the input channel to which you connected the AirPort Express audio cable and turn up the volume. Your iTunes' music should be playing now, bigger and louder and richer than it ever sounded through your computer's speakers.

▶ NOTES

Some stereo receiver/amplifier models must be set to accept a specific kind of optical input, such as one of multiple coaxial connections. Refer to your stereo system's instruction manual to configure it properly to receive the audio signal on the connected port.

Also, some stereo receiver/amplifier models exhibit a problem when synchronizing with the digital audio stream. If the stereo receiver is set to negotiate the digital audio codec automatically when a new audio stream begins, this can result in the first second or so of each track being dropped (AirPort Express sends no signal until a new song begins, and so the stereo must renegotiate the connection at the beginning of each song). If possible, disable automatic negotiation on your stereo, and set it to listen for a PCM stream.

5 Use a Second Computer to Relay Music to the AirTunes Speakers

AirPort Express doesn't come with a remote control, but that's because iTunes is intended to be the only remote it needs. This arrangement is especially useful if you have a public computer sitting in your den or living room. This computer can be used to control AirTunes playback even if the music you're playing is stored on an entirely different computer on the network.

First set up the computer with the large store of music to share its music library (as discussed in 58 **Share Your Music over the Local Network**). On the public computer near the AirTunes speakers, connect to the first computer's music library as described in 59 **Listen to Shared Music on the Local Network**. Finally, on the public computer, choose **Living Room Stereo** as the iTunes' output option. Now you can listen to the computer streamed wirelessly from the main music storage computer, and broadcast it back out again to your stereo speakers through AirTunes. How cool is that?

8

Maintaining Your Music Library

IN THIS CHAPTER:

iTunes' main advantage, what gave it the edge over existing MP3 player applications at the time it was released, is its database-oriented navigation system. With songs listed not by their filenames and folders, but navigated using the embedded ***info tags*** that group them into albums and artists so that they can be browsed more like physical CDs on your shelf, iTunes quickly pointed the way toward a richer world of data organized by its inherent criteria rather than by outdated, generic computing metaphors.

The features of iTunes are designed to let your music become organized naturally as you import or acquire it—the info tags are automatically applied to songs as you import them from CDs, and they're already embedded into each song you purchase through the iTunes **Music Store**. Yet this process isn't foolproof. It's possible for songs to get into your iTunes **Library** without having their proper info tags set. It's possible that, over time, through the trivialities of everyday computing life, your files might become accidentally moved or lost, or iTunes might simply lose track of them through something as simple as a wayward click or drag in the file system. In an ideal world, iTunes' song database can't become corrupted on its own—but what kind of an ideal world is it where hard drives crash, Internet connectivity is intermittent, and an inquisitive little brother might rummage through your computer and rename files while you're not looking?

This chapter presents a few procedures that will help you keep your iTunes **Library** in tip-top shape, organizing your music according to the best practices available for maximum efficiency in finding what you want. You'll see how to consolidate scattered files into your organized iTunes **Music** folder, how to fix broken song entries in the iTunes **Library**, and how to re-import a CD if there are encoding errors in the tracks you imported previously. These more advanced topics are intended to help you keep control of your digital music collection even in the face of a decidedly un-ideal computing world that's determined to make things difficult for you.

61 About Organizing Your Songs

✓ BEFORE YOU BEGIN	→ SEE ALSO
9 Import a Music CD into iTunes 11 Add a Music File to Your iTunes Library	69 Examine and Modify Song Information Tags

iTunes works just fine if you never touch any of the ***info tags*** yourself. You can import CDs while trusting to the information provided by the Gracenote CDDB query (as described in **9 Import a Music CD into iTunes**). You can purchase music from the iTunes **Music Store** and locate it in your library even if the artist name is spelled slightly differently from the way it's spelled in other songs by the same artist. You can import compilation CDs, in which each track is by a different artist, and let each artist be listed in the **Artist** column separately—in as frivolous a fashion as what can appear on discs such as Broadway soundtracks where the **Artist** field can contain long, unwieldy lists of names—or you can leave the entire disc's **Artist** field labeled, simply but unhelpfully, as **Various Artists**. Chances are you'll still be able to find the music you want, one way or another—if not by artist name, for example, you can always find an album by name in the **Album** list. These inefficiencies in the original info tags might not bother you at all; after all, there's always another way to find what you want in iTunes, as you saw in 33 **Find and Play Music**.

You might want to keep a few techniques in mind, though, beyond the ones covered by the tasks in this chapter, to help you keep your iTunes **Library** humming smoothly and efficiently. You can choose to ignore this advice, as you wish—but if you're bitten by the organization bug, as iTunes tends to inspire in people, you'll want to use these techniques to ensure that not just *you* can find all your music easily, but so can anyone else browsing your music, such as a remote iTunes user sharing your library (as explained in 59 **Listen to Shared Music on the Local Network**). Remember, what iTunes promotes is the legitimacy of the digital music medium; it wouldn't do to let people see your digital music collection in more disarray than your commercial CD collection!

Coalesce Artist Names

How is it spelled: **Emerson, Lake, and Palmer**? **Emerson Lake & Palmer**? **ELP**? Particularly if you've got tracks by the band that you acquired as MP3 files over the Internet from various sources, you might have this **Artist** field set to any of a seemingly limitless variety of spellings of the band name. Browse through the **Artist** list and you'll find that, in effect, the same band is listed several different times, each associated with only a small subset of the total tracks by that artist that you own.

Perhaps this doesn't bother you. But it should. What if a remote iTunes' user thinks he's navigated into your vast collection of Emerson, Lake, & Palmer music, only to discover that a few tracks are missing—not realizing that they're actually listed under **ELP**? It's common courtesy, to yourself and others (to say nothing of to Emerson, Lake, & Palmer) to organize all their music under the exact same band name so that it's all listed in the proper order, with a uniform level of respect for every song.

Now, the **Artist** fields that differ so subtly from each other are set in the individual songs' info tags; iTunes automatically and instantly displays all variations in the **Artist** list as collected from the songs themselves, and the larger grouping structures don't exist independently of the song files themselves. That makes it easier to keep things straight: All you have to do is fix a single song that has an aberrant spelling, and that spelling disappears from the listing, with the song snapping back into line with all the others by the same artist. An even better and more direct way to coalesce multiple spellings of an artist's name is to select all the songs by that artist—whether they're spelled correctly or not—and edit them all at once to set their **Artist** fields to the exact same value.

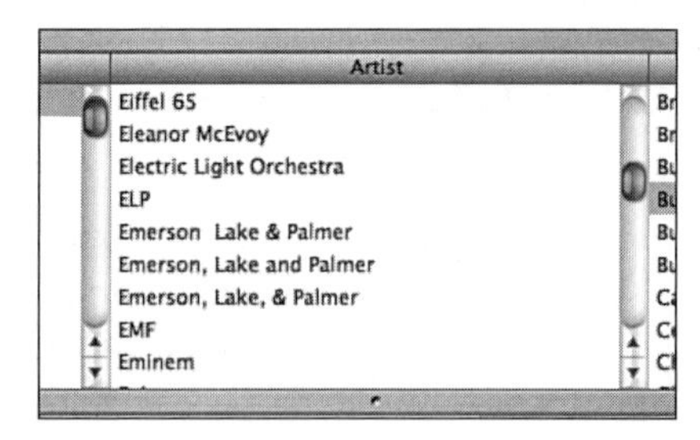

Selecting multiple artist entries with spelling variations.

61

Choose multiple artist entries from the **Artist** list by holding down the **Ctrl** key (in Windows) or the ⌘ key (on the Mac) as you click each one. The song listing area shows all the songs matching any of the selected artists. Don't click individual song entries to adjust them; instead, with the multiple artist groupings selected, choose **File**, **Get Info**. Click **Yes** in the dialog box that appears, confirming that you're sure you want to edit the information for multiple items.

In the **Info** window that appears, type the correct spelling of the artist name into the **Artist** field. iTunes fills in matching names from its database for you as you type; keep typing the name with the exact spelling, punctuation, and capitalization you want to use for all the selected songs until the correct text string is shown in the text box. Don't change any of the other fields, unless you want them to all have the same value as well (the **Genre** field is a good example of where this can be useful). Click **OK** to commit the changes and set all the selected songs to the same artist name.

Notice that the number of artists listed in the **Artist** list has now been reduced by as many superfluous alternate spellings as were represented in your music. Now there's only one **Artist** to select to get access to all your music by that same group.

▶ TIP

iTunes can recognize that some letters are merely variations on others. For instance, if an artist name in a certain song differs from the artist name in other songs only by capitalization, there won't be two separate artist listings in the **Artist** column. Similarly, vowels are grouped into single character families regardless of accents or diacriticals; this means that as far as iTunes is concerned, **Bjork** is the same thing as **Björk**. The completist in you, if he's really assertive, might compel you to fix these discrepancies even if they don't cause any superfluous listings—just select the artist by clicking the entry in the **Artist** list, edit the info tags for all matching songs, and set the **Artist** field to the spelling you want to set for all the songs.

Reduce Genre Variations

Another area where it pays to reduce the needless complexity of your iTunes **Library** is the **Genre** column. There is no universally accepted standard format for how genres are described; one set of songs might be listed as **Hip-Hop**, another as **Hip-Hop/Rap**, and another as **rap,hip-hop,urban**, depending entirely on who set the info tags in the songs in your library. If you're navigating your music by **Genre**, there's no way to know in advance which heading the music you want will be under. The best policy is to coalesce your genre variations into single, more all-encompassing categories.

From the **Genre** list, select an entry that you want to merge with another, more general entry. For instance, suppose that you have two albums under **Alternative Rock** and 15 under **Alternative**. You want to change the two wayward albums to fall in with the larger grouping so that they can all be reliably found in normal navigation, with a minimum of guesswork and blind hunting. Select **Alternative Rock**; then choose **File, Get Info**. Adjust the **Genre** field to read **Alternative** (you can select it from the drop-down menu or type until iTunes fills in the matching name for you). When you click **OK**, all the affected songs are updated, and the superfluous **Genre** entry disappears, with the albums and artists that were inside it now folded into the more general **Alternative** listing.

Organize Compilation Albums

What good is an album where every track is by a different artist? Especially if there are lots of different artists shown on each track, such as in an album of show tunes where each track's **Artist** field shows all the vocalists who performed on it? It may be entirely correct to have all these independent listings set in the individual songs, but it wreaks havoc on your **Artist** list; before you know it, the list is full of long, unreadable entries that are all but useless for navigating to the albums from which the songs originate.

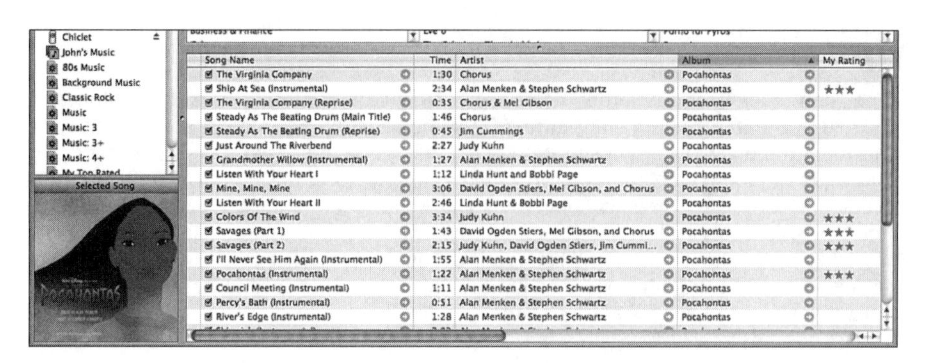

An album with tracks all by different artists, just aching to be marked as a ***Compilation*** *album.*

This is where the **Compilation** field comes into play. In iTunes, if you enable a special check box info tag called **Part of a compilation**, the song or album is organized in a different and much more useful way than normal songs or albums. Specifically, the entire album is found under a single **Artist** listing called **Compilations**, and all the individual and needlessly complex artist name entries are kept out of the **Artist** list. Similarly, the song files on the disk are organized into folders named for the album in which they appear, inside a folder called **Compilations**. This arrangement is much more efficient, whether you're navigating in iTunes or in the Finder or Windows Explorer, than digging into confusingly named folder trees named for long and complex artist names, only to find a single track inside each one. Compilations bring some sanity to albums where your only hope used to be to leave the tracks' **Artist** fields all set to **Various Artists**, which clearly isn't any good.

Navigate to an album whose tracks are all by different artists (use the **Album** listing to find it by name). Select the album name from the list and then choose **File, Get Info**. Select the **Part of a compilation** check box and click **OK**. The songs are updated; you should notice hardly any change in iTunes, except that the number of individual artists in the **Artist** list has been reduced by the number of different artists on the album. Now you can adjust each of the **Artist** fields, putting as much information into each one as you want, and your music navigation won't be made any more complicated no matter how much unique information you add. (This organizational structure is not currently available on the iPod.)

NOTE

For the **Compilations** grouping to be shown, be sure that the **Group compilations when browsing** check box is selected in the **General** tab of the iTunes **Preferences** window (choose **iTunes, Preferences** on the Mac and **Edit, Preferences** in Window to display the **Preferences** window). If this option isn't enabled, songs in compilation albums are organized into a **Compilations** folder in the file system, but the individual artists all show up in iTunes' **Artist** list.

Set Accurate Track and Disc Numbers

When browsing music in the **Library** view, it's often most useful to sort the songs based on the **Album** column. Doing so ensures not only that tracks are grouped together by the proper albums they come from, but that they're secondarily sorted according to their track numbers within the albums. With this organization, you can easily play an album all the way through by simply selecting it from the **Album** list and clicking **Play**; the tracks play in their original album order.

This behavior is true, however, only if the **Track Number** field is properly set in each of the songs. This field can take one of two forms: a single number, or a two-part number that also includes the total number of tracks on the disc (such as **7 of 12**). To ensure that the tracks are sorted properly, as well as to be able to set up ***Smart Playlists*** and other kinds of groupings based on the appropriate contents of these fields, it's important that each track have both its individual track number *and* the total number of tracks on the album set properly.

Select an album from the **Album** list. View the **Track #** column in the song listing area. If any of the tracks vary from the two-part **7 of 12** format, update them by setting the info tags; the best way to do this is to edit all the tags of the relevant tracks at once. Choose **File, Get Info**. In the **Track Number** fields, set the second number (and *only* the second number) to the total number of songs on the album. Click **OK** to set this value in all the tracks. Then select each individual song for which the track number isn't filled in; choose **File, Get Info** again and enter the appropriate track number for each song.

Multi-disc sets are also handled best by iTunes when they have the appropriate info tags set: in this case, it's the **Disc Number** field. Suppose that you have a three-disc set of songs by a favorite band. In the ideal case, all you'd have to do when playing this collection is select the single entry representing the entire three-disc collection from the **Album** list and click **Play** to play the whole thing from the beginning of the first disc to the end of the third. However, this usually isn't possible with discs imported using the basic information in the Gracenote database because the user-contributed information downloaded from there usually applies a superfluous suffix (such as **[1/3]**) to the album name for each disc instead of properly using the **Disc Number** fields. You can fix that, in what should be a familiar procedure by now.

First make sure that the individual disc number is set properly in each of the tracks. To do this, select an individual entry in the **Album** list representing a single disc in the set; choose **File, Get Info**, and set the first part of the **Disc Number** field pair to the appropriate number of the disc in the set. Click **OK** to save the changes to all the tracks on the disc. Repeat this step for all the discs in the set.

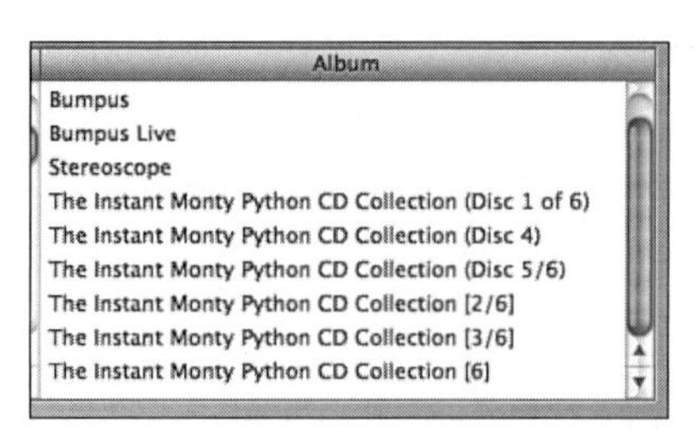

*Multiple discs from a single set, exhibiting superfluous variations in the **Album** list.*

Next, select all the different album entries representing the components of the three-disc set, holding down **Ctrl** (in Windows) or ⌘ (on the Mac) as you click each one. Choose **File, Get Info**. First set the **Album** field to an appropriate name for the entire collection, without any suffixes indicating the number of discs. Then fill in the second part of the **Disc Number** field pair, indicating the number of discs in the set (in this example, **3**). Click **OK** to save this information. Notice that the entries in the **Album** list collapse together into a single neat entry; selecting it shows you all the tracks from beginning to end within the collection. That's the way this kind of music was meant to work!

61

Work with Classical Music

There's one type of music that iTunes simply handles poorly: classical music. It just isn't designed for it. iTunes was developed with the modern organizational structure of popular music in mind: albums by individual artists containing a dozen or so songs each. This led to an obvious hierarchical structure for your library, with tracks grouped beneath albums, which are then grouped into artists and then genres. Yet when you think about how classical music is structured, it could hardly be any more different.

First of all, in classical music, the composer is far more important than the performer, which is usually defined as a certain symphony orchestra led by a certain conductor or featuring certain soloists. iTunes provides a **Composer** field, but it's not available as one of the **Browse** lists. The situation just gets worse from there: The concept of an "album" didn't exist in classical times, and instead of a dozen songs grouped into an album by a specific artist, the closest thing to it was a "work" (a symphony, concerto, or suite) consisting of only a few comparatively long pieces (or movements). These "works" were sometimes standalone bodies of music, but as often as not they were thought of as being part of a longer and ongoing lifelong body of work by the composer, or as entries in a series of themed works for a certain sponsor. To make matters still worse, these bodies of work are usually listed only by long, esoteric strings of numbers and identifiers, such as Beethoven's *String Quartet no. 9 in C op.59 "Rasumovsky" no.3*. Just imagine how that would look on an iPod!

▶ WEB RESOURCE

http://alanlittle.org/weblog/ClassicalID3.html

Alan Little discusses the ramifications of organizing classical music in the modern digital music paradigm.

Unfortunately, there's no good solution for this situation. iTunes and the iPod just aren't built for classical music. You can listen to digital versions of your classical music collection in iTunes just fine—it's just finding it that's a problem. You can use the **Search** bar to find music by a certain composer, or you can navigate the **Album** list to find the name of a work by its commonly known name (such as Holst's *The Planets*). But for music without the benefit of an easily readable and concise work title by which to find it, there's not a lot of recourse.

One possibility is to decide on an easily identifiable name for a given body of work—if one doesn't exist in common discourse, make one up if you have to—and assign that name to the **Album** field for the music. Don't adhere too closely to whatever name was assigned to the CD on which the music was published—more often than not, classical music CDs contain more than one work, often by different composers entirely. Instead, set your own name for the work, such as **Beethoven's Ninth Symphony**. It might not be very satisfying to classical music purists to see it listed in this way, but at least you'll be able to find it.

▶ NOTE

You can put the full, correctly formatted work title in the Comments field of the tracks on the album. If iTunes is updated in the future to better handle classical music, you can reorganize these tracks with the syntactically proper titles in front of you for easy reference.

62 Repair a Missing Song Entry

✔ BEFORE YOU BEGIN	→ SEE ALSO
33 Find and Play Music	66 Convert Audio Files to Other Formats 68 Find Music Files from iTunes' Entries 70 Eliminate Duplicate Tracks

Because iTunes is designed as a database of music, whose contents are really just pointers to the audio files on your disk, it has many advantages over pure "front-end" applications that play music files directly—and some disadvantages as well.

One of these latter is that if an audio file to which iTunes maintains a reference disappears—for any of a myriad reasons that this might happen—iTunes won't know where to find it. The reference in the library becomes a ***broken pointer***; it's still in the database, but it doesn't point to a valid file anymore.

▶ KEY TERM

Broken pointer—A song entry in the iTunes' database that points to a file that no longer exists or has been moved to another location so that iTunes can't find it. Broken pointers are marked with a ! icon.

▶ NOTE

The danger of broken pointers is much less on the Mac than it is on Windows. On the Mac, iTunes can keep track of files by their Unique File ID numbers, which locate them no matter where they are on the disk. In Windows, the Unique File ID doesn't exist, and iTunes can track a file only by its path. If you move a file on the Mac, iTunes can still find it; but in Windows, if the file system path is no longer correct for a file, iTunes can't play it.

This task describes how to fix a broken pointer, as well as how to fix a condition where a broken pointer is mistakenly directed toward the wrong audio file.

1 Attempt to Play a Missing Song

A broken pointer in the iTunes **Library** is marked with a ! icon next to its name in the leftmost column. This icon might not show up until you try to play the song; but iTunes periodically checks its internal database for consistency and displays the icon on any song whose corresponding audio file it can't find on the disk where it expects it to be.

Select the song and try to play it by double-clicking it or by clicking **Play**. iTunes pops up a dialog box telling you that the original file couldn't be found; it asks whether you'd like to repair the broken pointer by locating the file. Click **Yes**.

2 Navigate to Find the Original Song File

A file navigation window appears, in the style native to your operating system. Navigate your disk until you find the original file to which your iTunes' song entry pointed.

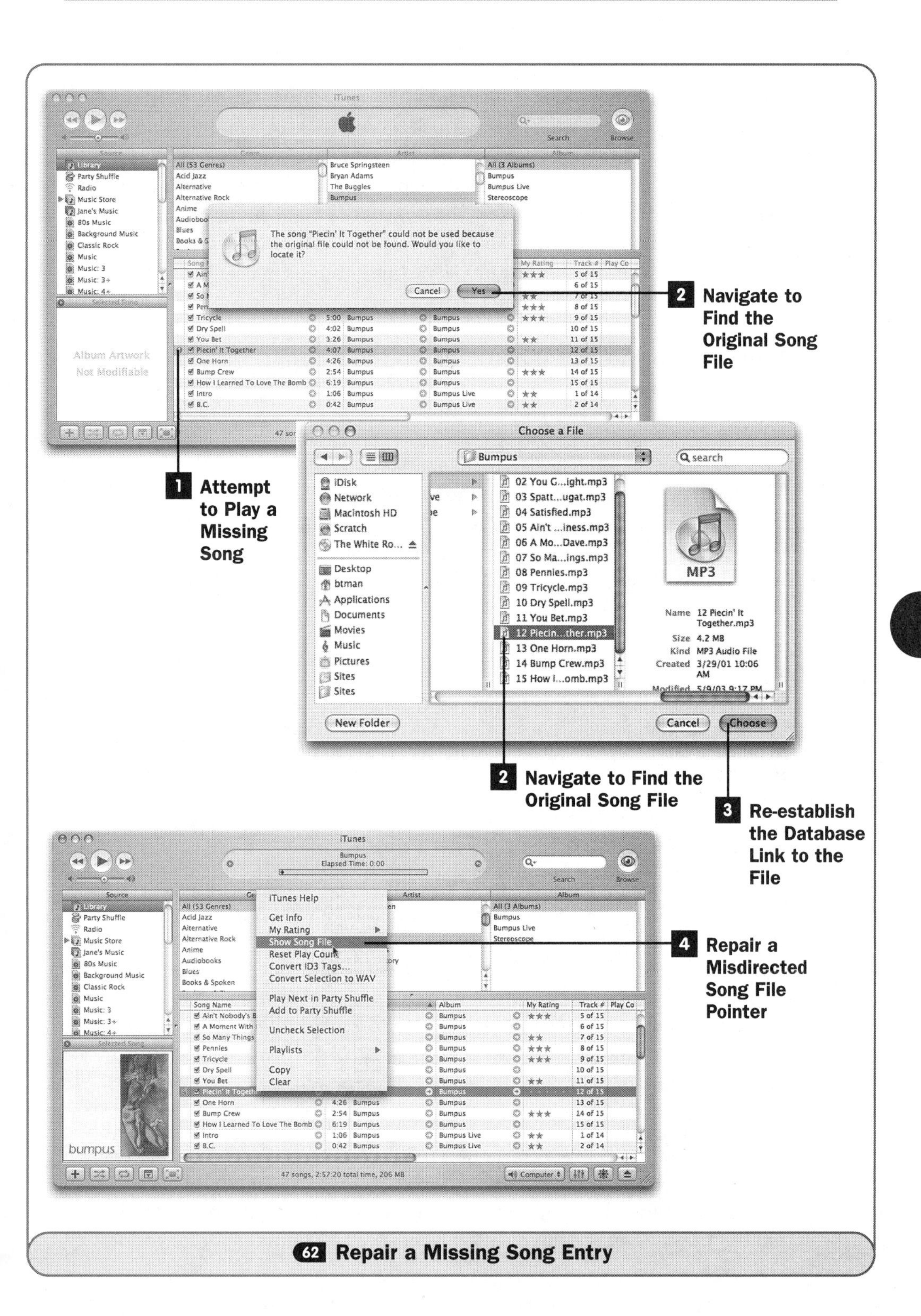

2 Navigate to Find the Original Song File
1 Attempt to Play a Missing Song
2 Navigate to Find the Original Song File
3 Re-establish the Database Link to the File
4 Repair a Misdirected Song File Pointer
The song "Piecin' It Together" could not be used because the original file could not be found. Would you like to locate it?
Cancel
Yes
Choose a File
New Folder
Choose

62 Repair a Missing Song Entry

Depending on what happened to the file, you might have to use different methods to locate it. First check the place where the file should be (in the appropriate folder inside the iTunes **Music** folder, for example) by navigating into subfolders until you see whether the file is in the folder it's supposed to occupy. Perhaps it has simply had its filename corrupted. If the file is not there, try searching your entire disk for any part of the filename or song name you can remember. (The Spotlight feature in Mac OS X Tiger can find lost music files where any of the embedded ***info tags*** as well as the filename match your search query.)

3 Re-establish the Database Link to the File

Select the original song file and click **Choose** or **Open**. If the file was deleted and you had to download a fresh copy, select that new file instead.

iTunes re-establishes the link in the database to the file you selected. Depending on your configuration, the file might be moved or copied automatically into your iTunes **Music** folder in the subfolder corresponding to the settings in the song's ***info tags***. See 12 **Import Your Existing Digital Music Collection into iTunes** for more information about configuring iTunes' behavior regarding the iTunes **Music** folder.

▶ NOTE

If the song file to which you choose to reattach the database entry doesn't have all the info tags filled out (for example, if it's a newly downloaded replacement copy), iTunes fills out all the missing tags from its own database entry. This is an excellent reason to make sure that your info tags are all as completely filled out as possible!

4 Repair a Misdirected Song File Pointer

Mistakes happen. They particularly have a way of happening in the wake of other mistakes, or when you're trying to repair the damage from a previous problem. One common thing that can happen is that you might accidentally re-establish the database link to the wrong music file—one that already exists in the iTunes **Library**. What happens in this case is that you end up with *two* entries in iTunes for the same file, with identical copies of all the same info tags (except for **Date Added**, **Last Played**, **Play Count**, and **My Rating**), and no database link to the original file for which you were trying to repair the entry.

One way to fix this is to simply import the file back into iTunes (see 11 **Add a Music File to Your iTunes Library**) and delete one of the redundant copies of the entry in iTunes, making sure to tell iTunes *not* to move the deleted file into the Trash. However, this solution is messy and external data for your re-imported song file such as the **Date Added** and **Last Played** stamps and the **My Rating** field is lost.

To re-establish the link cleanly and preserve all the unique song file information, do the following:

- Show the song file for the redundant iTunes entry (see 68 **Find Music Files from iTunes' Entries**). Select the copy with the **My Rating**, **Last Played**, **Play Count**, and **Date Added** fields corresponding to the original file whose link you were trying to repair (note that all the other info tags will be identical to the misdirected file).
- Move the misdirected file indicated by iTunes to a place where iTunes can't find it; on Windows, this means moving it to any other folder (such as your Desktop) or renaming it. On the Mac, you must move it to a different volume (your iDisk, a network drive, or an external hard disk—such as your iPod if you have it configured as an external drive) to defeat the Unique File ID.
- Try to play the song in iTunes. iTunes won't be able to find the song file; navigate to the correct original file (not the one you just renamed or moved to another volume), as described in step 2, and select it to re-establish the database entry. The song entry in iTunes regains its original info tags, imported from the file itself, and appears back in the proper place in the song listing.
- Move the second, misdirected file back into its original location. Play it in iTunes to be sure that its link is correctly established. You should now be up and running with both song files.

63

63 Re-import a Music CD for Improved Quality

✓ BEFORE YOU BEGIN	→ SEE ALSO
9 Import a Music CD into iTunes	64 Customize Importing Options 65 Import a CD in CD-Quality (Lossless) Format

Some CD drives are better than others. If you're the not-so-lucky owner of a drive with poor mechanicals or second-rate driver software, this condition is usually apparent in that the music you've imported from your music CDs are full of little clicks and pops that sound like dust on a vinyl record. Unfortunately, it has nothing to do with the cleanliness of the disc—it simply means that the drive or its driver software might not be capable of importing music cleanly at the selected data rate.

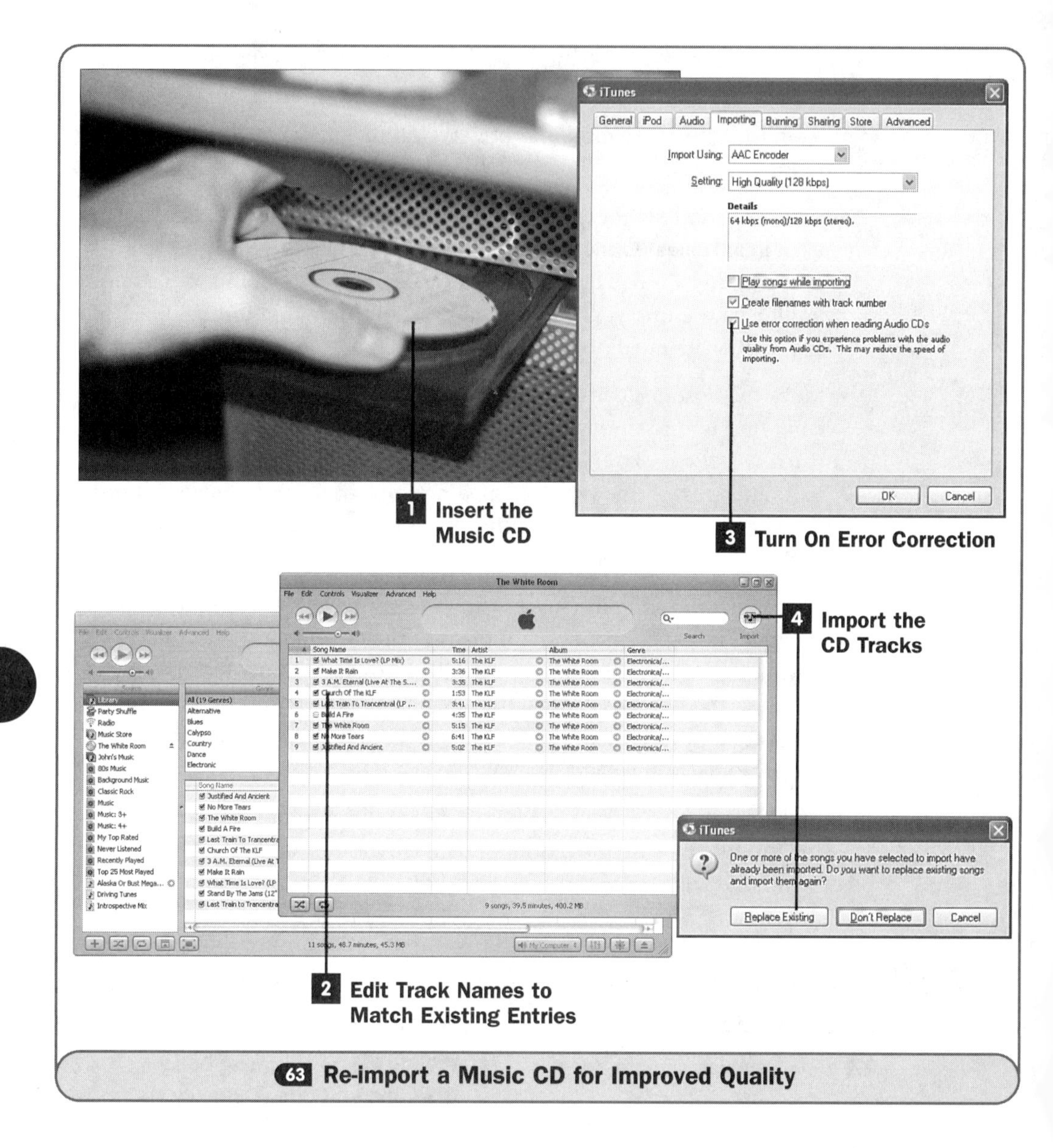

63 **Re-import a Music CD for Improved Quality**

▶ NOTE

This task shows how to re-import an audio CD to reduce the clicks and pops resulting from a fragile CD drive. If your CD is actually physically damaged, there's nothing iTunes can do to reconstruct the damaged data—it's lost for good, and importing the track will inevitably contain skips and errors. Look for a copy of the bad track in the iTunes **Music Store** instead—$1 for a single track is certainly cheaper than buying the whole disc over again. Of course, if the disc is actually smudged, scratched or dirty, you can buy a cleaning kit that can restore the disc to working condition before you import it again.

The good news is that you can re-import the CD using more sedate settings that are more likely to result in good sound quality. iTunes will simply replace your existing tracks with the newly imported ones, leaving all the info tags unchanged. Even the **Date Added**, **Last Played**, **Play Count**, and **My Rating** fields will remain untouched. If you import a bunch of CDs using an old computer with an inferior drive, and then you move to a new computer with a better drive, you can re-import your music files without losing the preference data you've been building up all this time. (See 94 **Back Up Your Music to CD or DVD** and related tasks for information on migrating your music collection from one computer to another.)

1 Insert the Music CD

With iTunes up and running and your connection to the Internet open, insert the CD you want to re-import into the CD drive. Wait for the track names to download from the Gracenote database.

2 Edit Track Names to Match Existing Entries

Double-click the CD in the **Source** pane to open it in another window; in the **Library** view, navigate to the album and view its tracks. You must update all the track names in the CD so that they exactly match the ***info tags*** of the existing iTunes entries—**Song Name**, **Artist**, and **Album**. If these track name elements don't match exactly, the newly imported tracks *will be added* alongside the old ones instead of replacing them. Use the two windows side by side so that you can copy and paste info tag data from the iTunes **Library** entries into the CD tracks.

3 Turn On Error Correction

Open the iTunes **Preferences** window (choose **Edit, Preferences** in Windows or **iTunes, Preferences** on the Mac). Click the **Importing** tab.

If you're re-importing the songs using the same drive you used previously, you might get better results by turning on error correction. Enable the **Use error correction when reading Audio CDs** check box. Music imported from CDs from now on might be of better quality, but it will take longer to import. Click **OK**.

4 Import the CD Tracks

Click **Import** in the upper-right corner of the CD window. iTunes notifies you in a dialog box that some of the tracks on the CD are already in iTunes, and asks if you want to replace them; click **Replace Existing**.

The CD tracks are imported and placed into the iTunes **Library** in place of the older versions. Play the tracks to verify that the new ones are free of the clicks and pops in the old versions.

If the newly imported music still has problems, it could be that you should replace your drive with a newer model. You can purchase a replacement optical drive very inexpensively ($50 or less), and you'll probably get more capabilities and speed to boot. It's certainly a more cost-effective solution than buying all your music over again from the iTunes **Music Store**.

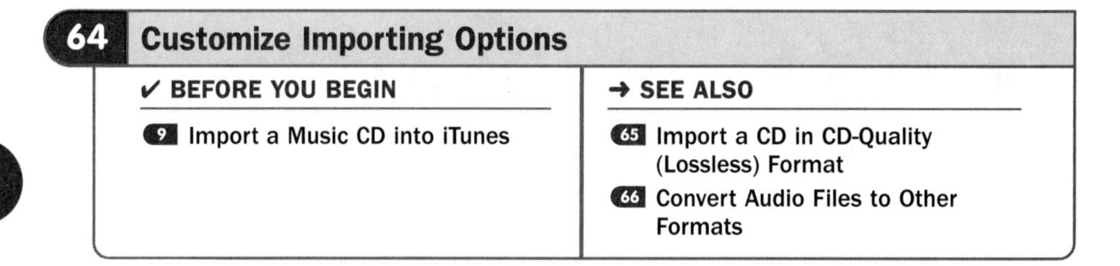

64 Customize Importing Options

✓ **BEFORE YOU BEGIN**

9 Import a Music CD into iTunes

→ **SEE ALSO**

65 Import a CD in CD-Quality (Lossless) Format

66 Convert Audio Files to Other Formats

Apple suggests that you use AAC ***format*** in its default ***bit rate*** settings to import your music CDs into iTunes. Because this is probably the format with the best balance of features and performance for most people's listening habits, iTunes is configured by default to this format. However, you can use any of several other file formats to create your new digital music files—most likely ***MP3***, to take advantage of the ubiquity of MP3 CD players—but also with the option of several high-quality ***lossless*** formats for those who prize audio quality over disk space frugality.

The importing options you can set in iTunes also determine the default destination format for when you convert audio files from other formats, as shown in 66 **Convert Audio Files to Other Formats**.

1 Open the iTunes Preferences

Open the iTunes **Preferences** window (choose **Edit, Preference** in Windows or **iTunes, Preferences** on the Mac). Click the **Importing** tab.

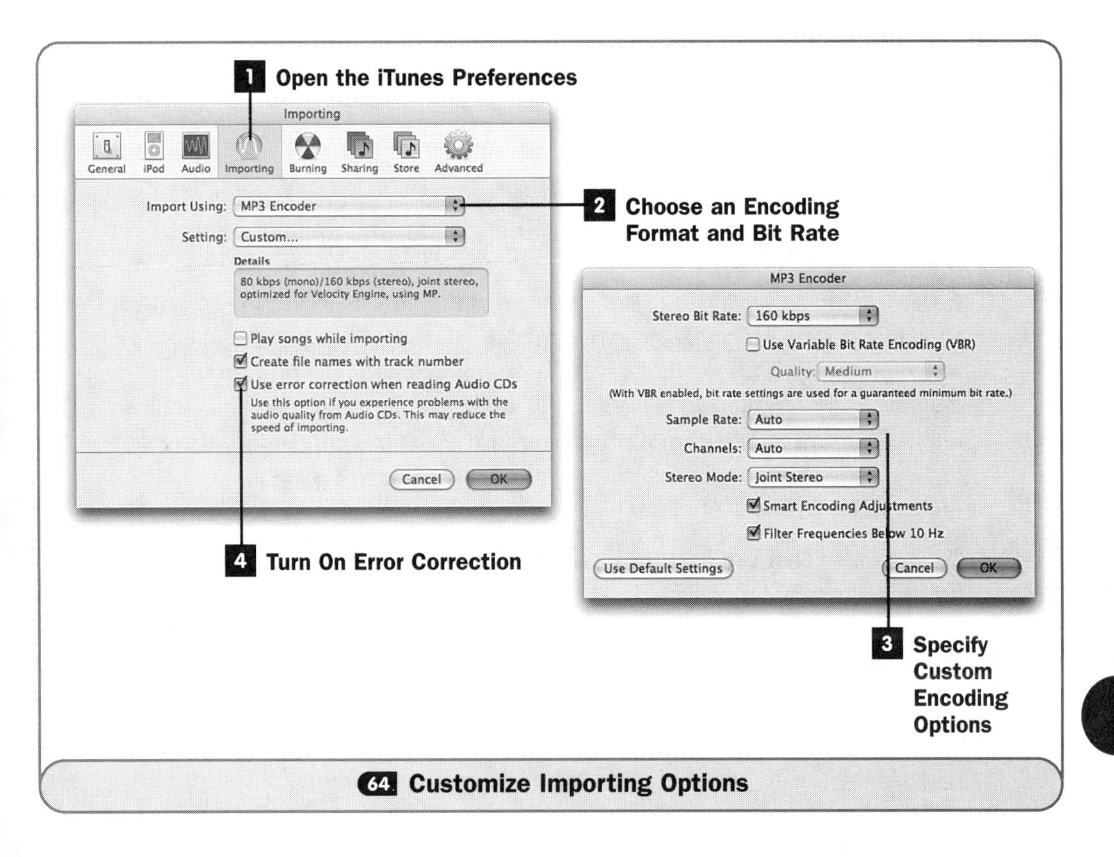

2 Choose an Encoding Format and Bit Rate

From the **Import Using** drop-down menu, choose an audio file format (an "encoder"). You might choose the **MP3 Encoder** to create MP3 files you can burn onto a data CD that will play in the car or on a portable MP3 CD player (see 54 **Create an MP3 CD**). You might select the **AIFF** or **WAV Encoder** options, to create uncompressed audio streams converted directly from the raw CDDA data, without any file-size reduction, for use in high-quality sound editing. Or you might opt for the **Apple Lossless Encoder**, which creates files about half the size of the original CDDA music, but with the same dynamic range and clarity (worthwhile if you're a hard-core audiophile).

▶ NOTE

Apple Lossless and AIFF formats are not supported on the iPod shuffle.

From the **Setting** drop-down menu, choose one of the available bit rates—the **MP3 Encoder** option, for example, has three different encoding quality settings from which you can choose. Most of the other formats have only a default **Automatic** setting and some **Custom** options you can tweak if you're an expert.

3 Specify Custom Encoding Options

Choose the **Custom** option from the **Setting** menu. This option is most useful if you've selected the **MP3 Encoder** option from the **Import Using** menu; the Custom setting allows you to adjust many of the parameters of the MP3 encoding policy. For instance, you can enable Variable Bit Rate (VBR) encoding, a popular technique that saves file size by reducing the bit rate in regions of the song that don't require as much sound resolution. You can also adjust the sample rate and number of channels, as you can with other encoding formats. Other options, such as **Smart Encoding Adjustments** and **Filter Frequencies Below 10 Hz**, are likely to be useful to experts only.

Click the **Use Default Settings** button to return to the default behaviors for the encoding format.

4 Turn On Error Correction

Back in the **Importing Preferences** window, enable the **Use error correction when reading Audio CDs** check box to ensure that imported CD music is subjected to several levels of checking as it's being copied and encoded. This option slows down the importing process, but on a fast computer such as a Pentium IV or a Power Mac G5, you likely won't even notice.

Click **OK** when you're done adjusting the settings. When you import CD music in the future, the music will be saved according to these settings.

65 Import a CD in CD-Quality (Lossless) Format

✔ BEFORE YOU BEGIN

9 Import a Music CD into iTunes
64 Customize Importing Options

→ SEE ALSO

66 Convert Audio Files to Other Formats
80 Use Your iPod as an External Hard Drive

People use iTunes and the iPod for the most amazing things these days. The makers of the *Lord of the Rings* movies, for example, used iPods to transfer in-progress audio and video clips to each other for editing and approval. (You'll see how to make use of your iPod's external hard drive function in 80 **Use Your iPod as an External Hard Drive**.)

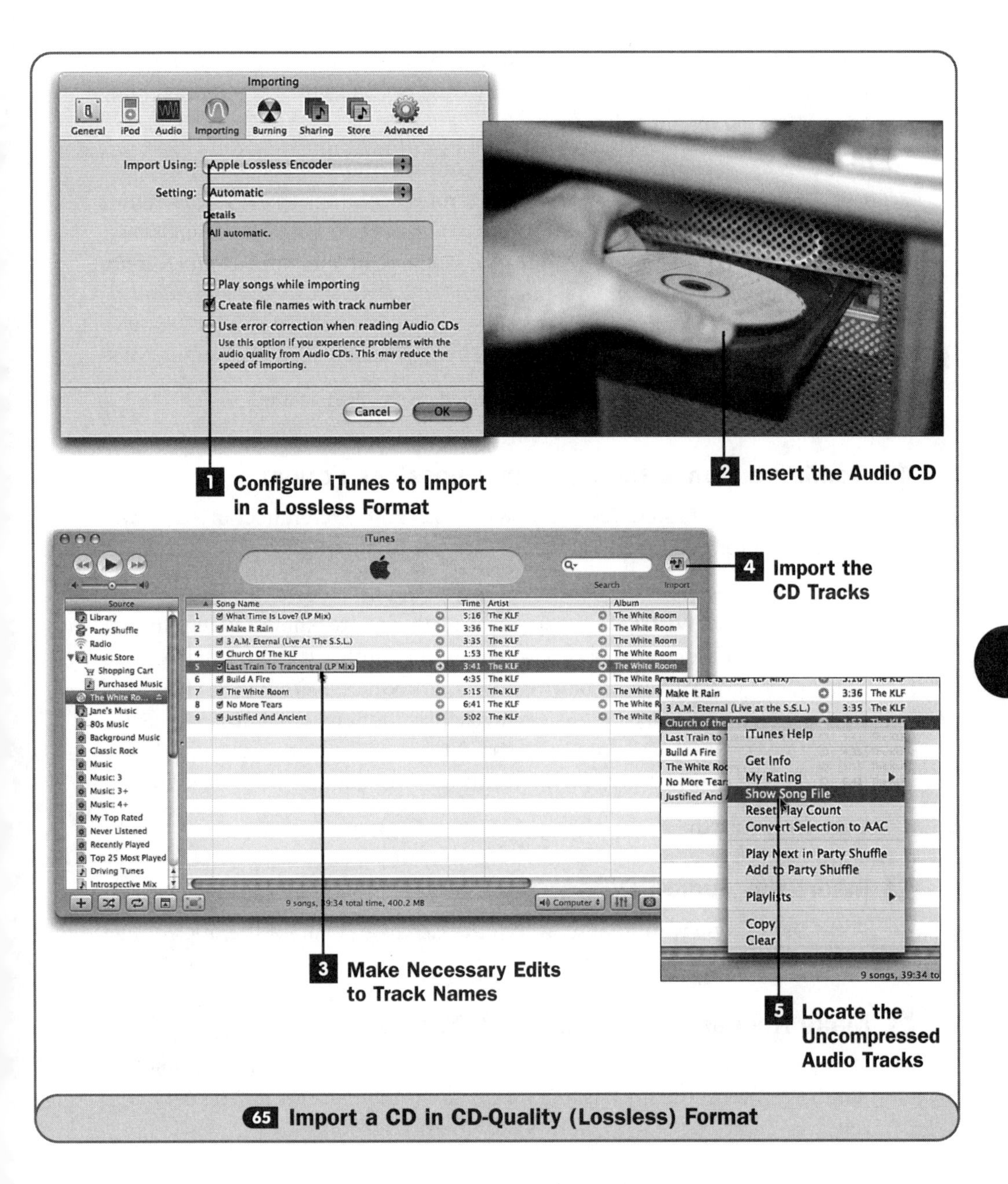

65 Import a CD in CD-Quality (Lossless) Format

It's easy to imagine that, in this capacity, it was important for the filmmakers to keep their audio clips in as pristine a format as possible to ensure that the clips could be edited and sent from studio to studio without any degradation in audio quality. This is the purpose for which ***lossless*** audio ***formats*** exist: ***AIFF***, ***WAV***, and the most recently developed one, Apple Lossless. These formats create audio files that are much larger than compressed MP3 or ***AAC*** files, but these pristine, CD-quality audio streams don't suffer from any quality loss as they're imported and exported from one format to another.

If your needs are such that you have to have a particular CD added to your iTunes **Library** in pristine CD-quality format rather than the space-saving compressed formats customarily used by iTunes, you can choose one of these lossless formats for your importing duties. Your iPod won't be able to hold as much music in these formats, but it'll sound a lot better.

▶ NOTE

Apple Lossless and AIFF formats are not supported on the iPod shuffle.

1 Configure iTunes to Import in a Lossless Format

Open the iTunes **Preferences** window (choose **Edit, Preferences** in Windows or **iTunes, Preferences** on the Mac). Click the **Importing** tab.

Choose a lossless format from the **Import Using** drop-down menu. Choose **AIFF Encoder** or **WAV Encoder** for cross-platform, uncompressed files that are no smaller than the raw CDDA files on the music CD itself. (AIFF is more Mac-oriented, WAV is more of a Windows standard.) Alternatively, choose **Apple Lossless Encoder** for lossless music files that are about 50% reduced in size from the raw CDDA data—these results are still about six times as large as compressed MP3 or AAC files, but this format definitely helps save space.

Click **OK** to use these new settings for future CD imports.

2 Insert the Audio CD

Insert the CD you want to import into the CD drive. Wait for the track names to download from the Gracenote database.

3 Make Necessary Edits to Track Names

Double-check the track name information downloaded from the Gracenote database against the track listing on the insert in your CD's jewel case; make any corrections to the track names that are necessary.

4 Import the CD Tracks

Click **Import**. iTunes imports the CD tracks and saves them to files in the chosen lossless format. These files are represented in iTunes in the same way as any other song files; the only way to tell the difference is the contents of the **Kind** field. (See 71 **Customize Which Information Columns Are Displayed** if the **Kind** column is not visible.)

5 Locate the Uncompressed Audio Tracks

You might want to use the imported AIFF or WAV files in an external audio-editing program. To do this, you must locate the original files on your hard disk. Select one of the imported song files and choose **File, Show Song File** to open a Finder or Windows Explorer window showing the original file in its location on the disk. You can then open the audio file in your favorite sound-editing software.

66 Convert Audio Files to Other Formats

✔ BEFORE YOU BEGIN	→ SEE ALSO
64 Customize Importing Options	65 Import a CD in CD-Quality (Lossless) Format

You can use iTunes to convert audio files from one ***format*** to another. For instance, you might have an AIFF file you created in an audio-editing program (such as GarageBand on the Mac) that you want to convert to MP3 or AAC format so that you can transfer it easily over the Internet and share with your friends. Because it's fairly likely that the motivation of any such format conversion is to have a listenable version of the converted audio file in your iTunes **Library** and iPod, iTunes does the conversion within the library itself. First you import the source file, then you convert it to the destination format (which is the same as the format you've selected for importing songs from music CDs, as shown in **64 Customize Importing Options**). Both the source and destination files are available in the iTunes **Library**, and you can then locate the original files with a single command for further external use.

66

1 Set the Default Importing Encoder to the Destination Format

iTunes can convert song files to your preferred destination format with a single command. However, before it can do this, you must define what your preferred format is. The format for file conversions is the same as the format you select for importing songs from music CDs.

Open the iTunes **Preferences** window (choose **Edit, Preferences** in Windows or **iTunes, Preferences** on the Mac). Click the **Importing** tab. Choose the desired destination format from the **Import Using** drop-down menu and use the **Setting** menu to specify any further encoding settings (as described in **64 Customize Importing Options**). Click **OK** when you've finished setting the default encoding format.

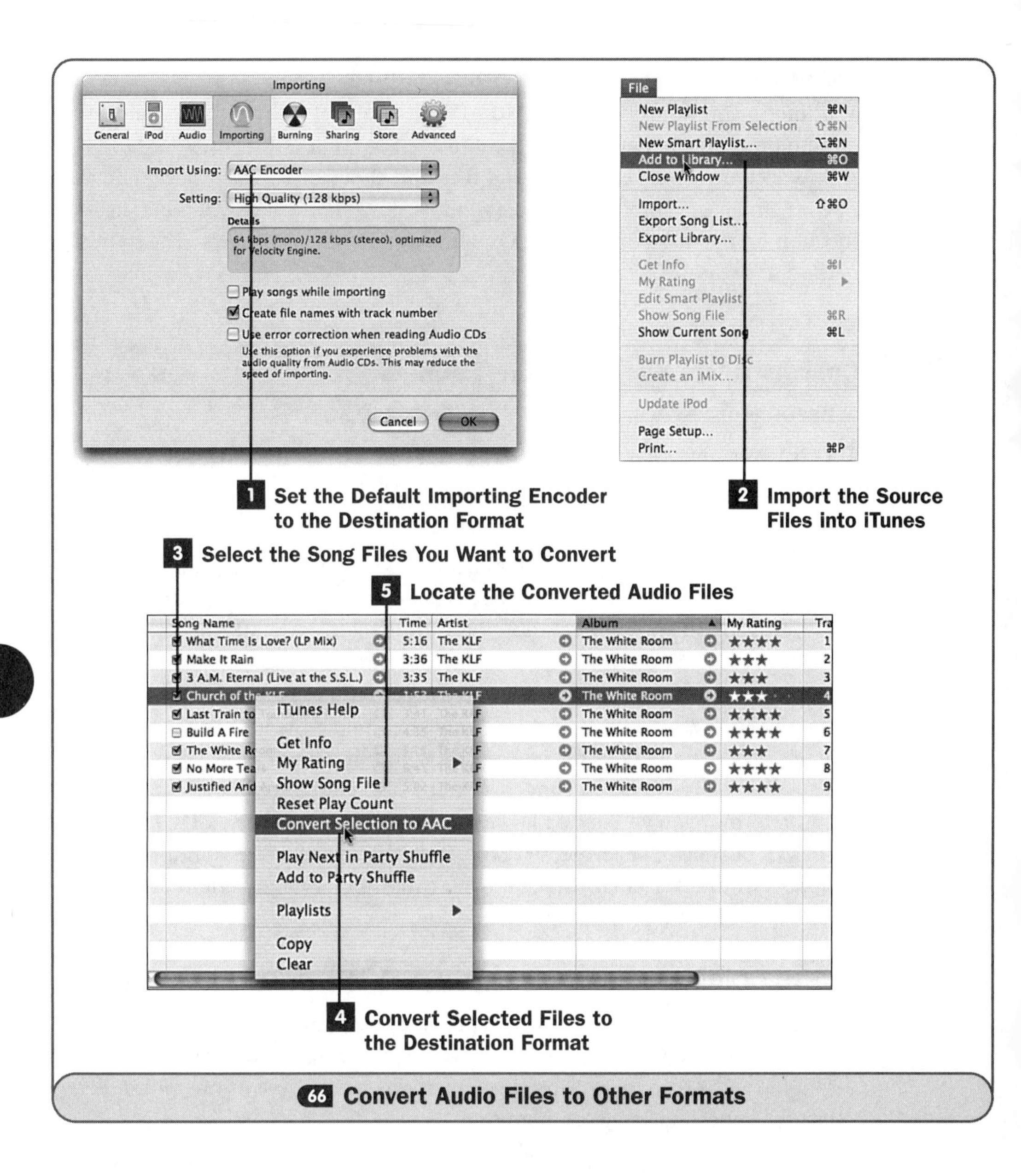

2 Import the Source Files into iTunes

Locate the audio file you want to convert. This file can be in any of the formats iTunes understands: ***MP3***, ***AAC***, ***AIFF***, ***WAV***, Apple Lossless, unprotected WMA (on Windows), or MPEG audio formats that predate MP3. You can even convert MIDI songs to your chosen sampled format using this method.

Add the file (or files, if you have more than one file to convert) into the iTunes **Library** as described in 11 **Add a Music File to Your iTunes Library**.

3 Select the Song Files You Want to Convert

Navigate to the newly imported files using the **Browse** lists or by sorting on the **Date Added** column. Click to select a single song file, or select multiple files by holding down **Shift** (or **Ctrl** or ⌘) as you click them.

4 Convert Selected Files to the Destination Format

From the **Advanced** menu (or the context menu that appears when you right-click the selected songs), choose **Convert Selection to *MP3*** (instead of *MP3*, the menu option will reflect the destination format you chose in step 1). iTunes converts all the selected files to the chosen destination format; the converted song files are shown in the iTunes **Library** under each of the songs from which they were converted.

5 Locate the Converted Audio Files

Select any of the converted song entries in iTunes and choose **File, Show Song File**. A Finder or Windows Explorer window opens to show you the location on the hard disk of the newly created file in your chosen destination format. You can now copy this file to a more useful location (don't delete it from the folder it's in, or it'll become a broken pointer in iTunes; instead, delete the song entry from iTunes itself and choose to have iTunes move the corresponding file to the Trash).

67 Consolidate Your Music Library

✔ BEFORE YOU BEGIN	→ SEE ALSO
2 Run iTunes for the First Time	68 Find Music Files from iTunes Entries
12 Import Your Existing Digital Music Collection into iTunes	70 Eliminate Duplicate Tracks

Consolidating your iTunes **Library** is a one-way operation that lets you clean up your hard disk after you've been using iTunes for a while and have added music files to it that might reside in various places all over your computer's hard disk. When you choose this option, iTunes finds all the music files that have been added to the library without being moved or copied to the iTunes **Music** folder, and copies them to appropriate locations in that folder on the basis of their info tags. After you've consolidated your library, you can recover disk space by deleting the original copies of your music files outside the iTunes **Library**. In the future, you can be assured that your iTunes **Music** folder contains all the music files in your collection (provided that you enable the **Copy files to iTunes Music folder when adding to library** option in the **Preferences** window).

1 Consolidate Your Music Library

Choose **Advanced, Consolidate Library**. A warning dialog box appears, asking whether you're sure you want to proceed, because this is a one-way operation that can't be undone. Click **Consolidate** to continue.

iTunes begins copying all the stray files into your iTunes **Music** folder. This process can take several minutes. When it's done, every song entry in your iTunes **Library** corresponds to a file that's properly organized by its **Artist** and **Album** *info tags* in your iTunes **Music** folder.

The next two steps illustrate a couple of configuration options that can help you keep your iTunes **Music** folder consolidated in the future.

2 Choose to Keep Your iTunes Music Folder Organized

Open the iTunes **Preferences** window (choose **Edit, Preferences** in Windows, or **iTunes, Preferences** on the Mac). Click the **Advanced** tab.

67

Enable the **Keep iTunes Music Folder Organized** check box. With this option enabled, every change you make to the info tags of a file in iTunes' interface is reflected immediately in the files themselves. Turn off this option if you don't want iTunes messing around with your files' names.

▶ NOTE

If you re-enable the **Keep iTunes Music Folder Organized** option after you had disabled it, iTunes must perform a check against all the songs in its library to make sure that all the filenames are accurate. This process can take a long time, and you can interrupt it by clicking **Stop**. However, it's a good idea to let iTunes finish making everything neat, so be patient.

3 Choose to Copy Future Imported Files to the iTunes Music Folder

The **Copy files to iTunes Music folder when adding to library** check box determines exactly what happens when you import a new file or group of files into iTunes' database. If the check box is enabled, iTunes makes a duplicate of each imported file and places it into an appropriate place in the iTunes **Music** folder, in subfolders based on the **Artist** and **Album** info tags. If this option is not enabled, the iTunes' database instead points to added music files wherever in the system they happen to be.

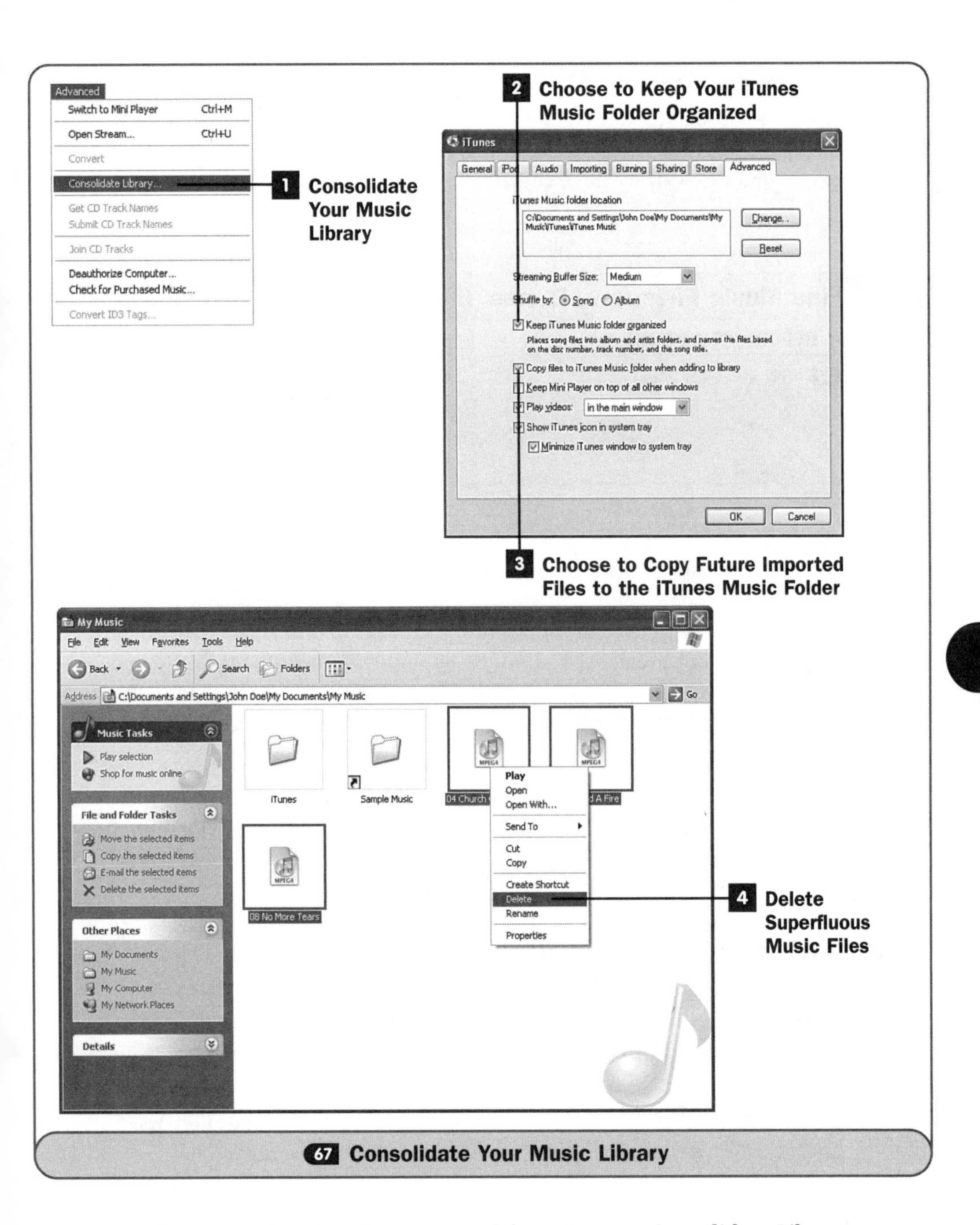

67 Consolidate Your Music Library

If you enable this option, you won't have to run a **Consolidate Library** process again in the future because all the music you add to iTunes will automatically be copied into your iTunes **Music** folder.

Click **OK** to commit your configuration changes.

4 Delete Superfluous Music Files

After the consolidation is complete, use the Finder or Windows Explorer to locate the original music files that were duplicated into the iTunes **Music** folder, and throw away these superfluous originals. Throwing away the originals lets you recover the (perhaps significant) disk space they consume.

68 Find Music Files from iTunes' Entries

✓ BEFORE YOU BEGIN	→ SEE ALSO
33 Find and Play Music	62 Repair a Missing Song Entry 66 Convert Audio Files to Other Formats 67 Consolidate Your Music Library

iTunes acts as an intermediary between you and the bare music files that make up your digital music collection. Its internal database structure translates the files with their austere names and folder paths into an easily navigable continuum of music, interlinked by **Artist**, **Album**, **Genre**, and other ***info tags***. You can accomplish most operations involving your music by simply dragging song entries out of the iTunes' song listing into other applications, particularly on the Mac where applications such as iMovie are designed to interoperate with iTunes.

However, this arrangement doesn't mean you won't ever have to find the original raw music files in their organized folders. You might want to attach an MP3 or AAC file to an email message, for example. You might have to upload a song file to your website. These operations require you to be able to find your way to the original music files to which the iTunes' database entries point.

1 Navigate to the Music You Want to Find

Using the iTunes **Browse** lists or the **Search** bar in the **Library** view, or any ***playlist*** or other music source in the **Source** pane, navigate to find an individual music file that you want to find on your hard disk.

2 Select a Song File to Find

Click to select the song file you want to locate.

▶ NOTE

You can't use this method to locate multiple files on the disk at once; if more than one song entry is selected, the Show Song File menu option is disabled.

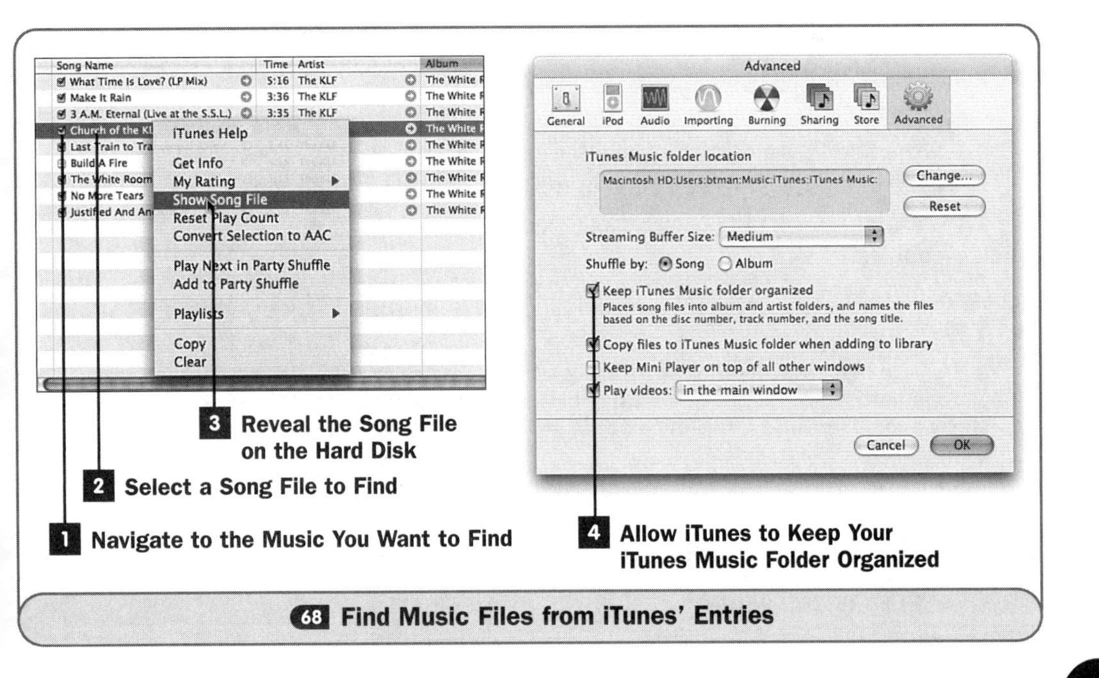

68

3 Reveal the Song File on the Hard Disk

Choose **File**, **Show Song File** (or right-click the song title and choose **Show Song File** from the context menu). A Finder or Windows Explorer window appears, showing you the selected file in its location on the hard disk. You can copy this file to any more useful location, such as your Desktop, for use with other audio-editing applications.

▶ NOTE

Don't move the file from its location on the disk, particularly if you use Windows. See 62 **Repair a Missing Song Entry** for more information on the consequences of moving a file and how to recover from it.

4 Allow iTunes to Keep Your iTunes Music Folder Organized

Note the path to the file's location. If you have enabled the **Keep iTunes Music Folder Organized** option in the **Advanced** pane of the iTunes **Preferences** window (open the window by choosing **Edit**, **Preferences** in Windows or the **iTunes**, **Preferences** on the Mac), you can be sure that the file can always be found by navigating first into your iTunes **Music** folder (inside the **Music** folder on the Mac, or in the **My Music** folder in Windows, then inside **iTunes**, where the **Music Library** database file is kept), then into the folder named for the artist of the song as set in its info tags. Open the folder corresponding to the album the song is on; inside that folder is the song file itself.

If the **Keep iTunes Music Folder Organized** check box is not enabled, you'll have to use the steps described in this task to find your music files because there will be no predictable way to locate them as there is when the option is enabled.

▶ TIP

If you have Mac OS X Tiger or an indexing system such as Google Desktop on Windows, you can quickly locate music files using their *info tags* with a Spotlight or Google search on your computer's disk. This approach is still not as elegant as using iTunes' folder hierarchy, but it'll do in a pinch.

69 Examine and Modify Song Information Tags

✔ BEFORE YOU BEGIN	➜ SEE ALSO
33 Find and Play Music	9 Import a Music CD into iTunes 14 Submit CD Track Names to the Gracenote Database

Song information tags, or ***info tags*** (also known as *ID3 tags* for MP3 files), are the heart and soul of iTunes. They're what give it the ability to organize your music in a richer and more meaningful way than simply by scrolling through folders looking for particular filenames. The info tags formulate the basis for the database queries that underlie every listing of song files, whether you're viewing an album or artist listing, a ***playlist***, a ***Smart Playlist***, or even just the **Browse** lists in the **Library** view.

As discussed in detail in 61 **Organizing Your Songs**, keeping your songs' info tags organized properly is a big part of what makes iTunes enjoyable to use. The more neatly you have your info tags specified in all your files, the easier it is to navigate iTunes and quickly and easily find the music you want to listen to.

iTunes provides several ways to edit your songs' info tags. You can modify certain textual info fields in place within the iTunes' song listing. Other tags, however, must be edited using the **Info** window, which shows you all possible info tags that can be set. The Info window can also be used to modify the info tags of large groups of song files all at once. Finally, iTunes gives you the ability to update the version and internal ***format*** of the ID3 tags in certain selected MP3 files, which corrects for limitations on field length and encoding format that can cause problems in MP3 files encoded with older software.

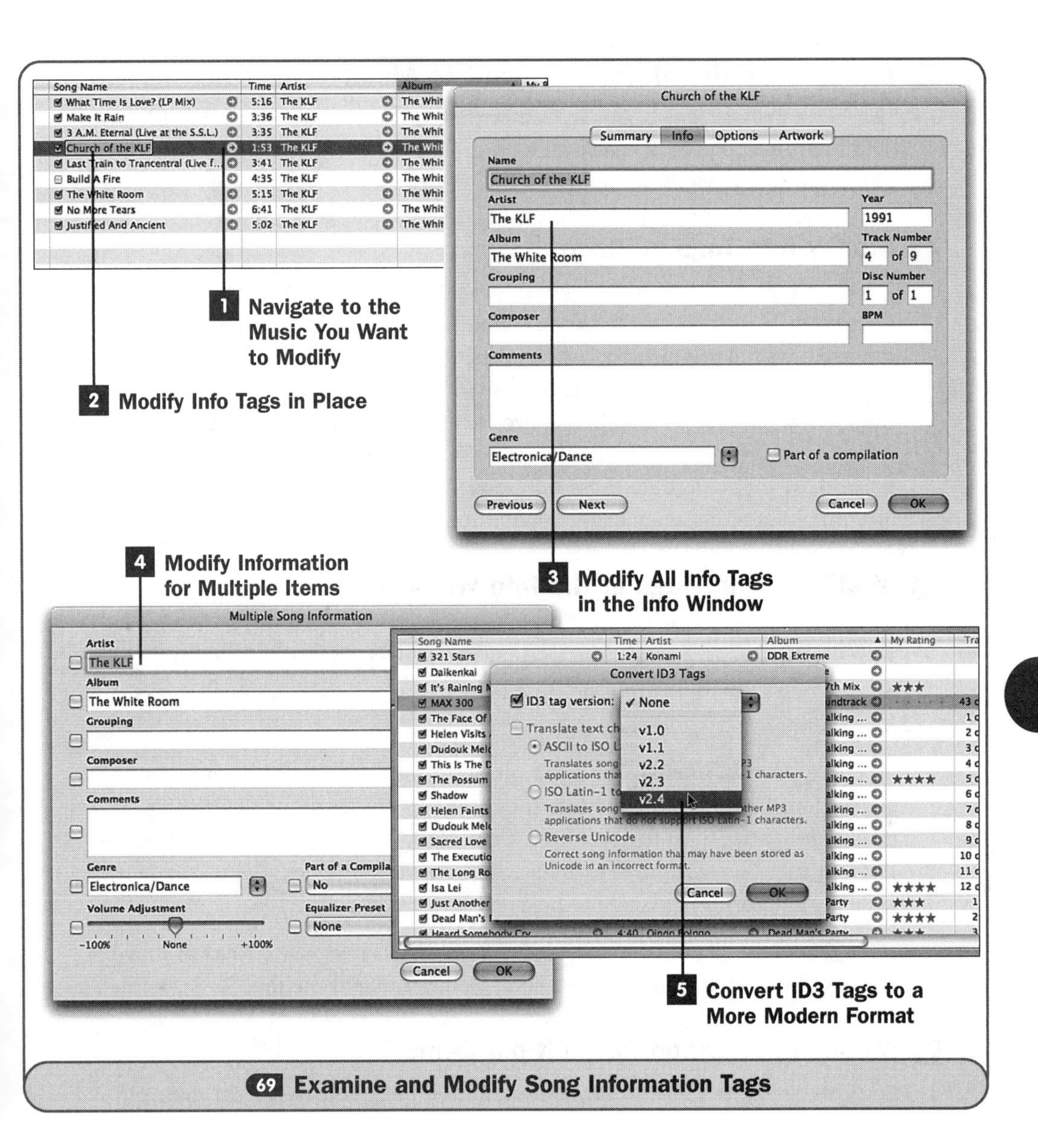
1 Navigate to the Music You Want to Modify
2 Modify Info Tags in Place
3 Modify All Info Tags in the Info Window
4 Modify Information for Multiple Items
5 Convert ID3 Tags to a More Modern Format
69 Examine and Modify Song Information Tags

69

▶ NOTE

Info tags can be set for any files in the iTunes **Library**. However, only certain file formats (specifically, *MP3*, *AAC*, and Apple Lossless) have the structural ability to store the info tag information inside the files themselves, in the *headers* (textual data at the beginning of a binary data file). Even these formats don't store the **Date Added**, **Last Played**, or **My Rating** fields, or certain other information such as preamp settings. For all other formats, the info tags are stored exclusively in the iTunes **Library** database itself, and the information is lost if the iTunes **Library** becomes unusable. See 97 **Restore Your Music Library Database from a Backup Copy** for more details on precautions you can take to protect your library's info tags.

1 Navigate to the Music You Want to Modify

Using the **Browse** lists or the **Search** bar in the **Library** view—or any ***playlist*** or other music source in the **Source** pane—navigate iTunes to find an individual music file whose info tags you want to modify.

2 Modify Info Tags in Place

For certain textual info tags, such as **Song Name**, **Artist**, **Album**, **Genre**, and **Composer**, you can edit the tags by simply clicking them in the song listing area and typing the new text (then pressing **Return** or **Enter**). This is the most straightforward way to modify the info tags that most directly affect navigation (the contents of the **Genre**, **Artist**, and **Album** lists depend on querying for every unique member of each of those fields in the entire library). Make changes to these info tags in a song entry, and the changes are immediately reflected in the navigation lists.

3 Modify All Info Tags in the Info Window

With a song file selected, choose **File, Get Info**. This command brings up the **Info** window; click the **Info** tab to show all the settable info tags for the file. Modify any of these fields that you like, but be sure you're putting in accurate information.

As you type in the **Artist**, **Album**, **Composer**, or **Genre** fields, iTunes makes suggestions by automatically filling out the remainder of the field with any matching values from the database it can find. As soon as you see the name filled in that you want to use, press **Tab** to move to the next field. Otherwise, keep typing until you've set the field the way you want it.

Click **OK** when you're done setting fields, or click **Previous** or **Next** to move backward or forward through the song listing and edit the tags for other files.

4 Modify Information for Multiple Items

You don't have to edit info tags one song at a time. It can be a lot more efficient—particularly if you want to make a change that affects all the tracks in a given album or by a certain artist—to select all the relevant tracks and then edit their info tags all at once.

Select multiple tracks whose tags you want to edit by holding down **Shift** as you click (for contiguous selections), or **Ctrl** or ⌘ (for non-contiguous selections). You can also select all the tracks in an album by selecting the album from the **Album** list, or all the tracks by an artist by selecting the name from the **Artist** list. Then, as before, choose **File, Get Info**.

The **Info** window that appears is slightly different from how it appears when you're editing just one file. In this version of the window, there's a check box next to every field that indicates whether the field has been modified while the window has been open. The check box is enabled if you make a change to any of the fields. Disable the check box on any field to prevent that field from being modified on all the selected tracks.

If a field has a value set in it, it means that all the tracks in the selection are set to the same value. Blank fields indicate that some of the tracks in the selection have different values for that field. Unless you're sure that you want to set all selected tracks to that same value, don't enter a value into a blank field!

Click **OK** to apply your changes to all the selected songs.

5 Convert ID3 Tags to a More Modern Format

Sometimes, an MP3 file that was recorded many years ago, or with very old software, might present difficulties when you try to set its info tags. A song name greater than 32 characters might become truncated, for example, no matter how many times you set it. This usually happens because the encoding software wrote info tags using an old version of the ID3 tag standard, which specified smaller limits on info tag lengths or text-encoding capabilities than is possible with modern info tags in newly encoded files.

▶ TIP

You can find out what ID3 tag version is used in any MP3 file by selecting it and choosing File, Get Info; on the Summary tab, the ID3 Tag information field reports the song's tag version.

Select an MP3 file whose info tags are giving you problems; choose **Advanced, Convert ID3 Tags** menu (or right-click the song and choose **Convert ID3 Tags** from the context menu). A dialog box appears, giving you several options for how to convert the ID3 tags. Choose a version number (the higher the better) from the **ID3 tag version** drop-down menu to upgrade the ID3 tags to a more modern format. (You might have to convert the tags to a version number smaller than the highest one available under certain circumstances, such as if you want to open the files in an application that doesn't support the most recent tag version.)

If the song's info tags contain non-Western characters that appear in the song listing area as question marks or unreadable symbols, select the **Translate text characters** check box and choose a conversion operation from the three options presented: **ASCII to ISO Latin-1** or its reverse operation, or the reversal of an incorrect Unicode text encoding.

Click **OK** to convert the info tags. You should now be able to set the fields to values with arbitrary lengths or character sets.

70 Eliminate Duplicate Tracks

✔ BEFORE YOU BEGIN

9 Import a Music CD into iTunes
12 Import Your Existing Digital Music Collection into iTunes

➜ SEE ALSO

62 Repair a Missing Song Entry
63 Re-import a Music CD for Improved Quality

A common issue that complicates the practice of keeping your iTunes **Library** cleanly organized is that it's very easy to accumulate duplicate songs in the library. From iTunes' perspective, a *duplicate song* occurs any time two or more songs share the same song name and artist. This usually results from the same song by the same artist appearing on more than one album that you've imported into iTunes (a common pitfall of having compilation or "Greatest Hits" albums in your library).

Normally this duplication doesn't cause any serious problems; but having multiple copies of a single song in your library makes it more likely that the song will come up in randomized (shuffled) playback, whether in iTunes or on the iPod, and it means that your **Play Count** field is inaccurate because it is split across two or more entries in the database. It's generally best to avoid having duplicate songs in your library. You don't have to delete them, though; just disabling the check box on a duplicate song means it you can exclude it from ***Smart Playlists*** or iPod synchronization, and you will generally listen to only the copy whose check box is enabled.

1 Choose a Music Source to View

Select the **Library** view or any ***playlist*** from the **Source** pane. Only the songs within the selected music source are analyzed for duplicates.

2 Show Duplicate Songs

Choose **Edit, Show Duplicate Songs**. The song listing changes to omit all songs that don't exist in matched pairs; the only listed songs are those with duplicates within the selected music source, where both the song name and the artist name are identical. For easiest viewing, sort the songs on the **Song Name** column.

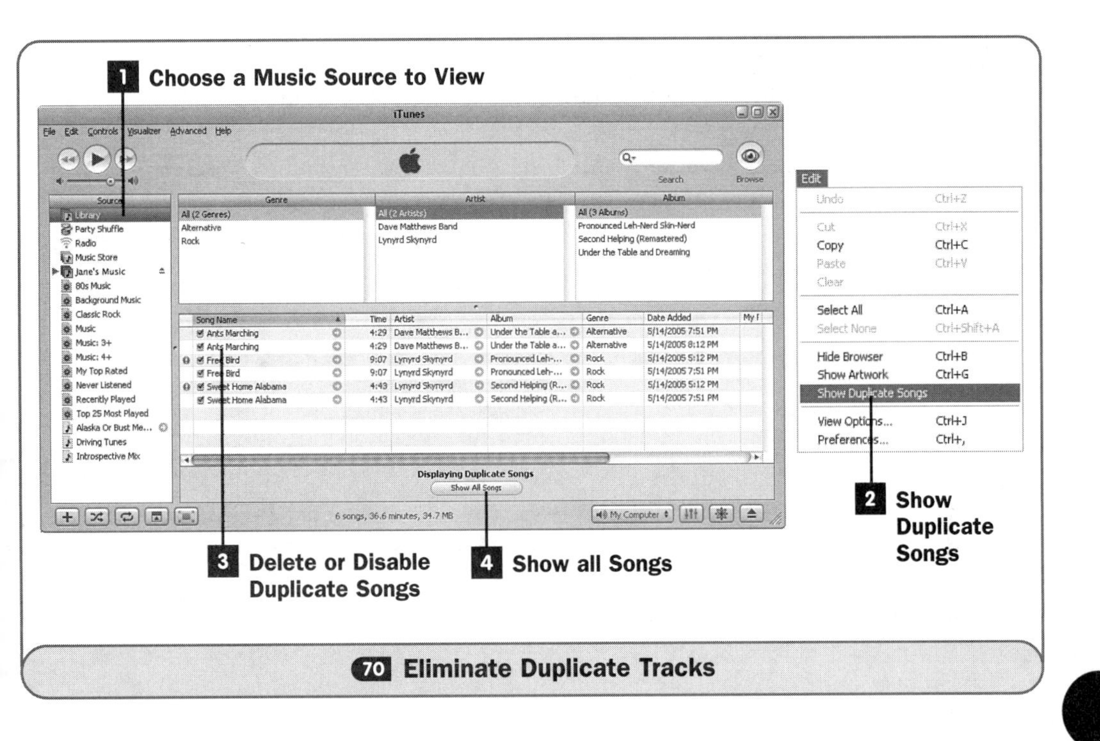

3 Delete or Disable Duplicate Songs

You can eliminate duplicate songs by deleting one of the copies from your iTunes **Library**. However, this approach means that you end up with incomplete albums. A better way to filter your music, perhaps, is to simply disable a duplicate song by disabling the check box next to one of the songs. (You might find it more sensible to disable the song that's part of a compilation rather than the one that's on an original album.)

Now that your duplicate songs are disabled, you can edit a Smart Playlist that you listen to a lot to ensure that songs where the check box is disabled are not included in the playlist; do this by selecting the **Match only checked songs** check box in the Smart Playlist's definition dialog box (select the Smart Playlist and choose **File, Edit Smart Playlist**). Similarly, in the **iPod** tab of the iTunes **Preferences** window (choose **Edit, Preferences** in Windows or **iTunes, Preferences** on the Mac), enable the **Only update checked songs** check box; this option prevents disabled songs from being transferred to the iPod and taking up space unnecessarily. It also prevents your Play Count from being spread across two or more identical song files.

4 Show all Songs

When you're done examining the duplicate songs in your library or other music source, click the **Show All Songs** button at the bottom of the song listing area or choose **Edit, Show All Songs**. This command returns you to the normal viewing and navigation mode.

9

Making the Most of iTunes

IN THIS CHAPTER:

It's the little extra features that make iTunes more than a simple music player: features designed not just to emulate the music-playing experience you'd get from your CDs, but to enhance it in new ways never possible before the advent of digital music. By skillfully using the ***info tags***, you can sift through your music to arrange it for playback just the way you want it. Taking advantage of iTunes' integration into both Windows and Mac OS X, you can control the playback and rating of your music from locations such as the System Tray and the Dock without going anywhere near iTunes itself. The result of weaving your computing in with your music enjoyment leads to a jukebox application that "learns" how to serve up music according to your tastes. To complete the picture, iTunes lets you really micromanage the finer points of playback of individual songs, selecting equalizer settings to enhance each one for its own musical profile. You can even install third-party ***Visualizer*** add-in software to create just the right visual atmosphere to go with the auditory treat in which your dedication to your music results.

71 Customize Which Information Columns Are Displayed

✔ BEFORE YOU BEGIN	→ SEE ALSO
2 Run iTunes for the First Time	69 Examine and Modify Song Information Tags
33 Find and Play Music	

iTunes displays your music in a tabular format, with every informational field associated with each song listed in its appropriate column. Just as with the file-navigation methods you're used to in your computer's operating system (**Details** view in Windows, or **List** view on the Mac), iTunes gives you complete control over which information columns are displayed, the order in which they're shown, and which ones are used to sort your listings of songs. These preferences are stored independently for each musical grouping listed in the **Source** pane—each ***playlist***, CD, iPod, and navigational view is preserved independently so you can be sure that when you select a music source, its contents are displayed just the way you want it for that particular selection of music.

1 Add or Remove Information Columns

While viewing any music source (the **Library** view, for example, or a playlist), choose **Edit, View Options**. This command brings up a palette with an array of check boxes, one for each possible information column. Select the columns you want to see and deselect the ones you don't. Click **OK** when you're done.

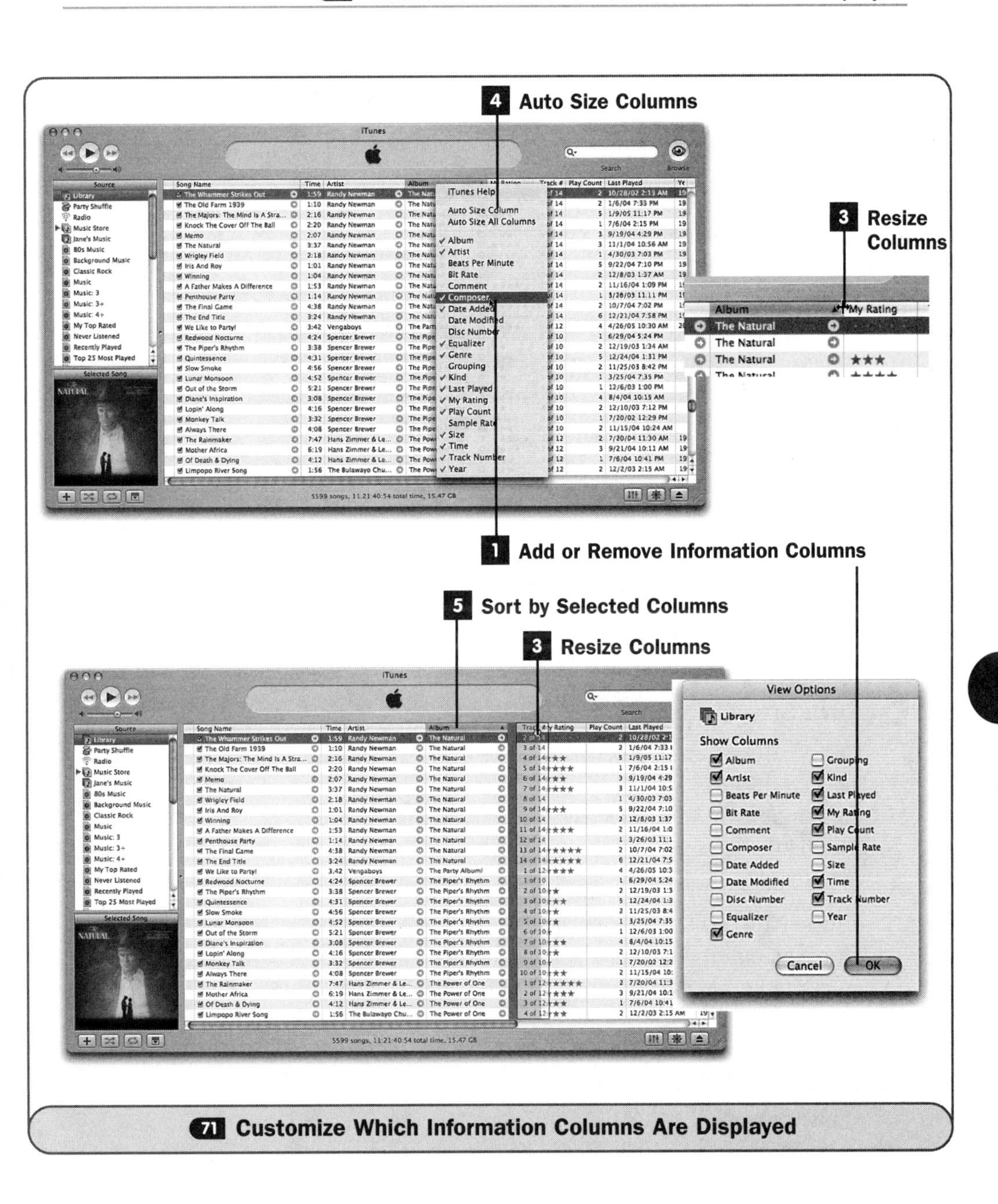

71 Customize Which Information Columns Are Displayed

▶ TIP

Another, more direct way to turn columns on and off is to right-click (or **Ctrl**+click) the header bar in the song listing area. The pop-up context menu shows all the column names, with check marks next to the ones that are displayed. Select a column name to toggle it on or off. Newly activated columns appear in the position where you clicked the mouse to summon the menu.

2 Change the Order of the Displayed Columns

Click and hold the header of a column you want to move to a different location. Drag the column left or right to insert it between a different pair of columns. You can relocate any column except for the **Song Name** and the first, unlabeled track-order column that appears in playlist views.

3 Resize Columns

You can manually change the width of any column. Position your mouse pointer in the header bar, over the vertical dividing line between any two columns. Click and drag left or right. The column to the left of the mouse pointer grows or shrinks accordingly; all the columns to the right shift left or right to follow it and are *not* resized.

▶ NOTE

You can make a column narrower than the text of the items within it; if you do, longer items are shown with an ellipsis (...). If you then edit their contents in place, the editable text is shown in its entirety, overlapping other columns while you type. You cannot, however, make a column narrower than the text of its name in the header bar.

4 Auto Size Columns

iTunes can automatically size a column to be just wide enough to contain the longest entry in it and no wider. Right-click (or **Control**+click) the header of the column you want to resize and choose **Auto Size Column** from the context menu. The selected column is immediately resized to optimally fit its contents.

Choose **Auto Size All Columns** from the same context menu to perform this operation on all displayed columns in a view at once. This gives you the maximum amount of complete, readable information in the smallest possible space.

5 Sort by Selected Columns

Click the header of any column to sort the displayed songs based on that column. The triangle to the right of the column's name indicates whether the sort order is ascending or descending. For instance, a text column (such as **Album**) is sorted alphabetically A–Z if the triangle is pointing up, and Z–A if the triangle is pointing down. Numeric columns such as **Track #** and **Time** work the same way with numeric sorting.

When you sort some columns, other appropriate columns are consulted for secondary sorting order. For example, if you sort on the **Album** column, the songs within an album are sorted according to **Track #** and separated by **Disc #**. If you sort on the **Artist** column, songs are secondarily sorted by **Album** and then by **Track #**.

72 Control iTunes from the Dock, Dashboard, or System Tray

✔ **BEFORE YOU BEGIN**

33 Find and Play Music
36 Rate Your Music

After you've got your music playing, set to a ***playlist*** that you can groove along with as you use your computer for other tasks, you don't necessarily want iTunes to be sitting there taking up space on your screen. It's taking care of the background music—you don't need to control it all the time. So you can hide it, minimize it, or switch to the **Mini Player** view to get it out of the way. Still, there will come those times when you want to skip a song you don't particularly like, assign a rating to a song you've never heard before, or just identify the song that's playing. You don't have to pull up the full-size iTunes' window to do this; you can access iTunes' basic playback controls, the rating system, and the title and other information on the playing song in a menu available from the System Tray (in Windows) or the Dock (in Mac OS X). In Mac OS X Tiger or later, there's even a Dashboard widget you can summon with a keystroke to get access to iTunes' basic controls for a quick volume adjustment or to skip to the next song.

1 Windows Only: Enable iTunes in the System Tray

If you're a Windows user, open the iTunes **Preferences** window (choose **Edit, Preferences**); click the **Advanced** tab. Enable the **Show iTunes icon in system tray** check box to display the iTunes' control icon in the System Tray, the box within the Taskbar in the lower-right corner of your Windows screen. Double-click this icon to quickly launch iTunes as well as to control it while it's playing.

▶ TIP

The **Minimize iTunes window to system tray** option, when enabled, means that when you click the **Minimize** button in the iTunes window, it disappears entirely from the screen and doesn't take up a slot in your Taskbar. Instead, double-click the iTunes' icon in the System Tray to return the window to full size.

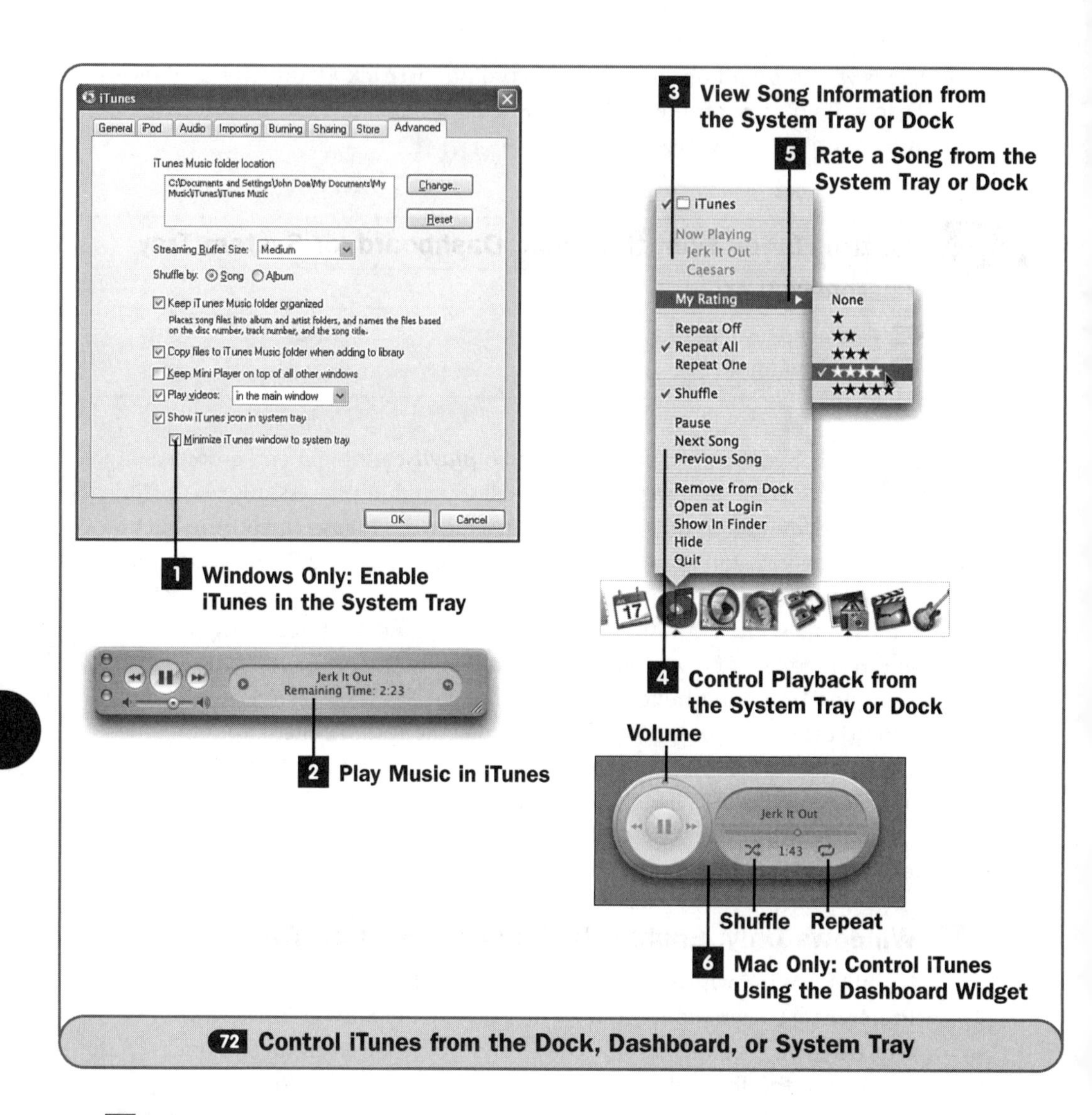

72

2 Play Music in iTunes

For both the Mac and Windows versions of iTunes, using the **Library** view or a playlist, play your music as you normally would.

3 View Song Information from the System Tray or Dock

While a song is playing, right-click (or **Control**+click) the iTunes' icon in the Dock (on the Mac) or the System Tray (in Windows). A menu appears with a number of different control options for iTunes, as well as a readout of the song's title, artist, and album name. These items are grayed-out because they are informational items rather than controls.

4 Control Playback from the System Tray or Dock

The context menu has **Play** (or **Pause**), **Next Song**, and **Previous Song** controls that correspond to the playback control buttons in iTunes itself. Using these controls, you can skip from song to song or pause the music without having to restore the entire iTunes' window.

You can also use the **Repeat Off**, **Repeat All**, or **Repeat One** options to choose the Repeat mode; click the **Shuffle** option to turn randomized playback on and off.

5 Rate a Song from the System Tray or Dock

From the context menu, open the **My Rating** submenu and choose a star rating for the currently playing song; choose **None** to clear the rating. The rating you choose is immediately saved into the iTunes' database.

6 Mac Only: Control iTunes Using the Dashboard Widget

If you have Mac OS X 10.4 (Tiger) or later, there's another quick way to control iTunes playback: the Dashboard. Activate the iTunes' Dashboard widget as you do any other widget: Press the configured Dashboard hot key (**F12** by default), or click the **Dashboard** icon in the Dock; open the widget bar by clicking the circled + icon in the lower-left corner; and drag the iTunes' widget from the bar to any position on the screen. This iTunes' widget shows the currently playing song name and presents controls for playing and pausing, skipping forward or back, controlling the volume (drag the circular ring left or right), scrubbing to a particular location in the song, or toggling the **Shuffle** or **Repeat** mode. You can even change to a different playlist by clicking the **i** icon to flip the widget around and access the controls on its back.

73 Train iTunes to Play Your Favorite Music

✓ BEFORE YOU BEGIN	→ SEE ALSO
35 Create a Smart Playlist 36 Rate Your Music 47 Rate Your Music on the iPod	48 Transfer Only Preferred Music to the iPod

The iTunes' features you've learned about throughout this book can be combined to give you intricate control over your music. Although it's certainly possible to micromanage your ***playlists*** to play exactly the music you want to hear, sometimes it's the element of surprise that makes listening to music in iTunes so much fun: just letting iTunes pick out a song you haven't heard in years, or that you didn't even realize you had. Simply playing songs at random, in **Shuffle** mode, can be fun too. But you don't want iTunes serving up bad songs with the good ones. This task shows you how, with the dutiful use of star ratings and ***Smart Playlists***, and your natural listening habits recorded by iTunes over a long period of time, you can train iTunes to serve you songs that surprise you *and* that are guaranteed to be the kind of stuff you want to hear.

1 Rate Your Music

As described in 36 **Rate Your Music** and 47 **Rate Your Music on the iPod**, assign a star rating to each song in your iTunes **Library** as you listen to it. Be sure to sync your iPod with iTunes on your computer after each time you play and rate music on the iPod to ensure that the ratings are accurately reflected in the iTunes **Library**.

2 Create a Smart Playlist for Highly Rated Music

Create a Smart Playlist (see 35 **Create a Smart Playlist** for details); define the playlist's criteria to include the requirement that matched songs have a rating of three stars or higher (you can adjust this threshold according to your taste). Name this playlist, for example, **Top Rated**.

3 Listen to Music Over a Long Period

Play music from the iTunes **Library** or on your iPod, using whatever playlists or music sources you like, for a period of weeks or months. Skip songs you don't want to hear. When you listen to a favorite song, be sure to allow it to play all the way through to the end so that its **Last Played** date stamp and **Play Count** field are recorded properly. Sync your iPod with your computer after each time you play music on the iPod to ensure that these fields are accurately reflected in the iTunes **Library**.

Over time, you'll see that your favorite songs are also usually your most frequently played ones, as you can verify by sorting the songs in your library using the **Play Count** column.

4 Create a Smart Playlist for Frequently Played Music

Create a Smart Playlist that's defined as matching only a certain number of your most frequently played songs. Do this by specifying as the only criterion that the playlist should be limited to a specified number of songs (say, **500**—however large you want your pool of "favorite songs" to be) and selected by **most often played**. Name this playlist, for example, **Most Often Played**.

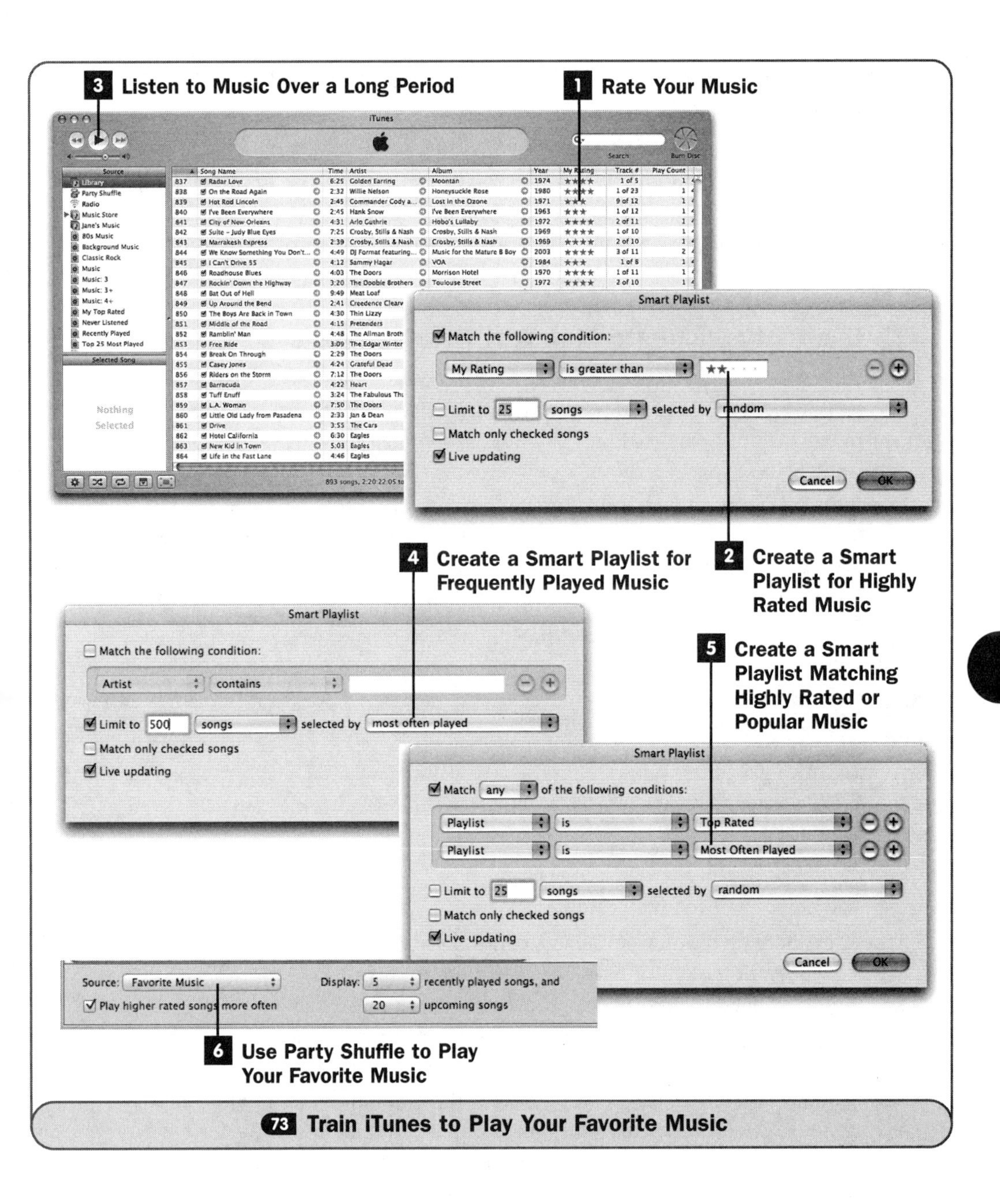

▶ TIP

You can use or modify the model Smart Playlists that come with iTunes (which include **My Top Rated** and **Top 25 Most Played**) for steps 2 and 4 of this task.

5 Create a Smart Playlist Matching Highly Rated or Popular Music

Create a third and final Smart Playlist called **Favorite Music**. This playlist should have two criteria: songs that are in the playlist **Top Rated** *or* songs that are in the playlist **Most Often Played**. (Make sure that the **Match any of the following conditions** option is selected at the top of the Smart Playlist definition.)

6 Use Party Shuffle to Play Your Favorite Music

You can now play music from the **Favorite Music** playlist, with **Shuffle** mode enabled (click the second button from the left under the **Source** pane), to be regaled with unexpected songs pulled from either your **Top Rated** playlist (matching songs you rated highly) or your **Most Often Played** playlist (matching songs you voluntarily play a lot). The surprise inherent in this method might suit you fine, or you can use Party Shuffle mode (see 39 **Use the Party Shuffle Playlist**) to choose a customizable list of songs from the **Favorite Music** playlist at random. Just remember: The more you listen to your music, the better the **Favorite Music** playlist will reflect your tastes.

74 Adjust the Global Equalizer

→ **SEE ALSO**

6 Configure Your iPod for Your Headphones or Speakers
60 AirTunes: Connect iTunes to a Stereo with AirPort Express
75 Adjust Equalizer Settings for Individual Songs

iTunes includes a "graphic equalizer" controller that lets you adjust the volume levels of different regions of frequency response to compensate for the specific strengths and deficiencies of your speaker system. If you have a set of large, powered speakers with a subwoofer connected to your computer, for instance, you'll want to boost medium-frequency ranges and let the amplifier handle the deep bass. If you have only a small set of speakers, you might want to boost the bass response relative to the medium and high ranges to compensate for the speakers' lack of low-range power. If you're using ***AirTunes*** to broadcast your music wirelessly to an external amp and A/V system, you'll want to disable iTunes' frequency modifications entirely and let the amp do the work.

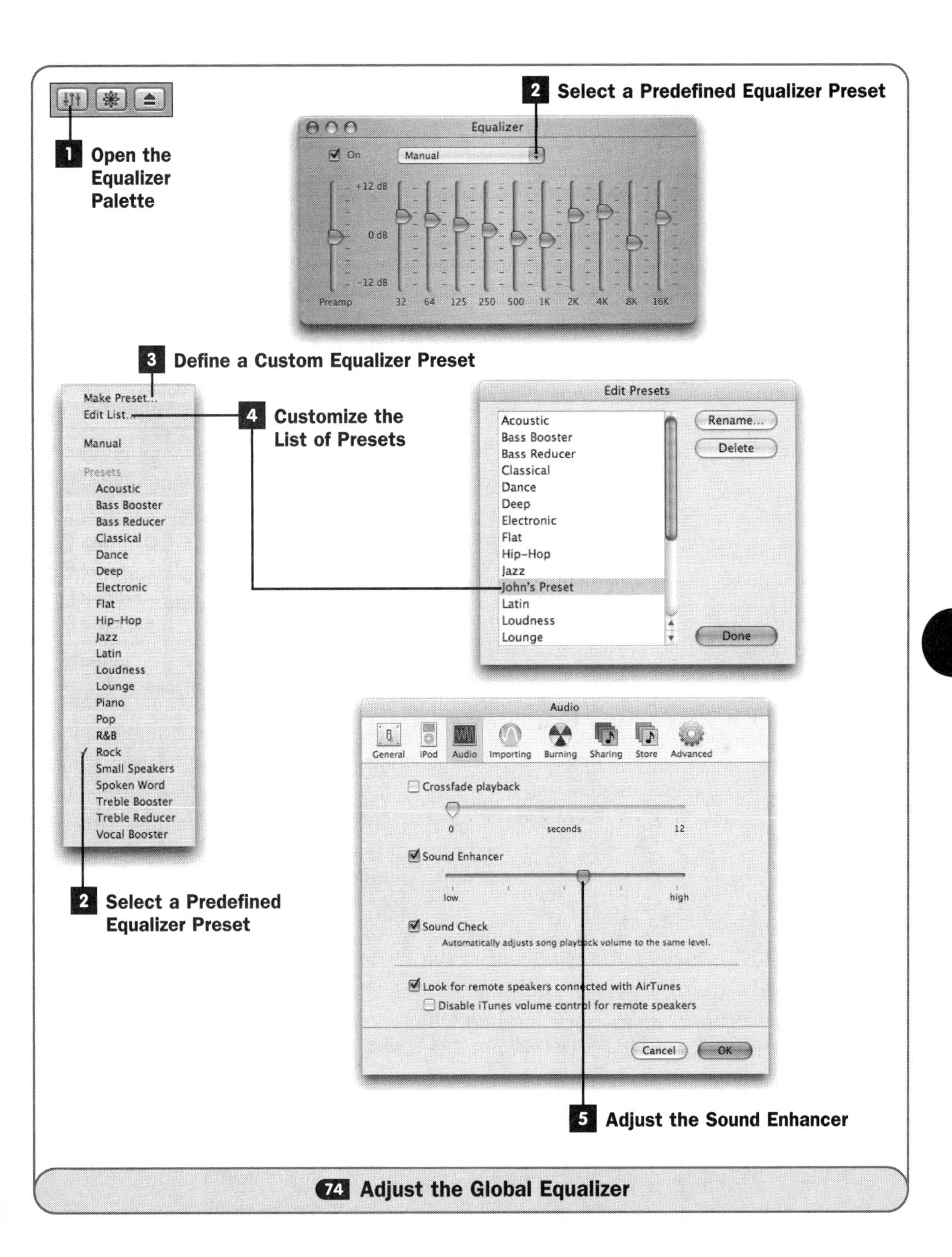

74 Adjust the Global Equalizer

Different styles of music require different adjustments to the output frequency ranges as well; for instance, you'll want to amplify certain medium ranges to strengthen vocal tracks, or suppress the middle in favor of the extreme high and low ranges for Rock or Latin music. However, genre-specific equalizer presets are best addressed in 75 **Adjust Equalizer Settings for Individual Songs**; this task instead describes how to configure iTunes in general for your speaker setup.

1 Open the Equalizer Palette

Click the **Equalizer** button in the lower-right corner of the iTunes' window (the graphic with three vertical sliders). This action brings up the **Equalizer** palette, a floating window with many sliders, each representing a narrow frequency range and shown in order from the lowest-pitch (at left) to highest-pitch (at right). You can manually move these sliders to control sound output in various ranges, or you can choose a *preset* (a predefined set of frequency-range volume adjustments) from the drop-down menu.

▶ TIP

The On check box in the Equalizer palette controls whether the equalizer settings are consulted at all as music is sent to the speakers. Disable this check box to send unmodulated, flat signals to the output channel. Use the Preamp slider to adjust the overall signal level across all frequency ranges if necessary.

2 Select a Predefined Equalizer Preset

Choose an appropriate preset matching your speaker setup from the drop-down menu. Presets designed to address specific kinds of output configurations are **Bass Booster**, **Bass Reducer**, **Deep**, **Flat**, **Loudness**, **Small Speakers**, **Treble Booster**, **Treble Reducer**, and **Vocal Booster**. All other presets are designed for specific styles of music and shouldn't be set in the global equalizer unless you plan to listen to only a particular kind of music for a while and then restore the **Equalizer** back to its original settings.

▶ NOTE

Equalizer adjustments are applied in real-time to the music that's playing, so you can select different presets while music is playing and immediately hear the effects.

3 Define a Custom Equalizer Preset

Drag any of the sliders up and down to make custom adjustments to the equalizer profile; the drop-down menu's selection changes to **Manual** as soon as you make any manual changes. Experiment to find out what parts of the music are affected by which sliders. For instance, vocals are at their strongest between 500Hz and 4KHz, and percussion is muddled unless the very highest frequency ranges (8–16KHz) are appropriately boosted.

When you have the sliders placed where you want them and the music sounds right, choose **Make Preset** from the drop-down menu. Enter a name for the new preset in the window that pops up. Click **OK**. From now on, you can find your custom preset by name in the list so that you can easily switch to it.

4 Customize the List of Presets

Choose **Edit List** from the drop-down menu. A window appears that lets you rename or do away entirely with presets you don't want anymore. Select a preset from the list and click **Rename** or **Delete** to alter the list's contents accordingly. Click **Done** when you're finished. Your changes are now reflected in the drop-down menu in the **Equalizer** palette, as well as in the **Equalizer** field for individual songs, as you'll see in 75 **Adjust Equalizer Settings for Individual Songs**.

▶ NOTE

If any songs are set individually to use presets that you rename or delete here, iTunes pops up a dialog box to confirm that the songs' presets will be reassigned or cleared accordingly. See 75 Adjust Equalizer Settings for Individual Songs for more information.

5 Adjust the Sound Enhancer

One final effect you can use to polish up your music's sound is the **Sound Enhancer**, an algorithm applied to all iTunes' output whose impact on your music can be increased or lessened. Open the iTunes **Preferences** window (choose **iTunes, Preferences** on the Mac, or **Edit, Preferences** in Windows); click the **Audio** tab. Enable the **Sound Enhancer** check box and tweak the slider to adjust the effect's intensity, which works by clarifying and sharpening the waveforms in the digital audio file to make the music sound more three-dimensional and immersive. This effect is applied in real-time; play music while you adjust the setting so that you can tell how it affects your music and where your taste indicates you should put the slider.

75 Adjust Equalizer Settings for Individual Songs

✔ BEFORE YOU BEGIN	➜ SEE ALSO
71 Customize Which Information Columns Are Displayed	6 Configure Your iPod for Your Headphones or Speakers
74 Adjust the Global Equalizer	

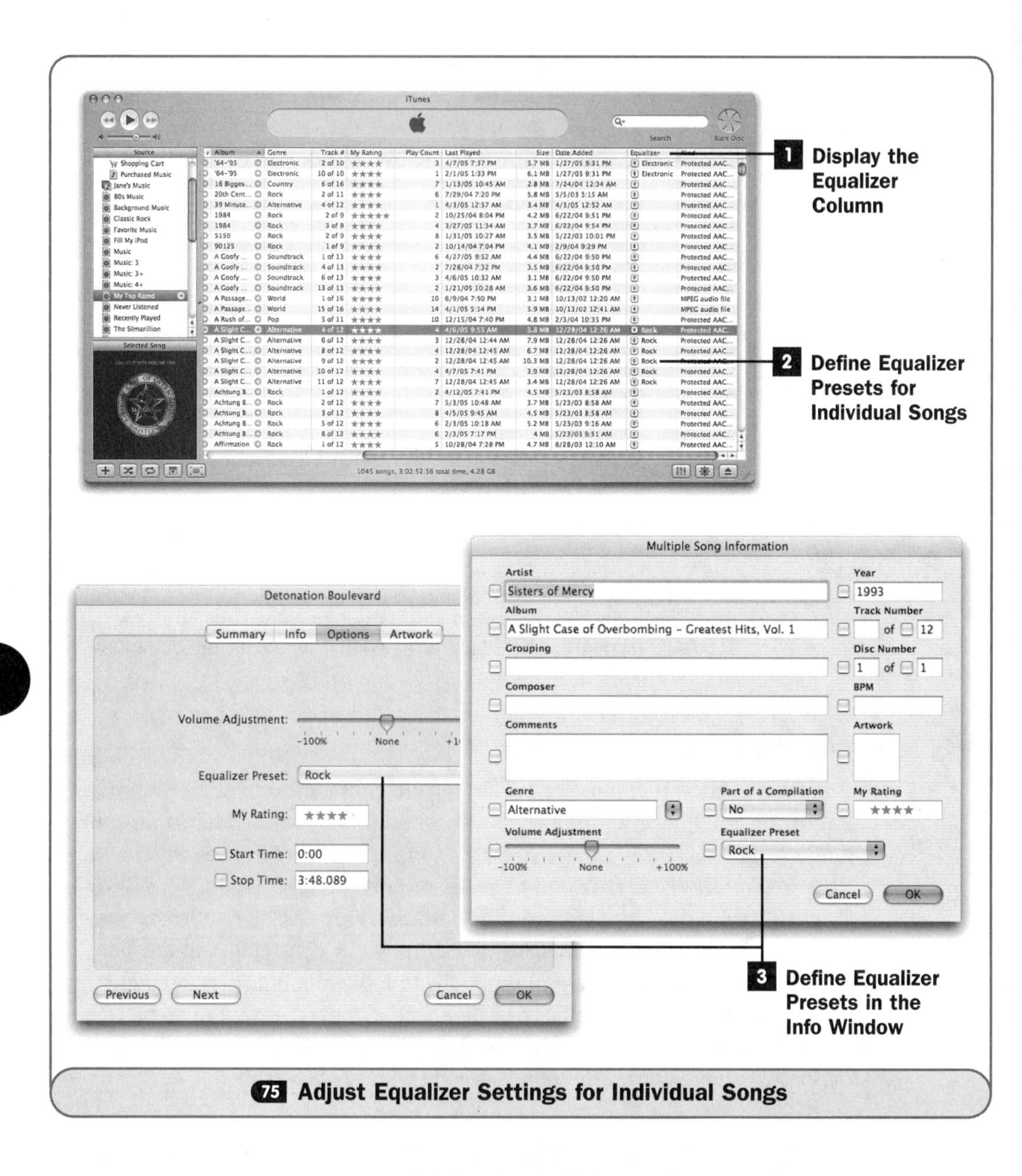

1 Display the Equalizer Column
2 Define Equalizer Presets for Individual Songs
3 Define Equalizer Presets in the Info Window
75

75 Adjust Equalizer Settings for Individual Songs

The **Equalizer** presets discussed in **74 Adjust the Global Equalizer** can be applied to individual songs. When you play a song with an **Equalizer** preset defined, that preset is used for output instead of whatever global equalizer setting is currently in effect. This feature is indispensable if you have a lot of music from different genres that require different amplification characteristics. Just set **Equalizer** settings for any tracks whose output balance you want to ensure is adjusted by a certain profile; as you play each such track, iTunes switches automatically to that profile for its duration, and then switches back to the global preset it had been using before.

▶ NOTE

Equalizer settings on individual songs have no effect when the songs are played on an iPod.

1 Display the Equalizer Column

In the music source or display mode of your choice (such as the **Library** view or a ***playlist***), display the **Equalizer** column as described in 71 **Customize Which Information Columns Are Displayed**. Scroll horizontally to that column's location or drag it to a position where it's visible.

2 Define Equalizer Presets for Individual Songs

Click the small up/down arrow icon in the **Equalizer** field of any of the song entries in the listing to reveal the drop-down menu full of available presets, the same as you see in the global **Equalizer** palette. Choose a preset appropriate to the song's genre or style from the list: **Rock**, **Electronic**, **Jazz**, **Dance**, **Acoustic**, **Classical**, **Spoken Word**—whatever best fits the track in question.

3 Define Equalizer Presets in the Info Window

You can also define a song's **Equalizer** preset without displaying the **Equalizer** column. Select the song and choose **File, Get Info**; on the **Options** tab, choose the appropriate preset from the **Equalizer Preset** drop-down list.

If you select several songs at once and choose **Get Info**, the **Equalizer Preset** menu is one of the configurable settings that you can apply to all selected songs at once.

76 Add a Third-Party Visualizer

✓ BEFORE YOU BEGIN

38 Use the iTunes Visualizer

iTunes comes with a ***Visualizer*** whose shifting shapes present such an ever-changing array of eye candy that you might never get tired of it. However, millions of people out there are using iTunes now, and their tastes in eye candy vary. Many third-party shareware software developers have created visualizers of their own which are packaged as *plug-ins*, or small encapsulated pieces of software that can be easily added to iTunes to enhance its capabilities.

This task shows how you can add a third-party visualizer to iTunes using as an example **G-Force** by Andy O'Meara, the visualizer on which the default iTunes Visualizer was based, and which has developed many of its own distinctive behaviors and features over the years. Many iTunes' users prefer G-Force's vaster array of unique and surprising effects over iTunes' more subdued ones.

▶ WEB RESOURCES

http://www.soundspectrum.com/

Home of G-Force, the most popular third-party visualizer plug-in for iTunes and other music players.

http://www.apple.com/downloads/macosx/ipod_itunes

The Apple Downloads site has links to many third-party visualizers, as well as other useful iTunes plug-ins. Note that not all software featured at this site is available for both Mac and Windows.

1 Download the Third-Party Visualizer

Visit the site from which the visualizer can be obtained (SoundSpectrum in this case, **http://www.soundspectrum.com**); download the visualizer, which is available as a free trial version and as a registered version with more features for a small fee. Download the installer package appropriate for your system.

2 Install the Plug-In

Follow the instructions in the downloaded folder or disk image to install the plug-in. In the case of G-Force, double-click the extracted **.exe** or **.pkg** file to run the installer program.

▶ NOTE

You must quit iTunes before running the installer for the plug-in.

3 Select the Third-Party Visualizer

Launch iTunes. In the **Visualizer** menu, you should now see a **G-Force** option along with the **iTunes Visualizer** option. Choose **G-Force** to switch to the newly installed visualizer.

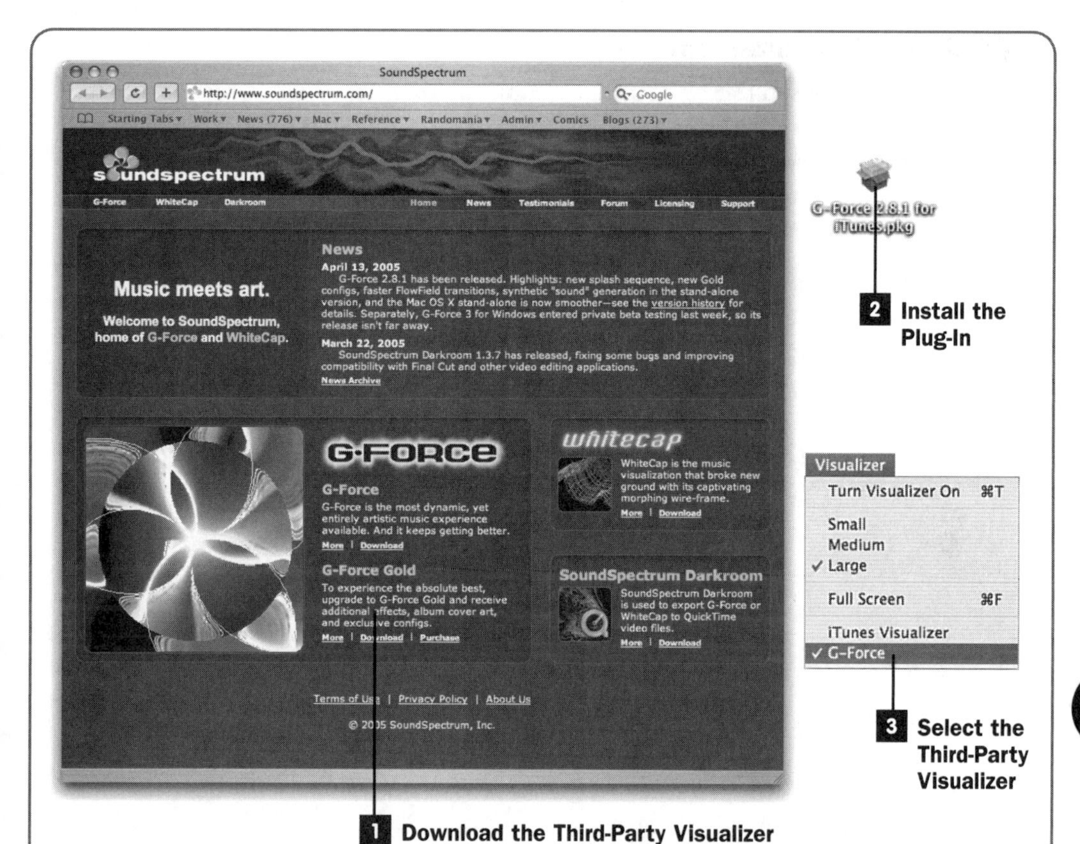

SoundSpectrum
http://www.soundspectrum.com/
Music meets art.
Welcome to SoundSpectrum, home of G-Force and WhiteCap.
News
April 13, 2005
G-Force 2.8.1 has been released. Highlights: new splash sequence, new Gold configs, faster FlowField transitions, synthetic "sound" generation in the stand-alone version, and the Mac OS X stand-alone is now smoother—see the version history for details. Separately, G-Force 3 for Windows entered private beta testing last week, so its release isn't far away.
March 22, 2005
SoundSpectrum Darkroom 1.3.7 has released, fixing some bugs and improving compatibility with Final Cut and other video editing applications.
G-Force
G-Force is the most dynamic, yet entirely artistic music experience available. And it keeps getting better.
G-Force Gold
whitecap
WhiteCap is the music visualization that broke new ground with its captivating morphing wire-frame.
SoundSpectrum Darkroom
G-Force 2.8.1 for iTunes.pkg
Visualizer
Turn Visualizer On ⌘T
Small
Medium
✓ Large
Full Screen ⌘F
iTunes Visualizer
✓ G-Force
1 Download the Third-Party Visualizer
2 Install the Plug-In
3 Select the Third-Party Visualizer

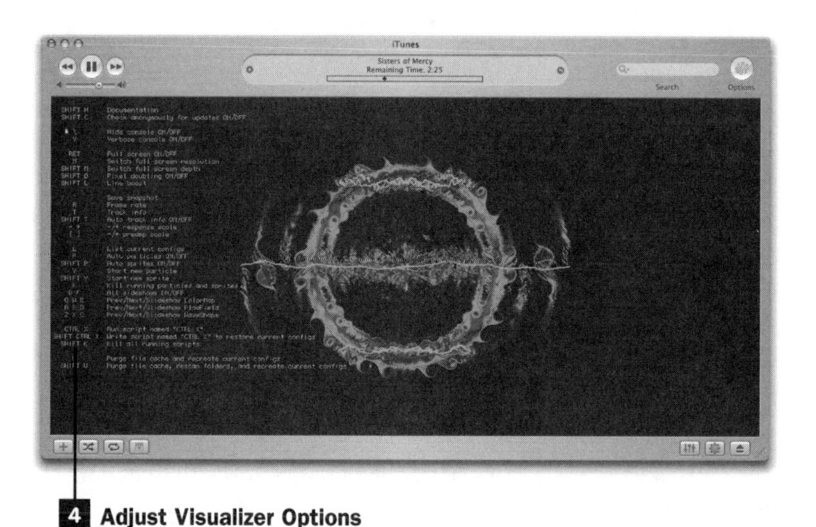

iTunes
4 Adjust Visualizer Options

76

4 Adjust Visualizer Options

Activate the visualizer by choosing **Visualizer, Turn Visualizer On** or by clicking the **Visualizer** button in the lower-right corner of the iTunes window (see 38 **Use the iTunes Visualizer**). Let it play according to its own internal scripts and heuristics; you'll probably find it entertaining enough to just leave it to its own devices.

Like the iTunes **Visualizer**, **G-Force** has a number of options you can select to customize its behavior. Some visualizers allow you to use the **Options** button in the upper-right corner of the iTunes' window to access their controls, but G-Force's options and help system is available only by pressing the **H** key. This command reveals a wealth of scripting and real-time control commands that are far beyond the scope of this book—refer to the visualizer's own documentation for more information on how to use these controls.

10

iPod Extras

IN THIS CHAPTER:

- 77 Carry Your Photos on an iPod Photo
- 78 Display Your Photos on a TV
- 79 Download Photos from Your Camera to Your iPod Photo
- 80 Use Your iPod as an External Hard Disk
- 81 Play iPod Games
- 82 Customize the iPod's Main Menu
- 83 Transfer and View Contacts
- 84 Transfer and View Calendar Events
- 85 Synchronize Contacts Using iTunes or iSync (Mac Only)
- 86 Transfer and View Text Notes

There's nothing much stopping the iPod from being a whole lot more than just a music player. It's got a spacious hard disk and large, high-contrast screen; it synchronizes with your computer through an easy-to-use Dock or cable; and it's small enough to fit unobtrusively on your belt. These characteristics all fit the description of any of the popular, full-function Portable Digital Assistants (PDAs) on the market today.

The iPod doesn't have an on-board method for feeding data into it (such as a keyboard or a stylus and touch-sensitive screen). It doesn't have a built-in camera or cell phone. But other than that, it's perfectly serviceable as a PDA, for some of the most popular reasons you'd carry one: viewing photos, carrying your address book full of people's contact information with you, reading text documents, even playing games. The iPod also makes a dandy portable hard disk you can use to back up important files from your computer. After you've been in a predicament in which your iPod came to the rescue by providing you an important phone number or resurrecting a backup copy of a critical file, you'll never think of it as a simple "music player" again—and you might never have to carry a traditional PDA as long as you've got your iPod.

77

NOTE

The tasks in this chapter all require the use of the iPod's screen, and thus do not apply to the iPod shuffle—except for 80 Use Your iPod as an External Hard Disk, which describes external hard disk use for both standard iPods and the iPod shuffle.

77 Carry Your Photos on an iPod Photo

✔ BEFORE YOU BEGIN	→ SEE ALSO
42 Transfer Your Music to Your iPod	78 Display Your Photos on a TV 79 Download Photos from Your Camera to Your iPod Photo 88 Temporarily Store Digital Photos on Your iPod

The top-of-the-line iPod model, the iPod photo, is equipped with a 65,536-color screen that turns the device into a lot more than just a music player. Its screen is ideal for showing off digital photographs, which fit with ease onto the capacious hard disk along with your music. Although the color screen enhances the rest of the iPod's normal functionality by adding richness and depth to the user interface (and album art as you play songs), the real benefit of the iPod photo is in the features surrounding synchronizing and displaying your digital photos.

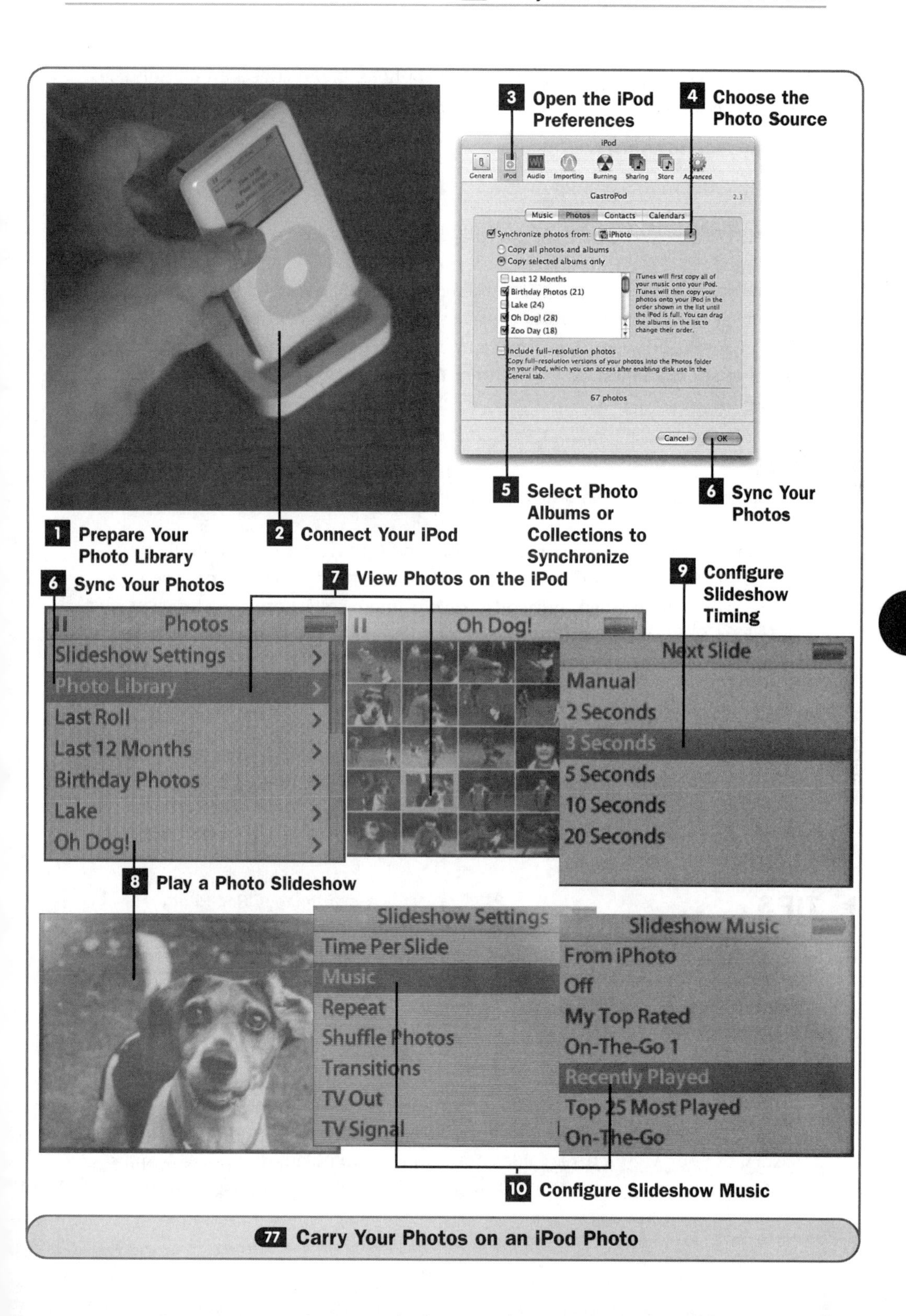

3 Open the iPod Preferences
4 Choose the Photo Source
iPod
General
iPod
Audio
Importing
Burning
Sharing
Store
Advanced
GastroPod
Music
Photos
Contacts
Calendars
Synchronize photos from: iPhoto
Copy all photos and albums
Copy selected albums only
Last 12 Months
Birthday Photos (21)
Lake (24)
Oh Dog! (28)
Zoo Day (18)
iTunes will first copy all of your music onto your iPod. iTunes will then copy your photos onto your iPod in the order shown in the list until the iPod is full. You can drag the albums in the list to change their order.
Include full-resolution photos
Copy full-resolution versions of your photos into the Photos folder on your iPod, which you can access after enabling disk use in the General tab.
67 photos
Cancel
OK
5 Select Photo Albums or Collections to Synchronize
6 Sync Your Photos
1 Prepare Your Photo Library
2 Connect Your iPod
6 Sync Your Photos
7 View Photos on the iPod
9 Configure Slideshow Timing
Photos
Slideshow Settings
Photo Library
Last Roll
Last 12 Months
Birthday Photos
Lake
Oh Dog!
Oh Dog!
Next Slide
Manual
2 Seconds
3 Seconds
5 Seconds
10 Seconds
20 Seconds
8 Play a Photo Slideshow
Slideshow Settings
Time Per Slide
Music
Repeat
Shuffle Photos
Transitions
TV Out
TV Signal
Slideshow Music
From iPhoto
Off
My Top Rated
On-The-Go 1
Recently Played
Top 25 Most Played
On-The-Go
10 Configure Slideshow Music
77 Carry Your Photos on an iPod Photo

77

To use these features, you must have an iPod photo, and a collection of digital photographs archived in one of the following applications:

- iPhoto (on the Mac)
- Adobe Album (on Windows)
- Adobe Photoshop Elements (on Windows)

You can also sync photos that are gathered into a single specific folder, if you don't have one of these applications. Another way to get your photos onto your iPod is to download them to it directly from your camera, using the iPod Camera Connector; see 79 **Download Photos from Your Camera to Your iPod Photo** for more information.

NOTE

The iPod photo can sync and display photos in JPEG, BMP, GIF, TIFF, or PNG format.

After your photos are loaded onto the iPod, you can browse them visually by selecting the **Photos** item from the Main Menu, then by selecting from the albums or collections synchronized from your photo collection. You can even start a slideshow of a selected collection of photos using background music from any of the ***playlists*** already on your iPod.

1 Prepare Your Photo Library

Using your favorite digital photo organizer application (iPhoto, Adobe Album, or Adobe Photoshop Elements), set up photo "albums" (think of them as photo playlists) to group your photos into appropriately named, themed collections.

TIPS

If you're using iPhoto, create slideshows from your albums and set them to music from your iTunes **Library**; your iPod photo can use this music setting automatically when displaying its own slideshows.

Try to limit your photo albums to less than about 200 photos; larger photo albums tend to display more slowly on the iPod photo.

If you don't have one of these applications, place all the photos you want to sync to your iPod into a single folder somewhere on your computer's disk, such as your **My Pictures** folder. You can use subfolders within this folder to create the equivalent of the "albums" used by the supported applications.

2 Connect Your iPod

Connect your iPod to your computer using the Dock or cable. Wait for it to finish synchronizing its information.

3 Open the iPod Preferences

Choose **iTunes, Preferences** (on the Mac) or **Edit, Preferences** (in Windows) to open the **Preferences** window. Click the **iPod** tab, then click the **Photos** tab within the window. You will see all the photo-syncing configuration options.

4 Choose the Photo Source

Enable the **Synchronize photos from** check box and choose the application where your photos are stored from the drop-down menu. If your photos are stored in a folder on your hard disk, choose that option and navigate to the folder's location in the navigation dialog box that appears. Select the folder by clicking **Choose** or **Open**.

5 Select Photo Albums or Collections to Synchronize

When you select your photo source, the box below the **Copy selected albums only** option becomes populated with the names of the albums you've created. If you have enough room on the iPod, you can choose to sync all the photos in your collection by selecting Copy all photos and albums. If you want to save some room on your iPod for music, choose the **Copy selected albums only** option and enable the check boxes next to each album you want copied to the iPod.

▶ TIP

The **Preferences** window says this as well, but it bears repeating: You can drag photo albums into the order you want them copied onto the iPod. This is important because iTunes copies selected albums in the displayed order onto the iPod until the iPod is full, without checking first to see whether it has enough space for all the selected photos. If the iPod fills up, some selected albums' contents might not be copied completely or at all. Putting the albums in a specified order can help ensure that certain photos make it to the iPod.

If you've got lots of room to spare on the iPod and want to carry full-resolution versions of your photos on its disk, enable the **Include full-resolution photos** check box. This option puts the large photo files into a folder called **Photos** on the iPod. See 80 **Use Your iPod as an External Hard Disk** to access this folder and the photos inside it.

6 Sync Your Photos

Click **OK** when you're done configuring the photo sync options. iTunes begins copying photos out of your organizer application, shrinking them down ("optimizing" them) to a size appropriate for the iPod's screen and TV output, and transferring them to the iPod's disk. Depending on the size of your photo collection and the speed of your computer, this process can take 20 minutes to an hour or more. iTunes shows you a status bar indicating its progress.

When the sync process is complete and iTunes indicates it's safe to do so, disconnect your iPod.

▶ NOTE

This procedure is relevant only for the first time you set up photo syncing. Each subsequent time you sync your iPod with iTunes, any new photos in your Photo Library or selected albums are copied to the iPod photo. You can click the Skip button to stop photos from being transferred, but they'll be sent anew to the iPod the next time you sync.

7 View Photos on the iPod

Choose **Photos** from the iPod's Main Menu. The subsequent menu lists all the photo albums you selected to transfer, including an option (second from the top) called **Photo Library** which contains every photo in your entire photo-organizing application (if you chose to transfer the whole thing). Select this option or one of the albums listed below it and press **Select**.

The contents of the selected group of photos are shown in a contact sheet (a set of small thumbnail images in a grid, 25 to a screen). Rotate the wheel to move the yellow selection rectangle to a photo you want to see, then press **Select** to view it at the full size of the iPod's screen. Press **Forward** or **Back** (or rotate the wheel) to move manually through the collection of photos, or press **Menu** once to return to the contact sheet.

8 Play a Photo Slideshow

Press the **Select** button while viewing a photo full-screen, or press **Play** while a photo album is selected in the **Photos** menu. A slideshow begins using the selected photo album and default presentation settings. Use the **Select** button to pause and resume the slideshow, or use **Forward** and **Back** to skip through the photos at your own speed.

9 Configure Slideshow Timing

Press **Menu** repeatedly until you arrive at the **Photos** menu; choose **Slideshow Settings** to view the presentation options for your slideshows.

These options include whether the photos in the grouping should be shuffled (randomized), whether the slideshow should repeat after it's done, and whether a horizontal "wipe" effect should be used in transitions between photos. You can also define the timing between slides, as well as the background music to be played.

To set the time between slides, choose **Time Per Slide**, and in the subsequent screen choose a number of seconds from **2** to **20** for each photo to remain on the screen. You can also choose **Manual** to specify that the slides won't advance unless you press the **Forward** button. Press **Select** to make your choice.

10 Configure Slideshow Music

To play music during your slideshow, return to the **Slideshow Settings** menu and choose **Music**. You can pick a playlist to use in the background of each slideshow (the iPod does the equivalent of beginning a new playback of the selected playlist at the beginning of the slideshow; if you're shuffling your music, a different song comes up each time). Alternatively, choose **From iPhoto** from the **Slideshow Music** screen to allow your slideshow settings in iPhoto (if you're using it) to dictate the background music for the iPod, or choose **Off** to play no music at all.

The next time you start a slideshow, it will use these newly defined settings.

78 Display Your Photos on a TV

✓ BEFORE YOU BEGIN	→ SEE ALSO
77 Carry Your Photos on an iPod Photo	79 Download Photos from Your Camera to Your iPod Photo

Running a slideshow on your iPod photo is a fun way to pass the time—on your own. After all, with only headphones to deliver the musical accompaniment, and only a little two-inch screen on which to show your photographic genius, who else can share it with you?

The answer is in the iPod photo's ability to direct its photo slideshows to the composite A/V jack on the top of the unit or to the S-Video jack on the back of the iPod photo Dock—and from there to a TV set. This output option lets everyone in the whole room enjoy your photos at full TV resolution (a far cry from the dozen megapixels of your digital camera, but still far better than the iPod's screen), as well as your selected background music. Equipped with the appropriate cable, your iPod becomes a presentation device suitable for showing off anything from your vacation memories to a business demonstration.

78

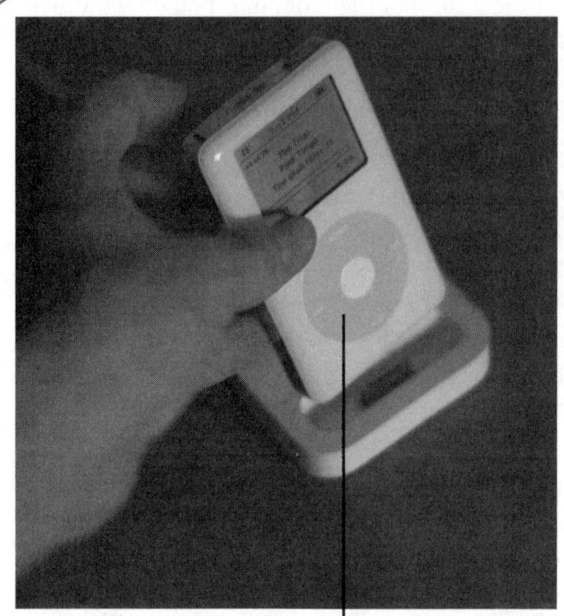

3 Specify TV Output Mode

Slideshow Settings

Time Per Slide	>
Music	>
Repeat	On
Shuffle Photos	On
Transitions	On
TV Out	Off
TV Signal	NTSC

2 Specify TV Signal Format

1 Sync Your Photos with Your iPod Photo

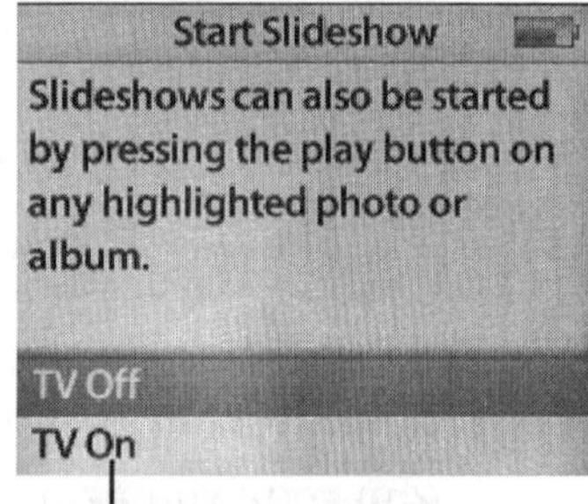

5 Begin the Slideshow

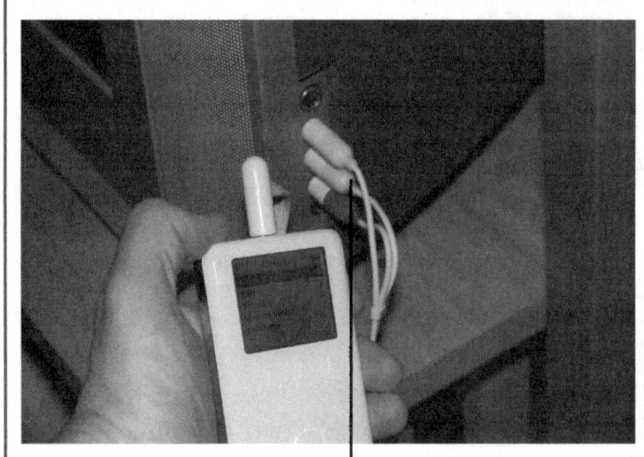

4 Connect Your iPod to the TV

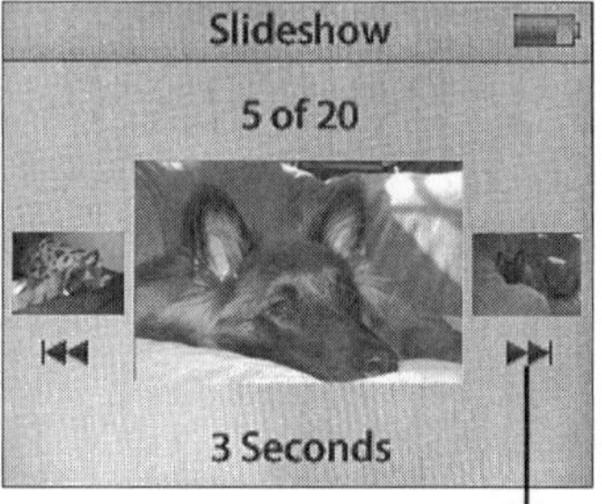

6 Control the Slideshow from the iPod

78 Display Your Photos on a TV

▶ NOTE

To connect your iPod photo to the TV, you need either a composite A/V cable (available from Apple for $19.00) or the iPod photo Dock ($39.00) and a standard S-Video cable. S-Video provides much better video quality than composite video does. Make sure that you use Apple's own composite A/V cable; other kinds of composite A/V cables won't work.

1 Sync Your Photos with Your iPod Photo

As described in 77 **Carry Your Photos on an iPod Photo**, load your photos onto the iPod photo. Be sure to set up a separate album containing the photos you want to display in your slideshow.

2 Specify TV Signal Format

From the iPod's Main Menu, choose **Photos**, then **Slideshow Settings**. At the bottom of the menu, highlight **TV Signal** and press **Select** to toggle between **NTSC** format (appropriate for North America or Japan) and **PAL** format (appropriate for Europe or Australia).

3 Specify TV Output Mode

The **TV Out** option has three settings: **Off**, **On**, and **Ask**. When set to **Off**, any slideshow you start is played back on the iPod's screen, with its sound directed to the headphones. If the **TV Out** option is set to **On**, the audio and video are directed to the connection to the TV, and the iPod's screen instead shows control information for the slideshow, letting you use the iPod as a sort of remote control for the TV presentation.

If you set the option to **Ask**, the iPod presents you with a choice at the time you start the slideshow, asking whether to play it in the iPod's screen or on the connected TV. This option is appropriate if you like to alternate between showing slideshows on the TV and on the iPod's screen, and want to choose which one is appropriate each time you start a slideshow.

▶ NOTE

Set other slideshow options as described in 77 Carry Your Photos on an iPod photo.

4 Connect Your iPod to the TV

Connect the composite A/V cable to the iPod's output jack; connect the other end of the cable to the TV's composite audio and video jacks. Alternatively, if you have the iPod photo Dock and an S-Video cable, connect the cable to the Dock and the TV's S-Video jack, and place the iPod into the Dock.

5 Begin the Slideshow

From the **Photos** screen, highlight the photo album you want to use for the slideshow and press **Play**. Depending on whether you set **TV Out** to **On** or **Ask** in step 3, you might be presented with a screen asking whether to turn TV output on or off. Choose **TV On**.

6 Control the Slideshow from the iPod

The slideshow begins playing on the TV. On the iPod, instead of seeing the slideshow itself, you see an informational screen displaying the current photo, the previous and next photos in the sequence, the number of the current photo in the slideshow, and a readout indicating how much longer the iPod will show the current photo. Use the **Forward** and **Back** buttons to advance or retreat through the photos, and press **Play** to pause and resume playback.

When the slideshow is done, press **Menu** to exit it, and disconnect the cables.

79 Download Photos from Your Camera to Your iPod Photo

✔ BEFORE YOU BEGIN	→ SEE ALSO
77 Carry Your Photos on an iPod Photo	88 Temporarily Store Digital Photos on Your iPod

Suppose that you're on vacation. You've been taking photos like there's no tomorrow, and your digital camera's memory card is filling up fast. You're only three days into a two-week road trip. What do you do? Buy more memory cards? Pack a laptop and download all the photos every time you fill up the card? If you have an iPod photo, there's no need: For $29.00, you can get the iPod Camera Connector, a little white adapter from Apple that lets you empty your camera directly into the iPod photo whenever the camera gets full. The iPod stores the photos in their full resolution from the camera, and uses the same internal format as the camera's memory card so that you can download the photos from the iPod into your computer when you get home. Meanwhile, while you're on the road, you can use the iPod photo to review each day's batch of photos, on its own screen or on a TV (see **78 Display Your Photos on a TV**).

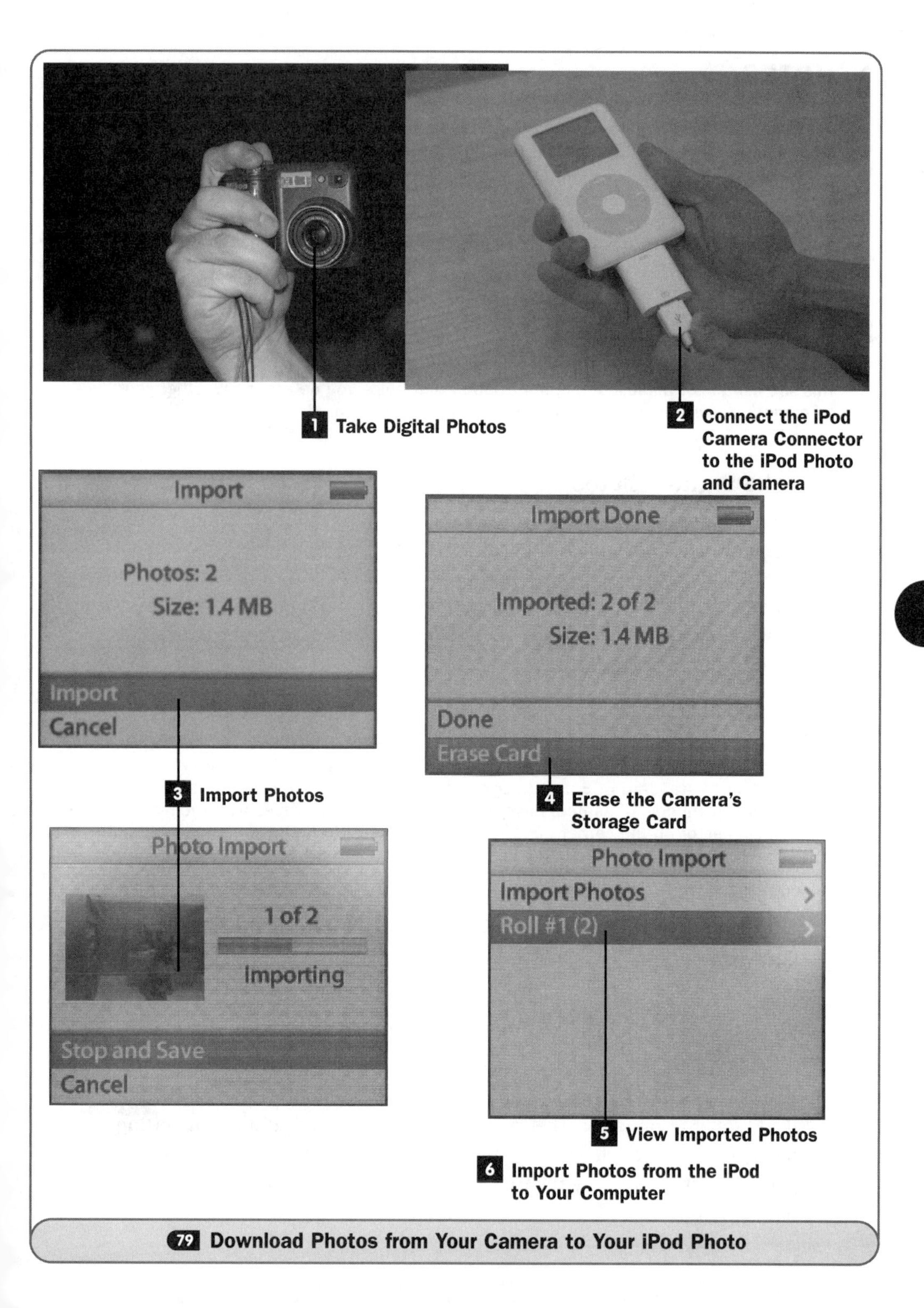

79 Download Photos from Your Camera to Your iPod Photo

▶ NOTES

You need an iPod photo with at least version 1.1 of the iPod photo software to use the iPod Camera Connector. Visit **http://www.apple.com/ipod/download/** to download the latest updater, and see 99 **Update Your iPod's Firmware** for instructions.

The iPod Camera Connector has the drawback of using up your iPod's battery power very quickly. It's a good idea to keep the iPod near a source of recharging power (the AC adapter or a computer to which you can attach the iPod using the Dock or cable) if you plan to use the Camera Connector a lot.

▶ WEB RESOURCE

http://www.apple.com/support/ipod/photos/

This site contains troubleshooting information that helps you determine whether your digital camera model will work with the iPod Camera Connector.

1 Take Digital Photos

Take pictures using your digital camera. Fill up the internal memory card, being aware of how much capacity it has and how much free space there is on the iPod photo. Remember that you can't delete music or photos from the iPod without a computer to connect it to, so you can't adjust how much space is available while you're away from home. Be sure to leave plenty of space for all your photos!

▶ TIP

Be sure to carry the camera's USB connection cable with you; the iPod Camera Connector has a standard USB port to connect to the camera, the same as on a computer, but different models of cameras use different kinds of USB cables with their own styles of connector on the camera end. You won't be likely to find a spare, and without one, you won't be able to download your photos.

2 Connect the iPod Camera Connector to the iPod Photo and Camera

Plug the iPod Camera Connector into the iPod's dock connector (logo facing front). The iPod immediately switches to an **Import** screen that says there's nothing to import.

Plug the camera's USB cable into the camera and into the other end of the iPod Camera Connector. The camera should go into its natural "importing" mode, the same as when you connect it to your computer. The iPod, meanwhile, reports how many photos there are to import along with their collective size.

3 Import Photos

On the iPod's **Import** screen, highlight **Import** and press **Select**. The photos are transferred from the camera to the iPod, each one displayed as a thumbnail icon as it is copied to the iPod's disk. This process takes several minutes, especially if your camera's card is full.

▶ TIP

At any time during import, you can select Stop and Save to interrupt the process and preserve all the photos transferred so far, or select Cancel to delete everything transferred up to this point.

4 Erase the Camera's Storage Card

At the end of the import process, you're given the option to erase the transferred photos from the camera's memory card; highlight **Erase Card** and press **Select** to do this. If you don't want to erase the photos from the camera's memory card, select **Done** instead.

5 View Imported Photos

The photos you imported are available from a screen called **Photo Import**, found on the **Photos** screen above your **Photo Library** and albums. Inside this screen is the option to import more photos (if you select this option, return to step 2), or to view an album called **Roll #1**. (The album's name is followed by the number of pictures in that album.) View this album as you would any other, as described in 77 **Carry Your Photos on an iPod Photo**.

As you import more "rolls of film" from your camera, each roll or album is added to the list: **Roll #2**, **Roll #3**, and so on.

6 Import Photos from the iPod to Your Computer

When you finally get home from your trek, you'll want to move the full-resolution photos from the iPod into your favorite photo organizer application (iPhoto for Mac users, or Adobe Album or Adobe Photoshop Elements for Windows—although any software that imports photos from a digital camera will work). After you've loaded photos onto the iPod photo from your camera, the iPod photo acts like a digital camera when it's connected to your computer; your photo software will think it's another camera and download the photos from it accordingly.

Connect the iPod to the computer using the Dock or cable. After it syncs with iTunes, launch your photo organizer application and import the photos as you normally do from your camera. Be sure to erase the "camera's" contents from the iPod (using the photo organizer's mechanism for doing so) when you're done transferring!

▶ NOTES

You might have to set up the iPod as an external hard disk for the photo software to recognize it as a camera-like device. See 80 Use Your iPod as an External Hard Disk for more information, and remember to unmount the iPod from your computer when you're done transferring photos.

If you can't get your photo software to download the photos automatically, set up the iPod as a hard disk and navigate into its DCIM folder to copy the photos from it to your computer.

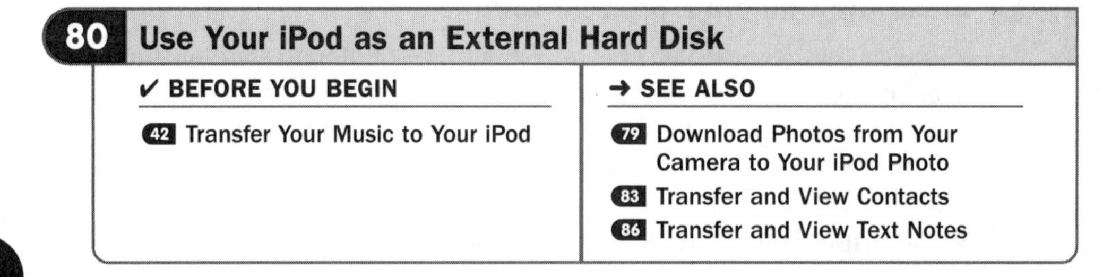

80 Use Your iPod as an External Hard Disk

✓ BEFORE YOU BEGIN

42 Transfer Your Music to Your iPod

➜ SEE ALSO

79 Download Photos from Your Camera to Your iPod Photo

83 Transfer and View Contacts

86 Transfer and View Text Notes

Ever since the iPod's original introduction in 2001, even those few people who were unimpressed with it as a music player immediately saw its usefulness in a more general sense: as an external hard disk drive. By connecting it to the computer over FireWire (and, later, USB 2.0), an iPod serves as 5 to 60 gigabytes of portable storage space, enough to hold anything from a collection of movie clips or business documents to a complete operating system installation that can be used to boot a series of computers in a lab. Today, as always, the owner of an iPod can use part of it to store and play back iTunes' music, and fill the rest with whatever files she wants to carry with her in her travels.

Many of the iPod's extra features (text notes, contact information, synchronized full-resolution photos, and so on) take advantage of its secondary guise as an external hard disk. Although you can't access the music files on an iPod without special software (see 98 **Copy Your Music from the iPod Back to iTunes**), special folders on the iPod's disk are used for certain specialized kinds of information that you place there manually or that is put there by software. Whether you have a full-sized hard-disk-based iPod or the "keychain USB drive" iPod shuffle, this task explains how to unlock this side of your music player's personality.

1 Connect Your iPod

Connect your iPod to your computer using the Dock or cable. Wait for it to finish synchronizing its information.

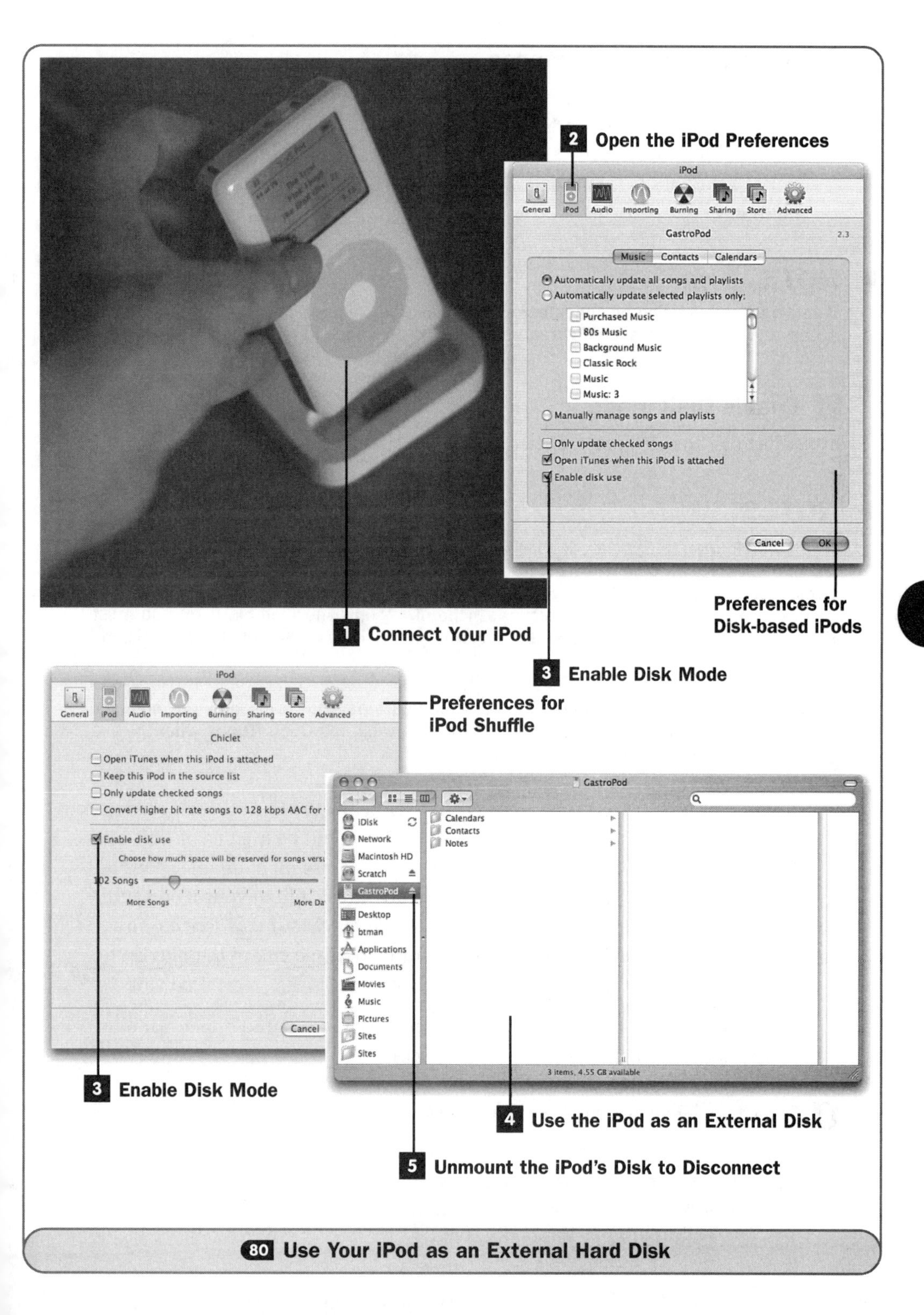

80 Use Your iPod as an External Hard Disk

2 Open the iPod Preferences

Choose **iTunes**, **Preferences** on the Mac or **Edit**, **Preferences** in Windows to open the **Preferences** window. Click the **iPod** tab, then (for all iPods except the iPod shuffle) click the **Music** tab from the tabs within the window, if it's not already selected. This action displays the iPod's general configuration options.

▶ NOTE

If you're using a version of iTunes before 4.8, click the **General** tab within the window to access the iPod's general configuration options as described here.

3 Enable Disk Mode

Select the **Enable disk use** check box.

▶ NOTES

If you enable **Manual** sync mode (see 43 **Use a Large iTunes Library with a Small iPod**), the iPod is automatically put into disk mode and must be manually unmounted before you disconnect it. Also, if you switch back to one of the two automatic sync modes (synchronizing all your music, or synchronizing only specified playlists), you must manually disable the **Enable disk use** option to make the iPod unmount automatically after synchronizing with iTunes.

You might want to prevent iTunes from launching automatically every time you connect your iPod, particularly if you've enabled disk use. Disable the **Open iTunes when attached** check box to accomplish this.

If you're using an iPod shuffle, use the slider below the **Enable disk use** check box to define how much of the 512MB or 1GB should be used for music, and how much for data. (Full-size iPods automatically use all available space not used for data to sync music.) If there's already music filling your iPod shuffle and you reduce the amount of space available for music, you'll be asked whether iTunes should remove enough music from the end of the playlist to make room for the specified amount of data.

Click **OK**; the iPod becomes enabled as an external disk and appears mounted on your computer among the other disks.

4 Use the iPod as an External Disk

Copy files to and from the iPod as an external disk, as you would any other disk. For instance, you can keep a copy of your résumé on your iPod shuffle, or a folder full of favorite pictures on your iPod mini; simply connect the iPod to another computer to access those files.

▶ NOTE

If the other computer has iTunes installed on it, it might launch and ask you whether you want to delete all the music from your iPod and sync it with that computer instead. Click No to prevent this from happening.

5 Unmount the iPod's Disk to Disconnect

From now on, the iPod does not automatically unmount from the computer when it's done synchronizing with iTunes, as it did before. Now, before you disconnect the iPod from the computer, you must unmount it as you would any externally connected disk. If you don't unmount the iPod, you risk data loss or corruption.

On Windows, right-click the **Unplug or Eject Hardware** icon in the System Tray, open the window showing connected devices, select the iPod, and click **Stop**. On the Mac, drag the iPod's icon to the **Trash** (which becomes an **Eject** icon). Alternatively, click the **Eject** icon next to the iPod's name in the Finder's sidebar, or right-click in Windows or **Control**+click on the Mac the iPod's name and select **Eject "*<iPod name>*"** to unmount it. When the **Do not Disconnect** icon disappears from the iPod's screen, it's safe to unplug it.

81 Play iPod Games

✔ BEFORE YOU BEGIN	→ SEE ALSO
46 Find and Play Music on the iPod	82 Customize the iPod's Main Menu 92 Enhance Your iPod's Battery Capacity

Nobody will ever mistake the iPod for a Sony PSP or a Nintendo DS, nor will it ever take the place of one of those devices—but Apple has not left us high and dry when it comes to frivolous ways we can pass the time when we're accompanied by nothing but our iPods. Listening to music is great, and arguably nothing does it better than the iPod...except that music without something visual to focus on isn't effective as a way to keep entertained. If you don't have an iPod photo for browsing pictures, or you don't want to spend your time paging through your contacts or text notes, you can always turn to the array of simple video games packaged with the iPod.

These games are all designed to work with the iPod's interface—they work using the rotary wheel and the middle button, just like some of the best classic games from the days of joysticks and sub-8-bit graphics. Some of the games (such as the Music Quiz) specifically take advantage of the iPod's nature as a music organizer and database storing everything in your iTunes **Library**.

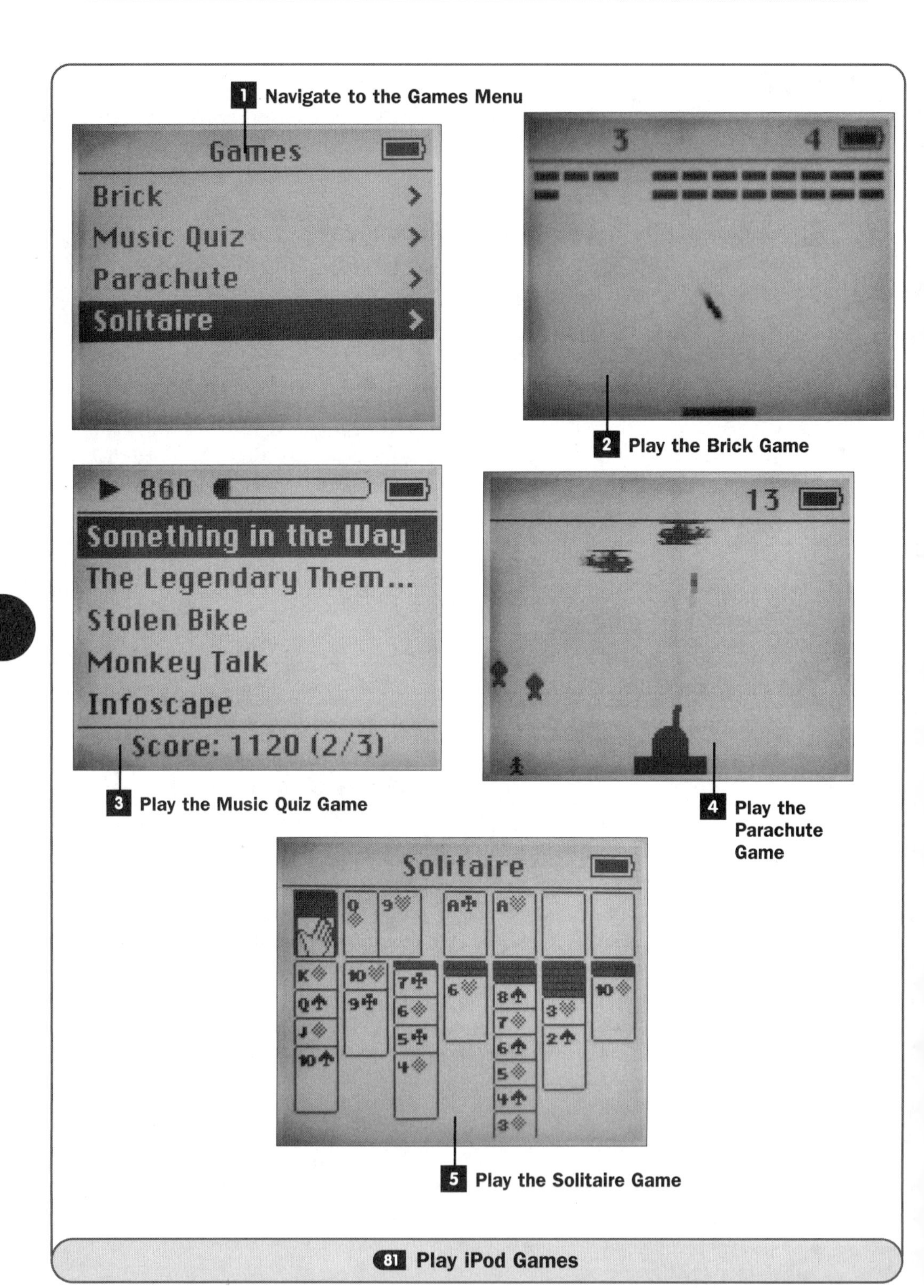
1 Navigate to the Games Menu
Games
Brick
Music Quiz
Parachute
Solitaire
3
4
2 Play the Brick Game
860
Something in the Way
The Legendary Them...
Stolen Bike
Monkey Talk
Infoscape
Score: 1120 (2/3)
3 Play the Music Quiz Game
13
4 Play the Parachute Game
Solitaire
5 Play the Solitaire Game
81 Play iPod Games

81

▶ NOTE

In the **Brick** and **Parachute** games, you must press the **Select** button to begin playing. For all games except **Music Quiz**, it's possible to have your iPod playing music in the background as you while away the time.

1 Navigate to the Games Menu

From the Main Menu, select **Extras**, then **Games**. You'll see the selection of four standard iPod games: **Brick**, **Music Quiz**, **Parachute**, and **Solitaire**. Play any of these games by scrolling to it and pressing **Select**; end a game by pressing **Menu** to return to the **Games** screen.

2 Play the Brick Game

Brick, originally the only game on the iPod and available only through a hidden, secret command, is a variation on the old "Breakout" arcade game programmed in 1976 by none other than Apple co-founder Steve Wozniak. The concept is simple: Use the wheel to move the paddle back and forth and deflect the bouncing "ball" back up to the top of the screen, where it strikes a wall of bricks and breaks each one it touches, earning you points. You lose a "life" if the ball gets past your paddle. Keep the ball moving as long as you can and break all the bricks to advance to the next level, where the ball moves faster, the paddle is smaller, and the brick wall is thicker.

▶ TIP

On 1G and 2G iPods, access the Brick game by navigating into the **About** screen (in the **Settings** menu) and holding down the **Select** button for several seconds.

3 Play the Music Quiz Game

Music Quiz is a game unique to the iPod in which you're presented with five song titles in a list. The iPod plays a randomly selected clip of music (about 10 seconds long) from the middle of a song whose title is somewhere in the list. You must identify the song as quickly as possible, highlight the correct title, and press **Select**. You earn points for each correct answer, and score higher the faster you respond. (You can use the **Play/Pause** button to pause the game at any time.)

NOTE

Because the iPod must access its disk to select five new random titles for each round, the Music Quiz game is one of the most disk-intensive activities possible on the iPod—and one of the fastest ways to run down the battery.

4 Play the Parachute Game

Parachute lets you engage your itchy trigger finger by putting you behind a defender's gun while helicopters drop paratroopers on you. Aim the gun using the wheel, and fire using the **Select** button. Shooting a paratrooper before he reaches the safety of the ground is worth one point, and shooting a helicopter is worth two. Each shot you take costs you one point, though, so simply filling the air with lead won't get you anywhere.

5 Play the Solitaire Game

Solitaire is mostly a game of patience. You use the wheel to browse back and forth through the displayed cards, and press **Select** to draw cards from the deck or pick up cards to move them from one pile to another. The game only allows you to draw three cards at a time (rather than a single card), meaning that it's easy to find yourself in an unsolvable game; if you do, just press **Menu** and then re-enter the game to reset the cards.

NOTE

The games on the iPod photo are in full color, giving them that extra bit of "kick" beyond their counterparts on the regular iPod; other than that, though, they're the same.

82 Customize the iPod's Main Menu

✓ BEFORE YOU BEGIN	→ SEE ALSO
42 Transfer Your Music to Your iPod	87 Record Voice Notes
46 Find and Play Music on the iPod	

You'll spend a fair amount of time at your iPod's Main Menu. This screen gives you top-level access to your music, extra features, settings, and quick commands such as **Shuffle Songs** and **Backlight**, as well as (when music is playing) the **Now Playing** screen. This arrangement of options is designed to give you the maximum amount of useful control over your music and data, while fitting all the options on a single screen.

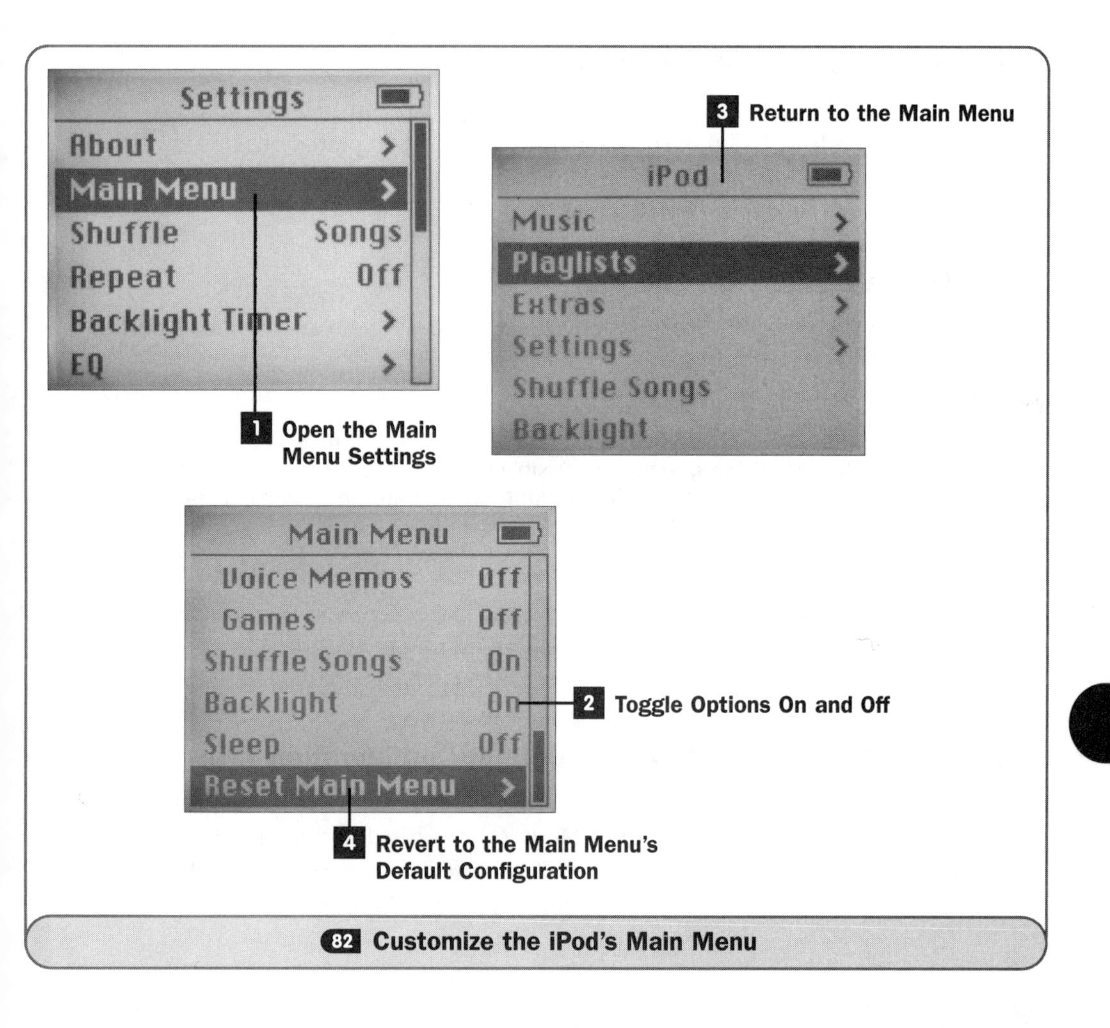

82 Customize the iPod's Main Menu

As you use the iPod, however, you might find that the default options on the Main Menu are insufficient for your needs. You might want top-level access to your **Playlists**, for example, or your **Contacts**, or you might not ever use the **Shuffle Songs** command and want to get rid of it. Thoughtfully enough, Apple allows you to turn on and off any of the individual options within the **Music** or **Extras** screens, allowing you to place them on the Main Menu or remove them accordingly. Some of these options (such as **Voice Memos**) are available only if you configure them in this way. Just about the only thing you can't remove from the Main Menu is the **Settings** screen, where the Main Menu configuration screen is found.

1 Open the Main Menu Settings

From the Main Menu, select **Settings**, then **Main Menu**. This command opens up a list of all the iPod commands that can be placed on the Main Menu. All are marked **Off**, except for the ones that currently appear on the Main Menu, which are marked **On**.

2 Toggle Options On and Off

Highlight any command and press **Select** to toggle that command on or off.

TIP

Remember that the iPod's screen only holds six lines of text. **Settings** can't be toggled on or off, and the **Now Playing** option isn't visible unless music is playing; thus, if you enable more than the default four optional items, you'll be forced to scroll up and down on the Main Menu to see all its options.

3 Return to the Main Menu

Press **Menu** twice to return to the Main Menu and view your newly customized menu screen.

4 Revert to the Main Menu's Default Configuration

If you decide you don't like your customized Main Menu layout, return to the **Settings** screen, then select **Main Menu** (as described in step 1), and choose **Reset Main Menu** from the bottom of the list; choose **Reset** in the subsequent confirmation screen. This action returns the iPod's Main Menu back to how it appeared when you first bought it.

83 Transfer and View Contacts

✓ BEFORE YOU BEGIN	→ SEE ALSO
80 Use Your iPod as an External Hard Disk	84 Transfer and View Calendar Events 85 Synchronize Contacts Using iTunes or iSync (Mac Only)

If you've got an iPod, there's no need to rely on your "little black book" full of addresses and phone numbers or even your cell phone or PDA. Whether you're using Windows or a Mac, any "card" of contact information (as stored in the industry-standard vCard format, used by popular data-organizing software such as Palm Desktop, Microsoft Outlook or Entourage, Eudora, or the Mac OS X Address Book) can be transferred directly to the iPod and viewed on its screen.

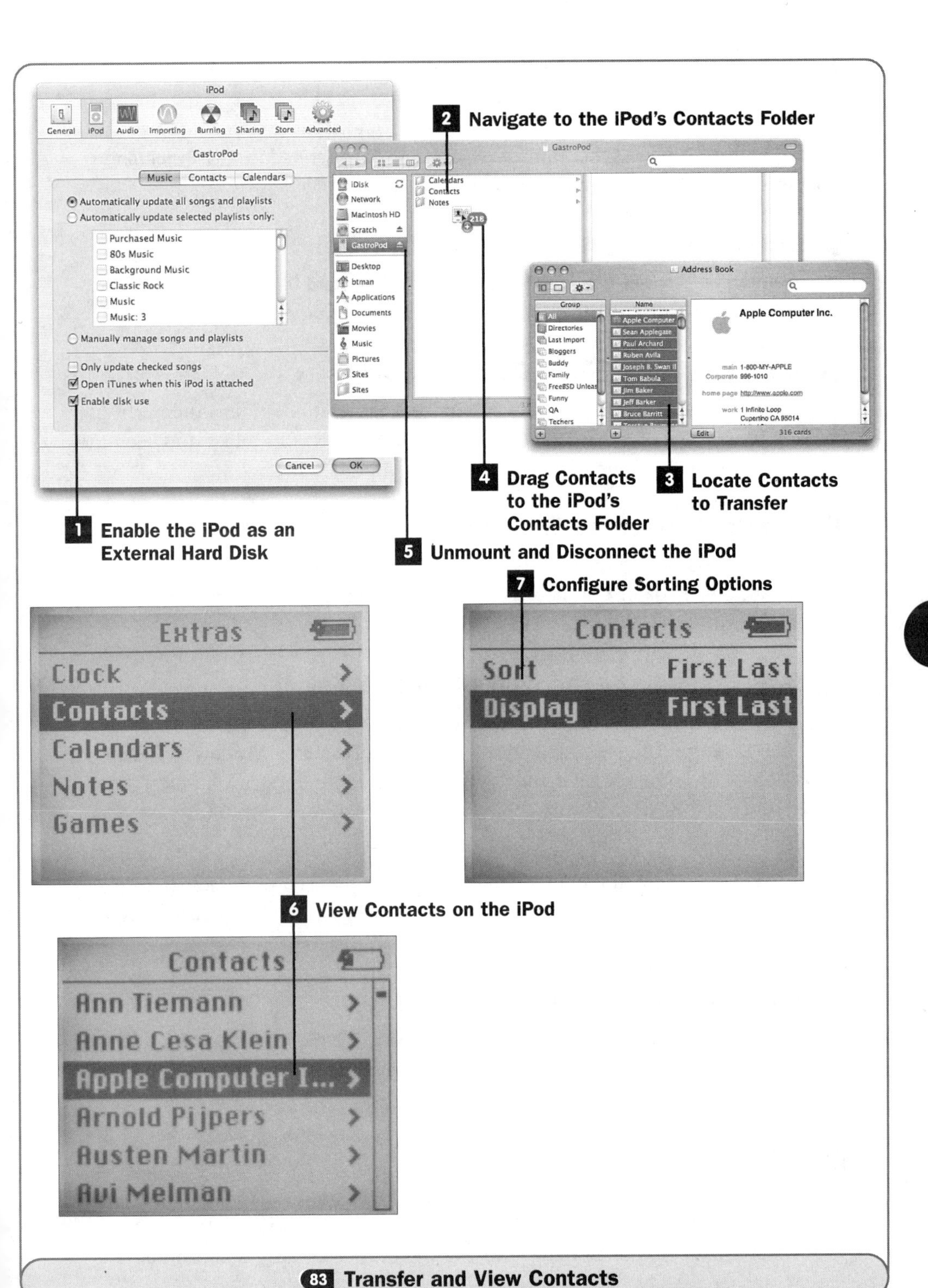

83 Transfer and View Contacts

This task describes how to load contacts into the iPod manually, using the **Contacts** folder on the iPod's hard disk. If you have a Mac, you can use the method described in this task, but you might find it far more efficient to use iTunes' built-in contact synchronization or iSync as described in 85 **Synchronize Contacts Using iTunes or iSync (Mac Only)**.

1 Enable the iPod as an External Hard Disk

As described in 80 **Use Your iPod as an External Hard Disk**, enable your iPod's external hard disk mode and attach it to your computer.

2 Navigate to the iPod's Contacts Folder

Open up the iPod's hard disk in a Windows Explorer or Finder window. In the top level of the disk is a folder called **Contacts**. Open this folder and keep the window open on your screen so that you can drag items into it.

3 Locate Contacts to Transfer

Open your data-organizing application where your contacts are stored. View the Address Book or Contacts section (if applicable), where your contacts are all listed.

4 Drag Contacts to the iPod's Contacts Folder

Most data-organizing applications will let you simply drag contacts directly from the application window into a folder in a Finder or Windows Explorer window. Drag individual contacts, or select multiple contacts and drag them all at once. The contacts are copied in vCard (.vcf) format into the **Contacts** folder.

If your application doesn't let you drag contacts directly to the folder, select the contacts and export them (the command is usually **File, Export**) to **.vcf** files in the iPod's **Contacts** folder.

5 Unmount and Disconnect the iPod

When you're done copying contacts to the iPod, unmount or eject the iPod as described in 80 **Use Your iPod as an External Hard Disk**, and disconnect it from the computer.

6 View Contacts on the iPod

From the iPod's Main Menu, select **Extras**, then **Contacts**. Your contacts are all listed alphabetically according to their names (first, then last). Use the wheel to scroll to the desired contact and press **Select**; all the information stored in the vCard for that person is displayed on the screen. Scroll using the wheel to see all of it.

You can't alter or add to any of the contact information stored on the iPod, nor can you transfer contact information from the iPod to any other device. However, simply being able to look up a phone number or address while on the go can be a lifesaver.

7 Configure Sorting Options

You can configure two aspects of contacts on the iPod: the order in which they're alphabetized in the **Contacts** screen, and the format in which their names are displayed.

From the Main Menu, choose **Settings**, then **Contacts**. Highlight the setting you want to change (**Sort** or **Display**) and press the **Select** button to toggle between the **First Last** and **Last First** name formats.

84 Transfer and View Calendar Events

✓ BEFORE YOU BEGIN	→ SEE ALSO
80 Use Your iPod as an External Hard Disk	83 Transfer and View Contacts 85 Synchronize Contacts Using iTunes or iSync (Mac Only)

Just as you can with contacts' addresses and phone numbers, you can carry your important calendar dates along with you on your iPod, reducing the need for yet another book in your pocket or PDA on your belt. Whether you're using Windows or a Mac, any "calendar" file (as stored in the industry-standard iCalendar or vCal formats, used by popular data-organizing software such as Palm Desktop, Microsoft Outlook or Entourage, Eudora, or iCal in Mac OS X) can be transferred directly to the iPod and viewed on its screen. The iPod can even beep or emit a silent alarm when your calendar events come due.

This task describes how to load calendars onto the iPod manually, using the **Calendars** folder on the iPod's hard disk. If you have a Mac, you can use the method described in this task, but you might find it more efficient to use iTunes' built-in calendar synchronization or iSync as described in 85 **Synchronize Contacts Using iTunes or iSync (Mac Only)**.

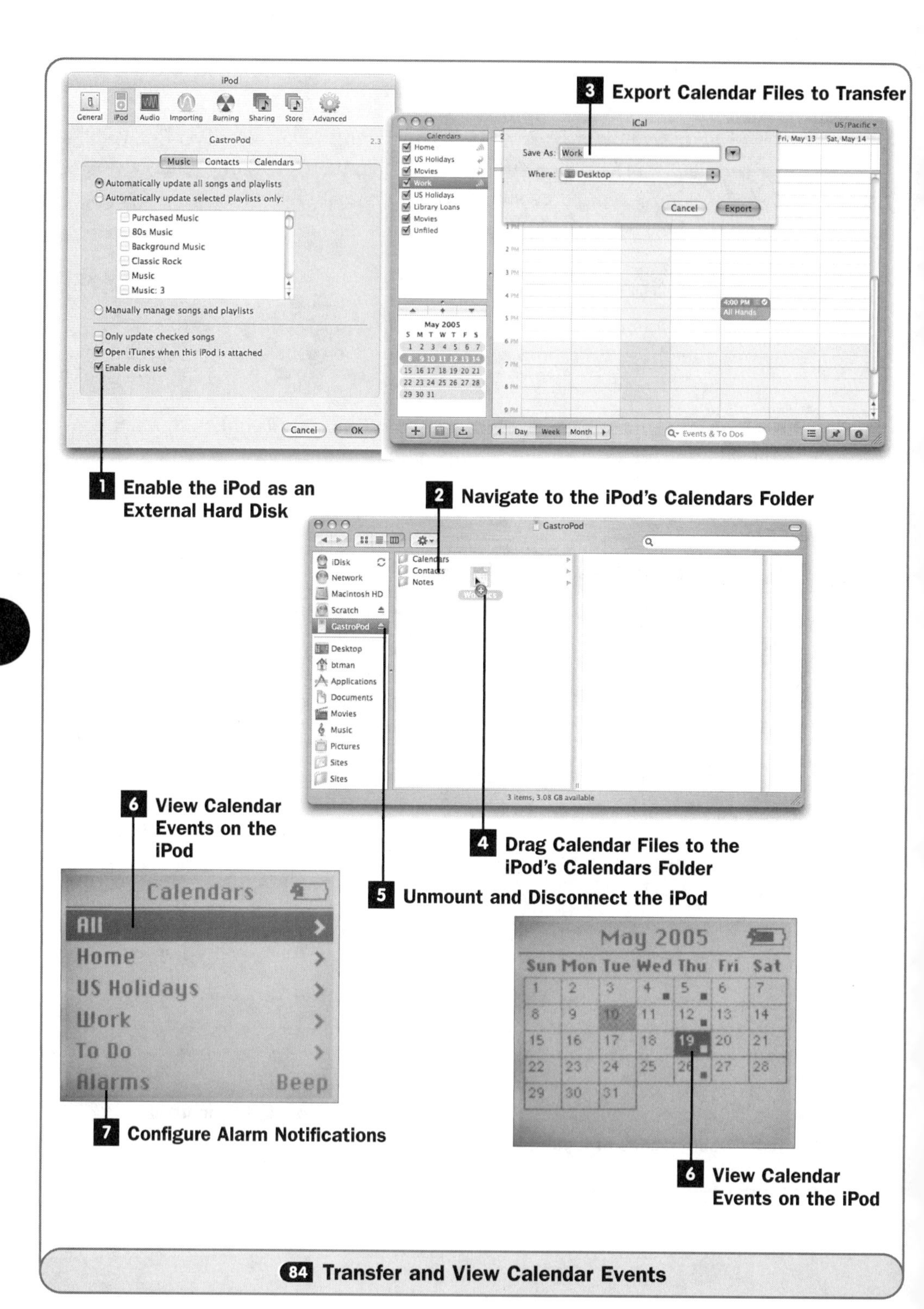

3 Export Calendar Files to Transfer
1 Enable the iPod as an External Hard Disk
2 Navigate to the iPod's Calendars Folder
6 View Calendar Events on the iPod
4 Drag Calendar Files to the iPod's Calendars Folder
5 Unmount and Disconnect the iPod
7 Configure Alarm Notifications
6 View Calendar Events on the iPod
Calendars
All
Home
US Holidays
Work
To Do
Alarms
Beep
May 2005
Sun Mon Tue Wed Thu Fri Sat

84

84 Transfer and View Calendar Events

▶ NOTE

To-do lists, a common feature of most popular calendaring software, can be transferred to the iPod only if you have a Mac and use iTunes 4.8 or iSync.

1 Enable the iPod as an External Hard Disk

As described in 80 **Use Your iPod as an External Hard Disk** enable your iPod's external hard disk mode and attach the iPod to your computer.

2 Navigate to the iPod's Calendars Folder

Open up the iPod's hard disk in a Windows Explorer or Finder window. In the top level of the disk is a folder called **Calendars**. Open this folder and keep the window open on your screen so that you can drag items into it.

3 Export Calendar Files to Transfer

Open your data-organizing application where your calendar events are stored. View the **Calendar** section (if applicable), where your calendars and events are listed.

Using the application's **Export** function (usually located in the **File** menu), export the calendar (or calendars) you want to transfer to your iPod. The output files should be in iCalendar (**.ics**) or vCal (**.vcs**) format; you can save them in any temporary location (such as on your Desktop) or directly into the iPod's **Calendars** folder.

4 Drag Calendar Files to the iPod's Calendars Folder

If you saved the exported files to a temporary location, locate the files on your computer's hard disk and drag them into the **Calendars** folder on the iPod. Wait for the files to be copied to the iPod's disk.

5 Unmount and Disconnect the iPod

When you're done copying calendar files to the iPod, unmount or eject the iPod as described in 80 **Use Your iPod as an External Hard Disk** and disconnect the iPod from the computer.

6 View Calendar Events on the iPod

From the iPod's Main Menu, select **Extras**, then **Calendars**. Your named calendars are all listed alphabetically, following an item at the top called **All**, which aggregates all the events from all your calendar files and presents them in a single unified view.

Use the wheel to scroll to the desired calendar and press **Select**. The iPod displays a calendar view of the current month, with a dot in each date where an event is registered; use the wheel to highlight a date and press **Select** to view the details of that date's events.

▶ TIP

If you continue rotating the wheel in the calendar view, it switches to the next month.

7 Configure Alarm Notifications

The iPod is set by default to emit a beeping alarm and display an event's details on its screen when a calendar item configured with an alarm setting comes due. You can suppress this beep, or turn off alarm notifications entirely, using the last item on the **Calendars** screen: **Alarms**. Highlight this item and press **Select** to toggle between **Off**, **Beep**, and **Silent** modes.

85 Synchronize Contacts Using iTunes or iSync (Mac Only)

84

✔ BEFORE YOU BEGIN	→ SEE ALSO
46 Find and Play Music on the iPod	83 Transfer and View Contacts 84 Transfer and View Calendar Events 86 Transfer and View Text Notes

If your computer is a Mac running Mac OS X 10.4 ("Tiger"), synchronizing your contacts and calendars is a feature built right into iTunes 4.8. In the **iPod Preferences** window you'll find **Contacts** and **Calendars** tabs that allow you to enable automatic synchronizing of all or selected contacts from your Address Book and calendar events from iCal. If you use Tiger, any time you connect the iPod to your computer, iTunes copies all your vital information to the iPod—not just transferring it to the device in one direction, but making sure that any changes or deletions you make in your Address Book or iCal data are reflected accurately on the iPod.

If, however, you don't have Mac OS X Tiger yet, you can still automatically update your contacts and calendars automatically—it just involves the use of a small utility built into Mac OS X Panther called **iSync**, which exists to keep your information synchronized to your various handheld devices (such as the iPod) and your other computers using .Mac. **iSync** can be configured to launch and sync your data every time you connect the iPod to your computer, or you can choose to launch it manually to sync whenever you want.

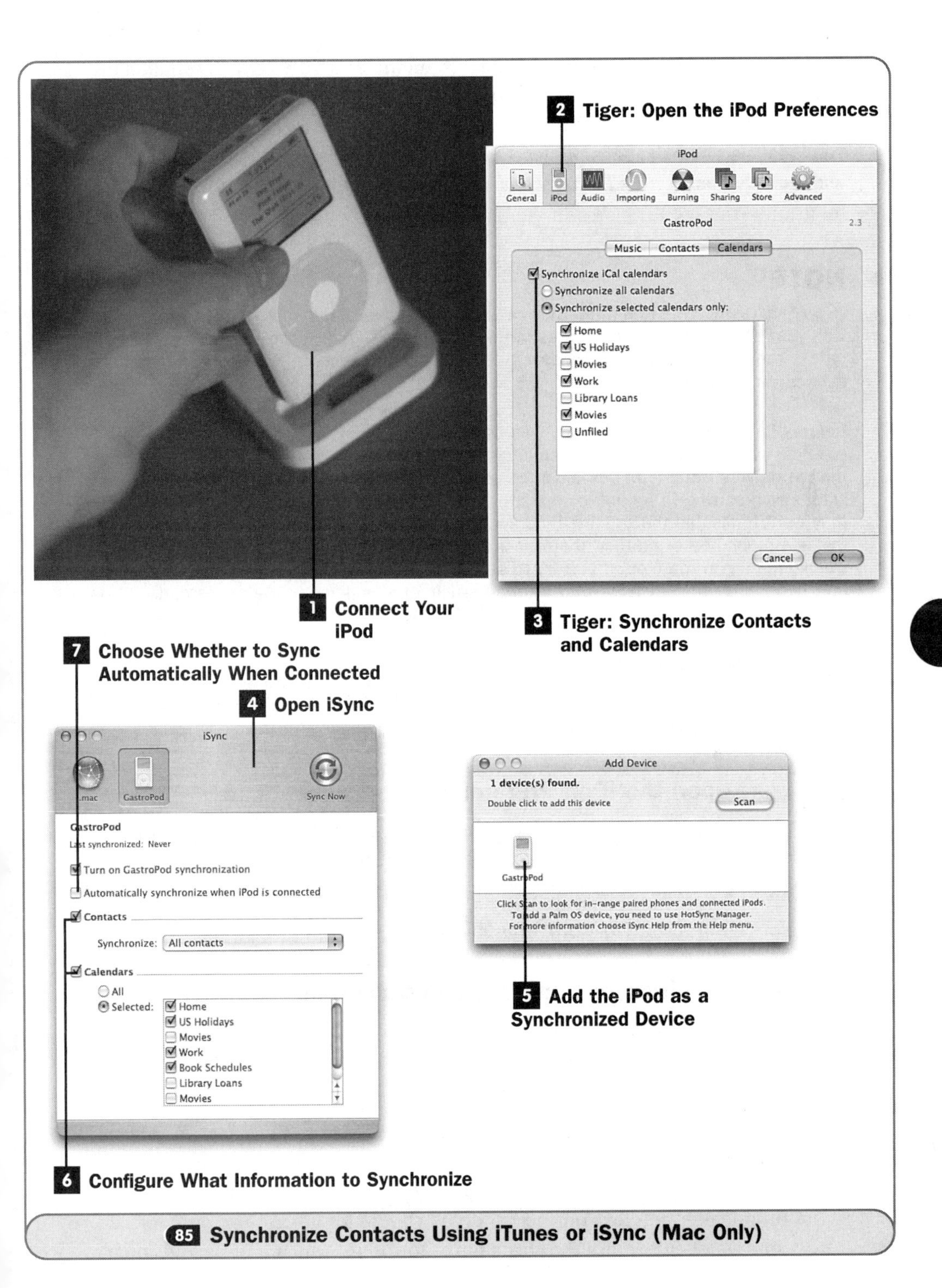
2 Tiger: Open the iPod Preferences
iPod
General
iPod
Audio
Importing
Burning
Sharing
Store
Advanced
GastroPod
Music
Contacts
Calendars
Synchronize iCal calendars
Synchronize all calendars
Synchronize selected calendars only:
Home
US Holidays
Movies
Work
Library Loans
Movies
Unfiled
Cancel
OK
1 Connect Your iPod
3 Tiger: Synchronize Contacts and Calendars
7 Choose Whether to Sync Automatically When Connected
4 Open iSync
iSync
GastroPod
Sync Now
Last synchronized: Never
Turn on GastroPod synchronization
Automatically synchronize when iPod is connected
Contacts
Synchronize: All contacts
Calendars
All
Selected:
Home
US Holidays
Movies
Work
Book Schedules
Library Loans
Movies
Add Device
1 device(s) found.
Double click to add this device
Scan
GastroPod
Click Scan to look for in-range paired phones and connected iPods.
To add a Palm OS device, you need to use HotSync Manager.
For more information choose iSync Help from the Help menu.
5 Add the iPod as a Synchronized Device
6 Configure What Information to Synchronize

85

This task covers both the built-in iTunes 4.8 method and the iSync method of syncing your data. This task applies only to Mac users with Mac OS X 10.2.8 or later, iSync 1.1 or later, and iCal 1.0.1 or later. If you have a Windows PC, or if your Mac's software is not updated to at least these versions, refer to 83 **Transfer and View Contacts** and 84 **Transfer and View Calendar Events** to transfer this information to your iPod.

NOTES

To-do lists (as used in iCal and other calendaring software) can only be synchronized with your iPod using the procedures in this task. To-do lists are copied automatically as part of the **Synchronize all calendars** option. Manually synchronizing your calendars does not transfer to-do lists.

Before Mac OS X 10.4 Tiger, **iSync** was used more extensively to sync your contact and calendar data through .Mac to keep your computers in sync, as well as syncing the information on your peripheral devices such as PDAs and iPods. Now, **iSync** is used exclusively for synchronizing PDAs and cell phones. If you have recently upgraded to Tiger, you may want to disable the existing iPod syncing in **iSync** and enable it in iTunes because this is a much neater method that doesn't cause two different applications to fire up when you plug in the iPod. If you try to set up iSync in Tiger with a new iPod configuration, it won't let you—it tells you that iPod syncing takes place in iTunes instead.

1 Connect Your iPod

Connect your iPod to your computer using the Dock or cable. Wait for it to finish synchronizing its music with iTunes.

2 Tiger: Open the iPod Preferences

If you're running Mac OS X Tiger and iTunes 4.8 or higher, choose **iTunes, Preferences** and click the **iPod** tab. Note that the **Contacts** and **Calendars** sections are available along with the **Music** section.

If you're not using Tiger or iTunes 4.8, skip to step 4.

3 Tiger: Synchronize Contacts and Calendars

In each of the **Contacts** and **Calendars** sections, select the check box to enable syncing of that body of information: **Synchronize Address Book contacts** and **Synchronize iCal calendars**.

Below the main check box in each of these sections are radio buttons allowing you to choose between synchronizing all your contacts or calendars, or synchronizing only selected contact groups or named calendars. Choose the appropriate option for your needs. If you choose to synchronize only selected groups or calendars, use the check boxes to specify which groups and calendars to send to the iPod.

Click **OK**; iTunes copies your contacts and calendars to the iPod and will synchronize any changed information the next time you connect the iPod to the computer. You're now done with this task; the rest of the steps are not relevant to users of Mac OS X Tiger.

4 Open iSync

if you're not using Tiger or iTunes 4.8, navigate into the **Applications** folder and double-click **iSync** to launch it.

5 Add the iPod as a Synchronized Device

From the **Devices** menu at the top of the screen, choose **Add Device**. iSync detects the iPod and reports its name and connection method. Double-click the iPod to add it to iSync's list of synchronized devices.

6 Configure What Information to Synchronize

Click the iPod's icon in iSync to open its configuration panel, if it's not already open. There are check boxes indicating whether iSync should synchronize your Address Book contacts (and which groups to synchronize), your iCal calendars and to-do lists, or both sets of information. Disable the appropriate check boxes if you don't want to synchronize certain data.

7 Choose Whether to Sync Automatically When Connected

Another selected check box is **Automatically synchronize when iPod is connected**. With this option enabled, iSync launches and synchronizes your contacts and calendars with your iPod whenever you plug it in. If you're already synchronizing your music with iTunes automatically and you enable this option, both iTunes and iSync will launch at the same time when you connect the iPod, fighting for your attention. You might want to disable this check box if you want iTunes to get priority. If you do, however, you must manually launch iSync and click **Sync Now** whenever you want to sync your information. Otherwise, enable the check box, and both applications will launch and sync at the same time.

▶ TIP

If you want to make sure that your information is synchronized every time you connect the iPod, leave the **Automatically synchronize when iPod is connected** check box enabled and disable the **Open iTunes when attached** check box in the **Music** section of the **iPod** pane in the iTunes **Preferences** window. You'll need to launch iTunes manually to sync your music, or choose **File, Update iPod**.

8 Sync Information with the iPod

Click **Sync Now**. iSync transfers all new and changed information to the iPod. When it's done synchronizing, you can safely disconnect the iPod and view the contacts and calendars as described in 83 **Transfer and View Contacts** and 84 **Transfer and View Calendar Events**.

86 Transfer and View Text Notes

✓ BEFORE YOU BEGIN	→ SEE ALSO
80 Use Your iPod as an External Hard Disk	83 Transfer and View Contacts 84 Transfer and View Calendar Events

You might not be able to jot down notes on it as you listen to your favorite music, but the iPod does allow you to *read* any text files you place in the special **Notes** folder on its disk. These text files can be anything from brief shopping lists or workout regimens to whole articles downloaded from the Web. The only restriction is that they must be saved in plain text (**.txt**) format.

1 Enable the iPod as an External Hard Disk

As described in 80 **Use Your iPod as an External Hard Disk**, enable your iPod's external hard disk mode and connect the iPod to your computer.

2 Navigate to the iPod's Notes Folder

Open up the iPod's hard disk in a Windows Explorer or Finder window. In the top level of the disk is a folder called **Notes**. Open this folder and keep the window open on your screen so that you can drag items into it.

3 Save Text Files to Transfer

If the text files you want to transfer to the iPod are not already in plain text format, you must export them to this format using their native applications (such as Microsoft Word). Using the application's **Export** or **Save As** function (usually located in the **File** menu), export each file you want to transfer to your iPod. The output files must be in plain text (**.txt**) format; you can save the files in any temporary location (such as your Desktop) or directly into the iPod's **Notes** folder.

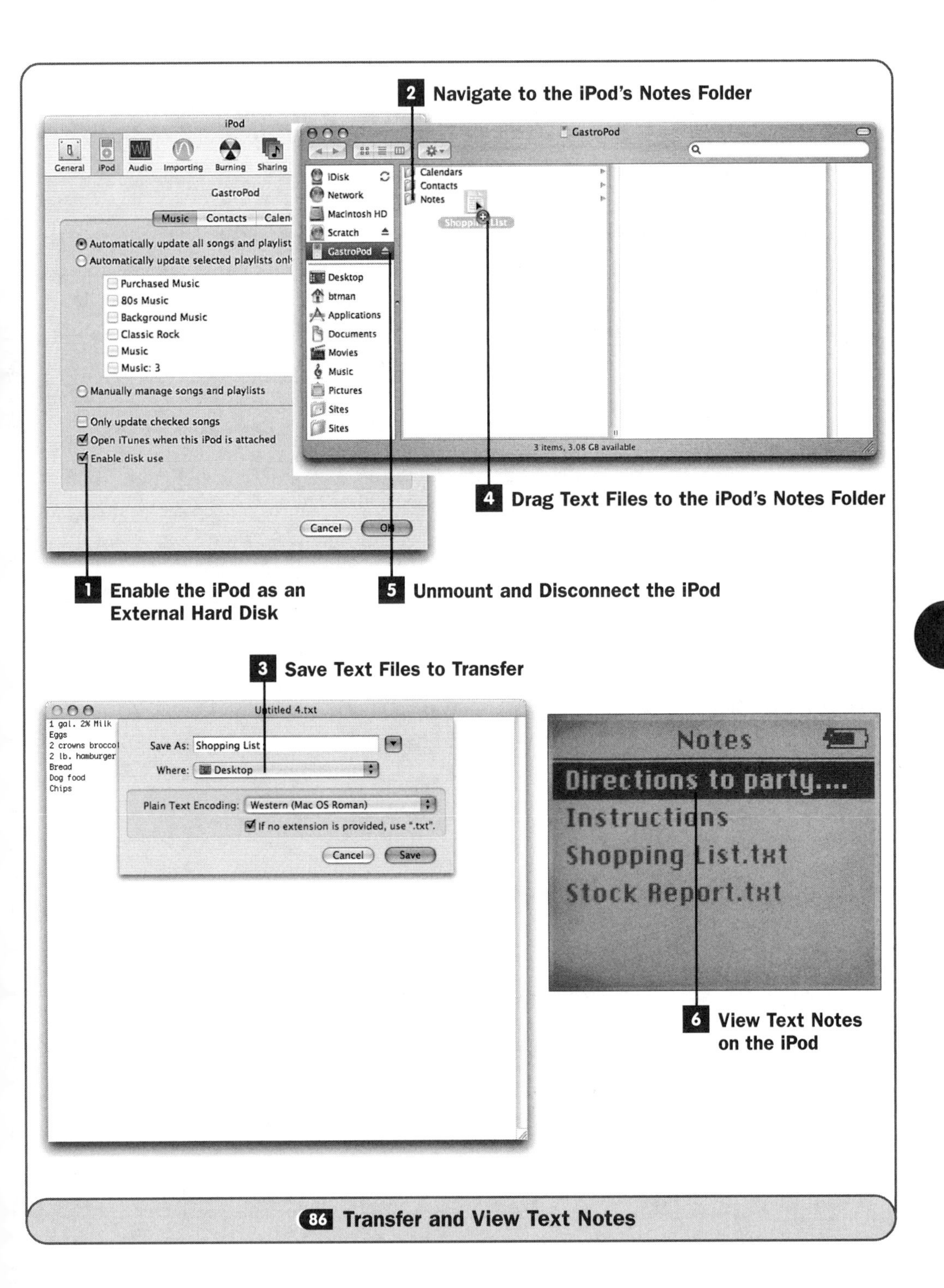
2 Navigate to the iPod's Notes Folder
iPod
General
iPod
Audio
Importing
Burning
Sharing
GastroPod
Music
Contacts
Automatically update all songs and playlist
Automatically update selected playlists onl
Purchased Music
80s Music
Background Music
Classic Rock
Music
Music: 3
Manually manage songs and playlists
Only update checked songs
Open iTunes when this iPod is attached
Enable disk use
Cancel
GastroPod
iDisk
Network
Macintosh HD
Scratch
GastroPod
Desktop
btman
Applications
Documents
Movies
Music
Pictures
Sites
Sites
Calendars
Contacts
Notes
3 items, 3.08 GB available
4 Drag Text Files to the iPod's Notes Folder
1 Enable the iPod as an External Hard Disk
5 Unmount and Disconnect the iPod
3 Save Text Files to Transfer
Untitled 4.txt
1 gal. 2% Milk
Eggs
2 crowns broccol
2 lb. hamburger
Bread
Dog food
Chips
Save As: Shopping List
Where: Desktop
Plain Text Encoding: Western (Mac OS Roman)
If no extension is provided, use ".txt".
Cancel
Save
Notes
Directions to party....
Instructions
Shopping List.txt
Stock Report.txt
6 View Text Notes on the iPod
86 Transfer and View Text Notes

4 Drag Text Files to the iPod's Notes Folder

If you saved the exported files to a temporary location, locate the exported files on your computer's hard disk and drag them into the **Notes** folder on the iPod. Wait for the files to be copied to the iPod's disk.

5 Unmount and Disconnect the iPod

When you're done copying text files to the iPod, unmount or eject it as described in 80 **Use Your iPod as an External Hard Disk**, and disconnect the iPod from the computer.

6 View Text Notes on the iPod

From the iPod's Main Menu, select **Extras**, then **Notes**. Your text files are all listed alphabetically by their filenames. Highlight a file and press **Select** to read it; use the wheel to scroll through the file's contents.

11

iPod Add-Ons

IN THIS CHAPTER:

If there's any sure indication of the runaway success of the iPod, it's in the incredibly vast market that has emerged for third-party add-on gadgets you can buy to turn your iPod from a simple music player into anything from an alarm clock to a boom box, to double or triple its battery life, to record and play back voice memos, and especially to bring your vast iTunes' music collection with you in the car for your daily commute or a thousand-mile road trip. The iPod's versatile design, with a controller socket in the top next to the headphone jack, and the Dock connector at the bottom carrying all kinds of signals to and from the unit, make third-party enhancement a slam-dunk.

Companies such as Griffin, Belkin, Bose, Monster, Sonnet, XtremeMac, JBL, and many others both well-known and obscure have jumped onto the iPod bandwagon to bring you the tools for making the iPod just what you need it to be. The tasks in this chapter describe some of the most popular methods for meeting the most common iPod-enhancement needs. Although some solutions are served by only a single unique company or product, others have a variety of possible products that compete for your business, and new products are entering the market all the time; talk to a Mac or iPod sales professional or one of the folks at the Genius Bar at any Apple Store to make sure that you're getting the best product in the field you're interested in.

▶ NOTE

The tasks in this chapter describe add-on accessories available for 3G iPods and later (iPods with a Dock connector). Many accessories available for the full-size iPod are also available in versions compatible with the iPod mini, and some work equally well with both. Earlier versions of iPods, without the Dock connector, have fewer options for accessorizing them, and they are generally not addressed here. Most accessories are also not compatible with the iPod shuffle.

▶ WEB RESOURCE

http://www.apple.com/ipod/accessories.html

Apple's iPod Accessories site features purchasing links for some of the most popular and highly recommended gadgets to add to your iPod.

87 Record Voice Memos

✔ BEFORE YOU BEGIN	→ SEE ALSO
46 Find and Play Music on the iPod	90 Listen to Your iPod in the Car

If you're a writer, teacher, student, researcher, or just someone who likes to get quick thoughts recorded for posterity, one gadget you might find indispensable in your daily life is a small and convenient voice recorder. With an iPod in your pocket and an inexpensive add-on accessory, you can have one.

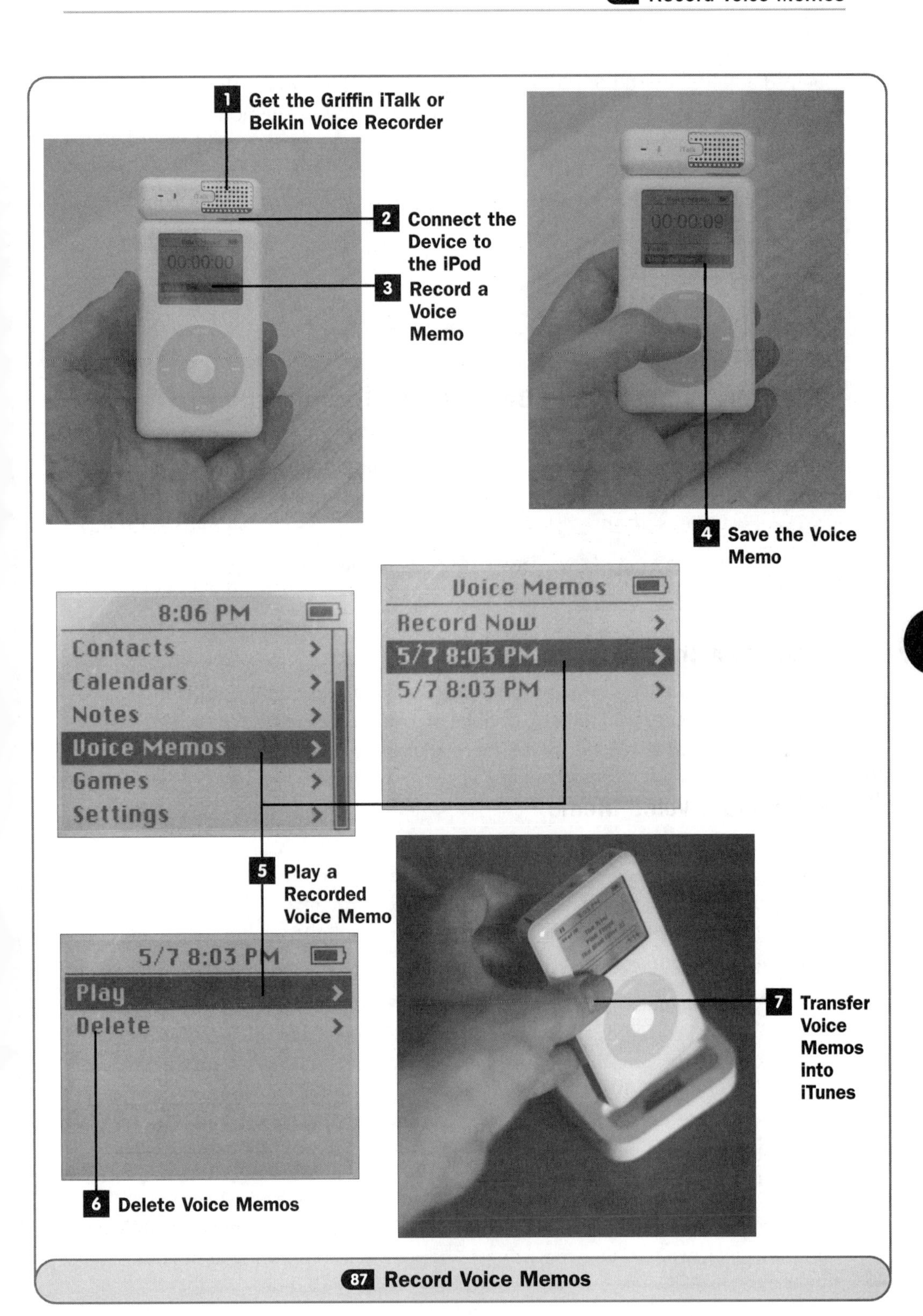
1 Get the Griffin iTalk or Belkin Voice Recorder
2 Connect the Device to the iPod
3 Record a Voice Memo
4 Save the Voice Memo
8:06 PM
Contacts
Calendars
Notes
Voice Memos
Games
Settings
Voice Memos
Record Now
5/7 8:03 PM
5/7 8:03 PM
5 Play a Recorded Voice Memo
5/7 8:03 PM
Play
Delete
6 Delete Voice Memos
7 Transfer Voice Memos into iTunes
87 Record Voice Memos

87

The iPod doesn't have a built-in microphone for recording your voice or any other sound, but its software does have support for third-party microphone accessories that unlock these features. Just connect the add-on device to the top of the iPod and begin recording. "Voice memos" you record in this way are stored in mono WAV format and can be transferred back to your computer to review at your leisure.

▶ **NOTE**

The iPod mini does not support recording voice memos.

1 Get the Griffin iTalk or Belkin Voice Recorder

The two most popular iPod microphones are the Griffin iTalk ($39.95) and the Belkin Voice Recorder ($34.95). Both work similarly, but the iTalk has a rather more seamless process for transferring voice memos back into iTunes. The illustrations for this task show the iTalk.

Visit the online Apple Store (**http://store.apple.com**) or an Apple retail store to pick up one of these devices.

2 Connect the Device to the iPod

Plug the microphone into the top of the iPod, making sure that the long round prong goes into the microphone jack and that the small tab goes into the rectangular hole next to it. (The speaker should face the front.)

3 Record a Voice Memo

When you connect the microphone, the iPod immediately goes into Voice Memo recording mode; the display shows the elapsed time in the recording, and there are two available options: **Record** or **Cancel**. **Cancel** leads back to the iPod's normal menu system; **Record** begins audio recording. Select the **Record** option and press the **Select** button.

Speak into the microphone, hold up the iPod to capture a lecture, or just set it down and let it record. The audio stream is recorded in mono WAV format at an 8KHz, 16-bit sampling rate, which consumes about 1MB per minute; this means if you have 10GB of unused space on your iPod, you can record voice memos for almost 67 hours (2.8 days) continuously before you run out of space. (If the iPod becomes full, you won't be able to record any more voice memos.)

4 Save the Voice Memo

You can pause the recording and resume it (select **Pause**, then select **Resume**); at any time, you can select **Stop and Save** to close the recording and save it on the iPod's disk. Press **Menu** to exit to the iPod's regular menu system.

5 Play a Recorded Voice Memo

While the iTalk or Voice Recorder is connected to the iPod, an item called **Voice Memos** is available in the **Extras** screen. Select this option to see all the voice memos you've recorded so far, labeled by the date and time of each recording. Highlight a voice memo and press **Select**, then choose **Play** to play it back through the microphone device's speaker; you can control it during playback as you would any song.

In the same **Voice Memos** menu, choose **Record Now** to record a new voice memo.

6 Delete Voice Memos

To delete a voice memo, select the voice memo in the **Voice Memos** screen and then choose **Delete** to erase it from the iPod.

7 Transfer Voice Memos into iTunes

When you synchronize the iPod with iTunes, the voice memos are automatically downloaded into your iTunes **Library** and placed into a ***playlist*** called **Voice Memos**; the recorded memos are automatically deleted from the iPod after they have been synchronized with the **Voice Memos** playlist as regular songs in the music database. If you enable disk mode (see 80 **Use Your iPod as an External Hard Disk**), you can access the voice memos in the **Recordings** folder at the top level of the iPod's disk.

▶ NOTE

The Belkin Voice Recorder might not synchronize your voice memos automatically into iTunes. If it doesn't, navigate to the iPod's Recordings folder, copy the contents to your computer, and add them into iTunes as described in 11 Add a Music File to Your iTunes Library.

88 Temporarily Store Digital Photos on Your iPod

✓ BEFORE YOU BEGIN	→ SEE ALSO
80 Use Your iPod as an External Hard Disk	79 Download Photos from Your Camera to Your iPod photo

If you aren't fortunate enough to have an iPod photo, you can still use your regular iPod to enjoy some of the convenience the iPod photo affords you as a digital photographer on the go: You can empty your digital camera's photos onto a monochrome iPod's disk for safekeeping until you get home from your vacation. Belkin makes two devices that serve to transfer photos and other data to your iPod: the Digital Camera Link ($79.99), which lets you connect your camera's USB cable directly to it; and the Media Reader ($99.99), into which you can load any CompactFlash, Secure Digital (SD), Memory Stick, MultiMediaCard (MMC), or SmartMedia card to transfer its contents to the iPod.

If you do have an iPod photo, refer to 79 **Download Photos from Your Camera to Your iPod photo** for a more elegant and cost-effective solution to this same need.

88

▶ **NOTE**

The iPod mini does not support importing photos.

1 Get the Belkin Digital Camera Link or Belkin Media Reader

The more inexpensive Belkin Digital Camera Link is best if you just want to transfer photos from your USB digital camera. Get the Belkin Media Reader if you want to transfer data other than just digital photos, or if you want to transfer digital photos from any of the six supported media types. The illustrations for this task show the Digital Camera Link.

Visit the online Apple Store (**http://store.apple.com**) or an Apple retail store to pick up one of these devices.

2 Load Batteries into the Device

Both Belkin devices require AA batteries, which are included: four for the Media Reader or two for the Digital Camera link. Insert them as indicated on your device's battery compartment.

3 Connect the Device to the iPod

Extract the connector and cord from the device and plug it into the iPod's Dock connector.

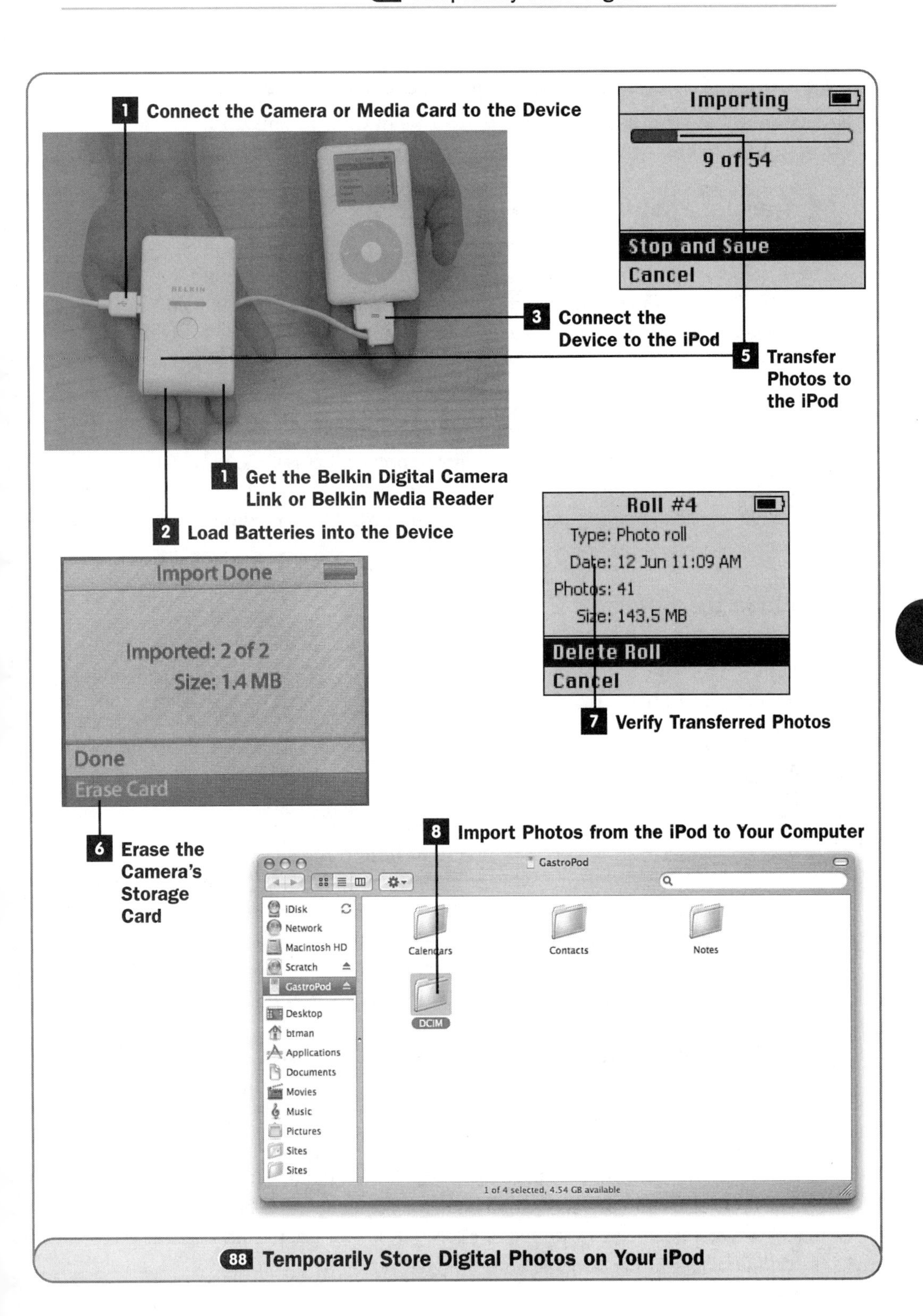
1 Connect the Camera or Media Card to the Device
Importing
9 of 54
Stop and Save
Cancel
3 Connect the Device to the iPod
5 Transfer Photos to the iPod
1 Get the Belkin Digital Camera Link or Belkin Media Reader
2 Load Batteries into the Device
Roll #4
Type: Photo roll
Date: 12 Jun 11:09 AM
Photos: 41
Size: 143.5 MB
Delete Roll
Cancel
Import Done
Imported: 2 of 2
Size: 1.4 MB
Done
Erase Card
7 Verify Transferred Photos
6 Erase the Camera's Storage Card
8 Import Photos from the iPod to Your Computer
GastroPod
iDisk
Network
Macintosh HD
Scratch
GastroPod
Desktop
btman
Applications
Documents
Movies
Music
Pictures
Sites
Sites
Calendars
Contacts
Notes
DCIM
1 of 4 selected, 4.54 GB available

88 Temporarily Store Digital Photos on Your iPod

4 Connect the Camera or Media Card to the Device

Connect the camera's USB cable to the Digital Camera Link, or insert the camera's storage media card into the Media Reader's slot.

5 Transfer Photos to the iPod

Press the button on the Digital Camera Link to begin transferring photos to the iPod. If you have the Media Reader, the iPod's display changes to a **Photo Import** screen similar to the one shown in 79 **Download Photos from Your Camera to Your iPod photo**, except without color. Choose **Import** to copy the photos to the iPod.

While the photos are transferring, the iPod shows a progress bar indicating how many photos are in the "roll" and how many have been transferred so far. Monochrome iPods do not display the photos themselves, however. There's a legend printed on the back of the Digital Camera Link that explains the different flashing signals of the LEDs and what they mean the unit is doing.

6 Erase the Camera's Storage Card

If you're using the Digital Camera Link, the photos are removed automatically from the camera's card at the end of the transfer; if you're using the Media Reader, select **Erase Card** from the screen that appears at the end of the download process.

7 Verify Transferred Photos

Navigate into the **Extras** menu, where a new **Photo Import** item has appeared. Select this option. On the **Photo Import** screen are listed each "roll" of photos you transferred from your camera, followed by the number of photos in each roll, such as **Roll #1 (12)**, **Roll #2 (42)**, and so on. Select one of these rolls to view the date on which it was taken, the number of photos in it, and how much disk space it consumes. You can also discard a roll of photos from your iPod by selecting it and choosing **Delete Roll**.

8 Import Photos from the iPod to Your Computer

When you get back to your computer, you'll want to move the downloaded photos from the iPod into your favorite photo organizer application (iPhoto for Mac users, or Adobe Album or Adobe Photoshop Elements for Windows—although any software that imports photos from a digital camera will work). After you've loaded photos onto it from your camera, the iPod acts like a digital camera when connected to your computer; your photo software will think it's another camera and download the photos from it accordingly.

Connect the iPod to the computer using the Dock or cable. After it syncs with iTunes, launch your photo organizer application and import the photos as you normally do from your camera. Be sure to erase the "camera's" contents when you're done transferring! Most photo software presents this option during the import process.

▶ NOTES

You might have to enable the iPod as an external hard disk before the photo software will recognize it as a camera-like device. See 80 **Use Your iPod as an External Hard Disk** for more information, and remember to unmount the iPod from your computer when you're done transferring photos.

If your photo software does not recognize the iPod as a camera, you can manually copy the photos out of the **DCIM** folder on the iPod onto your computer's disk to import them.

89 Use Your iPod as an Alarm Clock

✔ BEFORE YOU BEGIN	➜ SEE ALSO
5 Set the iPod's Date and Time	91 Turn Your iPod into a Boom Box with Remote Control

89

Taking your iPod with you on a vacation isn't just a matter of keeping entertained in distant locales—it's also a practical matter. You can use the iPod to make sure that you wake up each morning to a more pleasant sound than your phone ringing with a wake-up call from the hotel's front desk. The iPod can act as an alarm clock, beeping at a prescribed time, or you can hook it up to a set of compact portable external speakers and have the iPod begin playing music from a specified playlist at the set alarm time. You might like this arrangement enough to use it at home as well—so long, clock-radio!

▶ NOTE

Be sure to set the iPod's date and time before beginning this task; see 5 **Set the iPod's Date and Time** for details.

1 Set the Alarm Time

Navigate into the **Extras** menu, then select **Clock**, then select **Alarm Clock**. From the next screen, select the **Time** item. You're presented with a simple time readout (in 1-minute increments) that you can adjust by rotating the wheel. Set it to the time you want to wake up (making sure that the display screen reads **AM** if you want to set it for the morning) and press **Select** to set the alarm time. You are returned to the **Alarm Clock** menu.

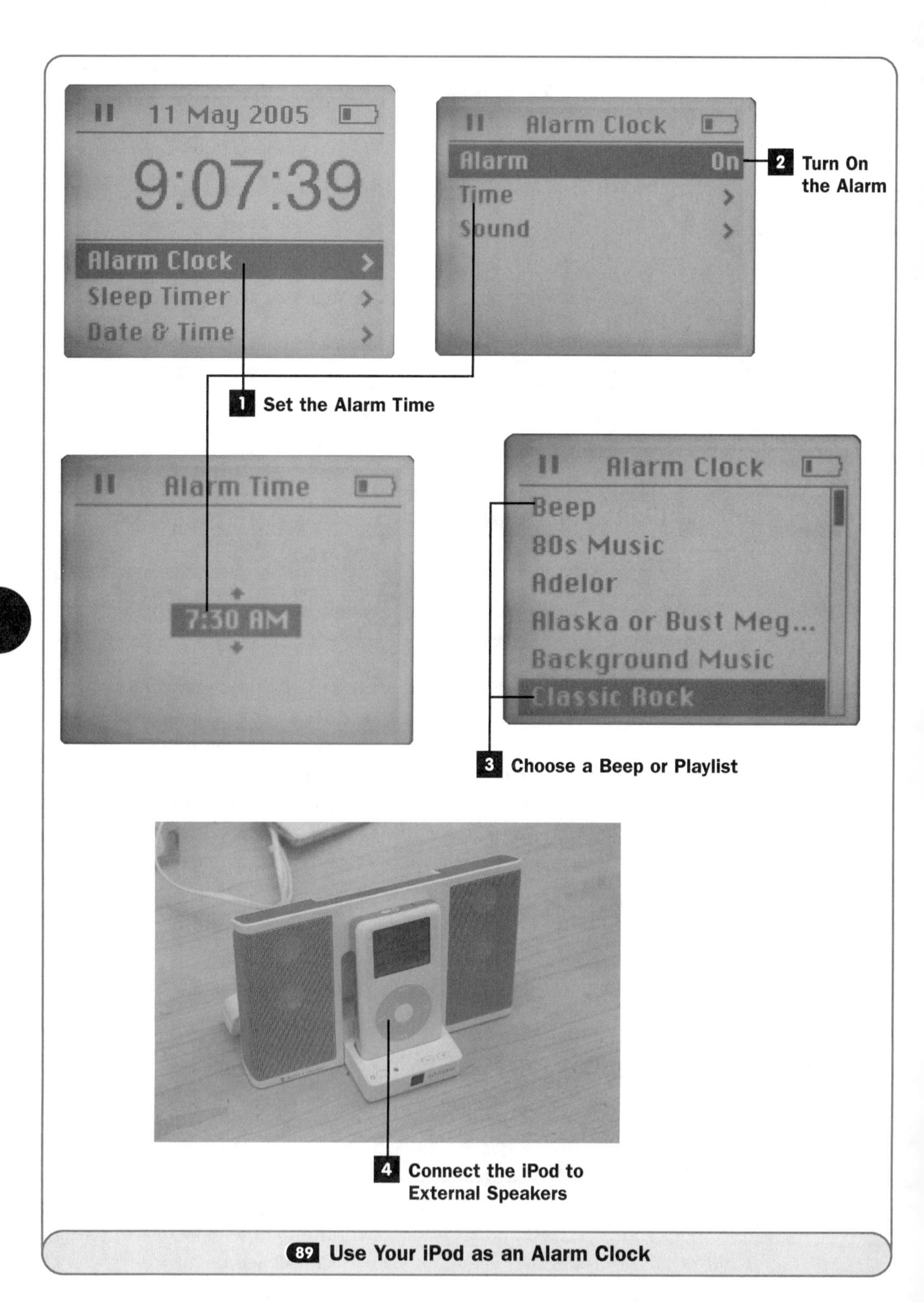

89 Use Your iPod as an Alarm Clock

2 Turn On the Alarm

After you've set the time of the alarm, you must turn on the alarm. Highlight **Alarm** and press **Select** to toggle the alarm clock function to **On**. The next time the iPod's internal clock reaches the set alarm time, it emits a melodic beeping cadence for several seconds—enough to wake up most people sleeping a few feet from it.

3 Choose a Beep or Playlist

If you don't like the beep and want to take your alarm clock to the next level, first invest in a set of small, portable speakers built for the iPod like the Altec Lansing inMotion iM3 ($179). In the **Alarm Clock** screen, choose **Sound**, and then select one of the listed ***playlists*** and press **Select**.

▶ TIP

You can use any set of powered or unpowered speakers you like, as long as they can be connected to the iPod Dock through its audio output jack or directly to the iPod's headphone jack. Speakers built for the iPod, with a built-in Dock, are probably the most elegant solution with the fewest wires.

▶ NOTE

If you have Shuffle mode enabled, the iPod selects a song at random from the playlist you choose when the alarm goes off.

4 Connect the iPod to External Speakers

The speaker system acts as an iPod Dock. Insert the iPod into the slot in the tray so that the Dock connector fits over the tongue in the slot. When the iPod's alarm goes off, it plays its music through the Dock connector and into the speakers.

▶ NOTE

Shut off the alarm music by pressing Play/Pause.

90 Listen to Your iPod in the Car

✔ BEFORE YOU BEGIN	→ SEE ALSO
46 Find and Play Music on the iPod	89 Use Your iPod as an Alarm Clock 91 Turn Your iPod into a Boom Box with Remote Control

Perhaps more so than any other place, people want to listen to their iPod music in their cars. It's an obvious place for it—giving you far more music capacity than MP3 CDs and far more personalized content than even satellite radio. Having an iPod in the car puts your time in the car back on your own terms, even when you're stuck in traffic.

Many automakers, such as BMW, Mercedes-Benz, Volvo, and Mini, have committed to integrating iPod connectivity into their cars. However, the solutions presented by these cars are a little less than ideal, and those of us without such privileged vehicles have to get by using one of the time-honored car-adapter technologies that are being made more and more iPod-friendly every day. This task looks at a few of the most popular configurations for hooking up your iPod to your car's audio system.

1 Use a Tape Adapter and Car Charger

Perhaps the most inexpensive solution for iPod-enabled motoring is a tape adapter. This device, sold by any of several companies (such as Monster and Sony) for $20 to $25, connects your iPod's headphone jack to your car's cassette tape deck.

Short of a direct stereo cable connection to your in-dash unit, this solution has the best audio quality available. However, there are plenty of drawbacks: There's an ungainly cord leading from your tape deck to the iPod. The iPod itself needs a separate charger, or at least some kind of protective case so that it doesn't get scratched as it sits in your car's center console. Most cars' tape decks have a tendency to noisily auto-reverse in between songs when they detect silence, interrupting the music. It's a hassle plugging in the dangling cable every time you get into the car. And many cars don't even have tape decks anymore.

▶ NOTE

If possible, disable your car stereo's auto-reverse feature while your iPod is connected; doing so prevents the tape deck from flipping the read head back and forth in between songs.

▶ TIP

Set your iPod to about 75–80% volume and control the volume of the music using the dash unit's volume control. Setting the iPod to this volume level is usually enough to drown out the inevitable hiss of the tape's motors and dirt on the pickups, and yet it's not high enough to cause clipping or distortion in the audio system. (The volume level is also low enough that you won't totally blow out your eardrums when you take your iPod out of the car and plug in your headphones without adjusting the volume first.)

1 Use a Tape Adapter and Car Charger

2 Use an FM Transmitter and Car Charger

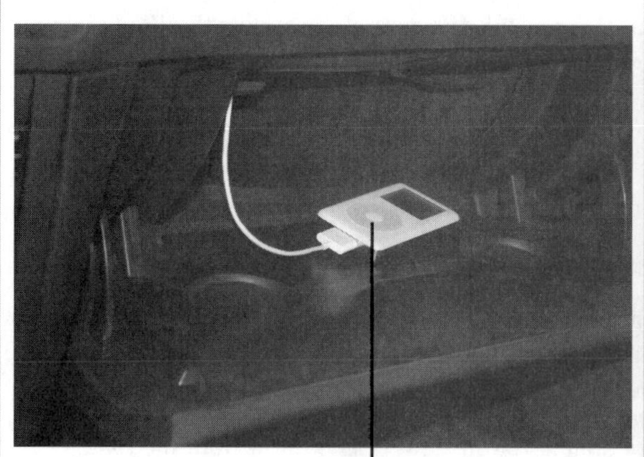

3 Use a Direct Wired Connection

90

You'll need a separate car power adapter to keep your iPod charged from the center console's cigarette lighter or power outlet while you listen to your music. Good choices include the XtremeMac Car Charger ($19.95) or the Belkin Auto Kit ($39.95), which includes an audio out jack for an FM transmitter.

2 Use an FM Transmitter and Car Charger

A somewhat more elegant solution than a tape adapter, yet one with some drawbacks of its own, is an FM transmitter. This device connects either to the headphone jack or the Dock connector of your iPod and broadcasts the audio output on a specified FM frequency that isn't used by a local radio station; just tune your car stereo to that frequency to pick up the iPod's signal. An inexpensive and popular example is the Griffin iTrip ($39.95). Some more complex FM transmitters even have integrated power adapters, such as the Sonnet PodFreq ($99.95) for full-size iPods and the Belkin TuneBase FM ($79.95) for the iPod mini.

Drawbacks of FM transmitters mostly have to do with signal strength and frequency response. As with any FM transmission, music sent from your iPod to your radio is subject to atmospheric interference, even if it's only inches away from the antenna or head unit; this can lead to static and broken sound, particularly in the higher registers. Furthermore, FM music by its nature has poor sound response in the upper frequency regions, meaning that your music will sound muted and dull, and instruments such as drums and vocals will be hard to hear properly. Finally (as though all this weren't enough), the iPod's **Sound Check** feature (see **40 Auto-Level Song Volumes**) is only in effect when music is played through the headphone jack; if your FM transmitter connects to the Dock connector, **Sound Check** is not applied, and your music may vary greatly in its output volume from one track to the next.

90

▶ TIP

Some integrated FM adapters, such as the DLO TransPod ($99.00) and Griffin RoadTrip ($79.00), feature rigid, adjustable stalks connecting the iPod in a cradle to the power outlet. This might suit your needs in getting unwanted cables out of the way; but also be sure to consider the value of having the iPod's cradle on a flexible cord so that you can pull it close to you to navigate or control your music. Remember, safety first—don't go for a solution that causes you to squirm around in your seat or peer away from the road for extended periods while you're barreling along at highway speeds!

3 Use a Direct Wired Connection

The most ideal solution, if you're lucky enough to have it, is a line-in jack in the in-dash unit itself. Just plug one end of a standard 1/8-inch stereo cable into the iPod's headphone jack, and the other end into the car unit's jack, and you'll be able to play your music without regard to frequency degradation or the idiosyncrasies of cassette tape adapters. However, you'll still have to deal with the dangling cords, both to carry the music to the car stereo, and to power the iPod through the charger.

The solutions put forth by automakers such as BMW and Mercedes-Benz tend to involve a Dock connector in the glove compartment, which conveys the ***playlist*** and song information to readouts on the dashboard and allows you to control playback using the buttons integrated with the steering wheel. Yet even these solutions aren't perfect—you get only very limited control over the iPod's navigation, song information displayed in the dash readouts is sparse at best, and the solution uses the Dock connector (which has no **Sound Check** leveling).

TIP

If you're the adventuresome type, you can wire a standard 1/8-inch audio cable directly into your car stereo's plug behind the head unit, which usually takes the place of a trunk-mounted CD changer in the input selection. This solution is only for experts, though—check the enthusiast sites for your car make and model to see if anyone in the ubiquitous discussion forums has advice for you. Chances are that *someone* will have tried hooking up an iPod to your car model!

Perhaps until Apple itself brings out its own custom-designed iPod-docking in-dash stereo unit, there will never be a perfect solution for listening to your iPod music on the road. Yet until that day comes, we have plenty of solutions that get the job done well enough for most of our needs.

91 Turn Your iPod into a Boom Box with Remote Control

✔ BEFORE YOU BEGIN	→ SEE ALSO
46 Find and Play Music on the iPod	89 Use Your iPod as an Alarm Clock
	90 Listen to Your iPod in the Car

As you've seen, an iPod can serve as the musical engine behind photo slideshows on a TV, as an alarm clock with music, as an endless supply of songs for your car—by this stage, it's hard not to see the iPod as a sort of "musical core" that can be plugged into just about anything to give it new sonic life. Perhaps the ultimate expression of that is in how you can construct an excellent bookshelf stereo system or "boom box"—complete with infrared or RF remote control—out of off-the-shelf components designed around a Dock-like receptacle into which you simply plug the iPod. Free of the tedium of CDs or the random chance of radio, you get all the control of your iPod's ***info tag*** navigation and your iTunes' ***playlists***, coupled with high-quality sound from good speakers and the convenience of remote control. Most of these speaker systems even charge your iPod while it plays. What more could you want?

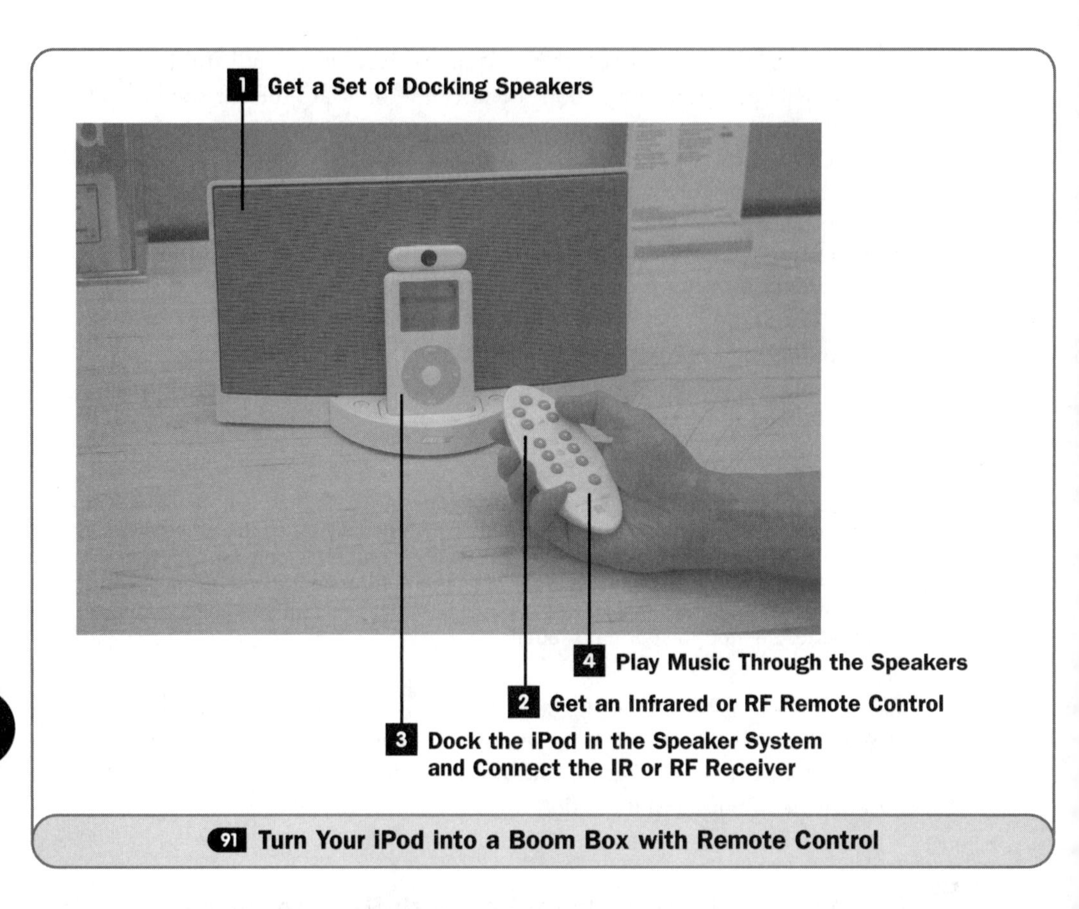
1 Get a Set of Docking Speakers
4 Play Music Through the Speakers
2 Get an Infrared or RF Remote Control
3 Dock the iPod in the Speaker System and Connect the IR or RF Receiver

91 Turn Your iPod into a Boom Box with Remote Control

1 Get a Set of Docking Speakers

Several companies make speaker systems designed to receive an iPod or iPod mini and reproduce its music with rich, deep sound. These include the portable JBL On Tour ($99.95) or Altec Lansing inMotion iM3 ($179), the round and stylish JBL On Stage ($159), and the imposing Bose SoundDock ($299). These speaker systems are all available and on display at most Apple Stores, if you want to see and hear them in action and choose the best one for your needs.

2 Get an Infrared or RF Remote Control

An infrared (IR) or radio-frequency (RF) remote control consists of two parts: a receiver that plugs into the top of the iPod and conveys your controls to the iPod's navigation system, and a remote control that sends signals to the receiver. Two popular products that match this description are the Griffin AirClick RF ($39.95) and the Ten naviPro ex ($49.95). The naviPro has more control buttons, whereas the Griffin AirClick has the convenience of RF signaling (which doesn't require direct line-of-sight to the receiver as an infrared device does).

3 Dock the iPod in the Speaker System and Connect the IR or RF Receiver

When you have your equipment together, plug the iPod into the speakers' Dock-like slot so that the Dock connector fits over the tongue in the slot. Then attach the remote receiver to the top of the iPod so that both prongs fit properly into the two jacks in the top of the iPod.

4 Play Music Through the Speakers

Using the remote, navigate the iPod's menus and select music to play. You can still use the iPod's click wheel and buttons to perform operations not available on the remote, but the remote gives you the convenience of skipping songs, pausing, or changing the volume while you relax across the room.

92

92 Enhance Your iPod's Battery Capacity

✔ BEFORE YOU BEGIN

Just jump right in!

→ SEE ALSO

77 Carry Your Photos on an iPod Photo

80 Use Your iPod as an External Hard Disk

Apple guardedly promises 12 hours of battery life from your iPod or iPod shuffle. As we all know, such rosy estimates are seldom entirely accurate, even for products as good as the iPod. Even if you do regularly get half a day out of a charge on your iPod, what good does that do you after a long red-eye flight from San Francisco to London, or in the middle of a weekend backpacking trip?

Fortunately, available devices let you bulk up your iPod's battery capacity—sacrificing its svelte size and elegant shape in favor of extra playback time when you need it most. Belkin makes a Battery Pack ($59) that takes four AA batteries and provides an additional 12 to 15 hours of life for full-size iPods (not the iPod mini); and Apple's iPod shuffle Battery Pack ($29) extends the life of your iPod shuffle by up to 20 hours with two AAA batteries. The Belkin TunePower ($79.95) is a rechargeable battery pack that supports full-size iPods as well as the iPod mini.

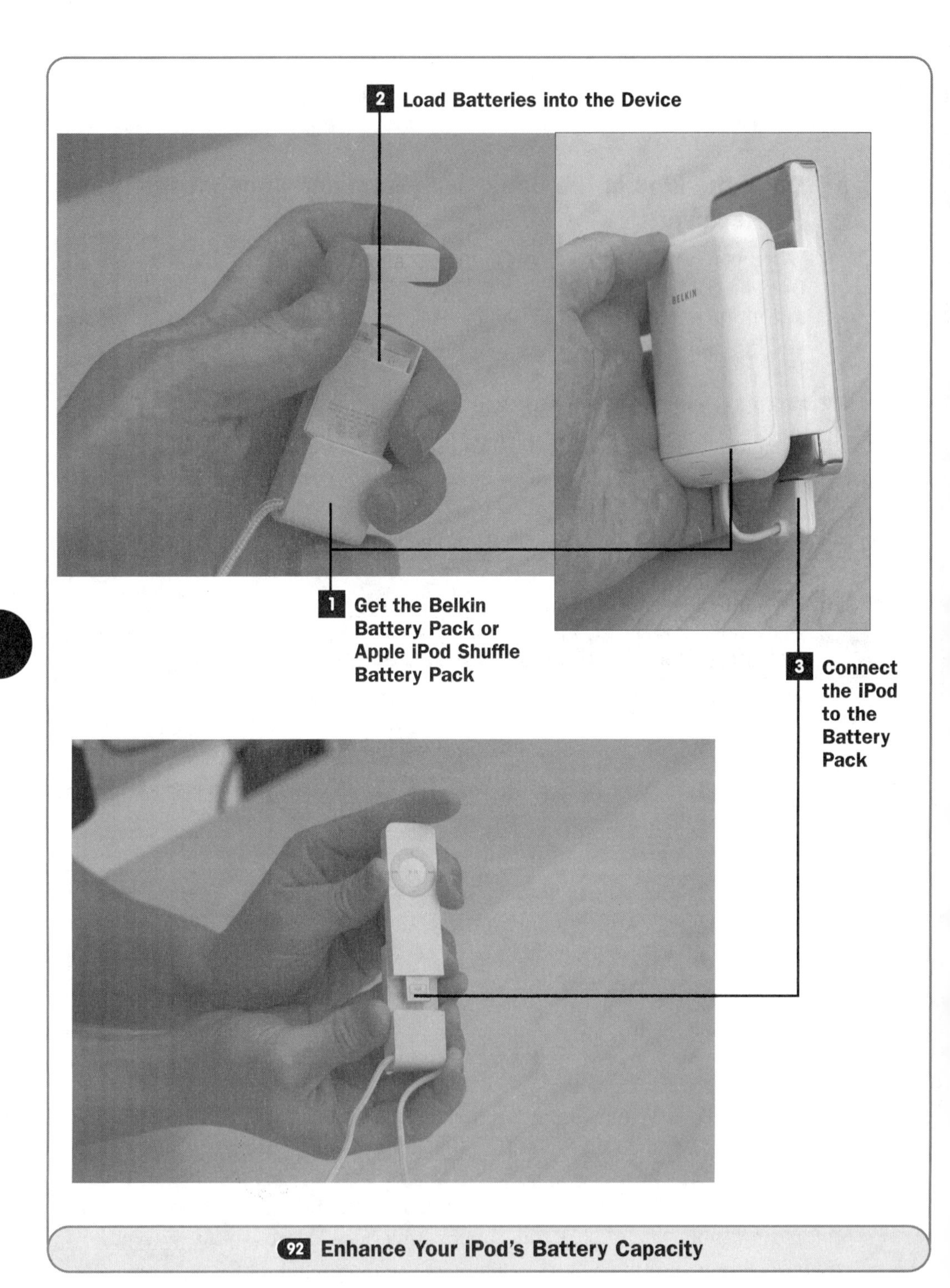
2 Load Batteries into the Device
BELKIN
1 Get the Belkin Battery Pack or Apple iPod Shuffle Battery Pack
3 Connect the iPod to the Battery Pack
92 Enhance Your iPod's Battery Capacity

1 Get the Belkin Battery Pack or Apple iPod Shuffle Battery Pack

Pick up the external battery module from your local Apple Store or other retailer. Be sure to get a device that's compatible with your model of iPod.

2 Load Batteries into the Device

Most iPod-compatible battery packs come with batteries in the package. Open the case as directed and insert the batteries.

3 Connect the iPod to the Battery Pack

Each battery pack connects to the iPod in a different way. The Belkin Battery Pack has two suction cups that attach to the shiny back of the iPod while the shell grips the iPod's sides and a Dock connector plug attaches to the bottom. The iPod shuffle Battery Pack has a plug matching the USB connector so that you can slide it on the iPod shuffle just as you would the regular protective cap.

No further configuration is necessary—the iPod now draws power from both its internal power source and the external battery at the same time, wearing each down at a comparable rate (one will not be exhausted before the other, in most cases). Be sure to have replacement batteries on hand to refill your external battery pack when the iPod finally runs out of juice, or keep a charger with you if you prefer using rechargeable AA or AAA batteries.

93 About Third-Party iPod Software

✓ BEFORE YOU BEGIN

51 About the Care and Feeding of Your iPod

→ SEE ALSO

99 Update Your iPod's Software
100 Restore Your iPod to Factory Settings

As cool as the iPod is on its own merits, some owners just crave seeing how much more it can do than is officially intended. These people relentlessly seek out iPod "hacks," which often involve third-party code loaded onto the hidden "system" segment of the iPod's disk or its firmware to modify its operation to do anything from displaying custom status images to downloading your email for you to read on the iPod's screen or burning music CDs straight from the iPod.

These modifications are not supported or endorsed by Apple; indeed, running them may void your iPod's service warranty. Yet for the intrepid iPod owner, the prospect of downloading news feeds to read on the iPod or changing its battery meter to display a numeric voltage readout instead of a graphical bar is just too much to resist.

Almost since the very first days of the iPod's existence, sites such as iPodHacks.com and iPoding.com have showcased the very best (and all the rest) of the available modifications and third-party software designed to alter the iPod's intended functionality. If you're curious, keep an eye on these sites—they report not only on new developments in the iPod-hacking community, but also on news of upcoming iPod-related products and little-known tips and tricks you can use in the unmodified, shipping version of iTunes.

WEB RESOURCES

http://www.ipodhacks.com

http://www.ipoding.com

http://www.ipodlounge.com

http://www.ipodwizard.net

iPodHacks and iPoding are two of the oldest and most extensive sites that archive hacks and modifications for your iPod. iPodLounge is an excellent news site that aims to keep you abreast of all the happenings in the world of iPod accessories, as well as many in-depth tutorials for some of the iPod's more esoteric functions. The iPodWizard site hosts a utility that allows you to customize your iPod's graphics, among other tricks.

Some kinds of iPod hacks involve simple, non-intrusive modifications, such as copying files to your iPod's hard disk to unlock special debugging features. These kinds of modifications are not destructive and can easily be reversed. However, you should be especially careful of any hack that works by modifying or replacing the iPod's system software or firmware. Such hacks have the potential to permanently disable your iPod, and it might no longer be covered by your warranty if anything goes wrong.

This book won't make any recommendations for specific hacking tools—they're really best left as an exercise for readers who are keen on living dangerously. However, if you're determined to ride the ragged edge of the iPod lifestyle, you should always remember how to reset the iPod: Hold down the **Menu** and **Select** buttons simultaneously for several seconds (press the **Menu** and **Play/Pause** on 3G and earlier iPods). You should also know how to restore the iPod's software to the factory conditions (see 100 **Restore Your iPod to Factory Settings**). Any hacks that alter the iPod beyond where it can be restored to working order by these methods are just asking for trouble.

That said, though, the iPod user community at the sites mentioned earlier is extensive and helpful. Between them and the folks at the Genius Bar of your local Apple Store, chances are that you'll be able to find help no matter what predicament you land in.

12

Protecting Your Investment

IN THIS CHAPTER:

The rapidly growing popularity of the iTunes Music Store brings with it not just new versatility in how we enjoy our music, but also a whole set of new problems that had never existed before. If what you bought is not a physical product you can hold in your hands, but a data file on your computer's hard disk, what exactly is it that you "own"? How do you reassure yourself that you have actual possession of this valuable item? What does it mean for consumer ethics if you can make an exact duplicate of a song file that you bought, even if software prevents it from being playable on someone else's computer? And most importantly, what recourses are there if you lose your purchased music because of one of the inevitable glitches we've become used to in computing, such as a hard drive crash?

After a few months using the iTunes **Music Store**, you might find that you've sunk hundreds of dollars into downloaded music files—and if you own an iPod, that's so many hundreds more. You need a way to be sure that this investment isn't put at risk of loss, any more so than a collection of physical CDs would be.

The iTunes **Music Store** support staff stresses the great importance of backing up your music files to a permanent medium such as CDs or DVDs. If you don't, you might be able to cajole the support staff into letting you download your music again; but you can't count on this because Apple's official position is that once you've successfully downloaded your music, you'd better back it up—if it's lost, it's lost for good.

▶ NOTE

See 22 Check for Purchased Music for information on how iTunes can recover an incompletely downloaded music file; this is also the method used when the iTunes Music Store support staff gives you access to re-download a track.

The tasks in this chapter describe techniques for backing up your music—and restoring it to working condition—so that you won't ever have to go to the support staff with your hat in your hand and a plate of cookies, pleading with them to bring your music back to life. With the right precautions, you'll always be able to restore your iTunes **Library** from scratch even after a catastrophic hardware failure.

This chapter also discusses ways to keep your iPod in tip-top working condition, updating its software when new features or bug fixes are released by Apple, or restoring it to its factory configuration if that becomes necessary. You can even take an iPod whose shiny back has become depressingly scratched and breathe new life into it, ensuring that it'll retain its good looks as long as it provides the soundtrack to your life.

94 Back Up Your Music to CD or DVD

✔ BEFORE YOU BEGIN

35 Create a Smart Playlist
52 Create an Audio CD from a Playlist
53 Customize CD Burning Options

→ SEE ALSO

96 Restore Your Music from Backup
97 Restore Your Music Library Database from a Backup Copy

One of the most straightforward ways to back up your music is using iTunes itself and choosing to burn a series of data CDs or DVDs of a selected ***playlist***; all you have to do is make a playlist of all the music in your library and then make sure that you have enough blank CDs or DVDs to hold all the files.

▶ TIP

A recordable CD holds 650 or 700 MB of data; a recordable DVD holds 4.7 GB. Use the readout at the bottom of iTunes' **Library** view to see how big your music collection is and calculate how many blank discs you'll need to have handy.

You'll want to perform this backup task on a regular basis, at least once a month—and particularly after you go on a buying spree and add a lot of new tunes to your library. Although backing up your music library might eat up a lot of blank discs—and cost you several dollars and a lot of time and clutter each time you do it—no doubt you'll agree that the value of restoring a thousand dollars' worth of purchased music from your careful backups is abundantly worth the initial hassle.

▶ NOTE

Backing up your song files (and other materials downloaded from the iTunes **Music Store**, such as digital booklets and music videos) preserves all the ***info tags*** embedded in the files themselves but doesn't save external song data such as equalizer settings, start and end times, and the **Date Added**, **My Rating**, **Last Played**, and **Play Count** fields. It also doesn't save your playlists. To preserve this information, you must back up your iTunes **Music Library** file, as shown in step 5 of this task. Refer to **97 Restore Your Music Library Database from a Backup Copy** for information on restoring your iTunes database file and the irreplaceable information in it.

1 Open the Burning Preferences

Open the iTunes **Preferences** window (choose **iTunes**, **Preferences** on the Mac or **Edit**, **Preferences** in Windows). Click the **Burning** tab to display the options for burning discs.

Verify that your CD or DVD burner is recognized by iTunes as explained in **53 Customize CD Burning Options**.

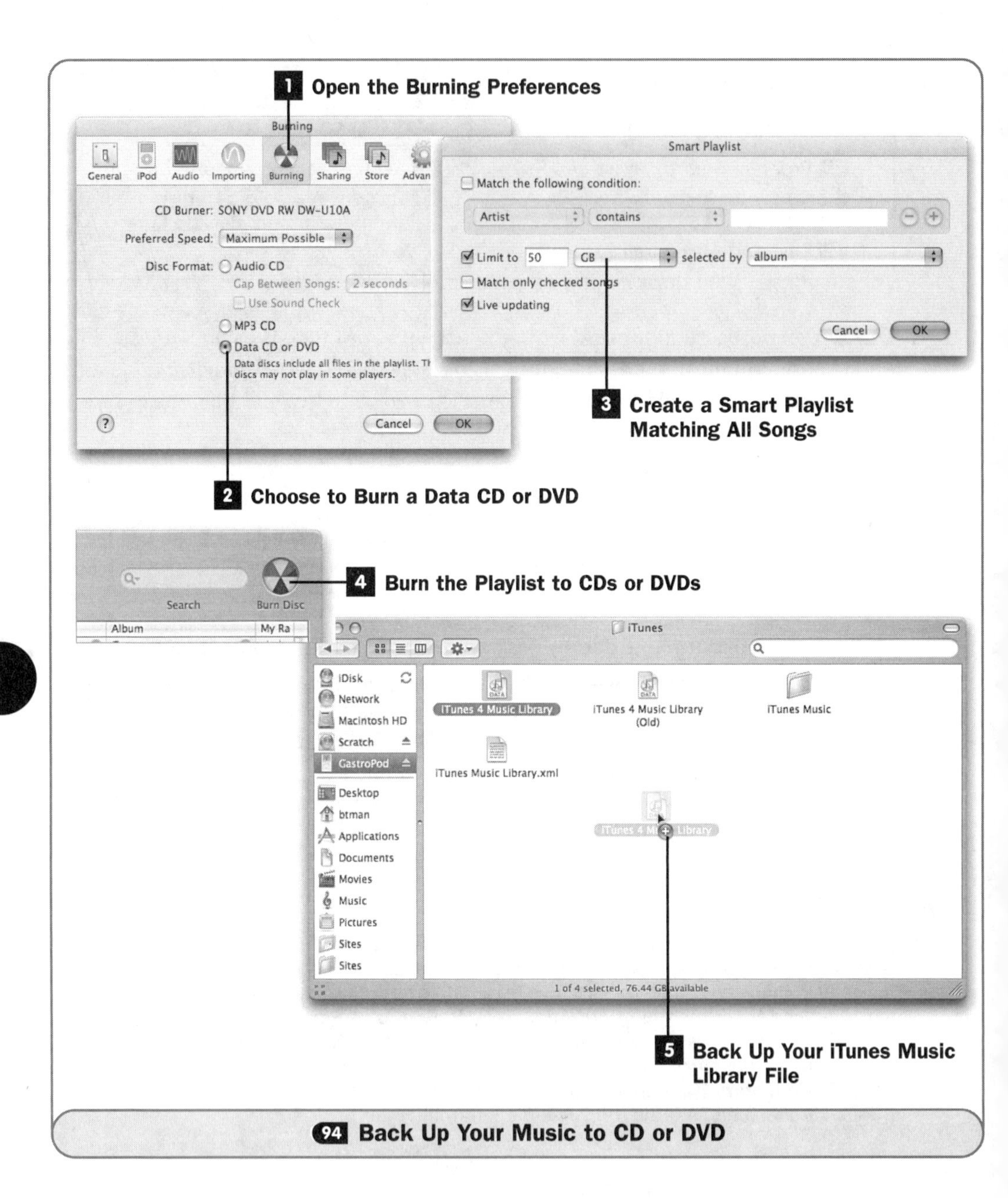
1 Open the Burning Preferences
2 Choose to Burn a Data CD or DVD
3 Create a Smart Playlist Matching All Songs
4 Burn the Playlist to CDs or DVDs
5 Back Up Your iTunes Music Library File
94 Back Up Your Music to CD or DVD

2 Choose to Burn a Data CD or DVD

Enable the **Data CD or DVD** radio button. This option creates discs that contain all the files in the playlists you burn, not just MP3 files (as occurs if you select the **MP3 CD** option); the **Data CD or DVD** option burns copies of protected AAC files, QuickTime movies, Apple Lossless files, and everything else iTunes recognizes, and is intended primarily for backup purposes.

Click **OK** to close the **Preferences** window.

3 Create a Smart Playlist Matching All Songs

As described in 35 **Create a Smart Playlist**, create a ***Smart Playlist*** with criteria chosen such that the playlist contains all the files in your iTunes **Library**. One easy way to do this is to disable the **Match the following condition check box**, enable the **Limit to** check box, and set the limit to a size larger than the total size of your iTunes **Library**. Choose an appropriate **selected by** setting, such as **album** or **artist** (this option helps you sort your burned CDs or DVDs in sequence).

Click **OK** to create the playlist; give it a suitable name such as **Everything**.

4 Burn the Playlist to CDs or DVDs

Select the playlist in the **Source** pane of the iTunes' window and click the **Burn Disc** button in the upper-right corner of the window. In the same manner as described in 52 **Create an Audio CD from a Playlist**, iTunes automatically detects that the playlist is longer than can fit on a single disc, and asks whether you want to burn the entire playlist to multiple data discs or to cancel the burn process and trim the playlist down to fit on a single disc.

If you choose to burn the playlist to multiple discs, iTunes burns as many tracks as will fit onto the first disc, and then prompts you to insert another blank disc to continue. This process continues until all the tracks in the playlist have been burned onto discs. Be sure to label the discs appropriately so that you don't forget their sequence!

▶ NOTE

The discs you burn are laid out with every file in a single flat folder at the top level of the disc, instead of organized into hierarchical folders as in the iTunes **Music** folder on your computer. This arrangement makes it possible for some players to read them sequentially. However, it's unlikely that such players will read DVDs, and *none* will play protected AAC files.

▶ TIP

You might want to print a track listing of the playlist and mark which discs contain which set of songs; this list can be very helpful when you want to restore selected songs from the backup set. See 55 **Print a CD Jewel Case Insert with Album Art** for more information about printing track listings.

5 Back Up Your iTunes Music Library File

Your music is now all backed up safely—but only your music files themselves, with their internal info tags; your playlists and external database information such as the **Last Played** and **Play Count** fields and your star ratings are not preserved. If you experience a hardware failure and have to restore your music, you won't get all your accumulated personalized data back if you stop now. To preserve this information, you must back up your iTunes **Music Library** file, found inside the **iTunes** folder inside **My Music** (in Windows) or in the **Music** folder (on the Mac).

▶ NOTE

Refer to 96 **Restore Your Music from Backup** for information about restoring your music files and to 97 **Restore Your Music Library Database from a Backup Copy** for restoring your personalized information from a preserved **iTunes Music Library** file.

Insert a writable CD into your computer's CD drive. Choose to open a writable CD window for copying files to be burned. This option varies according to your operating system: In Windows, it's **Open writable CD folder** using Windows Explorer; on the Mac, it's **Open Finder**. (You might have to double-click the disc's icon to open its window.)

In a second Windows Explorer or Finder window, navigate into the **iTunes** folder in your **My Music** or **Music** folder. Select the **iTunes 4 Music Library.itl** and **iTunes 4 Music Library.xml** files and drag them into the writable CD window. When the files are copied, burn the CD by choosing **File, Write these files to CD** (in Windows) or by clicking the **Burn** button below the window's title bar or in the sidebar (on the Mac). The database files are burned to the disc. Eject the disc, label it, and store it along with your backup discs of the music files.

▶ NOTES

The **iTunes 4 Music Library.itl** and **iTunes 4 Music Library.xml** files contain identical information and are updated simultaneously with every change you make. Technically, you need only one of these two files to restore your iTunes **Library** fully, but the files are quite small and there's no harm in preserving both. In Windows, you might have to turn off the **Hide file extensions for known file types** option (choose **Tools, Folder Options** and then click the **View** tab) to distinguish between the two files.

On the Mac, the **iTunes 4 Music Library.itl** file appears simply as **iTunes 4 Music Library**.

95 Back Up Your Music Using .Mac Backup (Mac Only)

✔ BEFORE YOU BEGIN

20 Purchase Audio from the iTunes Music Store

➔ SEE ALSO

23 Authorize a Computer to Play Purchased Music

94 Back Up Your Music to CD or DVD

Mac users are naturally a little better served when it comes to using and protecting their iTunes' music—Apple can't help but be a little bit partisan. Mac OS X integrates with iTunes in ways that Windows can't, and if you're a member of Apple's .Mac service (for a $99 annual membership fee), you have access to a utility that makes backing up your iTunes **Library** a straightforward, painless, and even entirely hands-off affair. This utility is called **Backup**, and it's available to anyone with Mac OS X 10.2 ("Jaguar") or higher and a paid .Mac account.

▶ NOTES

.Mac trial users can download and run Backup, but the only available backup location you can select is **iDisk**. You must have a full paid .Mac account if you want to back up to CD, DVD, or to a mounted volume such as a hard disk.

Sign up for a .Mac account using the **Sign Up** button in the **.Mac** pane of the **System Preferences** application, or by visiting **http://www.mac.com**.

Backup works by aggregating related files together into collections called ***QuickPicks***, each of which can be selected or deselected for backup depending on your needs and the available storage space on your backup medium (CD or DVD, iDisk space, or a locally mounted or networked hard disk). Restoring backed-up files from the backup medium is as simple as selecting them from the backup repository and clicking a button.

If you have a .Mac account, you should be using Backup already to protect the important files all over your Mac; but even if all you're interested in preserving is your iTunes' music, Backup provides useful QuickPicks to serve your needs, and it's never too soon to start getting into the habit of using it regularly.

1 Download and Install Backup

If you don't already have Backup installed, you must download it from the .Mac website, **http://www.mac.com**. Open this site in Safari or another browser. Log in using your .Mac member name and password. In the navigation bar along the left side of the page is an icon for **Backup**; click this link to go to the **Backup** page. Click the **Download Backup 2** button. On the page full of download links that appears next, **Backup 2.0.2** appears in the third column, under **Explore**. Click the download icon (a down-arrow) to download the application.

Double-click the installer file when it's fully downloaded. Proceed through the installation procedure as directed.

2 Choose a Backup Location

Launch **Backup** from the **Applications** folder. You'll have to wait for a few minutes as Backup examines your disk and builds up its catalog of available files and determines the sizes of each of the QuickPicks, which are the collections listed under **Items** in the main Backup window.

From the menu at the top left, choose a backup location. You can choose **Back up to iDisk**, **Back up to CD/DVD**, or **Back up to Drive**. Pick a location that suits your needs and the backup hardware you have available.

NOTE

iDisk is generally not a good location for backing up your music files—there's not enough storage space available, and it's slow to access. CD/DVD is a good solution if you have a suitable burner, but you'll end up making a sequence of discs each time you back up your music, which can get unwieldy. Perhaps the best, neatest, and fastest solution is backing up to a hard drive—if you have an external FireWire or USB 2.0 disk, or a remote drive mounted over the network, you can schedule an automatic backup to that location that doesn't even require you to be present as the Backup utility does its work.

3 Select the iTunes Purchased Music QuickPick

There are two QuickPicks of use to you here: **iTunes Library** and **iTunes Purchased Music**. Both these QuickPicks include your **iTunes 4 Music Library** database file, but **iTunes Purchased Music** only includes files you've bought from the iTunes **Music Store**, omitting song files you've ripped from CD or imported through other means. If all your imported music is on CDs that you own, you might consider those purchased CDs to be your backup of those files, and you can save backup disk space by backing up only the purchased music from the iTunes **Music Store** that you don't have saved in any other form. If you have enough space on the backup location, however, you might choose the comprehensive **iTunes Library** QuickPick to back up all your music files to the same location. The **iTunes Library** QuickPick option preserves all your CD music's ***info tags*** as you've painstakingly set them.

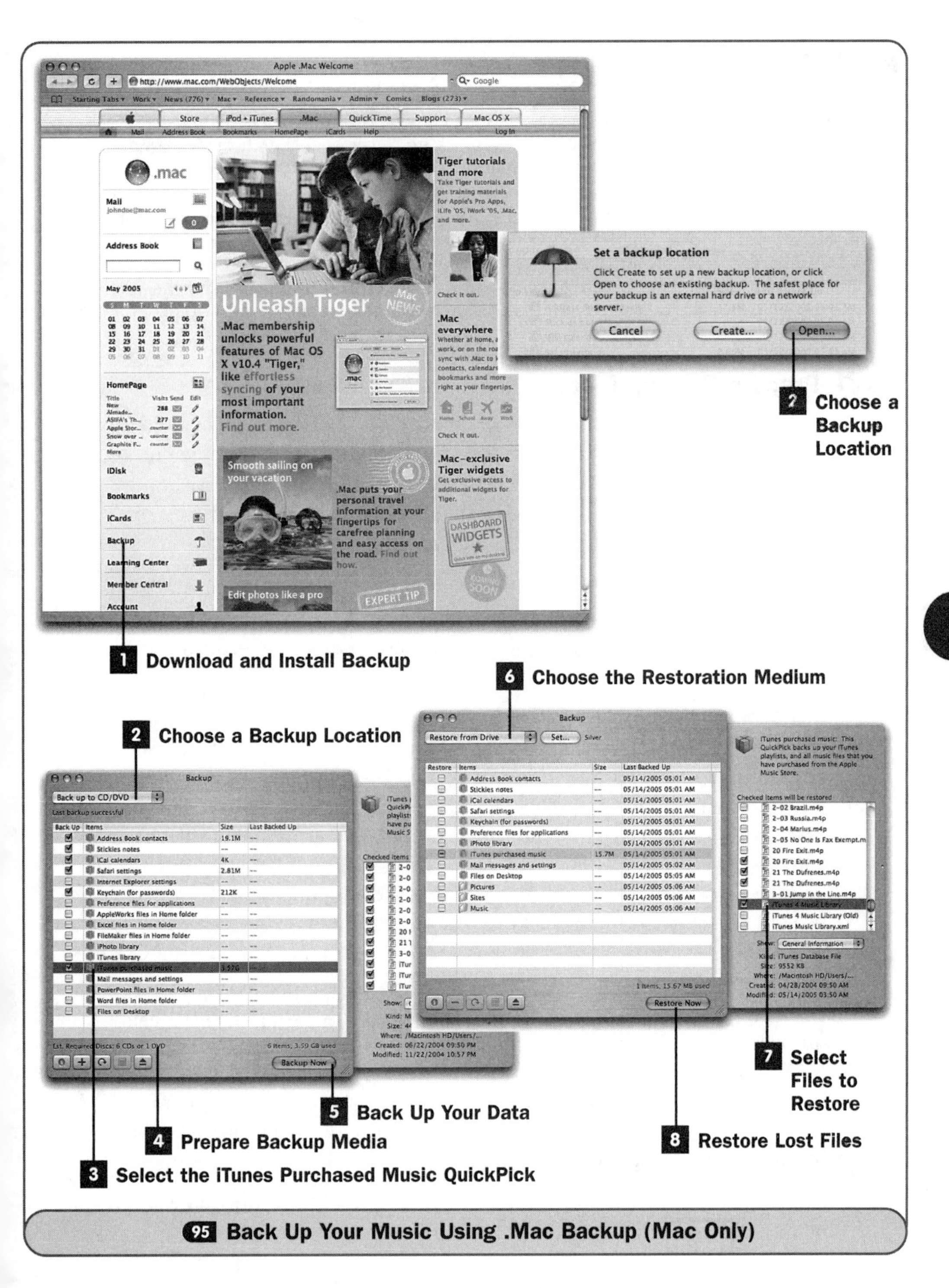

95 Back Up Your Music Using .Mac Backup (Mac Only)

▶ TIPS

It's possible—but unnecessary—to select both iTunes-related QuickPicks for backup; **iTunes Purchased Music** is a subset of iTunes **Library**. However, selecting both QuickPicks makes it possible to back up your entire music collection for safekeeping and then choose to restore only your purchased music after a data-loss incident.

If you choose to back up to iDisk, the only iTunes-related QuickPick is **iTunes playlist**, which lets you choose songs in a specific ***playlist*** to back up. This limitation is present because of the relatively small size of iDisk as a storage medium (250MB by default, although you can purchase more space up to a total of 1GB). If the playlist you select has too much music to fit into your iDisk space, you won't be able to back it up.

4 Prepare Backup Media

If you're backing up to CD or DVD, a readout at the bottom of the **Backup** window tells you how many discs will be required to hold the entire backup set. Make sure that you have the required number of writable discs handy, and that your drive can support burning the appropriate format (you can't burn DVD discs in a CD burner, for example).

95

If you're backing up to a drive, make sure that the drive is mounted on your Mac and you can navigate it in the Finder. Click **Set** at the top of the **Backup** window to navigate to the location on the desired disk and create an archive file for Backup to use.

5 Back Up Your Data

Click **Backup Now**. Backup begins copying files to the selected location. If you're backing up to CD or DVD, Backup prompts you to insert a new disc each time one is filled with data. You must be present throughout the backup process to feed your computer new discs. If you're backing up to a drive, however, you can walk away while Backup does its work unattended.

▶ TIP

Click the **Schedule** button (a calendar icon, fourth from the left at the bottom of the **Backup** window) to schedule automatic backups to a drive. A good policy is to run a backup once a week, at a time of day when the computer is not in use (for example, 5:00 in the morning). Backup is very processor-intensive and should not be run while you're working with other applications.

6 Choose the Restoration Medium

Suppose that the worst should happen—your hard disk crashes and you have to install a new one. Or suppose that you upgraded to a new computer and lost your old data, or that you accidentally deleted one of your song files from the iTunes **Music** folder. It's time to restore the lost files from your backup.

Launch Backup and then select **Restore from iDisk**, **Restore from CD/DVD**, or **Restore from Drive**, depending on where you backed up your music. If you backed up to a drive, Backup accesses the archive file and displays the list of QuickPicks found in the repository. If you backed up to CD or DVD, Backup prompts you to insert the first disc in the backup set. It reads the catalog information and displays the QuickPicks in the listing window.

7 Select Files to Restore

Select the **iTunes Library** or **iTunes Purchased Music** QuickPick (depending on which one you used to back up the files originally) and click the **Information** button (the blue **i** icon in the lower-left corner of the Backup window) to reveal the detail drawer. This drawer shows you all the files in the QuickPick collection that were found in the backup, listed alphabetically.

Scroll to the files you want to restore and enable the check box for each one. Be sure to select **iTunes 4 Music Library** for restoration if you want to restore all your iTunes database information, such as your playlists and star ratings.

▶ TIP

To restore all the files in the QuickPick, simply select its check box in the Restore column in the main Backup window. Otherwise a - is shown in the check box to indicate that only certain selected files will be restored.

96

8 Restore Lost Files

Click **Restore Now**. The selected files are copied from the backup repository and placed back in their original locations on the disk. (You are prompted to insert the appropriate CD or DVD if you backed up to that medium.) You should now be able to launch iTunes and use your music as though nothing had ever happened!

96 Restore Your Music from Backup

✓ BEFORE YOU BEGIN	→ SEE ALSO
11 Add a Music File to Your iTunes Library	62 Repair a Missing Song Entry
94 Back Up Your Music to CD or DVD	97 Restore Your Music Library Database from a Backup Copy

Murphy's Law (or one of its corollaries) implies that the surest way to prevent any disaster from befalling your computer or your music files is to keep regular backups. However, if you don't keep backups, even a minor data-loss event can be painful enough to give you a newfound sense of responsibility.

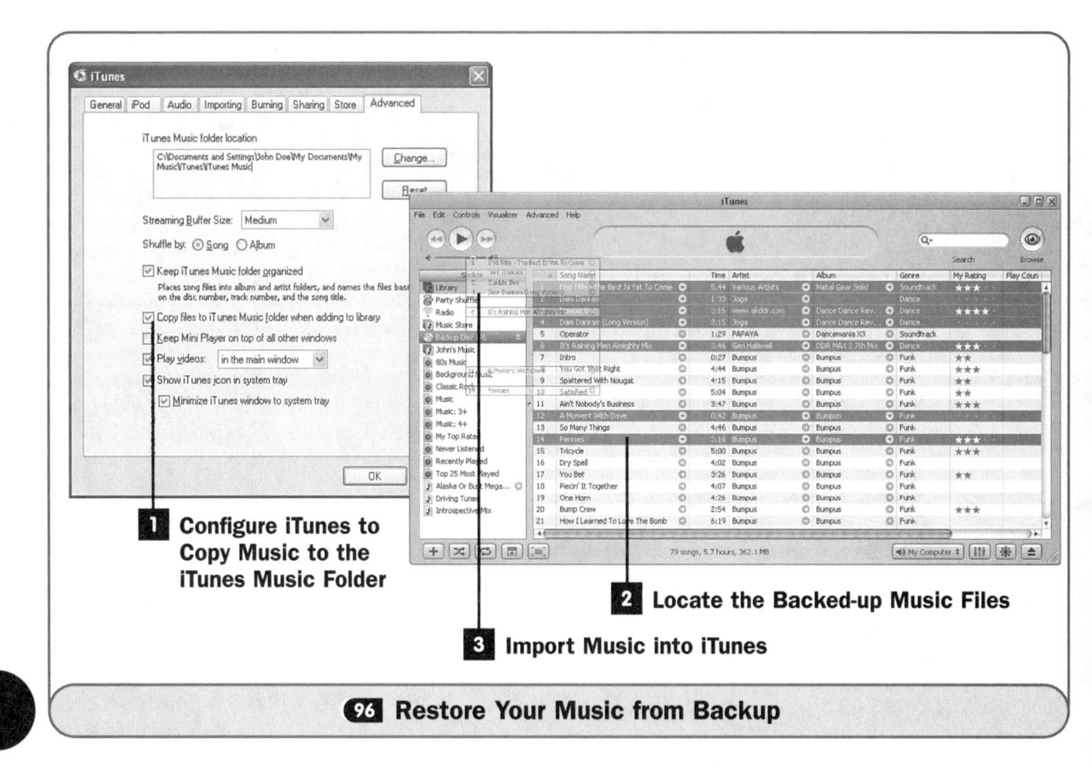
1 Configure iTunes to Copy Music to the iTunes Music Folder
2 Locate the Backed-up Music Files
3 Import Music into iTunes
96
96 Restore Your Music from Backup

Sooner or later will come a day when you need to rebuild your iTunes' music collection—whether all at once (as after a hard disk crash) or a few songs at a time. If you've been keeping backups by burning CD or DVD sets as described in 94 **Back Up Your Music to CD or DVD**, restoring this music can be a breeze—easier and quicker than creating the backups themselves.

▶ TIP

When you restore music from backup files, each song brings with it the information in its internal ***info tags***, such as **Song Name**, **Artist**, **Album**, and **Genre**. Remember that the info tags do not include external information such as the **Last Played** field and your star ratings, or your ***playlists***; this information is contained in the iTunes database file, which you can restore from a backup as described in 97 **Restore Your Music Library Database from a Backup Copy**.

1 Configure iTunes to Copy Music to the iTunes Music Folder

Open the iTunes **Preferences** window (choose **Edit**, **Preferences** in Windows, or **iTunes**, **Preferences** on the Mac); click the **Advanced** tab. Enable the **Copy files to iTunes Music folder when adding to library** check box, if it isn't already selected. This option ensures that iTunes copies your song files off the

CD or DVD and back into its **iTunes Music** folder, where the songs used to reside. Click **OK**.

2 Locate the Backed-up Music Files

Insert the disc containing the music files you want to restore. Music files are burned to data discs in the order specified in the all-encompassing ***Smart Playlist*** you created in **94 Back Up Your Music to CD or DVD**; if you printed out a track listing of the playlist at that time, you should be able to determine easily which disc has the songs you want.

The inserted disc appears in iTunes' **Source** pane and is automatically selected when the disc is mounted, showing you its contents. Navigate to the songs you want, using the **Browse** button to organize the songs by their ***info tags*** if necessary.

▶ NOTE

You can't change the info tags of song files on a data disc in iTunes; you must copy them to your hard disk before you can edit them.

3 Import Music into iTunes

97

Select the songs you want to restore; hold down **Shift** as you click to select a contiguous block of songs or hold down **Ctrl** or ⌘ to select multiple noncontiguous songs. Drag the songs from the CD's content listing to the **Library** item in the **Source** pane. The files are copied to the computer's hard disk and organized into their proper folders in the **iTunes Music** folder. If you go to the **Library** view and navigate the **Browse** lists, you'll find the songs right where they should be.

97 Restore Your Music Library Database from a Backup Copy

✔ BEFORE YOU BEGIN	➜ SEE ALSO
94 Back Up Your Music to CD or DVD	62 Repair a Missing Song Entry
96 Restore Your Music from Backup	98 Copy Your Music from the iPod Back to iTunes

The Music Library database file, found in the **iTunes** folder within the **My Music** folder (in Windows) or the **Music** folder (on the Mac), is the heart and soul of iTunes. Sure, you can recover all your actual *music* by simply copying your backed-up song files back into iTunes; but the Music Library database file (**iTunes 4 Music Library.itl** on Windows, or simply **iTunes 4 Music Library** on the Mac) is what stores all the extra information such as your ***playlists***, your star ratings, equalizer settings, and external fields such as the **Last Played** and **Date Added** fields. Without that information, all the personalization you've done to your iTunes music is lost, and you have to start building it back up from scratch.

This is why it's important to back up your iTunes Music Library database each time you back up your music files, as described in 94 **Back Up Your Music to CD or DVD**. It's a little extra work, but protecting the ways you've trained iTunes to play your favorite music might be every bit as important to you as protecting the music itself.

This task is useful in many circumstances such as when you're installing iTunes on a new computer. However, it's of particular interest when you have restored music from a backup (as described in 96 **Restore Your Music from Backup**), but you notice that your ratings and play counts have disappeared.

1 Quit iTunes

Because iTunes writes changes to the Music Library database file when you exit the application, you must quit iTunes (choose **File**, **Exit** in Windows, or **iTunes**, **Quit** on the Mac) before beginning this task.

2 Locate the Backed-up Music Library Database File

Find the CD, DVD, or disk location where your backup copy of the **iTunes 4 Music Library** file is. Open a Windows Explorer or Finder window that shows this file.

▶ NOTES

The **iTunes 4 Music Library.itl** and **iTunes 4 Music Library.xml** files contain identical information and are updated simultaneously with every change you make. You can theoretically restore your iTunes **Library** from either file, but the binary **.itl** file is preferred. In Windows, you might have to turn off the **Hide file extensions for known file types** option (choose **Tools, Folder Options** and then click the **View** tab) to distinguish between the two files.

In this task, **iTunes 4 Music Library** refers to the **.itl** file.

3 Copy the Music Library Database File into the iTunes Folder

In a second Windows Explorer or Finder window, navigate into the **iTunes** folder inside the **My Music** folder (in Windows) or the **Music** folder (on the Mac). Select all the files whose names begin with **iTunes 4 Music Library** and drag them out of the folder into a temporary location, such as your Desktop.

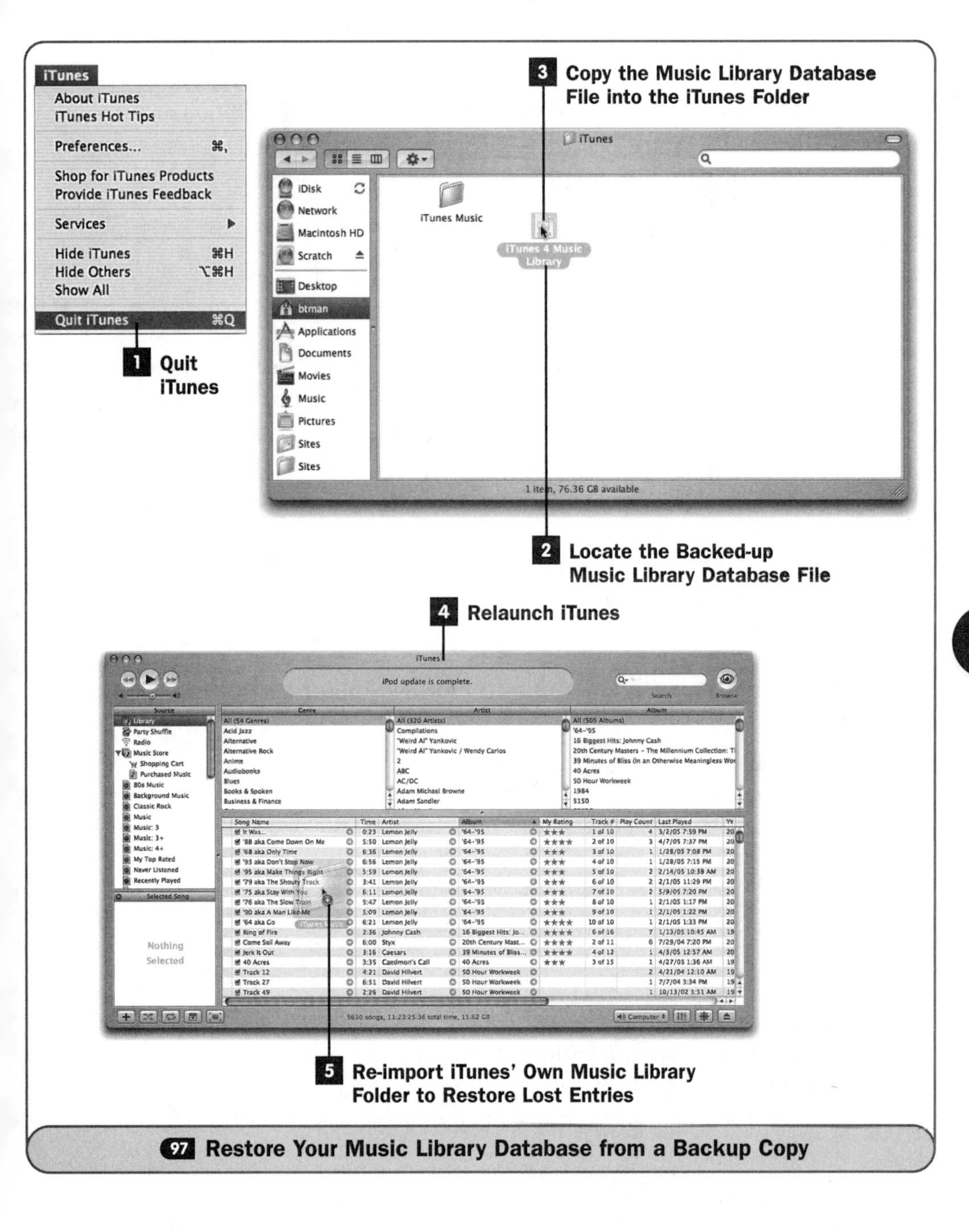

97 Restore Your Music Library Database from a Backup Copy

From the Windows Explorer or Finder window you opened in step 2 (the window onto the backup media), drag *a copy* of the **iTunes 4 Music Library** backup file into the **iTunes** folder window you just opened in this step. Be sure to drag a duplicate, not the original file itself. If the backup copy of the file is on a separate volume or a CD or DVD, a duplicate is created automatically. If the backup copy exists on the same disk, hold down **Option** on the Mac or **Ctrl** in Windows to duplicate the file as you're dragging it from one place to another.

4 Relaunch iTunes

Start iTunes. When you reopen the application, it reads the newly restored Music Library database file and shows the playlists and song information from there rather than from the file it had been using previously. If you restored a backed-up database file over a nearly empty one from a newly reinstalled copy of iTunes, your library should be populated with all the music you'd had before the database file was lost.

If all is well, you can throw away the old **iTunes 4 Music Library** files you dragged to the temporary folder or your Desktop. If anything goes wrong, however (for example, if the restored file has been corrupted somehow), you can go back to the previous state of the iTunes **Library** by quitting iTunes and then moving the temporary files back into place in the **iTunes Music** folder.

5 Re-import iTunes' Own Music Library Folder to Restore Lost Entries

There's one final housekeeping trick to perform. If you backed up your **iTunes 4 Music Library** file at an earlier time than your last backup of song files—or if you've been adding new music since reinstalling iTunes—you'll need to add those new songs to the restored library (because it won't yet know they exist). Fortunately, this step is an easy one.

In a Windows Explorer or Finder window, navigate into your **iTunes** folder and locate your **iTunes Music** folder, which contains all your organized music (including songs you've added or purchased since backing up your database file). Remember that iTunes can tell whether you've already added a certain file to the **iTunes Music** folder, and won't add a second copy if you try to import the file again. Taking advantage of this knowledge, simply drag the **iTunes Music** folder from its window into the song listing area of iTunes. (Note the + sign on your mouse pointer indicating that the folder's contents will be added to iTunes.)

When you let go of the mouse button, iTunes imports only those songs within the **iTunes Music** folder hierarchy that weren't already in its database. This process may take a few minutes, depending on the size of your music collection; but when it's done, you'll have all your music back to its normal state.

Any external data fields (such as the **My Rating**, **Play Count**, and **Equalizer *info tags***) you'd added to your newly acquired music will be reset, but those fields are still intact for all your other files, and you've now got all your music back at your fingertips.

98 Copy Your Music from the iPod Back to iTunes

✔ BEFORE YOU BEGIN	→ SEE ALSO
42 Transfer Your Music to Your iPod	94 Back Up Your Music to CD or DVD 80 Use Your iPod as an External Hard Disk

So that Apple could convince the record labels that iTunes and the iPod are not merely tools designed to help people steal music, the company had to engineer them in such a way that they couldn't be used for nefarious purposes—or, at least, not easily used for such schemes. Within the officially supported feature set of the iPod, you can copy music only from iTunes to the iPod, not the other way around. This arrangement prevents people from loading up an iPod with a diskful of tunes, sauntering to someone else's computer, and offloading fresh copies of all that music to someone who didn't pay for it. We all know that a resourceful thief can find ways around that missing feature, and such a thief won't be put off by the "Don't steal music" label that Apple rather optimistically puts on every new iPod. But by making it at least marginally inconvenient, Apple has ensured that the record labels will treat the iPod as part of a new and emerging legitimate market before they consider it a threat to their business.

However, theft isn't the only reason you might want to get music from your iPod onto your computer. The most obvious is as a backup; if your computer's hard disk crashes, and you've synchronized your music with the iPod, why worry? You've got a perfect mirror of your entire music collection on the iPod, complete with star ratings and ***playlists*** and all the rest of the personalized information on which you've come to depend. So why can't you just copy the music back onto your computer?

Apple doesn't support this kind of data transfer, but don't worry—third-party developers have stepped up to the plate to provide it where Apple can't. Small, dedicated utilities for low prices exist for both Windows and the Mac that let you copy your iPod's music right back into iTunes: **iPod.iTunes** for the Mac (€29.90, about $38), and **CopyPod** for Windows ($19.90).

Steps 1–4 in this task cover the use of iPod.iTunes for Mac users, and steps 5–10 describe the use of CopyPod for Windows users.

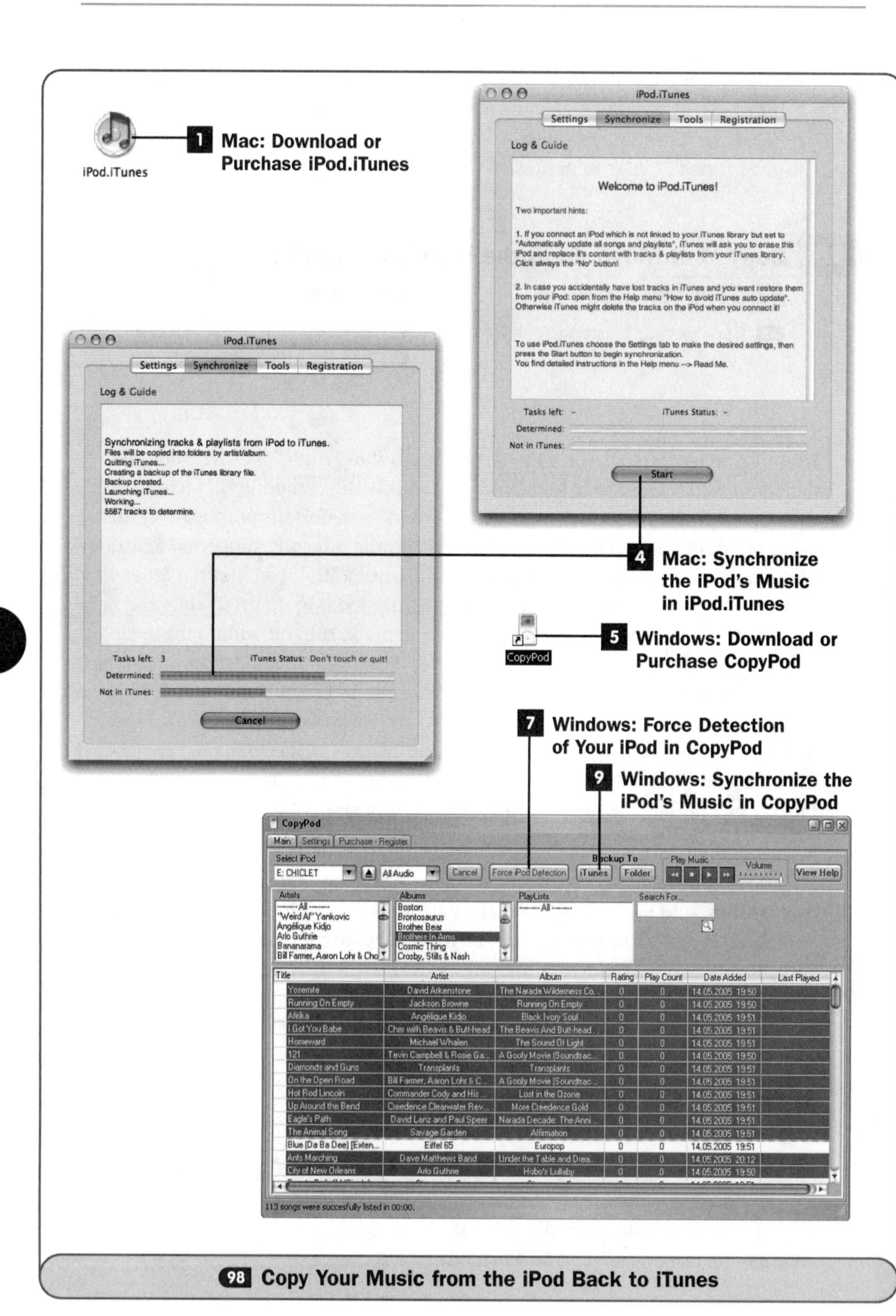

98

98 Copy Your Music from the iPod Back to iTunes

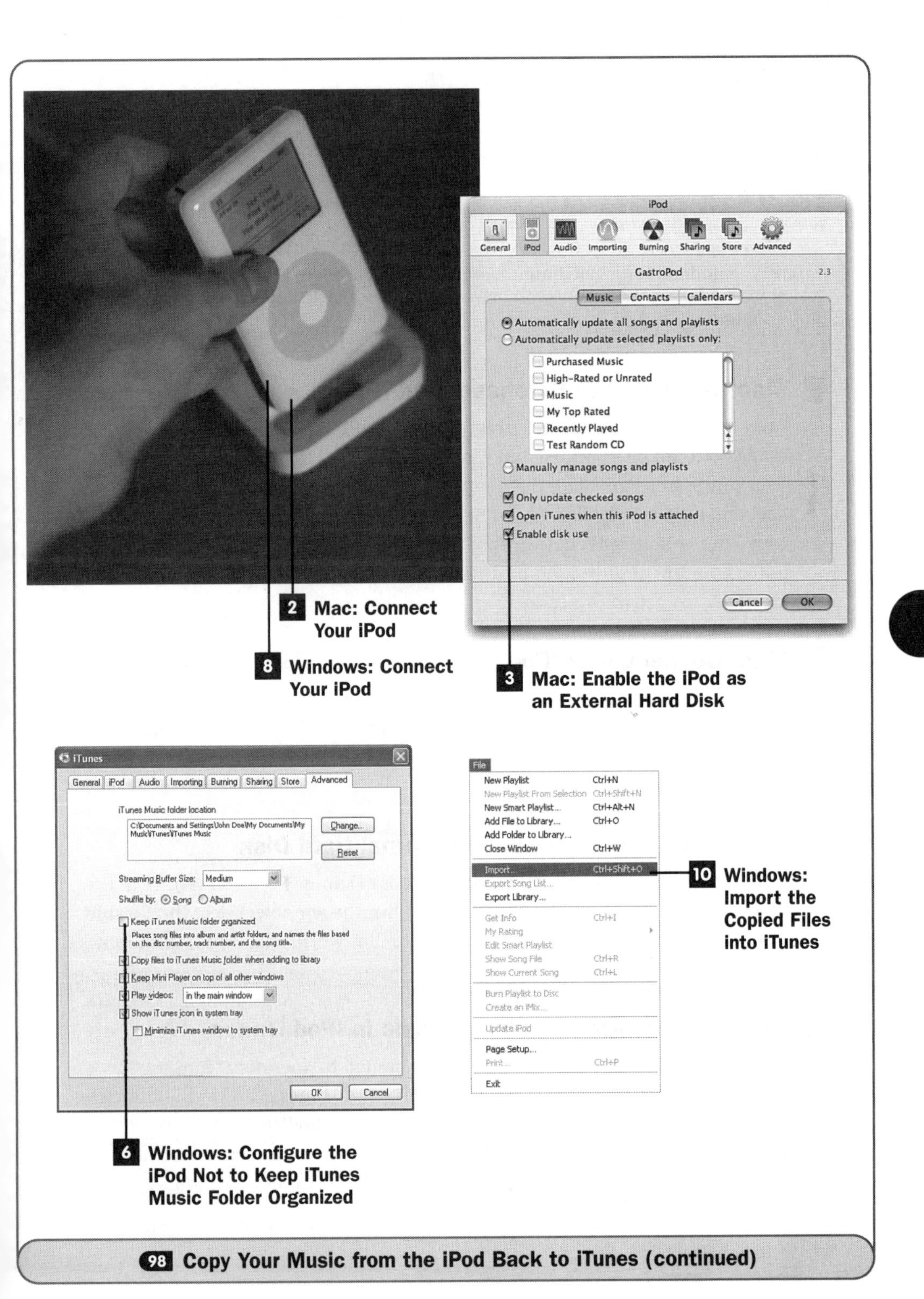

98 Copy Your Music from the iPod Back to iTunes (continued)

NOTES

If you're starting over with a new computer or a fresh installation of iTunes, and you connect the iPod to your computer, iTunes might try to establish a new "link" with the iPod—which means that it will delete all the music from the iPod and replace it with whatever is in the new iTunes **Library**. Always select the **No** option when presented with a dialog box offering to change the link and replace the iPod's contents (at least until you've successfully restored your iTunes **Library**)!

Naturally, restoring your music from the iPod won't recover any files that couldn't be copied to the iPod in the first place, such as MIDI files, QuickTime movies, or Internet Radio channels.

1 Mac: Download or Purchase iPod.iTunes

Go to **http://www.crispsofties.com**, home of the iPod.iTunes software. Follow the **Download** or **Purchase** links. Note that if you are trying to restore all your music from the iPod, the free trial version is not suitable because it deliberately skips copying about half the tracks from your iPod to iTunes. To copy your complete iPod, purchase the full version of iPod.iTunes, either as part of the initial download or after downloading the trial version by installing an activation code.

2 Mac: Connect Your iPod

Connect your iPod to the computer using the Dock or cable. When iTunes launches, it might warn you that the iPod is "linked" to another computer and offer to change the link to this computer and replace the iPod's contents with its own. Click **No**.

3 Mac: Enable the iPod as an External Hard Disk

Open the iTunes **Preferences** window (choose **iTunes, Preferences**); click the **iPod** tab, and then click the **Music** tab within the window. Select the **Enable disk use** check box. Dismiss the dialog box that warns you about unmounting the iPod and click **OK**.

4 Mac: Synchronize the iPod's Music in iPod.iTunes

Launch iPod.iTunes. This application is designed to operate in conjunction with iTunes, which runs in the background. iPod.iTunes quits and relaunches iTunes several times and creates some temporary ***playlists*** that it uses while copying the music. It's important that you not work with iTunes or quit it while iPod.iTunes restores your music. Just let iPod.iTunes do its job.

The **Start** button appears if conditions are correct for transfer. Click **Start** to begin the process.

First iPod.iTunes reads the iPod's contents and the iTunes **Library** to determine how many tracks on the iPod don't exist in iTunes; then it copies those tracks into iTunes, complete with star ratings and other external data (such as the **Last Played** and **Equalizer** ***info tags***). Finally it copies the iPod's playlists into iTunes, prefixed with the generic **From Mom's iPod** (which you can change in the **Settings** tab). This process can take a long time, up to or exceeding an hour depending on the size of your music collection.

▶ **NOTE**

Smart Playlists **copied from the iPod back into iTunes become regular playlists because the iPod can't distinguish between the two in its own database.**

Quit iPod.iTunes; go back into the iTunes **Preferences** window and deselect the **Enable disk use** check box. You can now begin reorganizing your recovered music if necessary—fix up your playlists, browse the newly imported tracks, and so on. When you synchronize your iPod again in the normal way, you can allow iTunes to establish its link with the iPod and copy its music back to the iPod's disk.

5 Windows: Download or Purchase CopyPod

Go to **http://www.copypod.net**, home of the CopyPod software. Follow the **Download** or **Purchase** links. The trial version is time-limited to 14 days; if you need to restore your music on a one-time basis, the trial version might suffice for your needs. (It's good to support software developers who produce useful software by paying for a registered copy, though, so if CopyPod helps you, please consider registering it anyway!)

6 Windows: Configure the iPod Not to Keep iTunes Music Folder Organized

Open the iTunes **Preferences** window (choose **Edit**, **Preferences**); click the **Advanced** tab. Disable the **Keep iTunes Music folder organized** check box to prevent iTunes from automatically naming folders and interfering with the restore process. Click **OK**.

7 Windows: Force Detection of Your iPod in CopyPod

Launch CopyPod. In the main window, click the **Force iPod Detection** button. This command prevents iTunes from launching and taking control of the iPod when you connect it.

NOTE

The Force iPod Detection button kills a background process that iTunes uses to detect when you connect the iPod; if you restart your computer, iTunes' iPod-detecting function is restored.

8 Windows: Connect Your iPod

Connect your iPod to the computer using the Dock or cable. CopyPod detects the iPod and asks if you want to list the songs on its disk; click **Yes**.

TIP

If CopyPod doesn't automatically detect your iPod, try selecting it from the **Select iPod** drop-down menu in the upper left corner of the CopyPod window.

9 Windows: Synchronize the iPod's Music in CopyPod

Select all the songs on the iPod by pressing **Ctrl+A**, or select only certain songs by navigating through the **Artists**, **Albums**, and **PlayLists** boxes and sorting the songs using the column headers as you would in iTunes. When you've selected all the songs you want to transfer from the iPod into iTunes, click the **iTunes** button under the **Backup To** label.

98

10 Windows: Import the Copied Files into iTunes

CopyPod creates two files on your Desktop, called **iPodBackupLibrary_1.xml** (which contains your song file information) and **iPodBackupLibrary_2.xml** (which contains your playlists).

Launch iTunes; choose **File**, **Import**. This command lets you select a catalog file in XML format and import the song files and other information it describes. Choose **XML files (*.xml)** from the **Files of type** drop-down list and then select the **iPodBackupLibrary_1.xml** file on the Desktop. Click **Open**. iTunes imports all the recovered files back into its library, reorganizing them into the proper folders.

Using the same method, import the **iPodBackupLibrary_2.xml** file; this file restores all your playlists.

NOTE

Smart Playlists copied from the iPod back into iTunes become regular playlists because the iPod can't distinguish between the two in its own database.

You can now go back to the **Advanced** pane of the iTunes **Preferences** window and enable the **Keep iTunes Music folder organized** option (if you had

had it enabled before restoring your music with this procedure). You're now back in business. You should restart your computer to restore iTunes' iPod-detection capability, and then you can sync your music back to the iPod in the normal way, this time allowing iTunes to establish its link with the iPod.

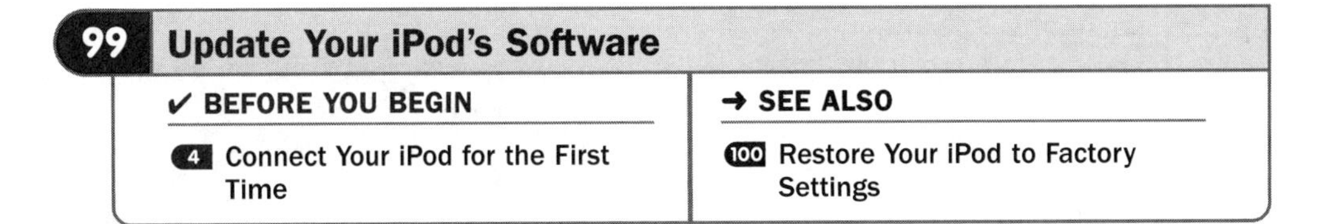

99 Update Your iPod's Software

✔ **BEFORE YOU BEGIN**

4 Connect Your iPod for the First Time

➜ **SEE ALSO**

100 Restore Your iPod to Factory Settings

Every few weeks, Apple issues an update to the software that powers the iPod, adding features and fixing bugs. Each such software release is delivered in the form of an "updater" that runs on either a Mac or a Windows PC, contains updates for all models of iPod in a single package, and gives you the option to either upgrade the software on your iPod or erase its disk and return it to the pristine factory condition.

It's important to keep abreast of iPod software updates for many reasons, not least of which is that some of the tasks in this book are not possible without the latest software installed on your iPod. Be sure to check regularly at the iPod software download page to see whether an update has been released.

▶ NOTE

If you're on a Mac, iPod software updaters are delivered through the **Software Update** mechanism (in the **Apple** menu) that also brings you updates to Mac OS X and your installed Apple software. Be sure to run **Software Update** regularly—it's how your Mac is protected against security vulnerabilities, as well as a convenient way to have necessary upgrades at your fingertips.

▶ WEB RESOURCE

http://www.apple.com/ipod/download/

Here is the iPod software download page, where you can get the latest iPod updaters for Mac or Windows computers.

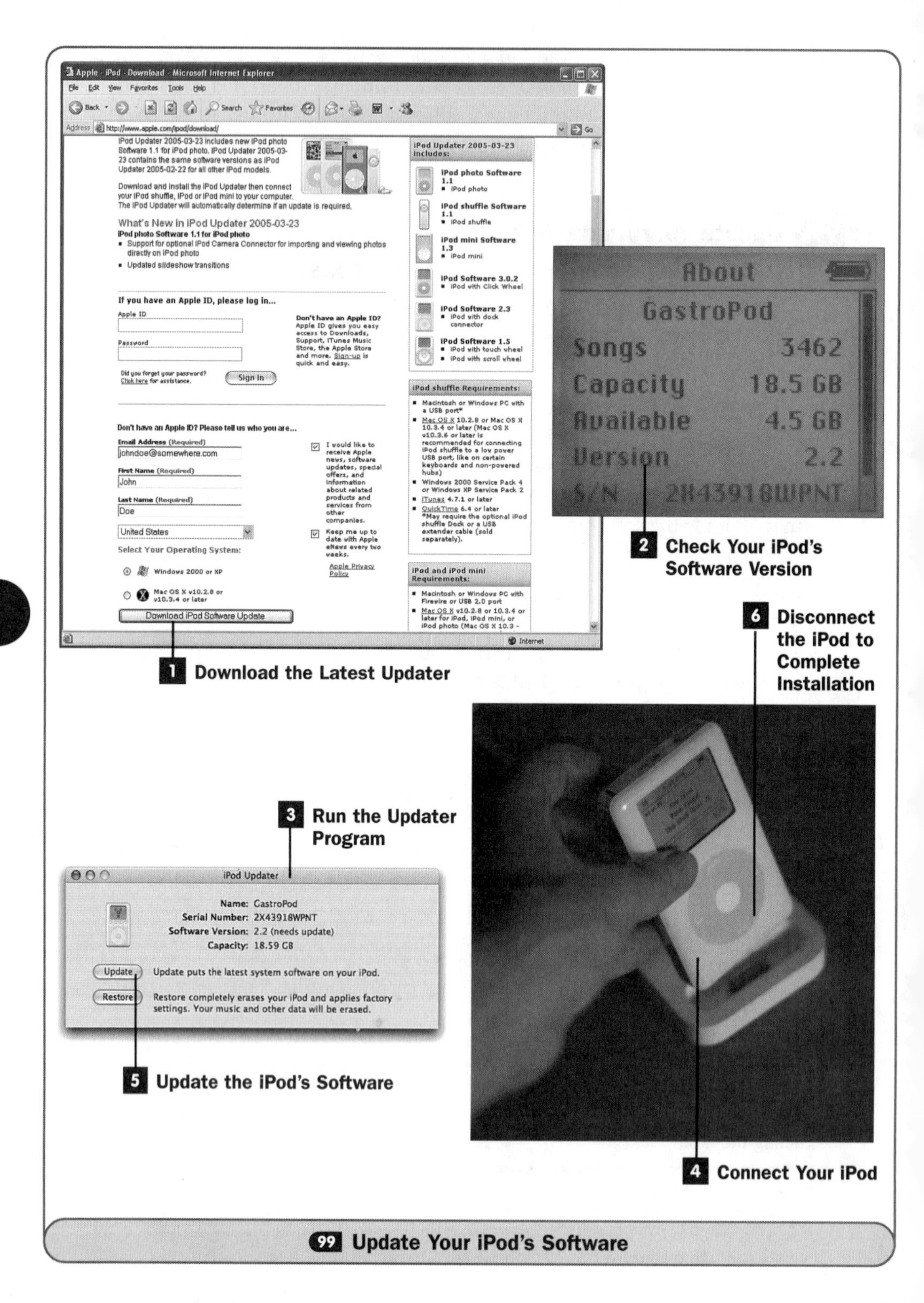
1 Download the Latest Updater
2 Check Your iPod's Software Version
3 Run the Updater Program
4 Connect Your iPod
5 Update the iPod's Software
6 Disconnect the iPod to Complete Installation
About
GastroPod
Songs 3462
Capacity 18.5 GB
Available 4.5 GB
Version 2.2
iPod Updater
Name: GastroPod
Serial Number: 2X43918WPNT
Software Version: 2.2 (needs update)
Capacity: 18.59 GB
Update
Update puts the latest system software on your iPod.
Restore
Restore completely erases your iPod and applies factory settings. Your music and other data will be erased.
Apple - iPod - Download - Microsoft Internet Explorer
http://www.apple.com/ipod/download/
What's New in iPod Updater 2005-03-23
If you have an Apple ID, please log in...
Download iPod Software Update

99 Update Your iPod's Software

1 Download the Latest Updater

Visit the iPod software download page. Apple requires you to identify yourself before you can download the updater, although this is not an authentication process and doesn't require you to be registered with any particular service; enter your name and email address in the fields at the bottom of the page, and indicate whether you want to receive promotional email using the two check boxes. Specify your computer's operating system using the radio buttons (your correct platform should be automatically selected). Click **Download iPod Software Update** to begin the download.

▶ NOTE

If you have an Apple ID, such as the login address you use to download music from the iTunes **Music Store**, you can use it to log in instead of supplying your name and email address.

When the download is complete, there is an installer program for you to run: **iPod.mpkg** on the Mac or **iPodSetup.exe** on Windows. Run this installer. When it's complete, the updater is available in the **Programs** menu in Windows, or in a folder called **iPod Software Updater** inside **Utilities** within the **Applications** folder on the Mac.

2 Check Your iPod's Software Version

On the iPod, navigate into the **Settings** screen, then select **About**. Check the **Version** number reported in the information screen.

3 Run the Updater Program

Launch the **iPod Updater** ***<date>*** program, either from its location on the disk or from the **Programs** menu in Windows. The first screen that appears reports the version numbers for each of the iPod models it supports; compare this version number with the version you saw on your iPod in step 2. If your iPod is up-to-date and you plug it in, the updater will tell you that no update is necessary (by comparing the version numbers, you can save yourself the trouble of continuing with this task).

▶ NOTES

Don't connect your iPod to the computer before you launch the updater program; doing so can cause the updater program to hang. Wait until the updater is running before connecting the iPod.

If you quit the updater without updating your iPod, you might have to manually unmount the iPod from the computer (by clicking Windows' **Unplug or Eject Hardware** icon in the system tray, or by clicking the **Eject** button next to the iPod in the **Finder** on the Mac) before you can disconnect the iPod safely.

4 Connect Your iPod

Connect your iPod to the computer using the Dock or cable. The updater heads off iTunes and prevents it from synchronizing your music while it's running. Your iPod's information, including whether its software needs updating, is displayed in the updater window.

5 Update the iPod's Software

If your iPod's software needs an update, the **Update** button is active. Click this button. (If you are running Mac OS X, you must enter an administrator's password.) The software is copied to the iPod.

6 Disconnect the iPod to Complete Installation

When you are directed to do so by the updater (and not before), disconnect the iPod from its Dock or cable. The iPod resets, and the firmware update automatically takes place, as you can see by the progress bar that appears on the iPod's screen. After 15 seconds or so, the iPod resets again and returns to the Main Menu.

▶ NOTE

In some cases, particularly with newer iPod models, you don't have to disconnect the iPod from the computer, even though the updater says you should. The iPod simply updates its firmware and returns to the Main Menu.

Quit the updater program and keep it around for future use, as in 100 **Restore Your iPod to Factory Settings**.

100 Restore Your iPod to Factory Settings

✓ BEFORE YOU BEGIN

99 Update Your iPod's Software

Perhaps your curiosity led you to install a "hack" that has resulted in an iPod that no longer boots or plays music correctly. Perhaps you've inherited a Mac-formatted iPod that you can't use with your Windows PC. Perhaps the iPod has mysteriously, on its own, seemingly gone crazy—unintelligible menu items, unresponsive controls, or the dreaded "folder with exclamation point" icon, which indicates that the system software on the iPod is no longer viable.

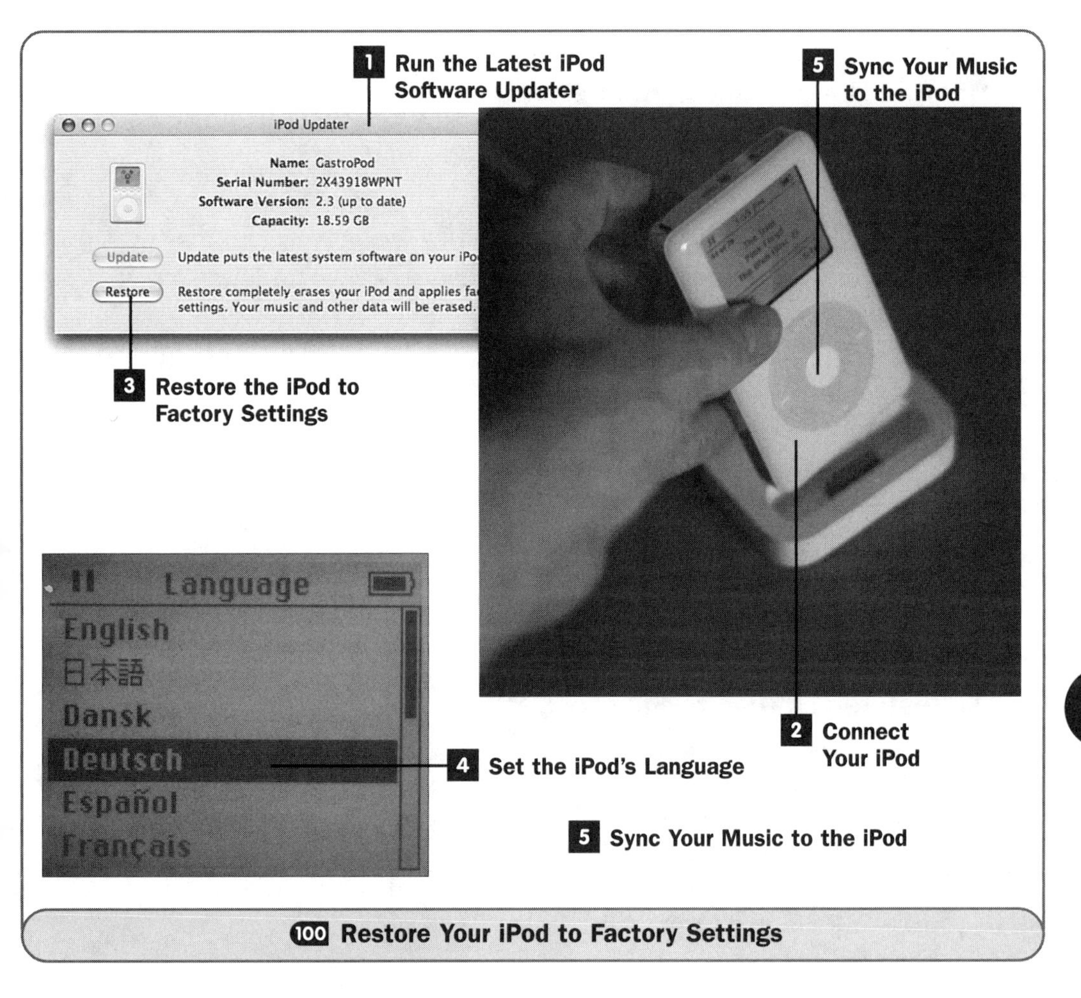

100 Restore Your iPod to Factory Settings

If resetting your iPod doesn't bring it back to its senses (hold down both the **Menu** and **Select** buttons for several seconds to reset it; to reset iPods older than the 4G model, hold down both the **Menu** and **Play/Pause** buttons), you might have to bring out the big gun: a Software Restore.

Restoring the iPod (using the same "updater" mechanism that was used in upgrading the iPod's software as described in **99 Update Your iPod's Software**) entails erasing all the contents of the iPod's disk, installing a new copy of the system software and firmware, and resetting its configuration to the state it was in when it first came out of the box. Before you embark on this process, however, make sure that you don't have any important files stored on the iPod in disk mode; anything there will be gone after the iPod has been restored. But at least the iPod will probably work again. See **80 Use Your iPod as an External Hard Disk** for more information about disk mode.

▶ TIP

Restoring the iPod formats the disk using the native format of the operating system on which you run the updater program—HFS+ for Mac or FAT32 for Windows. In this way, you can convert a Mac-formatted iPod into a Windows-compatible one, or vice versa.

1 Run the Latest iPod Software Updater

As described in 99 **Update Your iPod's Software**, download the latest copy of the iPod Updater from Apple's iPod software download site (**http://www.apple.com/ipod/download/**). If you're using a Mac, run the **Software Update** utility to make sure that you have all the necessary updates.

2 Connect Your iPod

Install the updater and run it. When the window reads **Plug in an iPod to update it**, connect your iPod to the computer using the Dock or cable. The updater window shows the vital information of your iPod, including its name and the current version of the software on it.

3 Restore the iPod to Factory Settings

Click **Restore**. (If you are using Mac OS X, you must enter an administrator's password.) The software is copied to the iPod and its disk is erased. When you are directed to do so by the updater (and not before), disconnect the iPod from its Dock or cable. The iPod resets, and the firmware update automatically takes place, as you can see by the progress bar that appears on the iPod's screen. After 15 seconds or so, the iPod resets again.

▶ NOTE

In some cases, particularly with newer iPod models, you don't have to disconnect the iPod from the computer, even though the updater says you should. The iPod simply updates its firmware and then returns to the Main Menu.

4 Set the iPod's Language

When the iPod returns to life, the first screen it shows is the language selection menu, just as it did when you first set it up (see 3 **Select Your iPod's Language**). Choose the language for your iPod.

Quit the updater software and unmount the iPod manually from your computer if necessary, by clicking the Windows **Unplug or Eject Hardware** icon in the system tray, or by clicking the **Eject** button next to the iPod in the Finder on the Mac. Disconnect the iPod from the Dock or cable.

5 Sync Your Music to the iPod

Connect the iPod to the computer once more. It's now effectively a brand-new unit, and iTunes treats it as such, giving you the opportunity to assign it a new name and register it, as described in 4 **Connect Your iPod for the First Time**. When you choose to update your music automatically, the iPod's disk becomes filled with the music in your iTunes **Library** once again, and—as a bonus—iTunes takes you to the Music Store where you can download free music as a welcome for "new" iPod users.

101 Turn a Scratched iPod into a Brushed-Metal iPod

✔ BEFORE YOU BEGIN	→ SEE ALSO
Just jump right in!	100 Restore Your iPod to Factory Settings

Not every problem you might have with your iPod has to do with the vagaries of software. It's just as much a concern for most iPod users to make sure that their hip little white music player keeps looking like new. Although Apple's sense of style can hardly be faulted for looks, it does perhaps leave something to be desired in the day-to-day practicality of maintaining those looks. Naturally, this means keeping that shiny stainless-steel back plate mirror-smooth and free of scratches.

The sad fact is that it's all but impossible to keep the back of your iPod looking pristine forever. But the good news is that, with a common kitchen scouring sponge or a piece of steel wool, a little bit of elbow grease and patience, and the fortitude to perform a little bit of seemingly destructive surgery on your beloved iPod, you can make it look just as good as when it was new, if in a slightly different way. All you have to do is give it a brushed-metal finish, and suddenly your iPod will not only be free of scratches, it'll be more resistant to new ones and to sweaty fingerprints as well. Performing this cosmetic surgery doesn't even void your warranty!

▶ WEB RESOURCE

http://members.optusnet.com.au/brushedipod/

Adam Podnar was one of the first to popularize the "brushed iPod" solution, and since then many iPod owners have embraced it as a compelling alternative look for their iPods.

▶ TIP

To experiment with different abrasive materials and brushing techniques before tackling your iPod, test the materials on the bottom of a shiny cookie sheet.

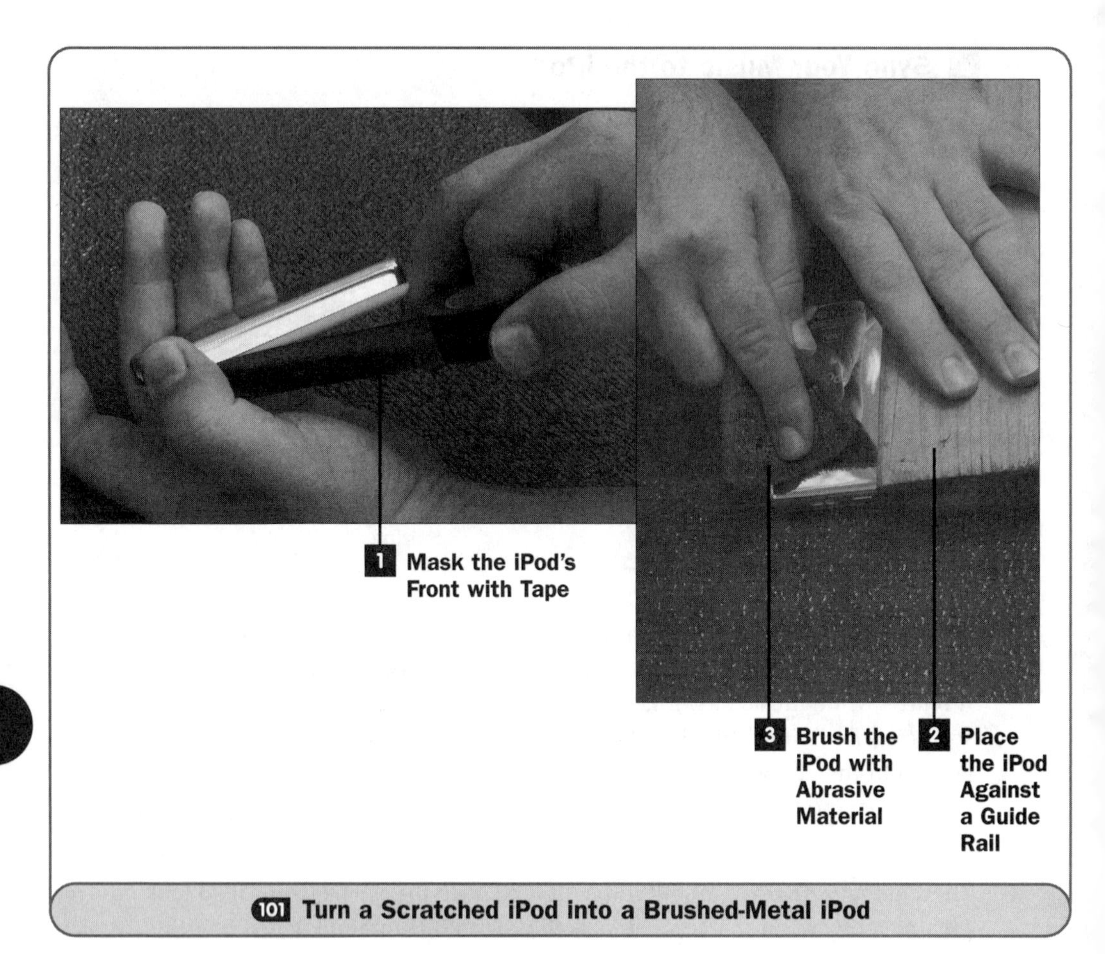
1 Mask the iPod's Front with Tape
3 Brush the iPod with Abrasive Material
2 Place the iPod Against a Guide Rail

101 Turn a Scratched iPod into a Brushed-Metal iPod

101

1 Mask the iPod's Front with Tape

Using electrical tape, mask the plastic front face of the iPod, aligning the edge of the tape carefully with the boundary between the plastic face and the metal back.

2 Place the iPod Against a Guide Rail

Place the iPod face down against a piece of wood or other firm surface.

3 Brush the iPod with an Abrasive Material

Using the rigid guide to keep your hand moving steadily in parallel strokes, brush briskly up and down the back face of the iPod with the rough side of a kitchen sponge, a piece of steel wool, some fine-grained sandpaper, or a foam sanding block. Experiment with pressure and technique until you see brushed lines appearing the way you want them to look. If you accidentally scrape sideways across the iPod's face, just brush in properly aligned motions over the mistake, and it'll soon be covered up.

▶ NOTE

The iPod logo and other text is engraved in the metal and is not harmed by this process.

The longer you brush, the better your iPod's surface will eventually look. Keep at it, sanding the short sides with more care until they match the back, and before long you'll have an iPod that not only looks as good as new, but that has a look all its own that none of your iPod-carrying friends will have!

▶ NOTE

Be sure to wash your hands after you're done brushing the iPod's surface. You'll have created a thin film of microscopic metal shavings on your skin, which is never a good thing to ingest.

Index

Numbers

A

B

C

D

E

F

G

H-I

J-K

L

M

N

O

P

Q-R

S

T

U-V

W-X-Y-Z

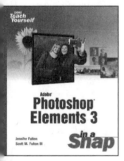

Key Terms

Don't let unfamiliar terms discourage you from learning all you can about the iPod and iTunes. If you don't completely understand what one of these words means, flip to the indicated page, read the full definition there, and find techniques related to that term.

Advanced Audio Coding (AAC) *A new digital audio format co-developed by Apple as part of the MPEG-4 definition; AAC has better quality than MP3, as well as optional built-in DRM.* **Page 8**

AirPort Express *One of Apple's brand of wireless Internet connectivity devices, a* **wireless base station** *that provides not just wireless (802.11g) connectivity but also an audio connection between iTunes and a set of speakers to which it's connected.* **229**

AirTunes *A feature of AirPort Express that broadcasts the capability to route music to a set of externally connected speakers to any copy of iTunes running on the network; any of these iTunes computers can choose the AirTunes speakers and play music through them wirelessly.* **229**

Audiobook *The digital equivalent of the spoken-word tape. It's a special kind of digital audio file that plays for a long time as its content (the text of a book or speech) is read. The file includes additional technology such that, if you pause listening to the audio stream, iTunes remembers where you left off and picks up again at that point when you resume listening. This technology even works if you move from iTunes to iPod as you listen to the audiobook.* **94**

Authorize *Register a computer over the network to be able to play protected AAC files purchased using a particular iTunes Music Store account.* **103**

Autofill *A technique for selecting just enough songs at random from a specified source to fill your iPod shuffle to capacity. With one button click, you can copy a whole new set of music to the device.* **171**

Bit rate *The number of bits per second consumed by an audio stream; the bit rate can be constant or variable, and if constant can be used to calculate how much disk space a song file will take up.* **52**

Broken pointer *A song entry in the iTunes database that points to a file that no longer exists or has been moved to another location so that iTunes can't find it. Broken pointers are marked with a ! icon.* **242**

Burn *To create a music CD using a writable disc (CD-R, CD-RW, or writable DVD).* **Page 3**

Burner *A CD or DVD drive capable of creating written, or burned, discs as well as reading them. Most modern computers are sold with CD burners, and many come with DVD burners as well.* **204**

CD-R *Writable compact disc. A CD-R can be burned once, and after that its contents cannot be changed. A CD-R or CD-RW can hold 650 or 700 megabytes of data, depending on the format.* **204**

CD-RW *Rewritable compact disc. A CD-RW can be burned multiple times, usually up to a few dozen times.* **204**

Compact Disc Digital Audio (CDDA) *The standard specification for mastering compact discs, which includes a specific format for the uncompressed audio data in each track.* **202**

Compression *Fitting more music into a fewer number of bytes by discarding unimportant musical data or indexing repeated patterns.* **51**

Crossfading *Having one track fade out at its end; the next track begins as the previous one is still fading.* **159**

Deauthorize *Revoke the ability for a computer to play protected AAC files purchased using a particular iTunes Music Store account, freeing up one of the available authorizations.* **103**

Deep discharge *Battery characteristics where optimum longevity and performance result from discharging the battery completely before recharging it.* **197**

Digital Rights Management (DRM) *Software algorithms that provide "copy protection" for digital music, usually enforced with digital "keys."* **12**

DVD-R *Writable digital versatile disc. A DVD can hold 4.7 gigabytes of data and generally costs significantly more than a writable CD. Data on a DVD is heavily compressed, making the format much more complex than that of a CD. Some DVD formats, such as DVD+RW and DVD-RW, can be written to more than once.* **204**